Sentimental Journey Home II (1938-1965)
Okie Boy, Texas Aggie

Arnold LeUnes

© Copyright 2018, Arnold LeUnes

All Rights Reserved

No part of this book may be reproduced, stored in a
retrieval system, or transmitted by any means,
electronic, mechanical, photocopying, recording,
or otherwise, without written permission
from the author.

ISBN: 978-1-64204-288-7

Jilly Pankey, formerly of the Art faculty at Texas State University and presently a freelance artist.

More of her work can be viewed at <u>www.jillpankey.com</u>

BOOK TWO

Sentimental Journey Home (1938-1965)
Okie Boy, Texas Aggie

American Life in the 1930's	1
Oklahoma: Home of the Red People	3
The Osage Indians	5
Famous Okies	7
Bartlesville, Dewey, and the Legend of Tom Mix	11
Bartlesville: The Town Jacob Bartles Built	11
Dewey: Jacob Bartles' Other Town	13
Tom Mix: Town Marshal, King of the Cowboys, and Silent Movies Idol	19
Family History	23
The Chamberlains	23
Richard Warren, the Mayflower Man.	24
"La Madama" Henrietta Chamberlain King.	29
Paul Richard (P. R.) Chamberlain.	30
LeUnes Family History	34
John and Gertrude LeUnes.	34
Gertrude LeUnes Meets Aimee Semple McPherson.	38
American Life in the 1940's	45
Borger, Texas	47
Borger Then and Now.	47
Six Memories of "Booger Town"	48
Carbon Black.	48
Tumbling Tumbleweeds..	49
Prairie Dog Town.	49
The Tornado Threat.	49
Gerald Myers.	50
My Mother and Father Get Divorced.	50
A Wonderful Childhood	53
Reflections on Resuming Life in Dewey	53
A Heavenly Haven for the Hopelessly Homeless.	54
Grandpa Chamberlain and the Cleveland Indians.	54

    House, Yard, and Neighborhood. 55
    Caretakers: Inola Harris and Henrietta and John Liss. 57
    The Bulldoggers Take An Early Stand Against Racism. 58
    Grandpa Chamberlain Breaks His Hip. 61
School Days, Lazy Summers, and Sports in the Life of a Young Boy 63
  School Days in Dewey 63
    Earl Marshall Provides My First Sex Education Lesson. 65
  Oklahoma Summers in the Late 1940's 68
    Grape-Nut Flakes, Cheerios, Post Toasties, and Pep Pins. 69
    Riding Bikes, Playing Marbles, and Shooting BB Guns. 70
    Polio, Nap Time, and *Fifty Famous Stories Retold*. 72
    Summer's Over: Back to School We Go. 75
  Sports in the Life of a Young Boy 76
    Baseball: Harry Caray, Stan "The Man" Musial, and the Redbirds. 76
    My Bubble Gum Baseball Card Collection. 78
    Football: The Oklahoma Sooners.. 80
    Football: The Men of West Point. 80
    Basketball: Robert "Cleats" McLeod. 81
American Life in the 1950's 83
Summers in Texas City, Texas 85
  Transitioning From Dewey to Texas City 85
  Texas City Vignettes 87
    A Bit of Texas City History. 87
    Heat, Humidity, Marauding Mosquitos, More Heat,
        More Humidity, and Petro-Chemical Pollution. 87
    Texas City Disaster. 88
    Water, Water Everywhere. 90
    Our Stepmother, June. 91
    Short Visits and Long Vacations. 93
    Little League Baseball. 93
    A "Fearsome Foursome": All Stars Carl Trepagnier,
        Jimmy Williams, Bobby Shosty, and Yours Truly. 97
Junior High School 99
  Talk About Life Transitions! 99
  Ova Farrow Asks My Class to Redshirt 100
  The Fearsome Mrs. Elva Myers 101
  George "Chief" Tyner 102
    The Cherokee Tribe, or the Tsalagi. 102
    "Chief" Tyner Provides an Unforgettable Civics Lesson. 104
  Acne, Blindness, Hairy Palms, and Insanity: The Evils of Masturbation 105
    Alvin "Bear" Smith. 106

- Politics and First Kisses ... 107
- Carl E. Davidson: My First Lesson in Sport Psychology ... 110
  - Mr. Davidson Becomes a Football Coach, If Unwillingly. ... 110
  - Pepsi, Peanuts, and Charles "Bud" Wilkinson. ... 112
  - Mr. Davidson Reveals a Strange Quirk. ... 113
  - Mr. Davidson Builds a Juggernaut. ... 114
- The Freshman Year ... 115
  - H. L. "Goob" Arnold. ... 115

Goober, Gonorrhea, and the Boys of Summer Go To High School ... 119
- Nicknames ... 119
  - Mike "Gonna" Rhea. ... 120
  - Frank "Johnny" Ringo. ... 124
  - Kenny "Red" Rigdon. ... 126
  - Elvis the Pelvis, Janice Golden, Marilyn Ruthrauff, and "Stink." ... 128
- High School Football: Coach Kester "Tractor" Trent ... 129
  - The Kid Needs Seasoning. ... 131
  - The "Oklahoma Jackrabbit" Breaks an Opponents' Neck. ... 132
  - No Post-Season Honors for Me. ... 135
  - A Final Tribute to Kester "Tractor" Trent. ... 137
  - Pros in our Midst: Opponents Who Went on to Stardom in the NFL. ... 140

Myrna Jo Brown, Princess of the Delaware Tribe ... 145
- The Delaware Indian Tribe, or the Lenni Lenape. ... 145
- Sports for Women in the 1950's. ... 148
- Our Relationship Goes South, and So Do I. ... 150

The Senior Year ... 153
- Doing Dumb Stuff. ... 153
- Ed Bishop and Easy Ed ... 153
- The Drug Stores ... 159

Memorable High School Teachers ... 165
- Marvin Leon Brown. ... 165
- Ralph Peck. ... 167
- Muriel Cearley. ... 168
- Jack "High Pockets" Hay. ... 170
- Miss/Mrs. Fry. ... 170
- Postmortem on our Teachers. ... 171

Racial Integration, "Hooter", Two-a-Days, and Our Final Season of Football ... 173
- Racial Integration Comes to Oklahoma ... 173
  - Lester E. "Hooter" Brewer. ... 175
  - The Dreaded "Two-a-Days." ... 177
  - The 1955 Starting Lineup.. ... 179
    - Right End. ... 180

Strong Tackle.	181
Weak Tackle.	182
Right Guard.	182
Center.	184
Left Guard.	185
Left End.	185
Blocking Back.	186
Wing Back.	186
Full Back.	187
Tail Back.	187
The Regular Season	188
The State Playoffs	189
Track and Field, Graduation, and Goodbye to Dewey, Oklahoma	193
Track and Field	193
I Tie the World Record in the Hundred-Yard Dash (Almost).	195
Racial Folklore.	197
The Track Season Continues.	198
The District, Regional, and State Track Meets.	199
High School Baseball.	201
Graduation and Goodbye	202

Undergraduate Days, Graduate School, and the United States Army

The Agricultural and Mechanical College of Texas	205
Bryan and College Station, Brazos County, and Texas A&M University	207
Goodbye to the Good Life	207
Things Begin to Settle Down	212
The "Bear", John David, and "The Sugar Land Express"	216
Everyday Life in the Corps	219
Jodie Calls.	219
Earning Their Master's Degrees in Hazing.	221
The Authoritarian Personality.	225
The Brain Drain.	227
First Semester Grades.	228
The Bonfire.	230
Positive Things, Good People.	232
Thumbing a Ride.	233
Outstanding Cadets.	235
Jack Lunsford, Class of 1957.	236
Thomas W. Adair III, Class of 1957.	237
Jon L. Hagler, Class of 1958.	237

  Ray Bowen, Class of 1958. 239
  Donald Cloud, Class of 1959. 240
  Melbern G. Glasscock, Class of 1959. 240
  William B. Heye, Class of 1960. 241
 That First Miserable Semester Comes to an End at Christmas, Sort Of 241
 Freshmen Come and Go 242
 Betty Grey Brightens the Day 243
The Sophomore Year 245
 Old Blue 245
 Hong Kong Flu Decimates the Student Body 250
 Gerald Avery 252
 Another Summer in Texas City 254
 Julia Catherine Jacobson Wins, Breaks My Heart. 256
My Final Two Years at A&M 257
 The Junior Year. 257
 ROTC Summer Camp at Fort Hood. 258
  Audie Murphy I Ain't. 258
  The Ku Klux Klan Comes to Summer Camp. 260
  Weekend Leaves with Larry Guseman. 261
 The Senior Year 263
  Mike Ogg, First Sergeant Nonpareil. 264
  Uncle Jimmy Serves Up Some Cold One's. 266
  Final Memories of A&M. 267
  What Are Friend's For? 267
 I Graduate!! 268
Favorite Professors 271
 The Motley Crew Earns Their Nicknames 271
  Milton "No Notes" Nance. 271
  Lloyd "Ivy League" Taylor. 273
  Jimmy Brautigam. 276
  Miss Barbara McKinney. 277
  "Cigar Dan" Davis. 277
  William Merl "Daddy-O" Dowell. 278
  Emil "Mammy" Mamaliga. 278
  Sid "Wolfman" Cox. 279
  Dr. Ewens. 280
  Walter Alphonso "Marvel" Varvel and Walter Andrew Varvel. 281
Friends and Classmates Killed in Vietnam: A Belated Tribute 283
 Floyd Kaase and Byron Stone 283
 Jim Vrba 284
 Other Classmates 285

- The Last Forgotten Soul 286
- American Life in the 1960's 287
- Summer of 1960 289
  - Falstaff Beer, "The Chief", and Brewmaster Tom Griesedieck 289
  - The Terrace Drive-In 291
- Graduate School, 1960-1961 293
  - Culture Shock Redux 294
  - The Koehler Boys and the KA's 294
    - Niggers and Jews and Sigma Nu's, A Hangin' from a Tree 296
  - The Boys in the Boarding House 298
    - Scrabble 299
    - TV Westerns 299
  - My Introduction to Graduate School 300
  - Barbara Laverne Blythe (March 11, 1952-May 28, 2017) 303
  - Hurricane Carla 304
- Uncle Sam Comes A' Calling 309
  - Fort Benjamin Harrison: The Winter of My Discontent 309
  - Good Old Fort Hood, Texas 311
    - Captain William "Bulldog" Turner, Sergeant Dean R. Gardner, the "Unknown Soldier", PFC Larry "I Don't Know if Natalie Would but I Would" Birr, and Specialist Five Art Parrack 315
    - The Fort Hood Boxing Team 319
    - Badminton: Old Sarge Teaches Me a Lesson in Sport Psychology 321
  - My Two Quasi-Combat Experiences 322
    - Cuban Missile Crisis, 1962 322
    - Operation Desert Strike, 1964 324
  - Natalie Jean LeUnes: Little One Born on Christmas 327
  - Minor Aggravations Add Up 328
  - The Creation 330
  - No More Active Duty for Me! 333
- Doctoral Student Days in Denton 337
  - The LeUnes Family Heads to Denton 337
  - Friends and Colleagues 338
    - Jonathan and Jerrianne 338
    - My Pals, John Ed and Sharon 341
  - Memorable Professors 342
    - Merl E. Bonney, Professor Without equal 342
    - Roy Q. Bellamy, Abnormalist 349
    - Dr. George Beamer Saves The Day (Or the Dissertation) 350
    - Other Wonderful Professors 351

PROLOGUE

Okie Boy, Texas Aggie

This book is essentially a recitation of assorted thoughts, memories, and reminiscences of my first twenty-seven years of life which covers my youth, adolescence, undergraduate college days, two stints as a graduate student, and my military service of which I am immensely proud. Highly salient is a lengthy discussion of growing up in Dewey, Oklahoma, and Texas City, Texas, in the 1940s and 1950s which are discussed at times in almost halcyonic and reverential terms. I then write of my four years as an undergraduate student at mostly military and all-male Texas A&M University (then the Agricultural and Mechanical College of Texas). To further flesh out the tale, I endeavor to regale the reader with reflections on my three years of graduate school at the University of North Texas (then North Texas State College) where I received my master's and doctoral degrees. I then bring this document to a close with recollections concerning my thirty-two month stint as a U.S. Army officer. My primary station for most of those nearly three years was Fort Hood near Killeen, Texas, with separate ten-week and four-week stops at Fort Benjamin Harrison in Indianapolis, Indiana, two months at Fort Stewart Georgia (near Savannah) preparing for an invasion of Cuba, and eight weeks or so in the Mojave Desert of California engaging in mock desert warfare.

In the intervening fifty-three years since the completion of the preceding, I have been a professor at Texas A&M University where I labor away in what was known for my first fifty-two years as the Department of Psychology and recently re-christened in 2017 as the Department of Psychological and Brain Sciences to better reflect the growing interest among my colleagues in issues related to brain and nervous system functioning. The half century-plus journey at A&M has been exciting, challenging, and fulfilling, and selected memories and reminiscences from that period can be found in my companion volume entitled "Stamping out ignorance in Aggieland: One professor's memories and reflections" The reference to stamping out ignorance is a tongue-in-cheek inside joke I share with several colleagues about the nature of our duties as professors. We often talk about stamping out ignorance, killing rats, and herding cats to define our roles. "Killing rats" is in the figurative not literal sense, though a number of my colleagues do conduct research using rats and they sometimes euthanize their subjects in order to better understand rat behavior and physiology and to make educated assessments about how these things relate to the human experience. In my own case, I work with humans and use the metaphor "killing rats" to cover the tying up of loose ends related to my work. As for "herding cats", keeping up with the sometimes unbridled and unfocused energy of the undergraduates who at times seem to be more centered on football, sorority and fraternity life, drinking and partying, part-time employment, volunteering with various agencies, and assorted other less academically oriented enterprises. All in all, however, they are delightful to work with and make being a professor one of the most rewarding jobs on the planet. As someone has said, in what other profession are you constantly being reminded of how wonderful you are. I am told how wonderful I am in some form or fashion virtually each and every day of the year, and I am thus blessed. Knowing your efforts to stamp out ignorance, herd cats, and kill rats actually pays off is highly gratifying.

We are here to educate and refine the unwashed and unwanted undergraduates who are quite intelligent but nevertheless rough around the edges due to their age and lack of real-world experience. It is sometimes hard to face the truth, but there are actually quite a few who are brighter than their professors but nevertheless in need of guidance and mentoring about matters related to their future in the workplace as well as their role as citizens who will hopefully go out and make the world a better place through their intellectual and humanitarian efforts.

But I digress as bit so let us go back to "Okie Boy, Texas Aggie." There is an extended coverage of the history of Oklahoma, ditto my home towns of Dewey and Texas City, and likewise the Chamberlain (maternal) and LeUnes (paternal) sides of the family. I also reflect on the elementary, junior high, and high school years, wonderful teachers I had, and the role of sports in the life of a reasonably gifted athlete who is the personification of the big frog in a small pond. Anecdotes related to these major themes abound.

A sizeable section of the remainder of the book is devoted to the four years I spent in College Station, Texas, attending what is now known as Texas A&M University. Going from provincial Dewey, Oklahoma, to a backwater, small, all-male, and mostly military environment of A&M was culture shock for me. The university at that time was small (5,500 students as opposed to the 65,000 now), backward, uninspiring, inhabited by a lot of good-old-boy professors with less than sterling academic credentials, and seriously lacking in the arts and the humanities. It is difficult looking back to call A&M a university when it lacked the basic arts and humanities, had only four courses in Psychology, and added its first Philosophy course in 1960. There was also terrible attrition in the student body due to the rigors of military life and the unregulated, out-of-control hazing of underclassmen that took place in the Corps of Cadets units.

In the late 1950s and into most of the 1960s, a revolution took place under the leadership of the World War II military hero, General James Earl Rudder, which transformed the university and dragged it, however reluctantly, into the twentieth century. Upgrading of the faculty and course offerings, the full admittance of women and blacks, and the lessening of the influence of the military aspect of the university were all critical components of this revolution. I am delighted to say the university is alive and well and regarded with great respect among academicians and the external business world alike. The voyage from what I have described in the 1950s to today has been exhilarating, and I have once again been blessed to be a small part of the evolution of A&M from mediocre cow college to major player on the world academic scene.

After graduating from A&M, I entered North Texas State College (NTSC) in the fall of 1960 where I received my master's degree in school administration a year later. I knew halfway through the degree I did not want to be a school administrator but the wheels had been set in motion to complete that degree and later orient myself in another direction for the doctoral degree. I had wonderful professors and met my first wife and the mother of my four oldest children while at NTSC.

Four months later, after barely surviving Hurricane Carla in Texas City, I found myself in the frozen tundra known as Indianapolis, Indiana, where I began my stint in the military at Fort Benjamin Harrison in Indianapolis, Indiana. The months were January, February, and March of 1962, and I was exposed to cold on a consistent basis that an Okie experiences only on occasion in the winter. I survived and moved on to Fort Hood in Killeen, Texas, where I spent the better part of my army stay. My thoughts on the army experience take up the remainder of the book, and lead us up to November of 1965 when I was offered a faculty position at A&M. As the trite saying goes, the rest is history and is captured in the companion volume entitled "Stamping out ignorance in Aggieland."

It is my fondest hope that the reader finds reminiscences of my youth to be reminders in some way of their own experiences. Also, I am hopeful the reader will want to invest in the companion volume in order to get a full understanding of what one beaten-up, old octogenarian Professor, Arnold LeUnes, thinks in retrospect about life for the past nearly eighty years as well as some more or less random thoughts on current events.

Happy reading!

American Life in the 1930's

Hitler Proclaimed Himself to be Chief of the German Military
Howard Hughes Set a Time Record For a Round-The-World Flight
Kate Smith Introduced the Song "God Bless America"
The Minimum Wage was Forty Cents an Hour
A Gallon of Gasoline Cost a Dime and a Loaf of Bread Nine Cents
Bette Davis Won an Oscar For Her Role in "Jezebel" and Spencer Tracy For His in "Boys Town"
"Flat Foot Floogie with a Floy, Floy" Topped The Music Charts
Boxing Champion Joe Louis Knocked Out The Great White Hope From Germany, Max Schmeling
The Dow Jones Average Topped Out at 132
The Average Price of a New House was $3,900
Electroshock Therapy was Introduced by Drs. Ugo Cerletti and Lucio Bini, Two Italian Physicians
The Life Expectancy was 59.7 Years
Newsman Peter Jennings, Singer Kenny Rogers, and Basketball Legend Oscar Robertson Born
So was Arnold Dallas LeUnes; At 0646 Hours On April 16, 1938, to be Precise

Arnold LeUnes

ARNOLD LEUNES AS INFANT

MOM AND INFANT LEUNES 1938

Oklahoma: Home of the Red People

"Illegal aliens have always been a problem in the United States. Ask any Indian."

Robert Orben, (1927-?), Comedy Writer and Magician

Oklahoma means "Home of the Red People" in the language of the Choctaw tribe, and I would like to open this section of this somewhat long verbal voyage with a brief description of the state and community where I spent the majority of my first eighteen years. My birth state has been widely misperceived as flat, desolate, and dry, due in great part to images originating from media representations of the Dust Bowl days of the 1930's. As is all too often the case with stereotypes, this one is also inaccurate. In reality, dense forests cover a fourth of the state; lush grassy plains rich in bluestem alfalfa cover the ground near the Osage Hills in eastern Oklahoma and these same plains are home to herds of resurgent buffalo; the eastern part is laden with beautiful man-made lakes that provide a myriad of outdoor activities. Granted, as one goes west, the terrain gets increasingly arid and craggy but nothing of the magnitude of those dreadful Dust Bowl days.

There are mountains galore; the Washita and Ozarks permeate much of the eastern part of the state, the Arbuckles the south, and the Wichita and Glass Mountains, probable remnants of the great Rocky Mountain range of another geological period, rise in the west. In general, then, Oklahoma feels a bit misunderstood and regards itself as a relatively undiscovered and underappreciated "Sleeping Beauty."

Prior to becoming the 45th state in the union in 1907, Oklahoma was known as the Indian Territory. This designation reflected the presence of the original indigenous tribes as well as those that came later from other parts of the United States, more often than not against their will. In the latter case, the Cherokees, Chickasaws, Choctaws, Creeks, and Seminoles, were relocated from their original homes in the southeastern part of the US to the Indian Territory. They have often been referred to by historians as the "Five Civilized Tribes", though the definition of civilized was defined rather narrowly and strangely. Essentially, the tribes were deemed civilized to the extent that they adopted the ways of the European white man who dominated this country from Colonial times and beyond. As part of being "civilized", they built homes, established schools, worked hard as farmers, and, in a number of cases, became good Christians. The conversion to Christianity, no doubt, was an essential part of the definition of "civilized" as spelled out by the dominant white settlers. Some Native American activists take umbrage at the term "civilized" because it implies that other tribes were somehow not civilized simply because they did not kowtow to the prevailing Indo-European, Judeo-Christian culture. I take similar umbrage because of the Christianity component imbedded in the definition; I know quite a few Christians who are not very civilized by any standard measure.

My experience with the "Five Civilized Tribes" is limited to one Creek and several Cherokees; to my knowledge, I never met a Chickasaw, Choctaw, or Seminole in the eighteen years I lived in

Oklahoma. Several Cherokees were friends and acquaintances in the Dewey area as I was growing up but it took me until the 1990's to make my first and only Creek acquaintance, a bright and engaging student at Texas A&M University named Nicole Durossette. Ms. Durossette brought much joy to my life for a two-year period in the early 1990's.

Nicole took several classes with me and co-authored a presentation on the psychological makeup of the greatest female athlete of all time, Mildred "Babe" Didrikson Zaharias, which we presented at a professional psychology conference in New Orleans. Nicole's mother was Anglo but the father was a full-blood Creek who made his living as an attorney. According to legend, Native Americans have long been unable to handle the white man's "fire water" (whiskey) and the good counselor was no exception, according to Nicole. I do not know why this story has stuck with me, but it has endured. The tale goes something like this: It seems that when she was six or seven years of age, Nicole and her father went to one of his favorite restaurants where he began to drink excessively. Before the evening was over, he was tipsy to the point that he forgot Nicole was with him, and he ended up going home, unwittingly leaving her alone in the restaurant. He eventually found his way back and retrieved his justifiably upset young daughter. All grown up now, Nicole has a master's degree in Psychology and is a Licensed Professional Counselor practicing in the greater Houston area. Unless things have changed recently, Nicole also manages real estate property, some of which is in the Bryan-College Station area.

Another prominent feature of Oklahoma was (and is) its oil industry that began in 1875 when George B. Keeler spotted "black gold" seeping from the ground near the south bank of the Caney River which constitutes the northern border of the city. Twenty-two years later, on April 15, 1897, a well in Bartlesville, the Nellie Johnstone Number One, was "born." This event led to a veritable explosion of drilling and exploration on the nearby Osage Indian lands, thus ushering in an era of unbelievable wealth and growth. Nearby Tulsa soon became known as the "Oil Capital of the World" and early oil barons with names like Sinclair, Getty, Phillips, Marland, and Gilcrease became household names in the petroleum industry throughout Oklahoma and world-wide.

Other major beneficiaries of the discovery of oil were members of the Osage Indian tribe who lived in and around Pawhuska in the heart of the Osage Hills, twenty-five miles west of Bartlesville. It seems their reservation sat right on top of one of the richest deposits of oil ever found in the US, and that discovery was a life-changing event for the members of that tribe. To flesh out our discussion of the Oklahoma oil boom and its effects, it might be informative at this juncture to take a brief look at the history and modern day status of these proud people, the Osages.

Sentimental Journey Home II (1938-1965)

SEAL, OSAGE NATION

The Osage Indians

The Preamble to the proposed Osage Nation Constitution reads as follows:

"We the Wah-zha-she, known as the Osage people, having formed the Clans in the far distant past, have been a people and as a People have walked this earth and enjoyed the blessings of Wah-kon-tah for more centuries than we really know.

Having resolved to live in harmony, we now come together so that we may once more unite as a Nation and as a People, calling upon the fundamental values that we hold sacred: Justice, Fairness, Compassion, Respect for the Protection of Child, Elder, All Fellow Beings, and Self.

Paying homage to generations of Osage leaders for the past and present, we give thanks for their wisdom and courage. Acknowledging our ancient tribal order as the foundation of our present government, first reformed in 1881 Constitution of the Osage Nation, we continue our legacy by again reorganizing our government.

This constitution, created by the Osage people, hereby grants to every Osage citizen a vote that is equal to all others and forms a government that is accountable to the citizens of the Osage Nation. We, the Osage People, based on centuries of being a People, now strengthen our government in order to preserve and perpetuate a full and abundant Osage way of life that benefits all Osages, living and as yet unborn."

This preamble provides a glimpse into contemporary Osage life and also serves as a reminder of the rich ancestral past of this most interesting tribe. The Osages, like the Tsalagi Cherokees and the Lenni Lenape Delawares discussed elsewhere, originally occupied vast areas in the heart of America. However, in 1872, the Osages were forced westward against their will by the U.S. government and ended up occupying land in the Indian Territory in what came to be known as Osage County. The Osages were a spiritual people, and believed in *Wah-kon-tah*, or the great mystery spirit. Also powerful in their lives was a legendary tale about the People of the Sky (*tzi-sho*) who would meet one day with the People of the Land (*hun-kah*) and form one tribe, the Children of the Middle Waters (*ni-u-ko'n-ska*).

The Osages were fierce warriors and accomplished hunters, and depended greatly on the buffalo for food, clothing, and other essentials. They also planted crops for harvesting once the hunts were completed in late summer. Unfortunately, their ancestral ways came into conflict with the mores and folkways of the white settlers, and eventually the Osages either chose to or were forced to live on reservations.

As noted earlier, in the late 1890's, a number of oil and gas companies commenced drilling in the Indian Territory. Over the next decade, hundreds of wells were drilled, many productive and some dry, but by the time Oklahoma became a state in 1907, the Osages were raking in huge royalties from the deals they had negotiated with several major oil companies. It is said that just making the quarterly royalty payments to the Osages kept eight company men busy for four or five days during each pay period. These royalties were known as "head rights", and they made the Osage the richest people in the world per capita by the 1920's.

I can remember as a boy hearing about the wealthy but reclusive Osages who lived on the reservation in Pawhuska, but I had no idea of the magnitude of the riches involved in those head rights. We also heard many tales of woe associated with having a lot of money but no jobs and few diversions. For the most part, the Osages did not stray far from the reservation in Pawhuska nor did they mix much with white people, unlike the Cherokees and the Delawares, many of whom chose integration over reservation life.

Today, the Osage Nation is made up of the Grayhorse, Hominy, and Pawhuska Indian Villages, and each retains considerable autonomy concerning traditions, customs, and history. Pawhuska, as noted earlier, is the capital of the Osage Nation and is home to 3,600 people (one third are Native American). The city lies adjacent to the eastern edge of the Osage Hills, twenty-five miles west of Bartlesville and thirty from Dewey, and apparently was named after an Osage chief, Pahucka, also called "White Hair." Legend has it that during a battle Pahucka earned his nickname from lifting a scalp he thought was the real thing but instead turned out to be a powdered wig, hence the name "White Hair."

As has been the case lately with a number of Native American tribes across the US, the Osages have invested in the legalized gambling business, with five casinos in place today. The umbrella organization for the casinos is called Osage Gaming, and it consists of operations in Hominy,

Pawhuska, Sand Springs, Tulsa, and Bartlesville (known there as the Osage Million Dollar Elm Casino). A number of other business, cultural, and social programs are available to preserve old traditions and otherwise enhance the lives of members of the present day Osage Nation.

Though there were many Osages in the area in which I lived, I do not remember knowing any of them personally. However, I did meet one during my freshman year, strangely enough, at Texas A&M University. The Osage in question was a Corps of Cadets junior named Chuck Revelette. He and I visited briefly on one occasion for maybe thirty minutes about Oklahoma and our respective home towns, but I never talked to him again during our time at the university. He did not seem interested in forming any kind of enduring relationship despite what I thought was an obvious Okie and Aggie bond. In retrospect, it appears that Chuck Revelette reflected the mores and folkways set in place by his reclusive, isolated tribal brothers and sisters.

Famous Okies

States also take pride in the production of musical luminaries and Oklahoma is no exception. It has given us country musicians such as Leon McAuliffe, Bob Wills, Reba McIntyre, Garth Brooks, Roger Miller, Leon Russell, Roy Clark, Conway Twitty, Hoyt Axton, Toby Keith, Mason Williams, Vince Gill, and Ronnie Dunn of Brooks and Dunn fame. Patti Page and Kay Starr, prominent female singers of the Big Band era, were from Oklahoma. The most famous of all folk musicians, Woody Guthrie, was said to be an Okie. So were prima ballerina Maria Tallchief of the Osage tribe and operatic soprano Leona Mitchell of Metropolitan Opera fame who is part African-American and part Chickasaw.

Famous stage personalities from Oklahoma include Gene Autry who, at the urging of Will Rogers, set out on a career in music in the 1920's. This show of support from Will Rogers led Autry to launch his singing career at radio station KVOO in Tulsa, one of my favorite stations as a kiddo. That gig and others eventually led Autry to fame and fortune in the old Western movies era. Other actors with Oklahoma roots included the idol of the silent films, Tom Mix, as well as Hopalong Cassidy, James Garner, and Chuck Norris. Norris, by the way, now lives on a ranch in Navasota, Texas, some fifteen miles from our home in College Station. There are occasional Norris sightings around the area, and he is often the subject of media attention for his television and film notoriety as well as his ultra-conservative political leanings.

Other famous personalities include the immensely talented black historian John Hope Franklin, the esteemed Indian activist Wilma Mankiller, and the accomplished civil rights activist, black leader, and author, Ralph Ellison. Dr. Franklin, a Harvard Ph.D. in History, Duke University Professor, and Presidential Medal of Freedom recipient in 1995, was born in Rentiesville and graduated from high school in Tulsa before embarking on his career as professor, author, and civil rights activist. Mankiller, the first female Chief of the Cherokee Nation, was born into abject poverty in Tahlequah. She became an author many times over, also a Presidential Medal of Freedom recipient, and professor at Dartmouth upon her retirement as tribal chief. As for Ellison, he was a native of Oklahoma City and yet another Presidential Medal of Freedom recipient. He was an avid civil rights advocate and author of the 1952 novel *Invisible Man* which explored racism in new and challenging ways.

Famous athletes from Oklahoma include baseball Hall of Famers Mickey Mantle, Warren Spahn (of "Spahn and Sain and pray for rain" fame discussed elsewhere), Johnny Bench, and Carl Hubbell. As well, the Waner brothers, Pepper Martin, and Allie Reynolds were prominent baseball players with Oklahoma roots. The Waner's, Paul "Big Poison" and Lloyd "Little Poison", are the only brothers to ever be elected to the Baseball Hall of Fame in Cooperstown, New York. Perhaps Henry Iba, the long-time legendary coach at Oklahoma A&M College (now Oklahoma State University), is its most famous basketball name, and the number of great football athletes who have passed through the University of Oklahoma are too numerous to mention.

Jim Shoulders, the five-time all-around professional rodeo performer of the year, and Hall of Fame bull rider "Freckles" Brown head the list of rodeo performers. The two rodeo stars undoubtedly owe a debt of gratitude to early cowhands who led cattle drives over the Chisholm Trail from Texas to the railheads in Kansas in the 1800's and early 1900's. These cattle drives gave rise to a cowboy lore that made the state a veritable Mecca for rodeos and wild-west shows. Jim Thorpe is perhaps the most famous Native American track and field athlete from Oklahoma. Thorpe, a member of the Sac and Fox tribe, was also a major league baseball player.

Five astronauts are Okies, the most of any state in the union. Finally, Wiley Post and Will Rogers are favorite sons of significance who unfortunately died together as the result of a plane crash in Alaska in 1935. Wiley Post was an important figure in the development of the airline industry in its early days, and his friend Will Rogers remains one of our country's richest sources of humor and quotable quotes about politics, human frailty, and everyday life.

Wiley Post was thirty-seven when he died and Will Rogers fifty-six. Post was born in 1898, and his good friend Rogers in 1879 on a large ranch near what is now Oolagah, forty-five miles southeast of my childhood home town of Dewey. Rogers dropped out of school in the tenth grade but went on to write six books, make seventy-one movies, and pen a syndicated column for 4,000 newspapers. He traveled around the world three times, made friends with Presidents and Kings alike, and spent a good portion of his life engaged in numerous humanitarian undertakings. He truly lived his life in the manner suggested by his most famous quote: "I never met a man I didn't like." Other famous Will Rogers bon mots are:

Sentimental Journey Home II (1938-1965)

"Make crime pay. Become a lawyer."
"A fool and his money are soon elected."
"I am not a member of an organized party. I'm a Democrat."
"The income tax made liars out of more Americans than golf."
"There ought to be one day, just one, when it is open season on senators."
"I don't make jokes. I just watch the government and report the facts."
"There are three kinds of men. The ones that learn by reading. The few who learn by observation. The rest of them have to pee on the electric fence for themselves."

OKLAHOM HUMORIST, WRITER, PHILOSOPHER WILL ROGERS

Bartlesville, Dewey, and the Legend of Tom Mix

Bartlesville: The Town Jacob Bartles Built

I was born at Memorial Hospital in Bartlesville, the county seat of Washington County, Oklahoma, in the heart of what was once known as the Indian Territory. The city was originally founded in the late 1890's by a Civil War veteran named Jacob "Jake" Bartles who is credited, however apocryphally, with being the first Oklahoman to grow wheat, operate a flour mill, have electric lights, and own a telephone. Bartlesville was initially made up of a flour mill and general store, but thanks to the leadership of its founder coupled with the discovery of oceans and oceans of oil on Osage Indian lands a few miles to the west, the fledgling city became a boom town.

JACOB BARTLES AND GENERAL STORE, EARLY 1900S

As noted earlier, Bartlesville leapt to instant notoriety in 1897 with the discovery of Oklahoma's first oil well, the Nellie Johnstone Number 1. Oklahoma quickly became the nation's leading oil producing state, and the discovery of those huge oil supplies in the Bartlesville area led to the founding of Phillips Petroleum. The company located its headquarters in Bartlesville, and was named after the oil baron Frank Phillips. Phillips' company thrived right from the start, and its substantial profits allowed him to build a 26-room mansion in 1929 aptly named the Frank Phillips Home. The mansion remains today as a museum dedicated to those early days of the oil and gas industry and the entrepreneurship and philanthropy of Frank Phillips.

Though Bartlesville has always remained relatively small in population (35,000 today), its influence was considerable because of the presence of Frank Phillips and his oil empire. Phillips Petroleum merged with Conoco a few years ago, thus becoming ConocoPhillips, and the corporate headquarters were moved from Bartlesville to Houston, Texas, a move that signified the end of an era for the small Oklahoma community.

One of the more distinctive features of the present-day Bartlesville skyline is the "tree that escaped the forest", the nickname for a dominating nineteen-story structure known as the Price Tower. H. C. Price was a wealthy citizen of Bartlesville and, like Phillips before him, greatly profited from harnessing and treating oil and gas. With some of those petroleum-related profits, Price commissioned a monument in his name to be designed by the famous architect, Frank Lloyd Wright, and it came to be known as the Price Tower. The edifice was completed in 1956 and was and still is the tallest structure in the city. Today, it houses a museum dedicated to the history of "Bartlesville, the City that Oil Built", as well as boutiques, art shops, and the like. Considerable national attention has been drawn over the past half century to the Price Tower and its famous designer.

In 2016, the *Houston Chronicle* ran a short feature in its travel section on Bartlesville and the Price Tower. In suggesting things the interested tourist might want to do, the writers of the piece added a blurb on what of interest is nearby. The blurb read: "Only a 10-minute drive away, the fun and funky town of Dewey is a throwback in time. Visit Linger Longer Antiques and Old Fashioned Soda Fountain, the kitschy Tom Mix Museum, Prairie Song Pioneer Village and the historic Dewey Hotel Museum." I never knew my little home town was "fun and funky" and a "throwback in time." Nor was I aware that the Tom Mix Museum to be discussed shortly was "kitschy." After I quit laughing, I emailed the piece to old Dewey friends, Frank Ringo and Mike Rhea, who seemed to enjoy the piece as much as I did.

Another area landmark mentioned in the travel article as a "Bartlesville to-do" with ties to Frank Phillips was the Woolaroc Museum, craftly named to capture the essence of the (woo)ds, the (la)kes, and the (roc)ks so prominently featured in the area landscape. Woolaroc, completed in 1925, is located in the Osage Hills some twelve miles southwest of Bartlesville on Highway 123. The 3,600 acre spread is home to many species of wildlife, including buffalo, elk, and longhorn cattle. Woolaroc also has a rustic lodge that, among other things, is testimony to Phillips' interest in animals. Though the walls are liberally decorated with animal heads and other likenesses, it is said that none of the trophies were gathered through sport hunting but rather from the natural deaths of the animals on display. In all, 108 sets of horns and ninety-seven animal heads are mounted on the walls of the lodge.

In Phillips' heyday, the lodge was a rustic retreat for dignitaries, movie stars, prominent businessmen, and more than a few outlaws seeking respite. To put it another way, Frank Phillips surrounded himself with friends from all walks of life, to include an unlikely assortment of captains of commerce, Catholic cardinals, and common criminals. Today, the museum houses an incredible collection of American West artifacts, and is a delight for tourists and historians alike. Of Woolaroc, the humorist Will Rogers once said, "When you are visiting the beauty spots of this country, don't overlook Frank Phillips' ranch and game preserve in Bartlesville, Oklahoma. It's the most unique place in this country."

There are other less famous yet intriguing sites and events of note in Bartlesville. One is the La Quinta Mansion, a 32-room structure built in 1930 for another oilman, H. V. Foster. The mansion has hand-painted ceilings, seven fireplaces, and a tower overlooking Bartlesville, and now serves as the campus of Bartlesville Wesleyan University, a private liberal arts Christian college. The city is also home to the annual OK Mozart Festival, a ten-day event held each year in mid-June. A relationship has been forged between Bartlesville and Mozart's birthplace in Vienna, Austria, and the fallout from that relationship has added much glamour and substance to the festivities. Finally, a tribute to the Native American heritage is held each fall in mid-September by the Delaware tribe which has been in the Bartlesville area since 1867. The three-day festival includes powwows, Native American arts and crafts, and a fashion show. The aforementioned Osages and Cherokees are also prominently represented at the festival as are other tribes in the area. I attended the event a few years ago and the Native Americans, their tribal dress, the dances and chants, and other features unique to Native American culture were enchanting reminders of my past and a melancholy trip back to the cherished days of my youth.

Dewey: Jacob Bartles' Other Town

The Caney River cuts a serpentine path just to the north of the Bartlesville city limits and the river and bridge serve to separate that city from my home town, Dewey, which is four miles away. Named after a naval hero of the Spanish-American war, Admiral George Dewey, the town was originally founded sometime in the 1890s by the aforementioned Jacob "Jake" Bartles, the visionary who was instrumental in putting Bartlesville on the map. Dewey was officially chartered as a city on December 8, 1905 and in 1908, became one of the major stops on the rodeo circuit, hosting what was known as the Dewey Roundup. At one time, rodeo cowboys apparently spoke of the Dewey event in the same reverential tones as those accorded the famous Calgary Stampede and the Cheyenne Rodeo Days. I vaguely remember the rodeo arena which had become old and decrepit by the time I was old enough to notice, and it was razed during my elementary school years to make

Arnold LeUnes

room for the high school. The latest reference I can find to the rodeo is 1946 and that date corresponds roughly with my memory of its demise, for I was eight years old.

The high school athletic teams inherited their mascot, the Bulldoggers, from those old rodeo days. My wife, Judy, likes to tell people we were not really the intimidating, to-be-greatly-feared Dewey Bulldoggers at all but rather the wimpy, bookish Dewey Decimals. I just cannot reconcile my image as an old Bulldogger and its bold suggestions of masculinity, macho mentality, and rodeo roughness, toughness, and tenacity with the thought of being a Dewey Decimal and its implied wimpishness. To add insult to injury, Judy still tells friends that my football teammates wore jerseys with numbers like n5r and 00.2a and so on. Sticks and stones may break my bones...

CEMENT PLANT SIGN

In addition to its famous rodeo, Dewey is credited with building the state's first airplane, licensing its first pharmacist, owning the first completely automated movie projector, and founding its first Oddfellows Lodge. The town cemetery bears the remains of one of Oklahoma's most notorious outlaws, Henry Starr (1874-1921), a distant relative of Belle Starr, arguably the most notorious female outlaw of her time. Henry Starr viewed himself as somewhat of a latter day Robin Hood, boasting of robbing only the rich but never the working man. He was shot and killed in 1921 while trying to rob a bank, and was interred in the Dewey Cemetery as requested. Several of my family members, hopefully more honorable than Henry Starr, are also buried there.

CEMENT PLANT

Another outstanding feature of Dewey in my youth was its major industry (aside from cattle and oil), the Portland Cement Plant, which lies dormant these days after many years as a major source of local employment. The plant was owned by a local businessman, Don Tyler, and my maternal grandfather, Paul Richard Chamberlain, was its chief chemist and superintendent for a time. Grandpa Chamberlain's employment at the plant, coupled with some wise investments, afforded him a very comfortable living for most of his life. Grandpa Chamberlain, in his role as plant chemist, actually developed a process that sped up the hardening process for cement, an innovation that supposedly revolutionized the entire industry. He and three collaborators, Waldo Tyler and Thomas Douglas of Kansas City, and Russ Loveland, also of Dewey, registered their innovation with the United States Patent Office in 1940.

A couple of vivid memories stand out concerning the cement plant. One was its sheer size; it seemed colossal as seen through the eyes of a young boy. The plant was a mile or so east of downtown Dewey and loomed on the horizon like a giant, off-white monolith, serving as a constant reminder of how much the local economy owed the cement industry. Dewey had paved roads and sidewalks before most cities in the area, and the Washington County Fairgrounds, our high school with its modern and spacious gymnasium, and the town library were all built from money generated by cement production.

Though not especially ornate or visually attractive, our gymnasium was state of the art, and it always stood out in stark contrast to the facilities of our competitors in the area. Rival cities such as Cleveland, Fairfax, Hominy, Pawnee, and Shidler were tax-starved in comparison with Dewey, with its taxation revenue from both the cement plant and Phillips Petroleum, and their schools were typically academically and athletically underfunded.

CONSTRUCTION, CEMENT PLANT

Another feature I remember well was the presence of maybe eight or ten modest houses in the shadows just south of the cement plant which housed most of the few Mexican-Americans in our town. They had names like Gutierrez, Macias, and Vargas, and most of the fathers worked at the cement plant and were thus able to provide a decent though hardly sumptuous standard of living for their children. One of those cement plant children, Johnny Gutierrez, went on to become a legendary Hall of Fame high school coach in Bloomfield, New Mexico, and the baseball field there is named for my high school classmate and dear old friend. In addition to his state recognition, Johnny was inducted into the National School Association Hall of Fame in 2012.

Though he retired several years ago after a long and distinguished career in teaching and coaching, Johnny continued to volunteer with the high school baseball team in Bloomfield. Then in

2012, just before school started, the school administration asked him if we would coach the ninth grade football team. Once again, Johnny was back at it, coaching the children of his initial group of players. When we get together at our rare class reunions (we have had maybe five or six all told), Johnny is my biggest cheerleader. He seems oblivious to the substantial gap between his recollections of my prowess on the football field and my actual accomplishments; I wish I had been half the athlete he thought me to be. John Gutierrez has one of the kindest hearts of any man I have ever met, and I am pleased as punch, as they say in Oklahoma, that good things have occurred in his life. There should be a lot more Johnny Gutierrez'es in this world.

Finding summer employment was not always easy for us young guys, and you pretty much took what you could find. A staple for employment was hauling hay. Farmers throughout the area always needed help every summer getting their hay out of the field and into the barn or off to market. It was awful work; the days were hot, the bales heavy, and the hay stuck to your skin like a hair shirt. However, we often took on the job because it offered us some spending money and, even more important, we thought it would build those large, bulging muscles so essential to success in football. Anything that prepared you for football was seen as a good thing. We were paid a dollar a ton for our efforts. As I remember, a bale of alfalfa hay weighed around seventy-five pounds, so every time thirty bales of hay were thrown on a flatbed trailer, we received a dollar. It was pretty much slave labor at its best and despite its supposed value in preparing us for the upcoming football campaign, we pretty much avoided going into the hay fields our last few years in high school unless there was absolutely no viable alternative.

I worked one summer as a laborer as part of a renovation project at the school. I must have pushed a thousand wheelbarrow loads of debris up a wooden ramp and out of the school building, only to turn right back around and bring in another thousand loads of cement and other materials for the much-needed renovations. Another summer, I was hired as a laborer to help repair Highway 75 near Dewey. I was paid the princely sum of one dollar per hour and often worked sixty-hour weeks or more. If I worked sixty-five hours a week, I was paid sixty-five dollars! Overtime? Forget it! Slave wages? A dollar an hour, period!

I toiled for a short while as a bricklayer's helper, and it turned out to be one of the worst jobs I ever had. The physical demands inherent in laying bricks were not nearly as much of an issue as having to put up with the endless, profane-laced abuse from the bricklayers. I was warned by others that bricklayers were blue collar prima donnas, and everything I heard was true and then some. Bricklayers were beyond impatient and impossible to work with; they weren't just impossible to please, they were insufferable! A helper could never haul enough bricks to make one of those ill-tempered bastards happy. They were, to put it in the vernacular, real assholes! I did not last long as a bricklayer's helper, and I knew beyond any doubt that when I left the worksite there was no amount of money that would get me to ever go back to that thankless job.

What appeared at first blush to be the job to end all jobs for a young guy, or at least this young guy, opened up in late July before my senior year of high school. It all began when Don Tyler, the owner of the aforementioned cement plant, called me to his office on Main Street. Just being invited to Mr. Tyler's office was both an honor and a source of considerable intimidation due to his status in the community; being summoned to meet him in his office was flat-out scary. He was cordial enough but very business-like, opening up our discussion with some kind words about my grandfather and all the good things he had done for Mr. Tyler at the cement plant. He told me he thought I was cut from the same cloth so he offered me a very responsible position for the next several weeks. I was to be the well-paid foreman of a work crew to be composed of compatriots of my choosing, and our task was to clear and burn some trees and brush on land owned by Mr. Tyler. I was flattered by his expressed confidence, and gladly accepted his generous offer. In the back of my mind, however, was the scary thought that the people I was going to hire and subsequently supervise were my friends who were known for their propensity to goof off, play tricks on each other, and engage in unbridled but mostly good-natured tomfoolery.

As a small example of their capacity for hijinks, at lunch the first day, one of the guys took off in the woods to go "Number Two", or take what some would today call "a dump" (what I now call a "W" in honor of our forty-third President). On the way to the privacy of the abundant trees, the perp picked up someone's work gloves and proceeded to use them as the receptacle for his peristaltic production. As you might guess, his unwitting victim was quite nonplussed when he put on his gloves to go back to work!

Over the next week or ten days, we cleared the designated rural real estate of downed branches, fallen trees, unwanted saplings and small bushes. Brush piles were created here and there for later immolation, and I generally felt we were giving Mr. Tyler an honest day's work for his money. But, as is sometimes the case in life, good times were not to last.

We finally reached the brush-burning phase of the operation in early August, maybe two weeks before the opening of fall football training which always signaled the end of our employability each summer. Burning the accumulated brush had gone swimmingly enough the first day or two, but things spiraled out of control one hot, windy August afternoon. That fateful mini-Apocalyptic day, the temperature was around 105 degrees, plus or minus two degrees, the skies were partly cloudy, the humidity low, and the seemingly sub-Saharan winds whipped up innocuous but aggravating dust devils. For those of you who live in more habitable environs and are deprived of their presence, a dust devil is a spiraling accumulation of dust and dirt blown about by sudden gusts of wind. I always thought of them as harmless mini-tornados that could not make it to the big-time.

My friends and I debated whether we should torch the brush piles or not, given the occasional winds that probably gusted as high as fifteen or twenty miles per hour. Finally, I asserted my authority as "boss" and opted in favor of going ahead with the burn. I thought I had sufficient personnel available to deal with any emergency should fire spread beyond a given brush pile, but that assumption proved to be erroneous! Almost immediately, the flames from one pile of brush jumped suddenly and with a vengeance to the surrounding grass and started a fiery, smoky path across an open field. My heart sank as I realized the possible consequences of my ill-fated decision.

For one thing, we were in grassland that stretched as far as the eye could see. We were also in oil country and there were several working rigs in the area.

The instantaneously out-of-control blaze was whipped into frenzy by the high winds, threatening everything in its path. In addition to the grasslands that were in peril, a small shed or two stood in its wake. More important, the fire was lapping at the edges of a couple of those aforementioned oil rigs which were calmly, rhythmically, and absent-mindedly pumping away, totally unaware of the danger lurking about.

Eventually, fire trucks showed up on the scene, and the blaze was extinguished by a mix of firefighters and Good Samaritans in a matter of a couple of hours with little or no damage to houses, barns, sheds, and oil rigs. That, of course, was a good thing but unfortunately acres of grassland had been reduced to ebony stubble.

The guys and I were hoping against hope that Mr. Tyler would be in one of those "Hey Boys, Shit Happens. Don't Worry About It" moods but we were not that lucky; he was an extremely unhappy camper! Deep down, I knew "Hey Boys, Shit Happens" moments were not in Mr. Tyler's DNA. Just as he had done several weeks before, he summoned me to his office and calmly and politely stripped me of my duties as straw boss, a decision that came as no surprise given the magnitude of my screw-up. On a more positive note, however, I learned a hard but valuable lesson about mixing fire, high winds, dried grassland, and piles of overheated and desiccated brush and trees.

Tom Mix: Town Marshal, King of the Cowboys, and Silent Movies Idol

Tom Mix, the famous cowboy star of the silent movie era, served as Dewey's town Marshal in 1912. Mix was born in Pennsylvania, an unlikely origin for a man who was to become Hollywood's "King of the Cowboys." Mix had little interest in school as a young boy, and dropped out in the fourth grade. It was about this same time that he happened to take in the famous Buffalo Bill Wild West Show, and he made a decision then and there to become a cowboy when he grew up.

A restless youth, Mix joined the Army in late adolescence in hopes of seeing action in the Spanish-American War. Overall, he adapted well to military life but was disappointed and perturbed about not being involved in actual combat in either the Spanish-American War or the ensuing skirmish, the Philippines Insurrection in 1901-02. In a fit of frustration about the lack of combat action, Mix went AWOL (Absent Without Leave), the military acronym for vacating one's post without authorization. For whatever reason, Mix was never pursued by the government for his dereliction of duty and, in a most unlikely turn of events, became a Texas Ranger in 1905. After a short time in law enforcement, Mix fulfilled his youthful dream of becoming a cowboy by working on a ranch in Oklahoma where he became quite adept at trick riding and roping. Brief stints with several Wild West shows followed, and he eventually drifted to California where he made his first movie in 1909.

Tom Mix had a number of marriages during this period (five in all), and his only child, Ruth Jane, was the product of the union with his third wife, a woman named Olive Stokes. Ruth Jane was born on July 13, 1912 while Mix was taking temporary leave from his acting career by serving as the town Marshal in my little old home town, Dewey. Mix actually lived on the opposite side of the street and down three or four houses to the north of my grandfather's home, and since I lived with my grandfather as a boy, this geographical proximity afforded me bragging rights with my friends even though Tom Mix and I never crossed paths. The fact that Mix's days in Dewey in 1912 and mine in the late 1940's and 1950's were three decades apart mattered little; he was still a famous neighbor as far as I was concerned. However, precious little was ever said about his living in the neighborhood, and I unfortunately have no anecdotes from family, friends, or neighbors to report from that short time Mix spent in Dewey.

Mix eventually left Dewey to return to the bright lights and the big city, and within a few years was a big star in Hollywood. At the pinnacle of his success, Mix was paid the princely sum of $17,500 a week, an absolutely incredible amount of money for that time. To give you some idea of just how much money Mix was making, that 1917 weekly salary of $17,500 would be the equivalent of just under $210,000 per week in 2015 dollars according to a website known as westegg.com. Mix eventually became a household name with an adoring American public, achieving legendary status of the magnitude of Hollywood superstars Lon Chaney, Charlie Chaplin, Rudolph Valentino, and Gloria Swanson. It has been estimated that Tom Mix made over $6 million dollars from his 300-plus movies and various other enterprises.

Mix was a Hollywood superstar for a decade but eventually found himself on the outside looking in due to the advent of talking movies. Mix, like several other stars of silent movies, did not make the transition to the so-called "talkies" well. The situation was further complicated by the fact he lost a fortune in the stock market crash in 1929. Always resilient, however, Mix retired from the movies in 1933 and moved to vaudeville theaters and the circus with his western act. The same year, he further reinvented himself, negotiating a financially lucrative contract in which his name was used for a radio show entitled *The Tom Mix Straight Shooters*. Another actor played his part, but the show was so successful it was a fixture on the radio until 1950, literally a decade after Mix's untimely and, in some ways, bizarre death. Tom Mix died in 1940 at the age of sixty while on his way to take part in a small vaudeville act in Phoenix, Arizona. He apparently was driving his beloved, bright yellow Ford Phaeton at excessive speed, lost control, ran off the road, and careened into a ditch where he sustained a fatal injury. Most authorities who have studied the life of Tom Mix believe he most likely would have survived the collision had he not stowed a heavy metal suitcase in the rear window of his car. The suitcase apparently became a lethal airborne missile when the car hit the ditch, striking Mix in the head, breaking his neck, and killing him instantly. That missile became known as the "Suitcase of Death" and it can be viewed today in the (kitschy) Tom Mix Museum in Dewey where other items associated with his life are on display.

By way of honoring his brief presence in Dewey, there is a one-day Tom Mix Festival held each September, beginning with the obligatory parade, followed by assorted Native American activities, a wild-west show, and day-long music. A five-kilometer run is also a part of the celebration, and I actually participated in the running of the third annual event in 1996. I ran mainly to escape my fortieth class reunion which was a dismal, dreary affair to be recounted shortly. I had the dubious honor of finishing the run in twenty-nine minutes and twenty-seven seconds which was about six minutes slower than my all-time personal best for that distance. This not-so-spectacular performance earned me a dead last finish in the men's 55-59 age group, and seventy-seventh out of eighty-nine total participants. The top runner, a twenty-five-year old by the name of Kurt Swanson, nosed me out by a mere twelve minutes and twenty-seven seconds!

DEWEY HOTEL AND MUSEUM

TOM MIX MUSEUM AND VINTAGE AUTOMOBILE

Family History

The Chamberlains

As we shall see shortly, little is known of my father's ancestry, so information about that side of the family is at best sketchy. My mother's ancestors, the Chamberlains, have provided a more complete and interesting description of that side of the family, though I would not describe it as particularly rich in detail either. It seems that there are two versions of the Chamberlain lineage, one put together by yours truly and another compiled by my cousin, Paul Chamberlain, of Conroe, Texas. The two accounts differ substantially in terms of the early family history but finally converge in the 1700's with the birth of Peleg Chamberlain (1736-1809) in Kent (Litchfield County), Connecticut. We shall start the proceedings with the LeUnes version, to be followed by that of Paul Chamberlain.

As best I can determine, the Chamberlain family roots in America are likely traceable to Richard Warren who was among the 102 passengers on The Mayflower when it made shore at Plymouth, Massachusetts, in 1620. Warren, later a businessman or merchant of some distinction in colonial Massachusetts, has been linked according to genealogical sources with perhaps as many as fourteen million people in this country. Among the more prominent descendants of Richard Warren are Civil War General Ulysses S. Grant, President Franklin Roosevelt, Astronaut Alan Shepard, author Laura Ingalls Wilder of *Little House on the Prairie* fame, actors Richard Chamberlain and Richard Gere, former Governor of Alaska and one-time Vice Presidential candidate Sarah Palin, and yours truly.

Having been a died-in-the-wool, yellow dog, liberal Democrat for all of my adult life, I am hesitant to acknowledge any possible blood relationship, however distant, with Mrs. Palin. Perhaps critics of my intellect will find solace in the ever-so-distant possible genetic link to the intellectually inert, idea-challenged, conservative cheerleader and all-around poster person for the Peter Principle. Of her intellect, social critic and humorist, Bill Maher once said: "Sarah Palin makes Joe the Plumber (a fleeting figure from the 2008 presidential election used by Palin as a symbolic representation of the "Average Joe") look like Aristophanes." A more comprehensive take on Mrs. Palin was provided several years ago by Janet Bagnall, a columnist for *The Gazette* (Montreal, Canada) who said, "Sarah Palin has been an exercise in Pygmalionism gone wrong. The most famous female politician in the world today is a vain and sanctimonious woman of boundless ambition and no vision." It is indeed a sad state of affairs when someone like Sarah Palin who turns out booboos faster than Apple turns out iPads can be trumpeted as legitimate Presidential material and a political pundit of the Republican persuasion.

I was appalled by a newspaper report which appeared in the Houston Chronicle in late 2009 or early 2010 in which a middle-aged woman from Central Texas blurted out to a reporter upon meeting Mrs. Palin at a political rally, "...I got so excited I nearly wet my pants." I have had a number of thoughts and emotions when meeting celebrities, dignitaries, and VIP's but wetting my pants at the prospect is not among them. What kind of a ninny is the woman? But then, perhaps our pants-wetting matron is representative of the type of woman who is enamored with Sarah Palin. I will give Sarah Palin credit for one thing: She's far from the brightest bulb in the chandelier but the woman knew how to take advantage of her celebrity status to make money, proving once again you do not have to be smart to become wealthy.

It is a source of fascination to see the speed with which the air has gone out of the Palin balloon over the past several years. She is seldom seen any more, the Republicans want absolutely nothing to do with her, and she is essentially (and deservedly) a has-been. It took the better part of three years for the gullible public which seems to relish being hoodwinked by quacks, charlatans, snake oil peddlers, and bogus political candidates to catch on to her act and reject it.

Richard Warren, the Mayflower Man. Richard Warren was born in England around 1850 and died in Plymouth in 1628. Genealogists, DNA experts, and other scientists and researchers possessing credentials far exceeding mine have been unable to turn up a trace concerning his ancestry prior to his coming to Plymouth. Given that the professionals have drawn so many blanks in their investigations of Richard Warren's pre-colonial life, I am content to look no farther. What is known is that he married an English woman named Elizabeth Walker on April 14, 1610 and they subsequently had seven children, apparently taking very seriously the Biblical admonition to go forth and multiply. In turn, the Warren children were also prolific, producing large families of their own. If enough people go forth and multiply, I guess you will eventually have fourteen million descendants! Few in the original *Mayflower* expedition can compete with the Warren legacy.

There were five female and two male children born to the Warrens and all survived to middle or late adulthood. The five females, Mary (1610-1683), Anna (1612-1676), Sarah (1613-1696), Elizabeth (1616-1670), and Abigail (1618-1693), were born in England and came to Plymouth in 1623 with their mother aboard a ship called *The Anne*. The two boys, Nathaniel (1625-1667) and Joseph (1627-1689), were born later in Plymouth. All the Warren children lived relatively long lives by standards of that era, and as stated above, produced many children in their own right.

Richard Warren was one of ten men who volunteered to go ashore to scout the Plymouth area before the other passengers left the relative safety of *The Mayflower*. Perhaps the most prominent among the members of the landing party was Myles Standish, the so-called "Hero of New England." Yet another prominent Mayflower passenger, though not in the landing party, was John Alden whose later rivalry with Standish for the hand of Priscilla Mullins gave rise over 200 years later to the famous poem by Henry Wadsworth Longfellow, *The Courtship of Myles Standish* (1858). Alden, a cooper or barrel-maker by trade, won the hand of Priscilla Mullins and they subsequently had ten children.

Sentimental Journey Home II (1938-1965)

Those early settlers wisely saw the need for some form of organized governance if they were to survive, and this realization led them to create what is known as the Mayflower Compact. The Compact was signed on November 11, 1620, in Provincetown Harbor on what is now Cape Cod by forty-one male colonists, among them Richard Warren. The document established a colony free of English law and was essentially designed to promote the common good through majority rule (even though the signers themselves were not a majority of the 102 people who made it to Plymouth on The Mayflower). In addition to Richard Warren, others signing the Compact included several men who were to take on considerable importance later in shaping the colony at Plymouth, namely William Bradford, William Brewster, and the aforementioned duo of John Alden and Myles Standish. Unfortunately, the hardships of *The Mayflower* voyage coupled with the privations encountered at Plymouth that first year took a huge toll on the early colonists, and only nineteen of the original forty-one signers lived through the winter in 1620. Richard Warren was among the survivors.

GREAT-GRANDFATHER JEHIEL CHAMBERLAIN
WIFE EDITH MAUD, AND PR CHAMBERLAIN

Arnold LeUnes

JEHIEL CHAMBERLAIN, FAMILY, FAMILY CAR, FAMILY CAT

GRANDMOTHER EDITH MAUD ALGER CHAMBERLAIN

Sentimental Journey Home II (1938-1965)

THE CHAMBERLAINS, PG, PR, PHILLIP, CIRCA 1945

L TO R PHILLIP CHAMBERLAIN, GERMAN SHEPHERD
CHIEF, MOM, PR, EDITH MAUD, PHILLIP CIRCA 1940

The possible (probable?) ancestral link between Richard Warren and the Chamberlain family goes as follows:

One of Richard Warren's sons, Nathaniel is the second link in the *Mayflower* ancestral chain;

Nathaniel Warren (1625-1667) married Sarah Walker, and they produced Alice Warren (1656-1692);

Alice Warren married Thomas Gibbs in 1767 and they produced Abigail Gibbs;

Abigail Gibbs (????-1741) married Jireh Swift in 1697 and they produced Jabez Swift;

Jabez Swift (1700-1767) married Abigail Pope in 1729 and they produced Abigail Swift;

Abigail Swift (1740-????) married Peleg Chamberlain (1736-1808) and the first tie to the Chamberlain *Mayflower* lineage was established. Abigail Swift Chamberlain and Peleg Chamberlain, in turn, produced Leander Chamberlain (1766-1822) who married Mercy Berry;

Leander Chamberlain and Mercy Berry Chamberlain produced Jehiel Chamberlain (1790-1839);

Jehiel Chamberlain married Lura Grenel (Luray Grennell?) Chamberlain and they produced my great grandfather, Jehiel Leander Chamberlain (1833-1924);

Jehiel Leander Chamberlain married Marion L. Atkinson in 1868 and they were the parents of my maternal grandfather, Paul Richard (P. R.) Chamberlain;

Paul Richard Chamberlain (1879-1949) married Edith Maud Alger (1879-1922) in 1908 and they produced my two uncles, Paul Gregory Chamberlain (1909-1988) and Phillip Lee Chamberlain (1913-1968), and my mother Marion Katherine Chamberlain LeUnes Berryhill Hunt (1916-1963);

Marion Katherine Chamberlain LeUnes and George John LeUnes (1917-2006) produced Arnold Dallas LeUnes (me). As stated elsewhere, I was born in Bartlesville, Oklahoma, on April 16, 1938 at 0646 hours. I weighed in at eight pounds, three-and-a-half ounces and was twenty-three inches long. This is where the saga began for me.

An interesting side note about the family can be traced back to Peleg Chamberlain and his wife, Abigail Swift in the middle 1700's. It seems the couple produced seven children, Leander, Rocksilana, Jirah, Swift, Lorany, Hannah, and Abigail. As noted earlier, Leander was the father of Jehiel who produced my great-grandfather, Jehiel Leander Chamberlain.

A particularly noteworthy descendant of this group of Peleg's children was a male child named Hiram who was born of the marriage of Swift Chamberlain (1764/5-1828) and his wife. Hiram Chamberlain (1797-1866) grew up with his family in Vermont as a cultured, well-educated, and religious man. He received a degree from Middlebury College in Vermont and, in 1825, graduated from the prestigious Andover Theological Seminary following a year of study at Princeton

Theological Seminary. Among his classmates at Andover were a number of important ministers or professors of the day including Edward Beecher (1813-1887). Reverend Beecher had a dozen siblings, the most notable being Henry Ward Beecher (1813-1887), the famous nineteenth-century clergyman, social reformer, abolitionist, and speaker, and Harriett Beecher Stowe (1811-1897), also an abolitionist and author of the iconic novel, *Uncle Tom's Cabin* (1852).

The Vermont Chamberlains were known as a religious lot. One of them, Remembrance, served the Lord as an evangelical missionary in Georgia. Another, Jeremiah, ministered in Mississippi, and Hiram's ministry eventually brought him to Texas. Hiram's decision to leave the comforts of New England for the unknown and unpredictable trials and tribulations of the south and west led him first to St. Louis, Missouri, then to Memphis, Tennessee, and finally to Brownsville, Texas, where in 1850 he set up the first Protestant church along the Rio Grande River.

That southern-most tip of Texas had long been the dominion of the Catholic Church and Hiram saw it as his Godly mission to alert Protestants to the evils of Catholicism. His views of religion were narrowly fundamental, believing that resolute self-denial and unwavering emotional adherence to one's duties were critical components of Christian piety. However, it is difficult to think unkindly of a man who was a staunch believer in the strict separation of church and state, perhaps the single most important protection against tyranny promoted by the founding fathers of this country (though it is not mentioned in the Constitution as some people think). He was also an ardent secessionist and served in the Third Texas Infantry as a Confederate Chaplain during the Civil War.

"La Madama" Henrietta Chamberlain King. Hiram Chamberlain married three times and his first wife, Maria Morse, bore him a daughter named Henrietta Maria Chamberlain (1832-1925). Henrietta was a lovely young woman with an incisive mind, traits that did not go unnoticed by a brash and dashing young Irish river boat captain and handsome part-time cowboy by the name of Richard King (1824-1885). Captain King, as he was known in those parts, was the owner and pilot of a steamship servicing the Rio Grande area who also dabbled in the cattle business, more or less as a hobby at first. Though unschooled and rough around the edges compared to the well-mannered, well-dressed, refined, and educated Hiram Chamberlain, Captain King was able to persuade the fundamentalist minister to let him marry the lovely and sophisticated Henrietta.

The wedding was a classic event, uniting a loud, hard-driving, profane frontier brawler with a lady of obvious class and upbringing. The ceremony took place on December 10, 1854 and for the honeymoon, Captain and Mrs. King spent four days on his small ranch in south Texas. She fell in love with the place and soon became known to the Mexican ranch hands working for Captain King as "La Madama", a nickname born of affection and admiration and one she carried to her grave some seventy years later.

It is fascinating to think the entire operation, soon to be known widely as the King Ranch, grew out of a small cow camp on Santa Gertrudis Creek near what is now Kingsville coupled with 15,500 acres Captain King bought from the estate of a deceased Mexican landowner for two cents per acre.

Captain King shrewdly parlayed this meager beginning with a few cows grazing on some desolate land into one of the largest ranch operations in the world.

A son was born to the couple in 1863 and his mother named him Robert E. Lee King, no doubt in honor of the storied Confederate General. Three other children, a boy, Richard, and three girls, Nettie, Ellen, and Alice Gertrudis, were born later, and the ranch prospered thanks to the good business acumen of Richard King and, later, that of Alice's husband, Robert Justus Kleberg. By the time Captain King died of stomach cancer in 1885, his ranch holdings included 500,000 acres, 10,000 horses, 20,000 sheep, and 100,000 head of cattle. The Captain died at the Menger Hotel in San Antonio and it is said that his ghost still haunts the hallways there. I stayed in the Menger several years ago, totally unaware at the time of the likely presence of Captain King's ghost. Looking back, however, I firmly believe the premises were "hainted."

After Captain King's death, Robert Kleberg managed the ranch for nearly fifty years, from 1885 to 1932, and expanded their land holdings to over a million acres. In turn, his son, R. J. Kleberg III, (Captain King and Henrietta's grandson), managed the ranch from 1932-1974. R. J. Kleberg was followed as CEO by James Clements and he held the position until 1988, at which time Darwin Smith took the reins. Smith's ascendancy to the CEO position represented the first time someone not related to Captain King had been in that position. The ranch has since taken on a corporate look with headquarters in Houston, some 200 miles to the north. It has maintained its considerable presence in agricultural pursuits but now has holdings in the petroleum, mercantile, and timber industries. Beginning three decades ago, the ranch became a visitor's site, with a museum and twelve-mile driving tour.

Henrietta grieved deeply over the death of her husband as would be expected, but eventually recovered following a long period of mourning. She spent her final forty years overseeing the ranch and engaging in religious, philanthropic, and humanitarian causes in the south Texas area. When "La Madama" died in 1925 at the age of ninety-two, the burial took place in the forty-acre Chamberlain Cemetery (named after her father, Hiram) in her home town of Kingsville. The hearse carrying "La Madama's" body was led to the cemetery by two hundred ranch hands dressed in their usual work clothes, a fitting tribute to one of the last pioneers and a most interesting (and wealthy) Chamberlain with distant ties to yours truly. A visit to the Chamberlain cemetery in Kingsville is one item on my abundant bucket list.

Paul Richard (P. R.) Chamberlain. Paul Richard Chamberlain, or simply P. R. as he was known to his family and friends, was our maternal grandfather. He was raised by his parents as an only child in Cleveland, Ohio, graduated from Case Institute in Cleveland, Ohio (now Case Western Reserve University), and was a chemist by academic training. As mentioned elsewhere, he eventually became the superintendent of the aforementioned Portland Cement Plant just east of the main center of Dewey, where he also was the chief chemist. He also served for a time as town mayor.

His father, Jehiel Leander Chamberlain, was the youngest of seven children born on October 4, 1833 of the marriage between Jehiel Chamberlain and Luray Grinnell. Jehiel Leander married

Marion L. Atkinson, fourteen years younger than he, on October 6, 1868 and they made their home first in Solon, Ohio, and later in Cleveland. The couple celebrated their fiftieth wedding anniversary in 1919, and Marion died shortly thereafter at the age of seventy-two. Jehiel Leander then moved to Dewey and lived with my grandfather until his death in 1924 at the age of ninety. Jehiel Leander and Marion are buried next to each other in the Willoughby Hills Cemetery, Lake County, Ohio. Maybe I need to add a visit to the bucket list…

L TO R ZENOBIA CHAMBERLAIN (PG'S WIFE), MOM, EDITH, PR, PAULA JO, YOURS TRULY, CIRCA 1945

PR AND COUSIN EDITH CHAMBERLAIN (DAUGHTER OF PG)

MOM AND GIRL'S SCHOOL CLASSMATES, CIRCA 1932

MOM IN DRY CANADIAN RIVER BED, PANHANDLE OF TEXAS, CIRCA 1945

GEORGE LEUNES, MOM, ME, PAULA JO, BUB, CIRCA 1944

I have not been able to turn up much about the life of Jehiel Leander other than he served in the 23d Ohio Infantry during the Civil War for three years and his rank when he left the service was Command Sergeant. Family lore always held that he was a General in the Union Army, but obviously that is not true. Commissioned officers in Jehiel's unit included, Rutherford B. Hayes and William McKinley; Hayes was a colonel at the time and McKinley a lieutenant.

As for Grandpa Chamberlain, he was a small man, maybe five feet five inches tall, slight in stature, with thick, snow-white, uncombed but not unruly hair. In his latter days, he was stooped and twisted due to scoliosis or osteoporosis (or both). Though Grandpa Chamberlain was not a tall man, it is said that he towered over his own father by a good six inches. He was a thoughtful soul, introspective, and not given to loudness, frivolity, or ostentation. I suspect he had his grievances with us at-times rowdy and rambunctious children, and he may have vented his feelings about us with our mother from time to time, but we were seldom even aware of his presence. He was, in a few words, quiet and reclusive. I will relate more about Grandpa Chamberlain shortly.

The investigative efforts of my cousin Paul Chamberlain paint a rather different picture of the family history, or at least the earliest parts of it. In his work, Paul has traced the family lineage all the way back to the year 1010 when our earliest known ancestor, Ralph Fitz Herlewin, was born. Herlewin was a native of Normandy, France, and he and his wife, Helesinde de Tancarville produced a son in 1040, William de Tancarville. He, in turn, sired a son by his wife Agnes Stigand in 1070, and that child became known as John Lord of Tankerville Chamberllin {sic}.

If one takes Paul Chamberlain's account at face value, the relocation of the Chamberlains from France to England began to take place in the last part of the eleventh century, probably tied in some way to the Norman invasion of that country in 1066. By the beginning of the twelfth century, all Chamberlain ties to the old country, France, had pretty much been severed. Around 1600, several Chamberlains found their way to Plymouth, Massachusetts, and five or six generations later, the two versions of the Chamberlain family history began to merge with some degree of clarity. There are many inconsistencies and an abundance of room for speculation concerning the specifics of the early family lineage, but a clear picture of the remainder emerged following the birth of Peleg Chamberlain in 1736.

Thanks to Ancestry.com, additional light of a more scientific nature has been shed on my background. In the spring of 2016, I submitted a vial of saliva to Ancestry.com for DNA analysis, and the results suggest a very strong British and western European ancestry on my part. According to their analysis, my ancestry is fifty-nine percent British, eleven percent Irish, and the remaining thirty percent is spread in small amounts among Eastern and Western Europe, North Africa, and other geographical locales. Clearly, there is a huge British Isles component to my ancestry.

LeUnes Family History

Much of what is known about the early LeUnes family is found in a terse, gut-wrenchingly sad memoir of sixty-seven pages penned by my paternal grandmother, Gertrude Spencer Chamberlain (May 27, 1882-October 27, 1922). She was born early that late May morning in 1882, and raised in an over-the-top fundamental religious environment. She says nothing of her childhood experiences other than terrible angst about religion, obsessing over whether or not she was always doing the right thing or being a properly pious person. In her mini-memoir, she makes brief mention of a marriage that took place when she was eighteen, a relationship fraught with trouble right from the start, with multiple separations and, eventually, divorce. She reports nothing about her life from the first marriage to the time of her second to my grandfather, John LeUnes (May 2, 1883-August 15, 1947). It was not until August 8, 1917, that she married Grandpa John (as we called him for the short time he was in our lives), and they lived most of their married life together in Arkansas City, Kansas.

Of her marriage to Grandpa John, she reports: "Somehow I married again. I did not intend to, but I did, and my new husband was very good to me. We went into business and prospered very fast, and all I could think of was a fine home and gardens." Though she never said so in so many words, the business she was referring to almost certainly was the family restaurant the two of them owned and operated in Arkansas City, Kansas.

John and Gertrude LeUnes. Grandpa John LeUnes was born in Sparta, Greece, and orphaned as a small child. He came to this country in 1894 as a pre-adolescent, speaking nary a word of English. After landing in New York and being processed through Ellis Island, he headed for the Greek section of the city where he quickly learned English, completed his schooling, and eventually found his way to Flint, Michigan where he opened a restaurant. He had a brother who stayed in New York City and, from all reports, prospered nicely as a jeweler. I once saw a picture of his brother holding a drawer full of diamonds and gold and silver jewelry he apparently kept in a storage box in the garage at his home. The cache was his life's work as well as a retirement hobby, and undoubtedly was worth many thousands of dollars. He reportedly never suffered theft of his beloved treasure despite what appeared to a young boy to be a decidedly laissez-faire approach to security.

GRANDPA JOHN LEUNES, GERTRUDE, AUNT VERA, GEORGE LEUNES, CIRCA 1920

GRANDPA JOHN LEUNES, WIFE GERTRUDE, CAR, PET

NEW HOME RESTAURANT

STEAKS AND CHOPS

Small Steak	.50	Pork Chops	.50
with onions	.75	Veal Chops	.50
with mushrooms		Veal Chops Breaded	.75
T Bone Steak	.75	Veal Cutlets Tomato Sauce	.75
with onions	1.00	Lamb Chops	.75
with mushroms		Pork Tenderloin	.75
Sirloin Steak	.75	Pork Sausage	.40
with onions	1.00	Fried Ham	.40
with mushrooms		Bried Bacon	.40
Porterhouse Steak	1.25	Hamburger Steak	.40
with onions	1.50		
with mushrooms		**Genuine Mexican Chili 20c**	
Double Porterhouse Steak for two	2.50		

EGGS AND OMELET

Ham and Eggs	.50	Bacon and Eggs	.50
Egg Omelet	.30	Ham Omelet	.45
Two Fried Eggs	.25	Cheese "	.45
Two Boiled Eggs	.25	Plain "	.35
Two Poached Eggs	.30	Spanish "	.75

OYSTERS IN SEASON

6 Oysters Fried	.50	Oyster Stew	.35
6 Oysters Raw	.25	½ Dozen, Stew Plain	.25
1 Dozen Raw	.45	1 Dozen Milk Stew	.60

MISCELLANEOUS

Milk Toast	.20	Bread and Milk	.15
Cream Toast	.35	Crackers and Milk	.15
Buttered Toast	.10	Corn Flakes and Milk	.15
French Toast	.25	Oat Meal and Milk	.15
Shredded Wheat	.20	Home Made Wheat Cakes	.20
Cup Cakes .10 Fried Cakes	.10	Waffles	.20

POULTRY

Spring Chicken, Whole Fried or Broiled	Spring Chicken, Half Fried or Broiled

HOME MADE PIES and CAKES 10c

NEW HOME RESTAURANT

FRUIT

Oranges Sliced	.15	Grape Fruit	.15
Oranges Whole	.10	Watermelon	.10
Sliced Bananas in Cream	.25	Cantaloupe	.10
Strawberries in Cream	.35	Peaches in Cream	.20

All Kinds of Fruit in Season

VEGETABLES

French Fried Potatoes	.15	Sweet Pickles	.20
Hash Brown Potatoes	.15	Sliced Cucumbers	.25
Lyonnaise Potatoes	.15	Sliced Onions	.10
Shoe String Potatoes	.15	Radishes	.15
Stewed Peas	.20	Celery	.25
Stewed Corn	.20	Lettuce	.25
Stewed Tomatoes	.20	Olives	.25
Sliced Tomatoes	.20	Sour Pickles	.15

SALADS

Potato Salad	.25	Chicken Salad	.50
Combination Salad	.25	Lobster Salad	.60

SANDWICHES

Hot Beef	.25	Hot Pork	.25
Swiss Cheese	.15	Ham and Egg	.25
American Cheese	.15	Fried Ham	.20
Boiled Ham	.15	Egg	.15
Hamburger	.15	Roast Pork	.15
Chicken	.25	Roast Beef	.15
Club Sandwich	.50	Sardine Sandwich	.25

DINNER

Clam Chowder Soup............ Vegetable Soup............

All Kinds of Soup

Roast Veal	Veal Stew
Roast Beef	Beef Stew, Vegetable
Roast Pork	Ham and Cabbage
Roast Lamb	Beef Heart and Dressing
Vienna Roast	Hamburger Steak
Fried Trout	Liver and Bacon
Fried Perch	Baked Macaroni
Fried White Fish	Beef Stew, Spanish
Fish Cakes	Spare Ribs and Kraut
Veal Pot Pie	

CHICKEN DINNER

Roast Chicken	Chicken Stew Dumplings
Chicken Stew Spanish	Fricasse Chicken

HOME MADE PIES and CAKES 10c

MENU, NEW HOME CAFÉ, ARKANSAS CITY, KANSAS

Grandpa John met Grandmother Gertrude Spencer, an Irish immigrant, while living in Flint, Michigan. The two of them left that city after a short stay because she wanted to live closer to her parents who had moved to Newkirk, Oklahoma, just south of the Kansas state line. John and Gertrude moved to nearby Arkansas City, Kansas, married shortly thereafter, and started the New Home Café, a restaurant that was well-received by the locals.

I had always assumed the cafe had a major Greek theme, given Grandpa John's heritage, but a recently discovered menu totally discounts that assumption. The menu featured what I would call down home American-style food, with nineteen kinds of meat, sixteen vegetables, fourteen different sandwiches, a huge array of soups and salads, oysters in season, "Genuine Mexican Chili", and several home-made pies and cakes. Nothing on the menu was remotely suggestive of Greek cuisine.

After getting settled in Arkansas City, Grandmother Gertrude and Grandpa John adopted two children, a female they named Vera Banita LeUnes (Walner) (March 18, 1909-December 1, 1997), and my father who was named George John LeUnes (October 30, 1917-September 29, 2006). Until I read Grandmother Gertrude's memoir, I was not aware that my father was just three days short of five years old when his mother passed away, and essentially was raised by Grandpa John and the older sister, Vera. Not having a mother at home may account for some of his self-reported adolescent proneness to impulsivity, "wildness", and lapses in judgment.

One example of this impulsivity occurred when he was sixteen. It seems he jumped on a freight train with the intent to ride the rails from his home to wherever it would take him. He eventually completed what turned out to be a several thousand mile round trip to Seattle, Washington, and back. Fortunately, his athletic talent served as a buffer for the adolescent impulsivity, and pretty much kept him on a straight and narrow path. He graduated from high school in 1934, ranking thirty-first in a class of 186. He was a good football player in high school and later played at Arkansas City Junior College. He also excelled in the pole vault, and would have qualified for the national championships his senior year in high school except for the fact that only two people per state could advance to the national finals and the top competitors in the event were both from his high school.

Well-kept secrets and how they are often surrounded with mystery and defended with tenacity is an interesting aspect of family folklore. One such example in our family, albeit untrue, was that our father knew nothing about his background prior to his adoption at an early age by John and Gertrude LeUnes. We LeUnes children were fed this line of bull throughout our lives, and believed it up until the death of our father in 2006. In looking through some of his papers shortly after he died, I learned that he was actually born in a hospital in Oklahoma City to an unmarried couple named Margaret Carter and G. A. Green, and was known until he was adopted on the twenty-fifth of April in 1918 as "Baby Carter". He was listed on the adoption papers as being four months old, though that information conflicts with his birth certificate which stated that he was born on October 30, 1917. It appears that he had to have been seven months old, not four, at the time of his adoption, and he made the transition from "Baby Carter" to George John LeUnes.

Grandmother Gertrude died of cancer in 1922, having been diagnosed with an operable and hence possibly curable stomach tumor. She was urged to undergo surgery to control the progression of the disease, but refused to accept medical advice and intervention. Instead, she turned to the blind faith that had guided her from virtually the moment she was born. To say she was over the edge when it came to religion would be a massive understatement. She truly believed to the very core of her existence up until the day she died God would heal her cancerous affliction through some sort of miracle, thus rendering surgical intervention superfluous. For the last several years of her life, the tumor grew in size and weight to the point where she sometimes had to place it in a wheelbarrow in order to walk around. I will return to this saga soon.

Grandpa John stayed on in Arkansas City after Gertrude's death and ran the restaurant for another ten years. He then deeded the restaurant over to another Greek family and moved to Tulsa where he opened yet another café. He died in Tulsa in 1947 and was transported to the family plot at the Riverview Cemetery in Arkansas City for burial. He, Gertrude, and my father are all buried there and several other family members will eventually join them at that site. My brothers, sisters, and I have politely declined my dad's offer to be interred alongside him and his parents. Judy and I both have a preference for cremation as a means of disposing of our earthly remains.

Gertrude LeUnes Meets Aimee Semple McPherson. Grandmother Gertrude's search for a cancer cure through divine intervention led her to seek the counsel of one of the leading religious figures and purported miracle workers of the early 1900's, Aimee Semple McPherson (1890-1944), or "Sister Aimee" as she was widely known throughout the US. Grandmother Gertrude first met Sister Aimee in St. Louis, Missouri, while seeking a healing miracle from the esteemed religious icon and faith healer. Grandmother Gertrude listened to two weeks of sermonizing in St. Louis, and though an actual healing did not take place, Grandmother Gertrude's belief in Sister Aimee's ability to perform miracles remained steadfast. She returned home from St. Louis in great spirits, unaware that fate was going to bring the two of them together soon, this time in Arkansas City. Their reunion took place in May of 1922, some five months before Grandmother Gertrude's death.

Sister Aimee McPherson was born in Canada at the end of the nineteenth century, and was immersed in fundamental religion by her mother from the earliest moments of her childhood. She spent her entire adult life as an evangelist, tent revivalist, and erstwhile faith healer, eventually founding in 1927 an evangelical Pentecostal denomination known as the International Church of the Foursquare Gospel in Los Angeles. The church's name came from the four-fold ministry which focused on Jesus Christ as Savior, Spirit Baptizer, Healer, and coming King. The church empire grew rapidly under her charismatic leadership, prospered greatly after her death, and by the year 2000 had an estimated eight million worshipers in 60,000 Foursquare Gospel churches in 144 countries across the world. US membership in 2006 was around 350,000 who worshipped in 1,875 churches. As of 2014, there were 6,500 credentialed Four Square ministers in this country alone. Clearly, Sister Aimee left a lasting, far-reaching legacy.

Sister Aimee achieved additional public notoriety because of her fervent opposition to the twin evils of alcohol consumption and the theory of evolution. She regarded evolution as one of Satan's vilest ploys to win over the hearts and souls of the American people, and this led her to become an avid supporter of William Jennings Bryan during the famous Scopes monkey trial in 1925. The Scopes trial, formally known as *The State of Tennessee v. Scopes*, was a landmark event in American history in which a high school biology teacher, John Scopes, was accused of unlawfully teaching evolution in his classes. The trial turned into a jousting contest between the two powerful attorneys, William Jennings Bryan representing the state of Tennessee and the lawyer defending Scopes, the inimitable Clarence Darrow. The end result of the Scopes deliberations was to open the doors to the teaching of evolution in American schools. Of course, Aimee McPherson was appalled at the results of the trial, and took her fight against evolution to the masses.

INTRODUCTION

IN SENDING out this little book, My First, I feel the need of reaching suffering ones whom otherwise, I could never reach.

I suffered so many years and wanted to read, or hear the testimony of someone who really had been healed.

I wrote several different publishers, and no one seemed to take any interest in my plea, therefore, by the help of God, I am going to reach everyone I can, by sending out this little book, for I want everyone to know what Jesus has done for me. He will do the same for you.

Our Dear Jesus is no respector of persons. He loves you, and has a special work for everyone, a work that no one else can do, that is why we ought to be careful and ask Jesus to lead us every day.

If this book will help you to trust Jesus more, to take him as your Daily Companion, then indeed I will be happy and asking Dear Jesus to Bless and Keep You, is My Prayer.

Some day in Glory, we can praise Him together.

GERTRUDE LE UNES

GRANDMOTHER GERTRUDE BOOK INTRODUCTION

Arnold LeUnes

GRANDMOTHER GERTRUDE AND ABDOMINAL TUMOR

A most interesting series of events transpired prior to Gertrude's second meeting with Sister Aimee. It seems that Grandpa John could see that his wife's death was imminent so he moved her back to Flint, thus allowing her to die in the city of her fondest childhood memories. In an effort to stave off her impending demise, Grandpa John reluctantly agreed to allow a team of surgeons in Flint to perform emergency surgery on the critically ill Gertrude. Few thought she would survive but ironically, she did, if only for a short time!

At the time of the surgery, Grandmother Gertrude weighed 176 pounds. After the surgical team finished removing the cancerous mass from her abdomen, she weighed eighty-seven pounds, or two pounds less than the eighty-nine pound tumor! Physician after physician indicated there was no way my grandmother could live another day following the surgery and if she did, it would be a miracle. The very thought that a miracle might be at hand was grist for my grandmother's mill, further fueling her religious fervor and fanaticism. Through a series of convoluted thought processes about the healing powers of blind faith, Grandmother Gertrude came to believe she had been granted additional life thanks to a religious miracle and would eventually be cured of all symptoms through prayer. This is where Sister Aimee McPherson entered the picture again.

In May of 1922, Grandpa John and Gertrude moved back from Flint to Arkansas City following her surgery and, as fate would have it, Sister Aimee was making a fourteen-day appearance in nearby Wichita, Kansas. Reports kept filtering back to Arkansas City during those two weeks about miraculous faith healings taking place at the Wichita revivals. Sister Aimee supposedly had cured stammering and stuttering in a minister, caused goiters to disappear from the necks of two women, restored sight and hearing to several dozen blind and deaf people, helped youths crippled by polio throw away their crutches and walk again, and, in what must have been her crowning achievement, convinced three hundred gypsies to accept Christ as their savior.

A series of reports about the miracles being performed by Sister Aimee in Wichita were filed with the local newspaper, the *Arkansas City Traveler*, and this feedback led the city ministerial alliance to pass a motion to formally invite the faith healer to Arkansas City once her important work in nearby Wichita was done. The decision was not altogether a popular one, with a couple of dissenting votes cast by more traditional religious practitioners perhaps blessed with better sense than their misguided peers in the ministerial alliance.

Prior to the Arkansas City revival, Grandmother Gertrude and three female friends drove over to Wichita to bear witness to the much-anticipated miracles that would soon be coming to their fair city. While at the revival, Grandmother Gertrude provided testimony about banishing the aforementioned cancerous tumor from her abdomen, which prompted Sister Aimee to pray over her condition. Grandmother Gertrude left Wichita convinced a miracle was in the offing, almost certainly when Sister Aimee came to Arkansas City to perform her magic.

In the midst of these emotional events, a powerful testimonial to Sister Aimee's healing powers was posted in an article in the *Arkansas City Traveler* by sports reporter, Joe Moore, on May 13, 1922. Moore reported he was allowed to pass under the rope separating Sister Aimee from her legions of admirers at the Wichita revival one evening, thanks in great part to intervention by Grandmother Gertrude who convinced the esteemed revivalist and new-found friend to minister to his case. It seems Mr. Moore had suffered an accident nine years earlier that left one of his legs several inches shorter than the other. This deformity required that he walk with the aid of crutches, which in turn caused him to suffer from back problems.

According to Mr. Moore's report, "Mrs. Gardner and Mrs. LeUnes came to me. They knelt beside me and prayed. I prayed with them. Mrs. Kennedy, mother of Mrs. McPherson, joined us in prayer. A strange feeling came over me. I know my face must have worn a beatific expression. I felt like a man born again." He went on to say, "Then they told me that my back was straighter than before, and that my coat, which generally fit me tight, was wrinkled and looser. I was not aware of this transformation because I was overjoyed at being able to walk unaided by crutches. I sat down but I couldn't keep still. I got up and strutted all around."

Flushed with the successes from her visit in Wichita, Sister Aimee accepted the gracious invitation from the Arkansas City ministerial alliance, agreeing to come to town on May 29 for just one evening to conduct a revival. In eager anticipation of Sister Aimee's visit, Grandmother Gertrude told her friends and acquaintances, "Mrs. McPherson does not ask for any guarantee. Mrs. McPherson earns her way by selling her books. I have brought some of these books to Arkansas City to sell for her. I am selling them out of gratitude for her coming here and for what she has done for me, as I was healed by the prayers of Mrs. McPherson." The books were *Divine Healing Sermons*, *Second Coming of Christ*, and *This is That*, the latter a collection of Sister Aimee's sermons. Her audiences were also encouraged to subscribe to *Bridal Call Monthly Magazine*. Grandmother Gertrude also offered her fellow citizens the opportunity to come to the family restaurant and purchase chairs for $25 apiece. In turn, each person's name would be inscribed on their chair for eventual installation in the tabernacle Sister Aimee was planning to build in Los Angeles, California. The tabernacle came to fruition five years later in 1927 and became the home of the aforementioned Foursquare Church.

Sister Aimee held forth as planned on Monday the 29th of May, 1922, and the headlines in the local paper the next day stated five persons had been healed during the previous night's proceedings. Among them were a partially blind woman, a young stutterer, a baby, a partially deaf man, and a woman suffering from a nervous breakdown. Despite these "successes", there were many who were disappointed by Sister Aimee's brief visit. Sister Aimee's mother hustled her off stage and out of town immediately after the completion of the service. Two rows of physically ill people expecting a miracle from the healer were left without so much as a good word, and tears flowed from the aged and infirm alike. Despite some major disappointments on the part of hopeful worshipers, the visit by Sister Aimee was declared a huge success and her legend carried on untarnished. She left Arkansas City, never to return again.

The last decade of Sister Aimee's life was stormy, with rumors of amorous escapades involving several men, including an alleged brief affair with the famous comedian, Milton Berle. She also got involved in power struggles with her mother and daughter over control of the Foursquare Church, fell out of favor with the press, got involved in a rocky marriage (her third), and eventually died under mysterious circumstances in California in 1944. It seems Sister Aimee had been scheduled to conduct a revival in Oakland, California, one evening, but was found dead in her hotel room that same morning by her son, Rolf. The cause of death was ingestion of a lethal dose of a barbiturate compound. Many believed her demise to be a suicide, but the coroner's official ruling was accidental death by drug overdose. With the death of his iconic mother, Rolf McPherson took up the reins of the religious empire Sister Aimee had created and managed it capably for nearly a half century.

Grandmother Gertrude died five months after those ministrations in Arkansas City. She believed to the very end that miracles were close at hand, imbedded somewhere in those prayers spoken so openly and eloquently by her iconic, faith-healing idol, Sister Aimee McPherson.

American Life in the 1940's

U. S. Population is 132 Million
The Annual Average Salary is $1300
The Annual Average Salary of a Teacher is $1450
World War II Creates First Great Exodus of Women in to the Workforce
55% of American Houses Have Indoor Plumbing
U.S. Supreme Court Gives Black Citizens the Right to Vote
Japanese Immigrants Placed in Internment Camps for the Duration of World War II
President Harry Truman Orders Atomic Bombs Dropped on Hiroshima and Nagasaki
Soldiers Returning From War Start the Baby Boom
Eniac, State of the Art Digital Computer Weighed 30 Tons, Stood Two Stories High
Big Bands of Glenn Miller, Tommy Dorsey, Benny Goodman Dominate Music Scene
Dr. Spock Writes *Common Sense Book of Baby and Child Care*
Decade of the Jitterbug, Tupperware, the Slinky, Zoot Suits, Rosie the Riveter
Heyday of Movies such as *Casablanca, Citizen Kane, Mrs. Miniver, Bambi,* and *Fantasia*
Five Million Americans Own Television Sets with Five-Inch Black and White Screens
The Magazine *Seventeen* Published For the First Time
Player Jackie Robinson Integrates Major League Baseball Thanks to Branch Rickey
Stan Musial of St. Louis Cardinals Highest Paid Pro Baseball player, $50,000 Per Year
Heyday of Boxing: Joe Louis, Willie Pep, Sugar Ray Robinson, and Ike Williams
Byron Nelson (PGA) and Babe Didrikson Zaharias (LPGA) Dominate Professional Golf
Some Northern University Football Teams Have Black Players

Borger, Texas

As noted earlier, the Phillips Petroleum Company headquarters were situated in Bartlesville, and many area citizens were employed by that immensely profitable enterprise, including my father. Phillips Petroleum also had major holdings in the Texas Panhandle, and the prospect of greater job opportunities led my parents to move in 1942 from Oklahoma, Home of the Red Man, to Phillips and Borger, Texas, in The Lone Star State.

We first settled in Phillips, Texas, and later in nearby Borger where I was to attend the first grade before moving back to Oklahoma after the breakup of my parents' marriage, a topic to be addressed shortly. The city of Phillips got its name from the oil company by the same name in 1938, and my father worked there from 1942 to 1945. My parents moved from Phillips to Borger when I was four or five years old and I have no memories of Phillips at all. Interestingly, in a sad footnote, a major explosion at the plant in 1980 caused damage so severe and widespread that the city of Phillips, Texas, was never rebuilt and no longer exists. However, a few memories do linger from the Borger days, and I will recount them at this point.

Borger Then and Now

Borger lies in the northwest part of the state, in the heart of what is widely known as the Texas Panhandle. The nearest large city is Amarillo, with a population of around 200,000. Interesting smaller towns in the area include Dalhart of "Smart Fart from Dalhart" and Dumas of "Ding Dong Daddy from Dumas" fame. Both cities are located a few miles away from Borger to the northwest. Hereford, home of the Whitefaces (in reference to Hereford cattle, a breed known for their reddish body color and snow white faces), and Happy, home of the Cowboys, are other notable area small towns. Whitefaces and Cowboys! It just doesn't get any better and any more Texan than that!

Borger sprung up as an oil town in late 1926 and was named for its founder, Asa Philip "Ace" Borger. The oil boom brought nearly 50,000 people to the area in search of the so-called "black gold." The town was nicknamed "Booger Town" because of the unsavory characters drawn to it, and soon became a haven for beggars, bootleggers, gamblers, prostitutes, and an assortment of down-and-outers and ne'er-do-wells. This situation was not unique to Borger; many boom towns have similar origins of a questionable nature.

Gambling houses, speakeasies, and brothels sprung up in abundance in "Booger Town", giving rise to a crime syndicate headed by a fellow named Richard "Two Gun Dick" Herwig who was ably assisted by a lieutenant, W. J. "Shine" Popejoy, so named because he was king of the Texas bootleggers. The syndicate prospered from revenue generated by the houses of prostitution, illegal moonshine operations, and gambling dens. Things finally got so bad that the Texas Rangers, led by Captains Francis Augustus Hamer and Thomas R. Hickman, were dispatched to restore order. The Rangers did manage to bring stability to the community but it was several years before Borger completely tamed down. Apart from his efforts on behalf of the citizens of Borger, Francis Hamer later became a legend in Ranger folklore for killing the notorious crime duo of Bonnie Parker and Clyde Barrow.

The Governor of Texas imposed martial law on Borger for a month in 1929 due to the murder of the District Attorney, John A. Holmes at the hands of an unknown assassin, and that imposition put a temporary crimp in at least some of the illegal activity. "Ace" Borger was shot to death in 1934 by an arch enemy, Arthur Huey, who was mad at "Ace" for not bailing him out of jail on an embezzlement charge. Huey put five slugs into "Ace" Borger and then took the man's own weapon and shot him several more times.

Borger has survived its unseemly origins and is now a major player in the oil and gas industry, and is the site of the world's largest inland petrochemical complex which includes Chevron-Phillips Chemical Company, ConocoPhillips Chemical Company, and Sid Richardson Carbon Company. It has also become a major distributor of agricultural produce, and the oil-related and agricultural industries have combined to create a vibrant community of around 14,000 generally law-abiding citizens.

Six Memories of "Booger Town"

Six recollections of the two-plus years spent in "Booger Town" stand out, memories nearly seven decades old and subject to distortion due to the passage of considerable time. Also, I was a first-grader at the time and one could ask just what does a six-year old remember about much of anything? I sometimes wonder how many memories of those people and events from the early 1940's are really my own and how many are recollections from others who have kept the stories alive through constant retelling. Such is the nature of many childhood memories, I am sure.

Carbon Black. All preceding disclaimers to the contrary aside, I vividly remember the carbon black problem. World War II spawned numerous war-related industries and one with which the Phillips plant was involved was carbon black production. In the 1940's, carbon black was used in the production of tires and in the refinement of certain petrochemical agents that were supporting the war effort. It is used today in the production of printer inks components, toners for xerox machines, and plastics, among other things.

What I remember most is the residue from the carbon black plant infiltrating every aspect of our lives. The stuff was sooty, as fine as graphite powder, and turned many a day into night when the atmospheric conditions were ideal for the formation of what the natives called "Black Dusters." This "black plague" surreptitiously seeped in under the doors and windows of area houses and deposited a tell-tale layer of fine, black dust on the window sills, counters, and other structures. There were no gas or electric clothes dryers around in the 1940's, so housewives typically dried their laundry outdoors on clotheslines. The intent, of course, was to keep the family in clean clothes, but more often than not, the well-meaning mothers were rewarded with a gray, gloomy return for their efforts. To this day, I think remnants of carbon black residue exist in the farthest recesses of my brain and nervous system. Perhaps some of my intellectual or character shortcomings are linked to my distant childhood and Borger's "Black Dusters."

Tumbling Tumbleweeds. The abundant tumbleweeds constitute a second "Booger Town" memory. During certain parts of the year, these happy ramblers rolled through town like fuzzy (furry?) oversized beach balls, pushed along on their erratic paths by the seemingly endless high winds of the Texas Panhandle. The tumbleweeds were more of a curiosity than a nuisance, and we kids loved watching them bounce along as they headed hither, thither, and yon. Some were small and others were huge, rolling along, distributing their seed to create the next generation of tumbleweed offspring, if you will.

Their omnipresence in the Panhandle of Texas made them the subject of a famous song, "Tumbling Tumbleweeds", which was popularized by the Sons of the Pioneers, a well-known musical group of the time period, and by the iconic cinema cowboy and singer, Gene Autry. The lyrics for this immensely popular ditty were borrowed from a poem that appeared in a University of Arizona literary magazine.

Prairie Dog Town. I also have fond memories of "Prairie Dog Town." I do not remember where we would go for sure to see these little burrowing animals, but I think it was somewhere near Canadian or perhaps Dumas. It was truly a joyous day when our father took us to watch these yappy, animated characters romp and play. The prairie dog is a member of the squirrel family, and is known to be extremely sociable and vocal. If threatened, they yip and screech and howl, retreating into their burrow until the threat, or what they perceive to be a threat, disappears. The prairie dogs were truly delightful to watch as they scurried about, bobbing and weaving, periodically popping their heads out of their burrows as if they were submarines upping their periscopes. I could not help but think as I watched the little varmints that we were the victims of a practical joke on their part, most likely the result of our inability to truly comprehend their loud, frenetic ways.

The Tornado Threat. A fourth memory is the constant threat of tornados. The Texas Panhandle and most of neighboring Oklahoma is known as "Tornado Alley", with a notorious reputation for the deadly twisters, particularly in the spring and summer. Though I never saw an actual twister in Borger, or anywhere else for that matter, the constant specter of one was intimidating thanks to our youthful imaginations fueled by exaggerations, old wives tales, and plain old misinformation from peers and adults alike. I still to this day have never seen a tornado, which is a bit of a miracle for someone who has spent twenty years or so of his life in the Texas Panhandle and the state of

Oklahoma. I have been in areas where tornados were sighted or touched down, seen their after-effects, but have yet to see one up close and personal, which is fine with me. I am perfectly happy to leave tornado-viewing/chasing to others of a more sensation-seeking persuasion.

Because of tornados, some of my friends jokingly suggest I should be banned from visiting Oklahoma City. I have been in OKC three times in the past three decades and each time the city was visited by one or more tornados. One of them killed a half dozen people and the others did considerable property damage. No wonder I am *persona non grata* in Oklahoma City!

Gerald Myers. Fifth, I remember having a friend named Gerald Myers. This memory is particularly vague as I did not get to continue the friendship because of an unanticipated departure from Borger after my first-grade year. As a hard core fan of Southwest, later Big 12, and now Southeastern Conference basketball, I have always wondered if the Gerald Myers who hailed from Borger and played for and later coached the men's basketball team at Texas Tech for many years is the same person who I counted as a friend in my distant youth. Our ages are roughly the same, and we graduated from high school in our respective home towns a year apart, so there is circumstantial evidence partially supporting the existence of a one-time friendship. I doubt I made as lasting an impression on Gerald Myers as he did with me seventy years ago because he could do cartwheels as a six-year old and I could not. Gerald Myers recently retired from his position as Athletic Director at Texas Tech, but if he ever comes to College Station again I will ask if he has any recollection of those halcyon days (if living in a city with a carbon black plant, tumbling tumbleweeds, and terrifying tornados can be called halcyon). Or, better yet, maybe I will get on the phone and ring him up!

My Mother and Father Get Divorced. Finally, I have vague recollections of the breakup of my parents' marriage. Even as a seven-year old, I remember our mother loading us children into the car to drive around Borger and see if we could locate our father who was late in returning home that eventful evening. She eventually found him hanging out at a local tavern, seemingly enjoying the company of another woman. Needless to say, my mother was not amused by his indiscretion, an argument ensued, and she departed the premises. I guess she made a decision at that point to file for divorce. In retrospect, one marital misstep seldom tips the balance in favor of a divorce, and I am sure there was plenty of past dirty laundry fueling her final decision. The eyes and ears of babes are seldom privy to the gory details of the dissolution of a marriage, and what we saw was probably the tip of the iceberg in what may well have been a continuously deteriorating relationship.

Shortly after that life-changing circumstance, my mother decided we would all move to Oklahoma to live with her father, our Grandpa Chamberlain, for a while (which turned out to be six years). We kids were left behind in Borger for a couple of days as our mother worked out details of the relocation. Once she was happy with the setup in Oklahoma, our father drove us from Borger to our new home in Dewey. Somewhere in western Oklahoma, he fell asleep at the wheel and hit a bridge. We almost certainly would have gone over the side into a small river or stream and possible death except my six-year old sister, Paula Jo (or just Jo), woke him up just in time to correct the steering wheel. We hit the bridge abutment head-on but fortunately at a relatively slow speed so no one was seriously injured, though some nerves were understandably jangled. Shortly after the accident, a Good Samaritan couple living nearby happened upon the accident scene and, after some deliberation, volunteered to put us up in their home for a couple of days of rest and recuperation. Meanwhile, our mother who was already in Dewey borrowed her father's car, drove to the home of the Good Samaritans, gathered us up, and off we went. The trip to Dewey signaled in the beginning of a new and exciting chapter in our young lives.

A Wonderful Childhood

Reflections on Resuming Life in Dewey

Grandpa Paul Richard Chamberlain played a quiet, unassuming, but significant role in the lives of the three LeUnes children prior to his death in 1949, and I would like to share some thoughts about him. I find it remarkable in retrospect that he let the four of us move into his home, for he had lived essentially alone for two decades following the death of his wife in 1922 and his live-in father in 1924. The sudden infusion of noise and energy generated by three rambunctious heathens after twenty years of virtual silence in the house must have been a big change for him.

PR CHAMBERLAIN "MANSION" 1920S

PR CHAMBERLAIN "MANSION" 1940S

A Heavenly Haven for the Hopelessly Homeless. As noted above, one of Grandpa Chamberlain's most magnanimous gestures was his willingness to allow my mother and us three children, ages seven, six, and three, to join his household in 1945 after the divorce. He provided willingly and well, and made few demands on us, or at least we were unaware as children are prone to be, of any excessive requirements. He did insist, however, on total silence in the house from 5:25 pm to 5:30 pm each weekday so he could hear the Dow-Jones stock market report on KWON, the Bartlesville radio station. He had invested in the stock market and done well, but like so many other investors of the times, took a big hit during the 1929 stock market crash. Over time, he was able to recoup his losses, and by the mid-1940's was able to provide nicely for himself and the uprooted family of his only daughter.

Grandpa Chamberlain and the Cleveland Indians. A second poignant memory is sitting with Grandpa Chamberlain and listening to stories about his beloved Cleveland Indians (aka "The Tribe"), one of the eight teams in major league baseball's American League at that time. He became an ardent Indian fan as a young boy growing up in Cleveland, Ohio, and like many of his baseball persuasion, despised the arch-rival Detroit Tigers. The Indians featured top players such as the legendary fireballer, Bob Feller, shortstop and player-manager Lou Boudreau, catcher Jim Hegan, outfielder Dale Mitchell (a fellow Oklahoman), and slugging second baseman Joe Gordon. These baseball stars became household names as I reached the age of eight or nine.

In the process of conveying his fervor for the Cleveland Indians, my grandfather introduced me to the nuances of baseball standings in the local newspaper, the *Bartlesville Examiner Enterprise*, which is still published today. As an eight-year old, I was puzzled when reading the sports section by the quirk in the baseball league standings whereby a team could be 3.5 games ahead of or 19.5 behind the league leader. That was a difficult concept to grasp, my simplistic and youthful reasoning being games are not played in halves but in wholes. Grandpa Chamberlain explained the conundrum in terms of simple arithmetic and I became the proud possessor of the mathematical acuity needed to figure out league standings. This accomplishment has served me well, though I suspect some Shakespearean sonnet, arcane trigonometric function, or invaluable Keynesian economic principle has been deprived of proper neural storage thanks to my childhood fascination with the complex mathematics of calculating baseball league standings and batting averages!

House, Yard, and Neighborhood. I vividly remember the neighborhood where I spent those formative years, residing at the north end of Dewey. We lived on Creek Street which connected us to the downtown area maybe a half mile away, and the roadway was lined with large trees that provided essentially what amounted to a canopy over its entirety. Grandpa Chamberlain owned the last house on the west side of Creek Street, a huge, resplendent three-story mansion with an adjoining yard that covered an entire city block. Some of the land nearest his house was maintained and manicured, but most of it was allowed to grow wild and natural. The yard was sufficiently spacious to allow for a football game on the south side of the house, but baseball required too much space so we moved those contests out into the pasture equidistant between our house and another on the far northwest corner of the huge lot. There was a primitive basketball court on the north side of the house which was more or less a replication of the stereotypical peach basket goal of the earliest days of that sport. It was a court only in the loosest sense of the word, and I suspect my failure to become a NBA basketball millionaire is somehow tied to that seldom-used, second-rate operation.

There was only one other house on the property, and it was basically "catty corner" from my grandfather's house. His large and elegant home was situated on the southeast corner of the big block and a much more modest frame dwelling was on the far northwest corner, maybe a quarter-mile away. My grandfather's house was huge and elegantly furnished, making it a great indoor playground though he no doubt never intended for it to be used for that purpose. The floors were always nicely waxed and we loved running into the foyer from the living room and sliding on our socks into the dining room, and vice versa via one of his expensive area rugs. We also thought getting from the second floor to the first was best accomplished by straddling the banister and sliding down; that seemed to make a lot more sense than using the steps as a means of descent. If we did use the steps, they were taken in groups of two or three, or even four as our legs got longer.

The house was fronted by a spacious, wide porch that provided a great place to play on extremely hot afternoons or cold, rainy days. My mother was fond, in a perverse sort of way, of telling about the time I was riding a tricycle around the spacious porch when Gary Cole gave me a running start, launched me into space, and sent me reeling down the concrete steps, asshole over tea kettle. I am positive she never truly forgave Gary Cole for that transgression.

Catalpa trees were located to the east and south sides of the house, and the worms residing on the lower sides of the spacious leaves chomped merrily away on what must have been for them a succulent feast. We kids would occasionally grab a catalpa leaf, put it to our lips, and suck on it, causing it to pop with a loud bang. Ah, how easily we were amused. Also, a world-class marble venue was located in the ample shade of the catalpa canopy, and many a life-or-death struggle was conducted there. Because of the shade, there was little grass, and this provided a nice, smooth surface on which to draw assorted sizes of marble rings in the dirt. We all knew the names for the marbles by heart, terms such as taws (or shooters), mibs, agates, steelies, and cats-eyes, and the battles to win those colorful, highly-coveted baubles were frequent and heated. I do not remember anyone being a particularly dominant marble player which made for some pretty even competitions. When not actively engaged competitively, we looked admiringly at each other's marble collections and negotiated almost daily trades.

Sandlot baseball, pickup basketball, and touch football games in the neighborhood were commonplace, in stark contrast to the youth sports of today which are highly regulated by the parents and other adults. I must confess a melancholy fondness for the days when we gathered eight or nine guys from the north side and meandered across town to see if a baseball game could be thrown together with our worthy adversaries from the south end. The equipment was minimal, and our meager collection of wooden bats was typically mended with a combination of nails and any kind of tape we could find. More often than not, it took both tape and nails to keep the bats functioning. Most of the time, the baseballs were stained brownish-green from continued exposure to dirt and grass. As well, their stitches were often frayed, which necessitated liberal use of medical or electrician's tape to keep them from unraveling. Tee shirts, eternally expendable, were willingly removed and placed on the ground to serve as bases. This act allowed the shirts to serve a much higher purpose than that for which our doting mothers had intended. Occasionally we would decide to go easy on the tee-shirts by drawing an outline of the bases in the dirt with a sharp stick. Of course, there were no umpires so ball and strike calls and determination of safes and outs were largely a matter of honor. There would be occasional disputes over some of the decisions, but diplomacy and the urgency of getting another time at bat, pitching another inning, or playing another go-round in the field usually prevailed. Winners were determined when everyone got too tired to continue or someone had to head home to eat the evening meal. How many evening meals have I eaten half-cold, all in the name of getting in one more inning or another turn at bat? A scolding for being late for supper was assured but lectures on rectitude were endured in the name of a greater calling, playing baseball. The transformation of one of us into the next Stan Musial or Ted Williams or Joe DiMaggio might be taking place, and we considered the every evening excoriation from our mothers to be lessons in what sport psychologists of today would call "mental toughness training."

Life during those days from roughly ages six to twelve was good, extremely so, almost Edenic, to be honest. We lived in a lovely, spacious, comfortable house, were fed in grand style, and life was largely blissful once World War II was brought to a halt and my parents' divorce became a thing of the past. We settled into a pattern in the late 1940's that did not change in any great measure for about five or six years with one fairly major exception to be discussed soon.

Caretakers: Inola Harris and Henrietta and John Liss. One of the things that made those years so wonderful was the presence of the caretakers hired by Grandpa Chamberlain to work around his home. For most of my elementary school years, he was able to afford a cook and housekeeper, and his hired help were among the highlights of my youth. One of these influential caretakers/cooks was an ample and amiable black woman named Inola Harris. Inola was quite large, weighing well over two hundred pounds. Every time I saw her, I just knew I was looking at Aunt Jemima, the cultural icon whose picture appeared on several breakfast products produced by the Quaker Oats Company in the 1930's and beyond. We kids were dead certain Inola Harris was Aunt Jemima in disguise.

In real life, Aunt Jemima was a black woman named Anna Robinson who was chosen in 1933 to represent Quaker Oats because she was large, outgoing, angel-faced, and projected the image of amiability and warmth the company wanted to foster to promote their product. Anna Robinson continued to represent Quaker Oats as Aunt Jemima until her death in 1951. As for look-alike Inola, she was a wonderful cook and thanks to her, we ate an abundance of southern home cooking, or what might be regarded as "soul food." I learned as a second or third grader to appreciate all of the more traditional and universally tasteful foods as well as the usually to-be-dreaded turnip greens, spinach, cauliflower, Brussels sprouts, cooked cabbage, sweet potatoes, yams, and broccoli, items anathema to the palate of most children and a fair number of adults. This condition has been referred to elsewhere as "Legume Anorexia", or a morbid fear of vegetables, but I never suffered from that affliction. Thanks in part to Inola Harris, to this day I will eat any traditional American food item except liver. Not even Inola's magic touch could conquer my abhorrence of that vile piece of meat; no one else since has been able to satisfactorily treat what I guess is a culinary character flaw either. People have always told me they know a secret method of preparing liver absolutely guaranteed to make it palatable to even the most skeptical critic. All approaches have failed miserably with me, but I thought I owed it to liver to not give up on it without a fight. I tried it every five years until I was forty, at which time I abandoned the cause for all eternity. I have since missed eight five-year periods, so I think liver is history for me!

Another salient memory of Inola is linked to the polio epidemic that struck terror in the hearts of caring parents everywhere, crippling so many young people during my childhood. The worst epidemic of polio took place in 1952, my fourteenth year; 58,000 people in the US contracted the disease, slightly over 3,000 died from it, and another 21,000-plus were left mildly to severely paralyzed. Dewey was not exempt from this plague, and I still remember a friend or two dying and others who were left with facial paralysis or permanent lameness from the worst form of polio, the bulbar type.

My mother and grandfather required Inola to make sure we three kids took a mandatory afternoon nap, a tactic designed as a small but vital part of a larger strategy to ward off polio. The standard anti-polio admonitions were: (1) do not swim in dirty or polluted water, and (2) do not get so tired that the immune system fails to ward off the disease, and (3) take an afternoon nap every day. I do not recall ever sleeping during those enforced, painful, and seemingly endless rest periods. We spent most of the time periodically harassing Inola, asking her every five minutes if it was time to get up and go outside again. Inola never gave an inch, always making us rest for two hours. I would yell down the stairs, asking Inola what time it was. Her standard answer without fail was, "Time for you to get back in that bed, boy."

Naptime had all the earmarks of a prison sentence, but given the number of local victims of the polio epidemic prior to the discovery of the Salk vaccine, it no doubt was a prudent policy. Inola Harris fully subscribed to the strategy or, at least, was a willing enforcer. Again, as I look back from the perspective of a father and grandfather many times over, the polio scourge surely struck terror in the hearts of 1950's parents. What a debt we modern parents owe to Jonas Salk and his associates who made the polio vaccine a reality.

Inola also gave me my first real glimpse, however small, into the viral social condition known as racism. Inola had what I assumed for maybe sixty years of my life was a son named Isaac who would occasionally come over from "Nigger Town", as the west side of town was "affectionately" known, to visit and play with us. My siblings and I greatly enjoyed having Isaac around but were puzzled at the response of my grandfather and mother to his visits. To wit, he was never invited into the house and, if thirsty, someone would fetch him a glass of water which he drank outside but never inside the house. He spent quite a number of evenings sitting on the back steps, waiting for us to finish the wonderful, sumptuous meals his mother had prepared so we could resume playing. When I inquired about why we as a family reacted toward Isaac and other blacks the way we did, my mother dismissed my query with a simple, "That's just the way things are. It's the natural order of things." There was never any malice in her tone, and I think she just viewed the world as organized that way. It is certainly the only world she had ever experienced, and I must confess I do not ever remember her saying anything with inflammatory racial overtones.

In the process of exchanging emails in 2012 with my oldest sister, Jo, she mentioned she had been in contact with a classmate who lent new insights into our understanding of Inola Harris and Isaac. It turns out I had been mistaken all those years, for Isaac was not a biological son of Inola's at all. Rather, he was a foundling who had been informally adopted by the good-hearted Inola and reared as her own. This bit of information was revealed to Jo by an old classmate of hers, Donald Joseph "D. J." Ogans, who also has a most interesting story.

D. J. Ogans grew up alongside Isaac in "Nigger Town" but eventually outgrew his modest, inauspicious origins. Post-high school, D. J. played in a blues band for eleven years and later started his own carpet business from which he retired after thirty-three years. At last report, the family enterprise was being operated by eight of Donald's twenty-three children (from three wives). There are reportedly fifty-four Ogans grandchildren. One of the goals D. J. Ogans set for his children was that they all graduate from college, and though I am not privy to the actual data about his success rate, it is rumored to be quite high. Some sources are adamant that his record was actually perfect which seems unimaginable.

The Bulldoggers Take An Early Stand Against Racism. Another email missive, also from my sister and dated September 14, 2012, lent even more insight into that black section of Dewey that was so mysterious to me in my childhood. It seems that during the fall of the year I was born, 1938, and long, long before the Civil Rights Movement grabbed a foothold in this country, a stand against racism was taken by the Dewey High School football coach and his team during the state playoffs. Homer Hill was the coach of the undefeated Bulldoggers (Decimals?) team, and they were continuing a successful run under his leadership, losing only seventeen games in the decade of the 1930's. The story goes that Coach Hill and his young "warriors" were preparing to play the Sand Springs Sandies in a Verdigris Valley playoff game in their home stadium near Tulsa. As the boys were warming up, Mary Popkess of the Pharmacy Popkess'es in Dewey came down to the sidelines and whispered to Coach Hill that the Bulldogger's number one football fan had been denied admittance to the game because he was black.

The black man at the center of the ruckus outside the stadium was Henry Kemps who made his living as a janitor and delivery man for various merchants in Dewey. In his spare time, he was a football fanatic and had not missed a Bulldogger game in the eighteen years prior to the incident in Sand Springs. After being turned away at the gate, Henry reconciled himself to the fact that he was not going to be able to watch his beloved Bulldoggers in their playoff match with the formidable Sandies. However, he wanted to be as close to the action as possible and be absolutely certain of its outcome, so he planned to wait outside the stadium until the game was over before heading back to Dewey.

Henry was well-liked by all who knew him, respected as a true gentleman, and had been the self-nominated, unofficial mascot for the football team for many years. Upon learning Henry would not be watching them in person that ill-fated day in Sand Springs, Coach Hill gathered his team together to talk about the situation. After a few minutes of weighing the pros and cons of their various options, Coach Hill and his players decided if Henry could not watch, they would not play. The coach and the thirty players who had suited up that day sprinted off the field just prior to the kickoff, leaving 4,000 fans gaping in wonderment. The boys then ran to Henry's car, lifted him on their shoulders, marched him on to the field, and sat him smack dab in the middle of their bench. After twenty, thirty, forty minutes of haggling among various school administrators and sports officials, play commenced with Henry in full attendance. The hotly-contested game ended in a 6-6 tie, but Sand Springs was awarded the championship because Dewey had a previous tie on their record and the Sandies did not.

After the game was over and everyone had gone back to Dewey, the team got in their cars and reconvened in "Nigger Town", circling Henry's house, honking their horns, whistling, whooping and hollering, and celebrating on his behalf. Black Henry Kemps and his wife were childless and the white Bulldoggers had become their surrogate sons. When Henry died in 1943, the entire football team attended the funeral and his obituary was four times bigger than any other published that day in the *Washington Countian*, Dewey's newspaper at the time.

This heartwarming vignette was contributed to *This Land Press*, a new media company based in Tulsa, by Anne Barajas Harp, a younger sister of Frank Barajas who was a freshman my last year in high school.

On a more depressing note, also contributed by Anne Sharp as part of the piece on Henry Kemps, there had been a race riot in "Nigger Town" twenty years prior to the Sand Springs fiasco that had a profound effect on racial relations in my little burg. It seems that a black man named Aaron Wardlaw killed Dewey's police chief, Walter Mull. As the news of the chief's murder spread, a band of white vigilantes marched on the jail with the intent to lynch Wardlaw. Upon finding that Wardlaw had been moved elsewhere for his protection, the vigilantes took their murderous venom over to the west side of town and burned the Antioch Baptist Church to the ground. As well, twenty-one homes were razed and dozens of black families fled under threats of death.

Eventually, peace and order were restored and Wardlaw was subsequently found guilty of murder. For their acts of retribution, thirty-six white men, including the mayor of Dewey, were found guilty of race crimes. Unfortunately, irreparable damage had been done to racial relations in the community, and several generations of black people learned to be quiet and subservient and stay out of the way of white people.

As I look back on these events and related ones, I do not recall my grandfather or mother expressing virulent racism or hatred of blacks through language or overt actions other than the preceding examples which, in the greater scheme of racial bigotry and violence, are relatively benign (if any manifestation of racism can be deemed "benign"). In any event, this exposure to Inola and Isaac was my up close and personal introduction to the very complex issue of racism in America. Though racial relations have come a long, long, long way in my eighty years, they have a ways to go in the next seventy-nine which my friends and, more significantly, the actuarial tables tell me I will not be around to observe and chronicle in my own modest fashion.

Speaking of "Nigger Town", as teenagers, my friends and I would on rare occasions hear the local yokels and rednecks talking boastfully of going "Nigger Knockin." The idea behind "Nigger Knockin" was to load up a sock with something formidable, maybe some marbles, ball bearings, or small rocks. Once the potentially lethal weapon was constructed, the "Nigger Knockers" would jump in a car, drive by black folks riding their bicycles or talking on a street corner, and try to take their heads off with their improvised weapon. I never heard of or knew anyone who actually went "Nigger Knockin" but it made for some interesting if perverse talk. Mostly, I think it gave some racist rednecks something to impress their small-minded friends with over a beer at Roaring Red's, a local dive masquerading as a saloon. Speaking of Roaring Red's, my siblings and I spent quite a bit of time there as children due to my mothers' propensity for consuming beer and her friendship with the proprietor.

Inola Harris eventually left the employ of my grandfather by choice, a sad moment for me for sure. The next caretakers, a middle-aged German couple named John and Henrietta (Hank) Liss, were his final ones. Their German heritage occasionally provoked some reasonably tepid anti-Nazi, anti-German discussion among the local citizenry. Memories of the horrors of World War II were still salient in the late 1940's, and suspicions about the motives of those "heinous Huns" (as well as the "Japs") lingered in the minds of Americans for many years afterward. I do not recall anything about John and Henrietta that remotely suggested they were Nazi sympathizers or anti-Semites. Mostly, they minded their business while taking good care of my increasingly ailing and feeble grandfather. As lagniappe, Hank spent considerable time indulging my childhood fascination with a variety of children's table games, mostly cards and Monopoly. She and I held almost nightly card games, what might have seemed in retrospect to be marathons to her, and I often triumphed. Henrietta seemed to take her losses in stride, and always applauded my mental acuity and card-playing skills. I was thrilled to have her approval and greatly appreciated her spending so much time with me. Those were good times!

Unfortunately, John and Hank Liss somehow got cross-wise with my grandfather and were let go, and a number of things apparently disappeared with them as they left town. Chief among the losses was an extensive coin collection featuring buffalo nickels and Indian-head pennies, both of which were prized for their increasing rarity.

After the Liss'es left, my grandfather employed no additional help, but those years with Inola Harris and Henrietta Liss were wonderful ones. Their separate tenures and departures still serve as cherished reminders of an interesting and idyllic period in my life.

Grandpa Chamberlain Breaks His Hip. Somewhat coincidental in time with the departure of John and Henrietta Liss, Grandpa Chamberlain fell and broke his hip. By reputation, he had been a force on the local tennis scene well into his late-fifties but had to abandon the game as he became increasingly frail. The consequences of falling at age sixty-five and the resultant broken hip represented quite a contrast to the agile tennis player of just a few years before. A broken hip has been a well-documented death sentence for many aged people, and my grandfather was no exception; it marked the beginning of the end.

One of the things I remember most about his last few years was Grandpa Chamberlain being bed-ridden and relegated to urinating in a bedpan much of the time. It was often my duty to empty the bedpan and replace it for later use; I became more familiar with the stench of urine than any small boy probably should. I suspect the chore would be less onerous for me today, but it was most unpleasant at the time.

There were a couple of Christmas mornings where I was not able to run downstairs with my siblings the very second we woke up to see what Santa had dropped off overnight because I first had to tend to my grandfather's bedpan and other needs. I know it was a small price to pay for his years of largesse and kindness, but I brought a touch of youthful selfishness to the task, and for that I am apologetic. It sure seemed unfair at the time, but for all my misgivings, I am positive no one enjoyed the situation less than he did. Grandpa Chamberlain's health inexorably deteriorated and he died in 1949 at age sixty-nine while my siblings and I were in Texas City, Texas, for the summer. I was eleven at that time.

It is unfortunate that I never really got to know either of my grandmothers and even in the case of the two grandfathers the relationships were brief and, in the case of Grandpa John LeUnes, quite superficial. Fortunately, while my exposure to Grandpa Chamberlain was brief, it had its meaningful moments, and I owe him a debt of gratitude for his astute tutelage about sports in general and baseball in particular and the example he set about leading an honorable and productive life. As viewed through the prism of a small boy, I saw Grandpa Chamberlain as a good, kind, gentle man.

YOUNG PR CHAMBERLAIN

L TO R FIRST ROW-BUB, YOURS TRULY, TWO
CHAMBERLAIN COUSINS (PAUL AND MARK), PAULA JO
SECOND ROW L TO R-AUNT ZENOBIA (PG'S WIFE), COUSIN
EDITH, PR, AUNT HELEN (PHILLIP'S WIFE), PHILLIP, MOM
CENTER-PG

School Days, Lazy Summers, and Sports in the Life of a Young Boy

School Days in Dewey

The school years from grades one through six were largely unremarkable, made up mostly of the day-to-day fun, mundane, nondescript life events that characterized growing up in the 1940's as a middle-class, small-town, Midwestern (Southwestern?) kid. After attending school my first year in Borger, Texas, I started the second grade in Dewey in late summer 1945, and my teacher was a gentle, middle-aged woman named Ida Allen. Viewing her through the sometimes myopic prism of youth, I was sure Miss Allen was at least ninety years old when we first crossed paths. With the perspective gained from additional years of observation and experience, I now know that she was middle-aged and not nearly the nonagenarian I had made her out to be. It also turned out that she taught my mother in the second grade, which was in 1923 or 1924, as well as one of my sisters fifteen years my junior, which would have been around 1960, give or take. That thirty-seven-year time period from 1923 to 1960 is not all-inclusive but strongly suggests that her teaching career spanned three or four decades.

Miss Allen showed up for our thirtieth high school class reunion in 1986, or sixty-plus years after my mother was one of her students, and graciously spent some time mixing with her former second graders. A highlight of the evening occurred when she produced the class attendance book from our second grade year and called roll in alphabetical order. Not everyone who had graduated from good old Dewey High was in that document but many were and, to a person, all would say they were most fortunate to have experienced the gentle and astute tutelage of Miss Ida Allen.

There was a girl in my second grade class by the name of Maxine Martin. Poor Maxine suddenly took sick early one morning in class, eventually upchucking her breakfast. Since I sat at the desk immediately in front of Maxine, I was directly in the line of fire and the prime target for her inopportune eruption. A cursory inspection of the back of my shirt and neck, however repugnant, revealed what appeared, in terms of both color and texture, to be the remnants of partially digested tomatoes. My peers, of course, were aghast at viewing the results of Maxine's misfortune (and mine). Maxine had red hair and a ruddy complexion, and through some sort of convoluted reasoning process probably understood only by seven-year olds, my peers tied the two physical features together, along with the vomiting of what may well have been tomatoes, to produce a nickname for the poor child. She was dubbed "Tomato Face" Martin, a nickname that lived on in perpetuity among her classmates. Poor thing!

Our third grade teacher was a lovely woman named Mrs. Poe Newton and the year passed with little of significance taking place, but an incident in the fourth grade is memorable. We had an unusually attractive teacher whose name unfortunately eludes me, and we were all in love with her because of her good looks and student-friendly teaching style. There was one problem; she was pregnant and eventually her condition got to the point that it could no longer be concealed and thus no longer tolerated by the school administration. Teachers in those more pristine, Puritanical times who showed the unmistakable, tell-tale signs of pregnancy were required to resign their position. Thus, our beloved teacher vanished suddenly and unceremoniously from our midst in mid-year. I guess in some circuitous bit of logic, her pregnancy was viewed as setting a bad example for us obviously worldly fourth graders. Implicit in this mindless nonsense, I suppose, was a misguided belief if we kids were aware of the pregnancy, we would then figure out our teacher was having sexual relations with someone, most likely a husband. By implication, all the fourth graders would then want to start doing the same thing our teacher had done. Thus, that evil symbol of what sexual activity can cause had to be removed before a Bacchanalian orgy broke out in the classroom, the cloakroom, or, heaven forbid, in front of God and everybody else on the playground. In reality, sex was the last thing on our overprotected little minds in the fourth grade. I doubt if one person in my class even knew what sex was since we were not prematurely bombarded with sexual information as children are today. To wit, the first of the two Kinsey reports, this one on male sexual behavior and published in 1948, did much to revolutionize how society looked at sexual behavior, but was certainly not on any suggested reading lists for a 1940's fourth grader!

My fifth grade teacher was a stern, at times mean, unpleasant and almost certainly unhappy woman by the name of Nann Lowe. Miss Lowe made life pretty miserable for us with her petty rules and stern, unpleasant demeanor. I always wondered if she liked children, or even if she liked life; I ultimately concluded she did not have much zeal for either. She was a spinster, seemingly a lonely woman, and rumors circulated a few years later suggesting she had taken her own life. The truth of the matter I do not know to this day, but I can assure you that the fifth grade was not much fun.

One thing stands out in my memory of that year apart from Miss Lowe's severity, though I cannot begin to tell you why. Our school was heated with radiators which lined the walls of the classrooms, the library, and other school facilities. On cold, wet, snowy days, and to her credit, Miss Lowe would require us to remove our soggy boots and coats and place them on or near those radiators. By late afternoon, our outer apparel was dry and warm which gave us a head start on fighting the cold as we departed for home at the end of the school day. I guess the fifth grade had to be pretty uneventful if one of the most vivid memories centers around cold boots and hot radiators, but being warm and dry on cold, snowy or rainy days felt pretty doggone good. I owe Miss Lowe for that one.

It was about this time, the transition year between the fifth grade and the sixth, when a transformative event took place in my life, truly an earthshaking, pivotal life-changer. It all began innocently enough when I started delivering the area newspaper, the *Bartlesville Examiner Enterprise*. One of the rituals for us "paper boys" was to convene each day at the post office on Dewey's Main Street where the newspapers were dropped off by the local distributor. Once retrieved and sorted, we folded them for delivery to our subscribers.

My tenure as a paperboy was brief for at least two reasons. One was that the weather in northeastern Oklahoma could be occasionally brutal in the winter, and delivering the paper on those frigid days when even the resident polar bears were in hiding was quite uncomfortable. This was particularly true on Sunday's when there was a morning edition as opposed to an afternoon one which was the case the other six days of the week. Though not cold on a continuous basis in the winter as in the upper tier of states, northeastern Oklahoma experienced weather as frigid as several degrees below zero. My recollection of an all-time coldest day was when I was fourteen and living on a dairy farm; it once got down to a minus nine degrees. We also would have a half dozen, maybe a dozen, snows each winter. Riding a bike to deliver papers in snow and freezing cold was not my cup of tea.

A second drawback to delivering newspapers, and a far more compelling one, was most of us made no money doing so. The distributor charged us so much per paper and our profits were predicated on getting large numbers of subscribers. This arrangement served the newspaper ownership well but did little for those of us down in the trenches, diligently distributing the news. The theory is all well and good but the practice suffered, mainly due to a handful of non-paying customers and sandbaggers. In order to collect our money, we had to knock on doors in hopes of visiting with our so-called paying customers. Some would never answer their doors even though we knew they were home. Others would sandbag, using lies, delaying tactics, and petty excuses in hopes you would eventually give up your collection efforts. Given our slim margin of profit from each paper, it did not take very many non-paying customers to reduce our take home pay to zero. I essentially broke even after several months of throwing the paper.

Earl Marshall Provides My First Sex Education Lesson. On a more positive note, we had a good time visiting with each other while folding our papers for later delivery, and it was during one of these gatherings that I was given my first and still-to this-day most vivid lesson in human sexuality, however impromptu. It seems there was this guy in our group whose name was Earl Marshall. Earl was in the same grade as most of us despite being two or perhaps three years older. I cannot remember if he was mildly intellectually disabled or if he simply lacked motivation for school. On the whole, he seemed a bit slower than the rest of us mentally, but not to a great degree. In the classification system we psychologists use, he would probably fall into the borderline group, IQ range of seventy to ninety.

Whatever intellectual or motivational limitations he may have possessed, to this day Earl Marshall remains a source of personal awe and wonderment for he was my first guru on the topic of human sexuality. I owe what little I know about the topic to those insightful musings and erudite, insightful pronouncements while folding newspapers almost seven decades ago. Being an older, obviously wiser and worldly chap, Earl went to great lengths to foster an image among his younger newspaper-folding companions suggesting he had plenty of experience with the more willing among the local womenfolk, or at least the ones near our age group. As part of his continuing attempts to bring the more uninformed among us up to speed on matters sexual, Earl waxed eloquent one day on the joys but also the dangers of heterosexual intercourse. In closing he issued a pronouncement, yea a stern warning from on high, to the effect that if one of us ever had sex with a girl, the doer of the dastardly deed (my words, not his) would be so tired and spent he would not be able to walk for thirty minutes (his words, not mine). Earl seemed authoritative enough and had me convinced I was in the presence of a true-blue guru, so I gave his admonition some serious thought. In a matter of no more than several nano-seconds, the following epiphany emerged from my sub-conscious mind: "What if there is a fire? What if the building catches fire? What do I do then? How do I get out of the house without burning up if I cannot walk?" I kept envisioning being reduced to ashes in some sort of pyrrhic cataclysm, no doubt a richly deserved fate for having lustful thoughts and succumbing to lascivious urgings. I guess my earlier religious training kicked in, suggesting death by fire as a proper punishment for someone of such obviously low character, someone so weak they would be unable to say no to the sex sin in the first place.

Whatever I have been and am now as a sexual being, I owe my condition to that 1950's tutorial from the mind and mouth of my mentor on matters masculine, Master Earl Marshall. He was, in a phrase, "da man!"

Mrs. Wilson was our teacher in the sixth grade, and she prepared us pretty well for the upcoming junior high years. The sixth grade is truly a transition year for both students and teachers. Anyone who has taught for a while will tell you fifth graders are sweet, loving, and manageable for the most part, but something happens, maybe that initial infusion of hormones, toward the end of the year and into the sixth grade, and they become completely different, often not very likeable people. My wife, Judy taught fifth graders for nearly three decades and I have heard her and assorted colleagues in the teaching profession wax eloquent on numerous occasions how something happens to fifth graders as they approach the sixth grade and early adolescence. In any case, Mrs. Wilson seemed to have the necessary resilience to handle us sometimes perplexing sixth graders.

I liked my teachers almost without exception, and I loved school itself. I was good at it and received plenty of accolades and pats on the back for my academic performance. School was a daily reminder for me that I was appreciated and valued; I was successful and made to feel worthy, things that not all kids get to experience. For many children, school is a constant symbol of their own personal and/or academic inadequacies. I liked getting stars by my name for good behavior, things like being punctual and turning in homework, as well as for personal hygiene things such as brushing teeth and combing hair. I suspect those stars are the only reason I ever brushed my teeth in those early school years. It sure was rewarding to see those stars pile up, and they lent partial support to the widely endorsed theory among psychologists and in-the-know teachers that using positive reinforcement to shape desirable behavior actually works!

I liked the compliments I received for my work, and the teachers were largely fond of me for both my academic performance and generally courteous demeanor. I would have never dreamed of acting up in class or talking back to an adult. I also got lots of strokes from my performance on standardized tests. I was always at or off the top of the chart on the achievement tests, particularly in reading, spelling, and arithmetic. I was (and am) an extremely rapid and voracious reader, and vividly to this day remember scoring at the college sophomore level on a reading achievement test when I was in the fourth grade. You can imagine how inflating such a performance could be to a fourth grader! I saw those data as a personal challenge to read more books from the town library than anyone else in my age group, and I suspect there were few who read more Bobbsey Twins books, Nancy Drew mysteries, sports novels, and even a smattering of the literature classics than I did. The school and town librarians were always applauding my voracious appetite for reading, and I lapped it up.

As for spelling, I do not think I ever made a grade below one hundred, and I won virtually every class or school spelling bee in the elementary school years. Even though I almost always scored perfectly on spelling tests and dominated the school spelling bees, I still was required to write each assigned word twenty-five times just like the poorest spellers in class. To cope with the ennui generated by such a stultifying, mundane, mindless task, I developed the habit of writing all words backwards, and soon became proficient with both writing and spelling them that way. If there had been a gnilleps eeb for kids who spelled words backwards, I would have won the national championship hands down. As it turns out, I have found little demand in the past seven decades for people who spell, write, or speak words backwards.

With regard to arithmetic, even today I can add, subtract, multiply, and divide numbers in most cases faster than other people can using a calculator. For example, a task such as figuring the average of six grades times two hundred students in a college class is a breeze for me. I consistently beat the person using a calculator on this task. Unfortunately, this arithmetic proficiency did not transfer over to the acquisition and retention of concepts in mathematics once I got into high school and college. I cannot to this day handle even the most rudimentary problems in algebra, geometry, or trigonometry, a deficiency whose roots are traceable, I think, to poor mathematics instruction in junior high and high school coupled with an absolutely colossal dose of indifference to the task on my part. But I can read, spell, and do basic life skills arithmetic like a computer.

I owe those teachers in the first six grades a huge debt of gratitude for their attentiveness, responsiveness, nurturance, guidance, patience, and endless support. Teachers do not become wealthy for their efforts, but their impact on young people is both substantial and eternal. I do not think we praise them enough but teachers should know that many of us greatly value their efforts on our behalf. Perhaps Lee Iacocca, the famous automobile executive and writer of the late twentieth century summed it up best: "In a completely rational society, the best of us would be teachers and the rest of us would have to settle for something less, because passing civilization along from one generation to the next ought to be the highest honor and the highest responsibility anyone could have." You go, Lee!

Another case in point about good teachers: My wife, Judy, in her "school marm" days was considered by many to be a master teacher and she accumulated awards and accolades to support that contention. Several years ago, she was asked to attend a dinner sponsored by A&M Consolidated High School in College Station to honor their best senior students. Each student honoree, in turn, selected a teacher to recognize who had been important to them along the way. Our local high school is blessed with large numbers of exceptional students, thanks in large part to the professors at the university who spawn them.

One of those elite students, a young lady named Ann Marie Panetta, requested that Judy attend the banquet as her guest and most memorable teacher. Most of the students invited a favorite high school mentor, but Anne Marie's choice was different in that she chose a fifth grade teacher. Though the group was a talented one, the speeches on behalf of favorite teachers tended toward predictable and mundane, with clichés about the teachers being on top of their subject matter, serving as role models, being inspirational and supportive, caring about kids, making a difference in one's life, and so on. Anne Marie's dedication speech, on the other hand, was laden with vignettes about those subtle teaching nuances that make for life changes and long memories, things like having animals in the classroom, teaching a section on black history for Black History Month, and hearing for the first time through a unit on women's history that young females should be proud of their gender and apologize to no one for being a member of the "weaker sex."

By the time Anne Marie was through, there was not a dry eye in the crowd. She brilliantly captured the essence of good teaching and the impact a teacher-mentor can have on the life of a bright and curious child. Anne Marie Panetta's words were in equal parts a tribute to herself as a brilliant and engaged young lady and another to a dedicated teacher with a true passion for trying to make a difference in the lives of children. Anne Marie Panetta graduated from the University of Texas in Austin and I lost track of her.

As a postscript to this discussion, sometime after the honors banquet, Judy attended a meeting of the local teachers, and became the focus of some good-natured ribbing from some of the high school coaches, most of whom are ostensibly social studies and/or history teachers. She was chided, good-naturedly, by the mostly coaches group for teaching about black history and the Civil Rights Movement, for discussing the roles and rights of women, and compassion for animals. She was told that those things were not really history; history was George Washington and the Revolutionary War, Abraham Lincoln, slavery and the Civil War, and World Wars I and II. That was real history!

Oklahoma Summers in the Late 1940's

A typical summer day in the 1940's began with a wake-up call from the birds roosting in the massive trees surrounding the house. Air conditioning was pretty much unheard of in those days, so in an effort to beat the heat, we kids often slept in a second-story screened-in porch overlooking the front yard. Since the humidity was not typically high in Oklahoma, or at least in comparison with the Texas Gulf Coast, the nights usually cooled down to the point that sleep was actually possible, maybe even comfortable. The screened-in porch beautifully served the purpose of keeping us cool and insect-free.

Grape-Nut Flakes, Cheerios, Post Toasties, and Pep Pins. Once up and about in the morning, I would fix myself a bowl or sometimes two of cereal to get the day going, and my favorites were Grape Nut Flakes, Post Toasties, Cheerios, or Pep, a less well-known cereal. Each of those cereal choices possessed its own unique charms. Grape Nut Flakes reminded me a bit of eating small, crunchy, edible rocks, particularly if they were softened with the cream skimmed off the top of a quart of milk. Milk in those days was delivered to the house, usually in quart bottles, and a nice two- or three-inch head of cream formed on the top of each bottle. This situation created a bit of a dilemma in which we were faced with two choices about what to do with the contents: (1) We could shake the bottle and equally distribute the cream throughout, or (2) leave the bottle alone and jockey with each other to see which of us would get to skim off the rich, thick, and tasty cream for their cereal. I often chose the latter alternative, an option made possible only if one was the first person downstairs for breakfast. Option two took on a measure of urgency if I was planning on eating Grape Nut Flakes, for those delightful breakfast chunks were rendered especially tasty by the presence of cream. It never once crossed my mind at the time that this behavioral quirk was in any way related to the consumption of huge quantities of fat calories and cholesterol.

In the case of Post Toasties, it was always a race against time to see if you could eat them before they became saturated with milk, though I noticed some people liked theirs on the soggy side. With regard to Cheerios, they were visually attractive because of their round shape, sort of like round, miniature, brownish, lifeguard rings floating about in a sea of milk. They were great to eat, and became much more so if you scattered some sliced, bite-sized bananas throughout. A change of pace, though not nearly so tasty, was to introduce fresh strawberries to the mix in lieu of the favored bananas. As for Pep, the cereal was incredibly bland but the blandness was offset by the fact that each box contained a small packet hidden among the grains of cereal, and inside these sometimes hard to find cellophane containers was a pin. Each pin sported the face of a famous cartoon character, and they were known as "Pep Pins." The idea of "Pep Pins" was no doubt a cleverly orchestrated advertising ploy emanating from Madison Avenue and designed to foster greater consumption of what I remember to be a rather pedestrian, not particularly tasty cereal. It was proof positive those Madison Avenue types knew exactly what they were doing; I probably doubled or tripled my consumption of Pep cereal for several years in order to get at those prized pins.

Insofar as my own personal childhood bartering agenda went, trading "Pep Pins" came in a close second to swapping the immensely popular and highly revered Topps bubble gum baseball cards. For some reason known only to the producers of Pep cereal and their henchmen on Madison Avenue, I always had an overabundance of pins carrying the likeness of The Phantom, a popular cartoon character of the period. Interestingly, The Phantom was the first cartoon character to wear the skin-tight outfit that became the trademark of comic book characters such as Superman, Batman, and other superheroes hell-bent on dispatching bad guys and righting the world's considerable wrongs.

It did seem a bit conspiratorial for the makers of Pep to create an over-supply of Phantoms, and it was a big letdown to open up a box and find one after another after another. Also, too many Phantoms on the market made for bad trading conditions; it is hard to make a good deal on something everyone else possesses to excess and also abhors as much as you do. Looking back, we were clearly unwitting pawns in a perverse Madison Avenue ploy to teach us lessons as young children about applied economic theory.

As I got older, Cheerios became my cereal of choice as part of a superstitious ritual. Through some convoluted mental process, I deluded myself into believing that eating Cheerios before a competition would contribute to exceptional performance in whatever sport I was playing at the time. However, an even stranger food superstition was that of an acquaintance in Bartlesville, Bob Ringo, who was an accomplished 800-meter runner in track. Ringo always prepared for meets by eating a healthy portion of sauerkraut. I was rather fond of the stuff in my own right, but the thought of dining on sauerkraut right before competing was mind-boggling at the time and remains so to this day. I cannot imagine running 800 meters on sauerkraut, but I cannot imagine running 800 meters under any circumstances. My lifelong friend, Frank Ringo, was never able to satisfactorily explain his cousin's weird, superstitious, pre-competitive predilection. I figure Ringo's sauerkraut and my Cheerios were performance-enhancing precursors to today's steroid compounds so popular among athletes, though a good deal healthier.

But, then, superstitious rituals in athletics often lack a credible explanation. Why do baseball pitchers studiously avoid the foul lines when jogging from the mound to the dugout? Or basketball players bounce the ball four times, not three or five, prior to shooting a free throw? Or athletes wear so-called lucky apparel, a la Tiger Woods at his peak donning his red shirt on the last day of golf tournaments?

Riding Bikes, Playing Marbles, and Shooting BB Guns. Once done with breakfast, we would read, go outside and play marbles, maybe take a bike ride around the immediate area, shoot almost always errantly at the unwitting but fortunate sparrows with our BB guns, or play catch with friends using our ragged old baseballs and beat-up gloves. Grandpa Chamberlain, being the baseball fan he was, sprung for an expensive first baseman's mitt on my tenth birthday, and that glove was my pride and joy for the next five or six years. It was a trapper's model, black, embossed with Phil Cavaretta's name.

The name Cavaretta held no special meaning for me then even though he was a star player. He was a Chicago Cub, and because of my loyalty to the St. Louis Cardinals, I did not know as much about the Cubbies. Cavaretta was a slick-fielding first baseman (and occasional outfielder), but his real strength was on the offensive side of the ball. He hit .355 in 1945 which earned him the National League's Most Valuable Player designation. Cavaretta played in the majors for twenty-two years, all but two with the Cubs. He spent his final two years with the cross-town White Sox, and ended up with a career batting average of .293, which is really quite an achievement. Though Cavaretta was a lefthander, they made gloves bearing his name for right-handed people like me, too. From the moment I first held that prized glove, my position in baseball, first base, was etched in stone. I played only that position until giving up baseball after my senior year of high school. In retrospect, I wish I had gotten hooked on a Joe DiMaggio or Stan Musial glove and cast my lot with being an outfielder. With my sprinter speed, playing outfield would have been a much better calling. There are 5' 9" outfielders but not many of that height ever end up at first base. Though less compelling, being right-handed did not help my first base case either.

Of all the sports I was probably best at baseball but I liked it the least. Part of my lack of fascination with the sport is no doubt traceable to playing in the spring where the weather can still be quite cool and the Oklahoma winds are sometime fierce and seemingly interminable. The never-ending gales and the dust they generated took a lot of fun out of the game. Also, most of the venues I played on were pretty primitive by today's standards. As noted elsewhere, I entertained the idea of resurrecting my baseball career for a brief time by walking on at Texas A&M but ultimately opted to do the same in track instead.

I treasured that Cavaretta model for many years, and it finally died from complications of abuse and old age. It had been rained on, spit on, spit in, spit at, hung, strung, restrung, patched, re-patched, and re-patched once again, and treated with massive quantities of various glove compounds. It was essentially gerrymandered together in its dotage by the glories of glue and the grace of the baseball gods.

As the summer unfolded and I rose from bed each morning, my mother would have the radio tuned to the local station which often serenaded us with delightful ditties such as "Sunny Side of the Street" and "Sentimental Journey." It was always reassuring to me as a kiddo to know that life was good on the "Sunny Side of the Street." The song was written in 1930 by Jimmy McHugh with lyrics provided by Dorothy Fields, and went as follows:

> "Grab your coat and get your hat
> Leave your worries on the doorstep,
> Life can be so sweet,
> On the sunny side of the street.
>
> Can't you hear that pitter-pat
> And that happy tune is your step
> Life can be complete
> On the sunny side of the street.

> I used to walk in the shade
> With my blues on parade
> Now I'm not afraid
> This rover has crossed over.
>
> Now if I never made one cent
> I'll still be rich as Rockefeller
> There will be gold dust at my feet
> On the sunny, sunny side of the street."

It was equally reassuring that someday we could look forward to the pleasures of a "Sentimental Journey." Bud Green, Les Brown (of Les Brown and his Band of Renown fame), and Ben Homer provided us in 1944 with the lilting lyrics to this oldie:

> "Gonna take a sentimental journey,
> Gonna set my heart at ease.
> Gonna make a sentimental journey
> To renew old memories.
>
> Got my bags, got my reservations
> Spent each dime I could afford.
> Like a child in wild anticipation
> I long to hear that 'All Aboard.'
>
> Seven…that's the time we leave at seven
> I'll be waiting up in heaven
> Countin' every mile of railroad track
> That takes me back.
>
> Never thought my heart would be so yearny
> Why did I decide to roam?
> Gotta take that sentimental journey
> Sentimental journey home."

What more could you ask of life than to live on the sunny side of the street with the prospect of taking a sentimental journey to eternal bliss somewhere along the way? It just did not get better than that for a 1940's small-town Okie boy!

Polio, Nap Time, and *Fifty Famous Stories Retold*. Afternoons, as noted earlier, were quiet time and my grandfather's cook, housekeeper, chief bottle washer and erstwhile detention officer, Inola Harris, made sure we rested to ward off the ravages of polio. We could hang out under the catalpa trees for a bit after lunch, maybe playing marbles, and generally following orders from an assortment of concerned adults to avoid the hot sun. As noted earlier, around 1400 hours, we were required to "take a nap" so as to not get too tired, weaken the immune system, and contract the dreaded polio. Inola would see to it we were at least out of sight and ostensibly taking a nap for a couple of hours, a penance period that seemed an eternity to a ten-year old. By 1600 hours, we would be off and running until suppertime. Usually, that meant a baseball game would break out somewhere, and we would play until the supper bell rang. Supper as we called it then (and I do to this day) was always wonderful due to Inola's culinary talents, and, despite the fact it usually occurred right in the middle of the most important baseball at-bat of one's life, I always looked forward to the supper hour.

After downing the evening meal, there usually was enough partial sunlight left to play hide and seek or generally putz around. At dark, we would go in the house where the much-dreaded bath was awaiting us, followed by another scourge of youth, bedtime. Often we were allowed to play in our grandfather's spacious house in the interim between the bath and bedtime, and our mother would play the piano (badly for the most part), or talk to us kids, or let us listen to the radio. Nine o'clock was lights out time. For me, what that really meant was my mother would turn out the lights and, as she left the room, I would immediately turn them back on so I could read a sports magazine or surreptitiously listen to the St. Louis Cardinals play the New York Giants or some other worthy baseball adversary on station KMOX out of St. Louis, Missouri.

My favorite reader as a boy was *Fifty Famous Stories Retold* which was written by Samuel E. Lowe and Viola E. Jacobson and published in 1920. The book was a collection of inspirational tales of famous historical figures, such as Leonidas, Diogenes, Alfred the Great, and William the Conqueror. I read each of those stories several hundred times at least, drawing inspiration from the messages the various stories conveyed. It became important to accomplish things in my life that would make Diogenes or Leonidas proud. Like Diogenes, I am also still searching for an honest man.

I lost my original copy of the book in one of the family moves, but was recently able to find a copy through a company specializing in old and out of print works. My fondest hope was that my then eight-year old, Lyndon, might find the tales as inspirational as I did. Unfortunately, he had a disdain for reading (which he fortunately outgrew at age twenty-six due to his love for history), and like many kids his age, found Eminem, 50 Cent, and the many times reinvented Snoop Dogg to be far more inspiring. In his defense, I think I am selectively forgetting that listening to Elvis in my day was to adults a sure sign Armageddon was just around the corner. Speaking of the end of the world, my one-time colleague (black), Frank Ashley, also a former Vice Provost for Academic Affairs at A&M, was fond of saying, "Armageddon can't be too far away when the best golfer in the world is black (Tiger Woods) and the best rapper is white (Eminem)." I doubt these words are original with Frank, but they spoke to racial bias and stereotyping of a time not so distant.

Arnold LeUnes

SISTER PAULA JO, BROTHER BUB, 1951

YOURS TRULY AND SISTER PAULA JO

Summer's Over: Back to School We Go. The summer routine ended with the start of school which ushered in a whole new set of rules and expectancies. Play time was allowed but being attentive to homework was obligatory. While I looked forward to homework during the elementary school years, my brother Bub (John) found it to be a plague. He was not good in school, enjoying pretty much only the social part. He was never a bad kid at school, just not very diligent. My sister Jo (Paula Jo) was somewhere in between the two of us. She was a most capable student and brought a lot of traditional stereotypical female conscientiousness to the enterprise. I do know that Bub and Jo, particularly Bub, got tired of hearing the litany from a succession of teachers that went roughly as follows: "Why are you not as good a student (or as smart) as your oldest brother?" I know the teachers meant well with their query, but it created resentment early on among my siblings. Life has a way of evening out a lot of issues, and those childhood jealousies or animosities have faded (I hope) into obscurity with the passing of years. The demands of more pressing life challenges have a way of making old childhood grudges and missteps pretty trivial by comparison.

YOUNGER DAYS

ASSORTED SCHOOL PICTURES OF YOURS TRULY, 1940S AND 1950S

Saturdays and Sundays were greatly anticipated, and were devoted to lighter activities. Religion was never really much of an issue with my mother, so we were seldom required to go to Sunday School or Church. I did do a stint or two at Vacation Bible School at the First Christian Church overseen by the Right Reverend Eugene Earls Butts. I suspect my mother hoped that Bible School would siphon off some excess energy as well as make me a better person by exposing me to the eternal verities of religion. I remember little of the experience other than I once constructed a fenced-in manger scene out of materials that would never stick to the intended surface. The blasted thing was constantly breaking up, falling apart, and perpetually in need of glue. As I look back, the project may well have been a metaphor for the way I looked at religion at that life juncture, and nothing seems to have changed in the ensuing seven decades.

Sports in the Life of a Young Boy

I loved all sports as a child, and from about age eight or nine to perhaps fourteen, baseball was my favorite. But then, baseball was America's Pastime, having little competition from other sports in the summer months in the 1940's and 1950's. Such, of course, is not the case today. The soccer invasion emanating from all parts of the globe has cut into the popularity of baseball in recent decades, as has the club movement where kids play their favored sport year-round from the age of six, seven, or eight. Simply put, baseball does not have total command over our summer imaginations as it once did.

Baseball: Harry Caray, Stan "The Man" Musial, and the Redbirds. There were only eight teams in the National League as of the 1940's, and the same was true of the "Junior Circuit", or American League, which had been created after the National League was formed. None of the sixteen clubs were located west of St. Louis geographically at that time.

I became a hard-core, dyed-in-the-wool St. Louis Cardinal fan around age nine or ten, thanks in great part to the presence of two people. One was the incredibly charismatic, eternally ebullient, and exceedingly extroverted Harry Caray, the baseball announcer for Station KMOX in St. Louis. The other person was my childhood hero, Stanley Frank Musial (1920-2012) of Donora, Pennsylvania. Musial was surrounded on the Cardinals team by a cast of players with immense talent and colorful nicknames, players such as Enos "Country" Slaughter, Harry "The Cat" Brecheen, Alfred "Red" Schoendienst, and George "Whitey" Kurowski. At shortstop was the man with the magic hands, Marty "Slats" Marion. Behind the plate were Del Rice and a chap named Joe Garagiola who went on to make a name for himself in the baseball broadcast booth after a fair-to-middling' playing career with the Redbirds.

Thanks to KMOX, we were able to pick up the games of both St. Louis teams, the Cardinals and the Browns, though the lowly American League Browns were of little interest. They won infrequently and had few talented players with whom to identify. We lucky Okies, at least those of us in the northeastern corner, were privileged to hear many of the Cardinal games in those years, basking in the glory of the "Redbirds" and a wonderful array of distinguished opponents from other teams.

But let's return for a minute to Harry Caray (born Harry Christopher Carabina in 1914). Harry cemented my already considerable love for the game of baseball with his often frenetic but always entertaining commentary. He made Cardinal players and opponents larger than life, and permanently imprinted the considerable baseball talents and, perhaps more importantly, the character of my childhood hero, Stan "The Man" Musial forever in my psyche. Musial was an immensely talented player and exemplified the best of being a good human being throughout his life, and I owe him a debt of thanks for being such a fantastic role model. I also thank station KMOX and Harry Caray for making Stan Musial and the Cardinals a formative part of my early life. Though I am no longer much of a Cardinal fan thanks to the passing of time and the creation of the Texas franchises in Houston and Arlington, I know in my heart of hearts that old-timers like Stan Musial, Harry Caray, and an assortment of other Cardinals of the past are still lurking in the subterranean sections of my psyche.

In 2011, a very feeble Stan Musial, decked out resplendently in a Cardinal red blazer and matching tie, was awarded the Presidential Medal of Freedom by President Barack Obama. Though he could not leave his wheelchair to accept the award, Stan the Man was a Cardinal all the way. Shortly after receiving the Presidential Medal, it was revealed that the seemingly indestructible Stan the Man suffered from Alzheimer's Disease. He died in 2012, but it took the inexorable effects of time and a crippling, catastrophic neurological illness to slow down Stanley Frank (The Man) Musial, aka the "Duke of Donora."

Harry Caray was ably assisted during part of his tenure with the Cardinals by a colorful ex-major league catcher, Charles Evard "Gabby" Street who brought years of experience as both player and successful manager to the broadcast booth. Caray was truly the voice of Cardinals baseball, and a small part of me died when he was dismissed in 1969 by the Busch family of beer brewing fame who owned the team. I was thirty-one-years old and consumed with more important life challenges by that time, but the Cardinals did not seem like the Cardinals any more without Harry Caray.

Harry reinvented himself and took on larger-than-life proportions when he moved to the Chicago Cubs in 1982, where he stayed until failing health forced him to relinquish his spot behind the microphone in 1997. He died a year after his full retirement in 1998, a month shy of his eighty-fourth birthday. During his time with the Cubbies, he developed a huge following with his good-natured bantering with the fans, ably abetted by his most capable color man, ex-pitcher Steve Stone. The always jovial and extroverted Caray was known for his affinity for the night life of the Windy City which led his fans to call him "The Mayor of Rush Street." Rush Street, of course, is Chicago's answer to Bourbon Street in New Orleans or Beale Street in Memphis.

In the booth, Harry developed several idiosyncrasies that added to his legend. One was the use of the phrase, "Holy Cow!" when referring to major moments or events in a game. He also popularized the chant, "It Might Be, It Could Be, It Is", whenever a Cubbie hit a homerun. And what fan of that era will ever forget Harry singing his sometimes off-key and always cacophonous rendition of "Take Me Out to the Ballgame" during the seventh inning stretch at Cub games? Though he was "a homer" and shameless promoter of his beloved "Cubbies", Harry Caray rightfully remains a baseball broadcasting legend. He was enshrined in the announcer's wing of baseball's Hall of Fame in Cooperstown, New York, in 1989. He was in my personal announcer Hall of Fame many years before that.

My Bubble Gum Baseball Card Collection. I saved bubble gum baseball cards from Bowman and Topps by the hundreds, perhaps thousands, during my childhood. The personal baseball card collection was populated with the likes of Jackie Robinson of the Brooklyn Dodgers and one of his staunchest defenders in the early days of baseball integration, PeeWee Reese. I also had some Gil Hodges's, Carl Furillo's, and Pete Reiser's. Since they were arch-enemies of the beloved Redbirds, it was hard to like the "Boys of Summer", beautifully chronicled in the wonderful book written by the ultra-conservative but verbally and intellectually gifted George Will. There is no denying that those Dodgers of that era truly played an inspiring brand of baseball. Also, American society owes a huge debt to the owner of the Dodgers, Branch Rickey, for bringing Jackie Robinson into the league in 1947, once again integrating baseball after a hiatus of some sixty years.

The first black professional baseball player is generally acknowledged to be John (Bud) Fowler who played for the minor league team in New Castle, Pennsylvania in 1872. Fowler was followed a decade later by Moses Fleetwood Walker who played for the Toledo (Ohio) Mud Hens in 1883, and as such, was the first black major league baseball player. He was joined later that same season by his brother, Weldy (also known as Weldey and Welday) Wilberforce Walker. Widespread racism forced the Walkers out of the game shortly after their debut, and no blacks played organized baseball in the all-white system until Jackie Robinson joined the minor league team in Montreal in 1945 and the Brooklyn Dodgers in 1947. One can only guess how many potential Hall of Famers never got to showcase their considerable talents in the major league spotlight because they were black.

There were many great players on the other teams in the National League in 1947 and each series would bring these different players to life via KMOX. In would come the Boston Braves, and the beloved Cards would have to face bubble gum luminaries such as Warren Spahn and Johnny Sain. Their manager, Billy Southworth, was said to have pitched those two guys whenever possible, thus giving birth to the managerial mantra mentioned earlier, "Spahn and Sain and pray for rain." Given that those two pitchers had forty-two wins between them in 1947 while the other three Braves starters accounted for only twenty-five, it is easy to see from whence Southworth's strategy arose.

Who from that era can forget those New York Giants and their heralded slugger, Big Johnny Mize? We Cardinal diehards held our breath every time Mize strode to the batter's box. The much feared Hall of Famer accounted for 359 home runs, or "taters", over his career, so I think our fears were justified. Bobby Thomson was a worthy accomplice to Mize's dirty work with 264 career home runs himself. Thomson, a Scottish immigrant, became forever famous with one swing of the bat that will live forever in the lore of baseball. Serious fans of baseball will remember he hit a home run in the bottom of the ninth inning of a deciding playoff game against the dreaded Dodgers in 1951 that clinched the pennant for the Giants and sent them to the World Series against the New York Yankees. The Giants entered the last inning of the deciding game down 4-1, scored a run and then Thomson unloaded what is now known as the "Shot Heard Round the World" with two runners on base to give the Giants a 5-4 win. It is not unusual even today to see video recapitulations of that famous home run. Bobby Thomson died on August 17, 2010 at the age of eighty-six.

Though not known for a dominating offense, the Cincinnati Reds were a force, led by Ewell "The Whip" Blackwell, feared for his herky-jerky, side-winding submariner delivery, and Johnny "Double No-Hit" Vandermeer, so named for his consecutive no-hitters in 1938, the year of my birth.

The Cubbies from Chicago won sixty-nine games and lost eighty-five that year in 1938, so they were not much of a threat to the well-being of our Redbirds. Stan Hack was wrapping up a career in which he hit .301, and "Peanuts" Lowery, Andy Pafko, Eddie Waitkus, and Bill Nicholson were threats to be reckoned with when they stepped into the batter's box.

Dragging up the rear in the National League that year were the Pennsylvania teams, the Philadelphia Phillies and the Pittsburgh Pirates. The Phillies were led offensively by Harry "The Hat" Walker. Harry had been dealt earlier that year by the Cards to the Phillies and hit .371 (lifetime .296). Colorful pitchers Lynwood "Schoolboy" Rowe and Dennis "Dutch" Leonard combined for thirty-one wins in fifty-three decisions, so they clearly were the go-to guys, the Steady Eddies, on the Phillies pitching staff. As for the Pirates, Ralph Kiner hit fifty-one home runs (career total of 369) and Hank Greenberg twenty-five. Other stalwarts were Wally Westlake in right field and Bobby Cox, for many years the manager of the Atlanta Braves, at shortstop. A notable pitcher for the beleaguered Pirates was Elwin "Preacher" Roe who won four and lost fifteen that year. Roe was subsequently traded to the Brooklyn Dodgers in 1948 and he went on to post ninety-three wins and only thirty-seven losses over the next seven years, posting a career best year of twenty-two wins and three losses in 1951. I suspect some red-faced General Manager may have kicked himself a time or three when thinking about the wisdom of trading the "Preacher Man."

Of the preceding players, Harry "The Hat" Walker led the league in hitting in 1947, which serves as a sort of microcosm for that era, with Kiner fourth and Musial fifth. Kiner and Mize both hit fifty-one home runs to lead in the power category, with Mize winning the RBI title over Kiner. Kiner led in slugging percentage and total bases. My man Musial was third in triples and hits and fifth in total bases. Blackwell led the league in wins with twenty-two and Spahn and Sain and Pray for Rain each had twenty-one. Blackwell also led in strikeouts, was second in earned run average (2.47) to Spahn's (2.33), second in fewest hits per nine innings (7.48), and second in shutouts (six) and third in innings pitched (273). Spahn, in addition to having the lowest ERA, pitched the most innings (290), and threw the most shutouts (seven). Blackwell threw twenty-three complete games, followed by Sain (twenty-two), Spahn (twenty-two), Larry Jansen of the Giants (twenty-one), and Dutch Leonard with nineteen. These complete game numbers are in stark contrast to the highly specialized relief game of today where anyone pitching a game from start to finish is viewed as a rarity. For example, there were 840 complete games pitched in major league baseball in 1944. In 2004, that number was 150. Cy Young who pitched from 1890 to 1911 is the all-time complete game leader with 749 complete games. In 2011, the career leader was Roy Halliday of the Philadelphia Phillies with sixty-one. In third place was forty-eight-year old Jamie Moyer who had thirty-three complete games, or roughly one for each year he pitched in the major leagues.

The American League, the so-called "junior circuit" was of interest, also, but not nearly as memorable as the National League despite my early mentorship under Grandpa Chamberlain. Certainly, the considerable feats of Joe DiMaggio and Yogi Berra of the dreaded Yankees, the "Splendid Splinter" Ted Williams of the Red Sox, and the flame throwing Bob Feller of the Indians, were topics of everyday conversation. I cannot remember how many arguments I had with my friends over who was the best player, Musial, Williams, or DiMaggio. I suspect my unwavering allegiance to Stan Musial blinded me to the gargantuan accomplishments of Ted Williams. I just would not back down on my loyalty to Musial as the best player of the era and maybe of all time. Looking back now, I can see that Musial was a fabulous player in his heyday but promoting him as the best of all time may be a stretch.

Football: The Oklahoma Sooners. Oklahoma Sooner football, under the capable stewardship of the handsome and debonair Charles "Bud" Wilkinson, was in its heyday in my youth. The unparalleled success of the Sooners captured the fancy of youth football players across the state, and we all aspired to be the next Darrell Royal, Jack Ging, Tommy McDonald, Merrill Green, Billy Vessels, Jim Weatherall, or a Boydston or Burris brother. Of the group, Tommy McDonald took on special significance for me, for he was about my size and speed and exemplified the best in football demeanor. He wore jersey number twenty-five, and as was the case with Stan Musial in baseball. I tried to emulate McDonald (and Musial) to the nth degree, choosing twenty-five for my football jersey number throughout junior high and high school.

Wilkinson's OU teams put together a forty-seven-game winning streak in the late 1940's, and it was easy to jump on the bandwagon and bask in the reflected glory of the "Big Red." I decided when I was maybe ten or eleven I was going to play football for the University of Oklahoma, so football pretty much became my favorite sport at that point. Since I had modest sprinter speed, I decided I would groom myself to be an outstanding running back for OU, perhaps even the next Tommy McDonald. My dream of gridiron greatness at OU never materialized due to a combination of lack of ability and absence of dedication, but it was fun to emulate my heroes and dream my dreams as a young boy.

Football: The Men of West Point. My earliest interest in college football, however, was focused not on OU but rather on the gridiron fortunes of the U.S. Military Academy, the Black Knights of West Point. Though their games were typically played many miles removed from the wilds of Oklahoma, we were somehow able to pick up radio accounts of their games in the late 1940's. This period in Army football immediately after World War II was glorious, and names like Arnold Tucker, Arnold Galiffa, Glenn Davis, Felix "Doc" Blanchard, John Trent, Bill Yeoman, and J. D. Kimmel became as familiar to me as those of my baseball heroes. Doc Blanchard, "Mr. Inside", and Glenn Davis, "Mr. Outside", dominated the sports headlines for several seasons, and they were awarded the coveted Heisman Trophy in successive years as college football's best player, Blanchard in 1945 and Davis in 1946. One of my early West Point heroes, Captain John Trent, was killed in the Korean War, and news of his death hit me hard as a kid. Yeoman went on to become a highly successful coach at the University of Houston and Kimmel enjoyed a long career in engineering before his death in 2009.

As a boy, I was not aware of the nuances of West Point recruiting which enabled them to dominate football in the late 1940's. One huge recruiting edge accrued via a technicality which made it possible in those days to play four years of college ball elsewhere and then be appointed to the academy and play four more years for the Black Knights. For example, Major General Harvey J. Jablonski, the Commanding Officer of my unit in the early 1960's, the First Armored Division, was said to have played four years at Washington University in St. Louis and four years at West Point. Also, older men who had served in the army during World War II sometimes received an appointment if they just happened to possess serious football talent. This liberal application of the rules created a "men against boys" scenario in college football for a brief time which worked to the huge advantage of the cadets of West Point. Of course, I was unaware of these shenanigans and subterfuges, and reveled in Army's successes for those few years. As time wore on, I switched my allegiances to the Sooners and enjoyed their many triumphs just as many Okies have done in the "Bud" Wilkinson, Barry Switzer, and Bob Stoops eras.

Basketball: Robert "Cleats" McLeod. For whatever reason, I never really had a basketball court setup that was worth much, so my friends and I pretty much played hoops a couple of blocks away at the home of Robert "Cleats" McLeod. Robert's dad was handy with a welding torch and he shaped a basketball rim out of a piece of steel and made a nice backboard to go with it, and most of our games throughout my childhood and adolescence took place there. Speaking of basketball, has anyone noticed that at the professional level today, the sport is just one headlock away from becoming professional wrestling? There are more muggings per square inch during an NBA playoff game than there are on the mean streets of Harlem in New York City or in south-central, gang-infested Los Angeles. The comedian, Rodney Dangerfield, has captured my feelings about that "sport" with the following paraphrase: "I went to a pro basketball game the other night and a wrestling match broke out."

Robert received his nickname in high school not for his prowess as a field goal kicker but rather for his sheer absence of kicking talent. He was pigeon-toed and basically had difficulty putting one foot in front of the other without doing a pratfall. Thanks to his inability to produce with his foot and the fact that no one else was any better, our football teams always ran or passed the ball for extra points. There was no such thing as a field goal in my six years of football at Dewey; I do not remember an opposing team ever kicking one against us either. This situation is interesting in view of the fact there was really no incentive to run or pass because an extra point, regardless of whether or not it was scored by passing, running, or kicking, was worth only one point in those days. We just did it the hard way, thanks to "Cleats" McLeod and our collective ineptitude in the kicking game.

American Life in the 1950's

Population of U.S. is 152 Million
The Average Annual Salary is $2990
A Loaf of Bread Costs 14 Cents
Cold War Starts and Bomb Shelters Proliferate
Jonas Salk Develops Polio Vaccine
Korean Conflict Begins and Ends
AFL and CIO Merge to Form Mega-Union with 15 Million Members
Alaska and Hawaii Admitted to the Union Making Them 49th and 50th States
Bestsellers were *Power of Positive Thinking, The Lonely Crowd, The Organization Man, Catcher in the Rye, East of Eden, Caine Mutiny, Giant, Atlas Shrugged*
Brown vs. Board of Education Ruling Passed by Supreme Court
Activist Rosa Parks Refuses to Give Up Seat on Segregated Bus in Alabama
Hula Hoops, Coon Skin Hats, Silly Putty, Poodle Skirts, Blue Suede Shoes Popular
Era of Crooners Dinah Shore, Nat "King" Cole, Perry Como, and Frank Sinatra
Elvis Presley, Jerry Lee Lewis, and Bill Haley and the Comets Dominate Radio
Lassie, Ozzie and Harriet, I Love Lucy, Guiding Light Major Hits on Television
Diary of Anne Frank, Cat on a Hot Tin Roof and *South Pacific* Dominate Broadway
Jose Ferrer (*Cyrano De Bergerac*) and Judy Holliday (*Born Yesterday*) win Oscars
Al Jolson, George Orwell, and George Bernard Shaw Die
Althea Gibson Integrates Women's Professional Tennis

Summers in Texas City, Texas

Transitioning From Dewey to Texas City

Upon completing the fourth grade in 1948, my siblings and I were introduced to a most significant life phase. To wit, we spent all but one of the next eight summers with our father and stepmother in Texas City, Texas. As noted elsewhere, my parents divorced in 1945, and this set up a situation whereby my siblings and I split time between two homes in the summertime. My mother, as noted much earlier in this chronicle, departed for Oklahoma, and my father left the barren Panhandle and Phillips Petroleum for the Texas Gulf Coast. Eventually, he established himself in Texas City, working for over a decade as Business Agent for the International Union of Operating Engineers (IUOE), Local 347.

GEORGE LEUNES, GALVESTON (TX) BEACH, CIRCA 1950

HALF-SISTER NANCY, GEORGE LEUNES, HALF-BROTHER GEORGE WAYNE,
UNIDENTIFIED INFANT, CIRCA 1960

Several years after moving to Texas City, our father felt comfortable enough with both his new marriage and increasingly sound financial situation to bring us to his home each summer starting in 1948. More often than not, we made the trip to Texas City via the Santa Fe Railroad from Ponca City, Oklahoma, to either Houston or Galveston. Making the trip by car from Dewey to Ponca City, (aka "Punkin Center", a local colloquialism used I suppose in reference to cities in Arizona, Colorado, and Kansas which actually were named Punkin Center), was a real adventure. We were chauffeured by our mother and Highway 60 has never been the same since!

We were obviously not old enough to transport ourselves to Ponca City, so that onerous chore became the province of our mother who had a morbid, beyond-the-pale fear of driving. The short eighty-mile trip to Ponca City would take two hours or more because my mother was terrified of on-coming traffic, among many other things, and at the first sight of an approaching car, would pull off the road and on to the shoulder until the threat passed. You can imagine on a busy day how long it might take to navigate eighty miles with her approach to dealing with traffic.

Once safely aboard the train, we relaxed and focused our thoughts on the upcoming three months in Texas City and the joy of being around our father and his new wife, June. At summer's end, our father would buy us enough clothes to last the next year and put us on a train bound back to Ponca City. We then got to experience my mother's traffic terror in reverse as we made our way to Dewey to resume our old way of life and begin school once again.

Texas City Vignettes

A Bit of Texas City History. I have chosen to write a few words about Texas City since so many years of my life and innumerable meaningful experiences are anchored there. The city was founded shortly before 1900 by three brothers from Minnesota who were, of all things, on a duck hunting trip to the marshlands along the Gulf Coast. It dawned on the erstwhile duck hunters, Jacob, Henry, and Benjamin Myers, that the area had the potential to become a major seaport. Upon returning to their home state, the brothers forged a financial alliance with some investors that enabled them to purchase 10,000 acres of Galveston Bay frontage. From this humble beginning rose the municipality of Texas City in 1893. Shortly after achieving city status, a man by the name of A. B. Wolvin convinced the federal government to create a twenty-five-foot channel to facilitate greater seaport activity. The project took a big hit when the horrific hurricane of 1900 stormed ashore, killing more than 6,000 people in nearby Galveston. The port was finally completed in 1905, ship usage expanded rapidly, and the city grew by leaps and bounds. By 1950, the city was home to slightly over 16,000 people, thus placing it in the top fifty in Texas in terms of population. As of 2010, the US census reported the city had around 45,000 residents.

The Texas City Refinery started operating in 1908, and three more refineries, Amoco, Union Carbide, and Monsanto Chemical Company, opened facilities there over the next several years. These petro-chemical operations played prominent roles in boosting the economy of Texas City and, later, supporting the war effort in World War II. Also assisting with the war effort was a local tin smelter operation, one of only three of its kind in the Western Hemisphere. At one time, the Texas City smelter literally provided almost all civilian and military needs for tin in the free world.

Heat, Humidity, Marauding Mosquitos, More Heat, More Humidity, and Petro-Chemical Pollution. Texas City was a hot and ungodly humid city, and by both day and night the mosquitoes roamed by the hundreds of thousands, or maybe it was hundreds of millions. Perhaps the Karankawa Indians had the place figured out before they became extinct in the 1850's. The tribe lived along the Gulf Coast and were said to cover themselves with mud to ward off both the heat and the voracious mosquitoes. It has been documented in the print media that the Gulf Coast mosquitoes, on occasion, have been known to clog up the nasal passages of herds of cattle, thus causing many to suffocate. Though I never felt at risk for asphyxiation by their presence, they often congregated in my bedroom at night. Their omni-presence deprived me of much-needed, restorative sleep, and in the dark stillness of night, they sounded like B-17's on a bombing raid. I think they extracted most of their much-needed supply of blood, however, from couples huddled in the front and back seats of automobiles parked at the drive-in movie, the entertainment rage of that era.

I liked Texas City, its warmth and humidity, its sultriness, the abundant ocean spray, and perversely enough, the smell of its refineries that loomed over most of the horizon. I always thought the odor emanating from the refineries was really the smell of money, though many, especially outsiders, found the aroma to be offensive. In retrospect, it is likely that the odors I was processing were really impending lung cancer, emphysema, and Chronic Obstructive Pulmonary Disease

(COPD) from petrochemical waste thrust by their stacks into the atmosphere. Putting a little different spin on the Texas City smog and smells, radio talk show personality and businessman Scott Delucia of our local radio station, WTAW, recently described Texas City as, "One of those hamlets along the Gulf Coast that glows in the dark."

I suspect my deceased eighty-eight-year old father's COPD was at least partially related to the air pollution. According to the U.S. Department of Health and Human Services website, the leading contributor to COPD is smoking cigarettes. However, spending years in environments in which lung irritants are present, i. e., refineries, also contributes heavily to the development of respiratory problems. My father brought seventy years of smoking cigarettes plus fifteen years of residing in Texas City to the COPD table.

Texas City Disaster. On the morning of April 16, 1947 (my ninth birthday, by the way), Texas City became the scene of one of the largest civilian catastrophes in the history of the United States. It seems a French ship, *The SS Grandecamp*, carrying 2,500 tons of ammonium nitrate fertilizer, was in port but ultimately headed back to Europe where the massive task of rebuilding a devastated Europe was taking place after World War II. Specifically, the fertilizer was to be used to assist farmers in their efforts to re-energize agriculture and feed the people of Europe, many of whom had been left homeless and starving by the ravages of the war.

The Texas City Disaster, as it became known in the media, began around 0800 in the morning of April 16 when smoke was spotted coming from *The Grandecamp*. The cargo in the ship's hold had become so heated that harbor water began boiling nearby. An hour after the smoke was first spotted, the fertilizer reached a flash point and the cargo detonated. Though it was port policy to require tugboats to tow burning vessels out into the harbor, the procedure was not implemented until it was too late.

A column of smoke arose from the eruption, reaching a height of around 2,000 feet. The explosion blew two small airplanes out of the sky, tossed a barge one hundred yards inland, leveled dozens of buildings, and propelled the ship's anchor all the way across town. The force generated by the detonation actually drove a fifteen-foot wall of water away from the refinery, and it later came rushing back as a mini-tsunami which continued inland for 150 feet, devastating structures and drowning numerous people in its path. The wall of water produced by the explosion in the refinery eventually reached one hundred miles out into the Gulf of Mexico.

Most of the city firefighters died in the initial blasts, and rescue workers labored through the night to find people trapped in the wreckage. As the ship continued to burn, a crowd gathered to watch the local firefighters douse the blaze, or so it was reported. Unfortunately, many of the onlookers were curious children who, like the adults, were unaware of both the nature and potential lethality of the cargo being transported by *The Grandecamp*.

Unexpectedly, the cargo of a second ship detonated an hour after midnight on the 17th, greatly compounding the mounting confusion and panic among the local citizenry and emergency personnel.

That second vessel, *The High Flyer*, was also loaded with highly volatile ammonium nitrate fertilizer, and the explosion led it to burn throughout the night. Efforts to tow it away from the refinery as dictated by port policy failed for whatever reason. The April 17 blast was considered to be the most violent of the explosions, and it wiped out a grain elevator, a warehouse, and a nearby ship, *The Wilson B. Keene*. A black oily mist rained down on nearby Galveston and other cities in the area, and seismograph readings of the explosion were detected 1,000 miles away in Denver, Colorado. The fires rapidly spread throughout the entire complex of refineries in the city, toppling buildings and trapping people inside.

It took over a week to extinguish the numerous fires, and months of cleanup were required to remove all of the rubble. Nearly 600 lives were lost, thousands more suffered an assortment of injuries, and the overall damages were estimated at $67 million. That cost figure would be the 2015 equivalent of around $700 million. The bodies of sixty-three people were never identified, and a monument known as Memorial Park and Cemetery was formally dedicated to their memory in the 1980's. The Information Center there has a pictorial account of the events of April 16 and 17, 1947.

It is a credit to the leadership of the community and a dedicated citizenry that they decided to rebuild, and they did so with a vengeance, and Texas City soon became a vibrant community once again. However, the memories of the events of 1947 remained powerful in the minds of those who lived through what appeared at the time to be the end of the world. Hal Boyle, a prominent World War II correspondent for Associated Press, stated he had only seen devastation of the proportions of the Texas City Disaster one other time in his four years of reporting on World War II. The devastation Hal Boyle was referring to was at Nagasaki where one of the two atomic bombs was dropped in August of 1945, ending the war with Japan.

The very same fertilizer compound which devastated Texas City that fateful April day in 1947 also killed fifteen people, wounded 160 others, and damaged 150 buildings in West, Texas, in May of 2013. Sadly, the same can be said for about the Oklahoma City bombing on April 19, 1995. In this instance, a disgruntled Army veteran and anti-government militant Timothy MacVeigh and his associates, Terry Nichols and Michael Fortier, loaded a Ryder rental truck with ammonium nitrate fertilizer, drove it to a selected point adjacent to the Murrah Building, and detonated its charge, wounding 800 people and killing 168 others, nineteen of whom were children. There were also three unborn fetuses among the casualties. The children were supposedly safely ensconced in a day care facility provided for government employees working in the Murrah Building.

The motive for the killings was to exact revenge on the U.S. government for the way it handled (mishandled?) the David Koresh cult in Waco, Texas, in 1991, and the Ruby Ridge incident in 1992 in Montana. For his part in masterminding the slaughter of innocents, MacVeigh was put to death by lethal injection in 2001. Terry Nichols was sentenced to prison for life without the possibility of parole, and Michael Fortier was given twelve years as part of a plea agreement in which he agreed to testify against his collaborators. Fortier was released from prison in 2006, placed in a federal witness protection program, and lives somewhere in the US with his wife and two children.

On a personal note, Fortier served some of his sentence at the federal prison in Fort Worth, Texas, where a former student and good friend, Dr. Michael "Mike" Sharp, was the chief psychologist. At one point in Fortier's tenure in Fort Worth, Dr. Sharp invited me up to Fort Worth to give a talk to his staff on promoting physical fitness in the workplace. I was a bit shocked at the security in place the day of my visit, and I soon learned why things were so tense. Mike indicated the heightened security measures were instituted because of the presence of Fortier up on one of the top floors of the facility, maybe the sixth or seventh. In any case, there were armed guards at each side of the first floor elevator, and each floor was treated with the same level of security. It was not likely Mr. Fortier was going to break out of that prison.

Water, Water Everywhere. As mentioned much earlier in my introductory remarks, Northeastern Oklahoma for the most part is flat or slightly rolling and filled with trees and lakes. However, the major bodies of waters were some distance away from Dewey so we spent very little time lakeside growing up. On the other hand, it was hard to escape water in Texas City and Galveston, and the wonderment of seeing it for the first time sticks indelibly in my memory.

GEORGE LEUNES, CIRCA 2000

Rather than have us ride the train the first year we spent in Texas City, our father drove us the 450 miles from Dewey to the Gulf Coast. To add a touch of adventure to the long drive, he went several miles out of his way to take us through Bridge City in far southeast Texas. The Rainbow Bridge 176 feet above the Neches River was the highest structure of its kind I had ever seen in my life. It was absolutely breathtaking though somewhat scary for a ten-year-old to mentally process the magnitude of it all. Nothing in my past experience provided me with anything resembling enough imagination to conjure up such an image; like so many other things in life, it simply had to be seen to be appreciated. The same thing was true for the Gulf of Mexico. For an Oklahoma flatlander, the Gulf was awesome; waves breaking close to shore, salt water smells tickling olfactory senses, big ocean-going vessels making their way across the distant horizon, and diving birds everywhere. Ah, the wonderment of it all as seen through the eyes of a child of ten!

We spent many a Sunday lolling about on the beach in Galveston during the next several summers. At the end of those fun, sun-filled and oft-sunburned days, we would rinse off the grit and grime at a nearby beach shower, make a fast run through a car wash to remove the salt spray so detrimental to the health of an automobile, chow down on a foot-long Coney Island hot dog at a nearby drive-in restaurant, and head for home and a real shower. Few showers in my life have felt better than those at the end of a long day at the gritty, grimy beach!

Our Stepmother, June. My father and his new wife, Teresa June, or just plain "June" brought stability to our lives, something in short supply back in Oklahoma where our mother's drinking problems were becoming more serious. June was perhaps twelve years younger than my father, in her early twenties and really quite an attractive woman. She had a pretty face, striking figure, and what looked to my twelve-year old eyes to be Betty Grable quality legs, equally fit for a calendar. For those of you not familiar with Betty Grable, she was a 1940's and 1950's movie star and World War II pin-up girl noted for her profoundly shapely legs. It came as little surprise that June had an affinity for wearing shorts which accentuated her best features.

Speaking of wearing shorts, many years ago my first wife Barbara and I were traveling in East Texas and stopped by a roadside flea market to look at baubles, doodads, gewgaws, and the usual assortment of plain old junk. We were barely out of our car before an impolite sixty-ish woman ordered us off the property, clearly offended because Barbara was wearing the dreaded societal scourge, shorts. Many years earlier, in the late 1940's or early 1950's, June had encountered the same thing during a family vacation in Mexico where wearing shorts was pretty much forbidden for women. My, haven't things changed in this regard?

During those early years in Texas City, my father typically worked eighteen hours a day seven days a week and traveled a quarter million miles a year as a part of his labor union business. His travels took him to Washington, D.C. on a number of occasions, but the majority of his trips involved visits to petrochemical facilities ranging from Lake Charles, Louisiana to the east of Texas City and over to Lake Jackson, Texas, to the south and west. Occasionally, he would even make a northern jaunt to El Dorado, Arkansas.

When in town, he spent time with us kids, and almost always was willing to play catch with a baseball for a few minutes over the lunch hour or at the end of the day. Though he was not around a lot, I frankly never felt neglected, largely because of the quality time he and I spent together and the company of his delightful wife, June. In addition to being easy for a young boy to look at, June was a devoted wife, great cook, and ready and willing card player. We spent many a night sitting on the floor playing Canasta, Solitaire, Battleship, and what have you. June, like the aforementioned caretakers of Grandpa Chamberlain, always made me feel very special, and that is something all children need. My siblings have fond memories of her today, but I do recall some minor jealousies on their part because she was not our "real mother", which is often the lot of the stepmother. In my own personal view, June was a generous, good-hearted woman and I am glad I got to spend some wonderful time with her.

STEPMOTHER JUNE, CHILDREN, STEPCHILDREN

Boy, could June cook! Oh, my goodness gracious, could she cook! She was raised in Marlow, near Duncan in south-central Oklahoma and just north of Wichita Falls, Texas, and her mother grounded her in the nuances of preparing good, simple, down-home country cooking. Her meals were seldom elaborate or expensive but they were always tasty and sumptuous. Most had six or seven courses, and were almost always followed by banana pudding or some other delightful dessert. I won lots of points with June and my siblings because I would consume my usual share of the food while anxiously waiting for everyone to finish up, at which point I would proceed to make sure there were no leftovers. I honestly do not think we ever ate a leftover during my late pre-teen and teenage years.

Short Visits and Long Vacations. During the first several summers we spent in Texas City, the family made short visits to area sights such as the San Jacinto Monument and the Battleship Texas in Pasadena and the Alamo in San Antonio. The San Jacinto structure was at the time second in height only to the Washington Monument, and was created as every Texan knows to commemorate the Battle of San Jacinto which ended the Mexican-American War in 1845, thus giving Texas its independence. Of course, the Alamo still serves today as a reminder of the valor of a band of heroes dedicated to the preservation of the American/Texas way of life during that same war.

We also visited dude ranches in the hill country of Texas, Carlsbad Caverns in New Mexico, and the Mexican cities of Monterrey and Cola de Caballo (Spanish for "Tail of the Horse"). I had absolutely no interest in riding a horse at the hill country dude ranch, much preferring to stay behind and gorge myself on cantaloupe and watermelon, and just fiddle around until the riders returned. I still like cantaloupe and watermelon and fiddling around more than I do horses.

Every time I look at a horse, I am reminded of the Freudian concepts of *Eros* and *Thanatos*. Freud theorized that we are possessed of a very strong wish to live called *Eros* and an equally powerful wish to die, or *Thanatos*. The wish to die is as powerful as the wish to live in Freudian theory because it represents a return to Utopia from whence we originally sprung. Ashes to ashes and dust to dust; such is Utopia, and we are all possessed of a powerful urge to recapture that Edenic state. Because *Thanatos* is a powerful force, people choose suicide, drinking themselves to death, running around with married women, or riding motorcycles or horses as manifestations of this compelling death wish. Every time I see a horse, I am fascinated by their often-resplendent coloration and yet intimidated by their muscular beauty. However, I am convinced to the very core of my existence that the thousand pound behemoths have an incredibly small brain programmed like a computer and loaded with only two thoughts, "I'm hungry," and "How can I harm a human today." The almost certain response when a rider straddles their powerful, broad backs is to first buck while concomitantly searching with both big, beautiful eyes for a fence post, the nearest available barbed wire, or a tree limb with which to dislodge or, even better, dismember their burdensome load.

Little League Baseball. It was important to my father that my friends and I have a place to play baseball during those summers in Texas City, and to that end, he became the driving force (so I was told) in obtaining a Little League charter for the community. Little League baseball originated in 1939 in Williamsport, Pennsylvania, and spread slowly throughout the nation as people began to warm up to the idea of organized youth sports. Initial concerns were voiced that such organized competition might damage the fragile psyches of our young people, but that simply did not occur. By 1950, my twelfth year, we had a league of eight teams in Texas City. Boys from eight through twelve were eligible to play, but given the huge differences in size and strength associated with those two age extremes, few if any of the younger kids were able to garner an open roster spot. Contrast that system with what is done today, with seniors, majors, minors, senior minors, junior minors, minor minors, coach pitch, tee ball, and assorted combinations and permutations sufficient to boggle the analytical capabilities of even the most powerful of computers.

As stated earlier, I had cut my teeth on baseball, thanks to the combined input from Grandfather Chamberlain, Stan Musial, Harry Caray, Station KMOX, The Sporting News, and Topps bubble gum baseball cards, so Little League baseball had considerable appeal as a place to validate my ability to play and enjoy the game. I thus started my virtually certain trek to baseball's Hall of Fame in Cooperstown, New York, by way of Texas City as a twelve-year old.

I was assigned to play for the Monsanto Red Sox and our practices were held inside the refinery still laden with signs of the devastating explosion in 1947 that killed nearly six hundred people. Twisted metal and burned out patches of grass served as vivid reminders of the fiery conflagration that had taken place three years earlier. It was a bit spooky to practice there, to say the least, and I was sure there were ghosts, maybe even "haints" residing in the refinery rubble, furtively watching us go through our paces.

I am not sure how well we did as a team that year, but I remember all too well being a Texas City disaster of my own with the bat. I think I got my only hit of the season, a triple, in the last game, accumulating many a strikeout prior to that breakout hit. I was not aware of it at the time but that triple set the tone for a whole new world of baseball for me. I broke out of my batting funk and actually became a hitter the following year, and a pretty damn good one at that, if I may be so presumptuous.

Stepping backwards in the batter's box with the left or right foot as the pitcher was delivered, or what is known as "stepping in the bucket", was what I did best in Little League. I once heard a concerned father at a clinic for Little League coaches and parents ask Mark Johnson, long-time coach at Texas A&M University and Sam Houston State University in Huntsville, what you should do if a kid is afraid of the ball and "steps in the bucket." Coach Johnson's terse answer: "Find the kid another sport." At that juncture in my baseball career, I was a most viable candidate for that "other sport."

Through all of those dark days with the bat, my father remained positive which was a huge help as I was pretty advanced in my ability to beat myself up over real and imagined shortcomings. In all my days in athletics, I still do not remember my father ever making a negative comment about any of my performances, poor or otherwise. That response, no doubt, makes him a statistical rarity among parents of youth athletes.

At the end of my seventh grade year, I once again returned to Texas City for the summer. In order to give us boys a place to play organized baseball now that our Little League days were over, my father spearheaded a movement to get a Texas Teenage League up and running. The program was for boys thirteen to fifteen, and the league was composed again of eight teams during the inaugural season in 1951. I played for the International Union of Operating Engineers (IUOE) Local 347 Buffs, sponsored by the labor union local of which my father was Business Agent. The team name was borrowed from the Houston Buffalos which at that time was a farm club for my beloved St. Louis Cardinals. Many a Cardinal had spent time in the minor leagues as a "Buff" in the 1940's and 1950's, biding their time and honing their skills in Houston with hopes of making it to the "big show", or the major leagues.

During my first practice as an IUOE Buff, I hit a booming triple off of a scary fireballer by the name of Raymond Dupuy who had obliterated most of his opponents for the preceding two years, striking out almost everyone he faced. Getting that triple off of one of his intimidating fast balls bolstered my confidence, and I never had much trouble hitting a baseball after that. Young Raymond Dupuy somehow lost his touch as he got older and faded into baseball obscurity, but he could sure bring it as a kiddo and getting a hit off of him early on gave my morale a substantial boost at a time when I needed it most. I hit sufficiently well after that to make the All-Star team for two years as a first baseman, and was among the top four or five league leaders in batting average.

In the middle of that initial season, I was fortunate enough to hit the first home run in the new Teen Age League Park. The blast came off of a fat pitch, a round house curveball, from Cleo Johnson and it was juiced with the bases loaded, a grand slam, or the old "grand salami" in baseball jargon. Unfortunately, I lost that ball and all of my youth baseball and high school football scrapbooks when our house was inundated by Hurricane Carla in 1961, which is related in some detail elsewhere.

During my second year, the Buffs advanced to the state tournament in Galveston where we finished second. One of my personal tourney highlights was putting on a career batting practice demonstration before one of the games. We were allowed only three pitches and I deposited all three on top of or off the side of a grain elevator some thirty to forty feet behind the fence. Watty Watkins, a long-time scout for the St. Louis Cardinals, was in attendance that day and saw my freaky display of power. He also had nice things to say about my future prospects, intimating that I might be the best first base prospect in my age cohort in Texas. I think he was just being nice, but the praise was welcomed anyway.

In the championship game, we played a team from Houston and I got to see my first legitimate curve ball, not one that is telegraphed from the time it leaves the pitcher's hand, the so-called "roundhouse curve" which Cleo Johnson threw to me earlier that season. This curveball was the real deal, the one that looks like a fast ball until it suddenly drops out of the hitting zone with a vengeance. At fourteen, I saw the handwriting on the wall, the face of the future. The curve ball was going to be my ruination and it was small consolation to know I would be in good company with a lot of other potential baseball players for whom that pitch was a harbinger of the end of their baseball careers.

In this regard, *Sports Illustrated*, in its May 29, 2017, edition ran a fascinating article concerning the history and current status of the curveball. The curveball, also known as the yakker, the deuce, the hook, the bender, the unfair one, Public Enemy Number One, Uncle Charlie, and Sir Charles to players, fans, and baseball aficionados, was apparently "invented" in 1867 and introduced to baseball by Candy Cummings, a 5'9", 120-pound amateur pitcher in a game against Harvard University. Attesting to the power of the pitch, fellow Okie and New York Yankee Hall of Famer Mickey Mantle once said after facing a fellow Hall of Famer curveball specialist, Sandy Koufax, said: "How in the fuck is anybody supposed to hit that shit?" I feel better now, knowing Mickey Mantle had his problems with the curveball, too. When I think back on my experiences with the yakker, I am reminded of the Muhammad Ali mantra, "Float like a butterfly, sting like a bee."

As if learning to hit a curveball was not enough, I received another lesson in the subtle nuances of pitching (and hitting) a baseball three years later while playing in an American Legion game in Tulsa, when I was seventeen. We were facing a Native American guy, tribe unknown, named John Postoak, and his pitches did not have enough velocity to break a plate glass window; his offerings were hour glass slow, teasing, taunting, tantalizing, and, unfortunately for us befuddled batters, totally under his control. I think my team got three weak hits off of Postoak, and all of my own swings were dismally feeble. I fouled pitches off of my shins and shoes; I popped up little weak foul balls over the dugout; I dribbled soft grounders off of home plate; Postoak literally twisted me in knots. In three at-bats, I probably hit the ball a combined 60 feet and 6 inches, or the distance from home plate to the pitcher's mound where Postoak reigned supreme with his frustrating assortment of total junk. I learned an important lesson from Postoak that day, namely baseball games can be won by pitchers without overpowering force if they are crafty and smart. Postoak was both, but I never heard of him again and have always wondered what became of his baseball career.

A few years prior to the Tulsa debacle, I witnessed a sterling performance from a real power pitcher, at least by high school standards. His name was Ralph Terry and he was from Big Cabin, Oklahoma. He came to Dewey as a high school senior to face the not-so-fearsome Copan Hornets from a tiny berg a few miles up Highway 75 north of Dewey. Terry pitched a perfect seven-inning no-hitter, striking out all twenty-one Hornet batters along the way. We all knew we were in the presence of a pretty special pitcher that day.

Terry later pitched for twelve years in the majors, mostly with the New York Yankees, and won 107 games and lost ninety-nine. He also pitched in five World Series. I wish I had been old enough to bat against him just to see what it would be like to face a future major leaguer. I still have that same urge even today, a "bucket list" item, if you will. I harbor no illusions about being able to hit the likes of Dallas Keuchel of the Houston Astros or King Felix Hernandez of the Seattle Mariners or Clayton Kershaw of the Los Angeles Dodgers, but I would love to stand in the batter's box, bat cocked as if I could hit, and see what a baseball looks like when a major leaguer spins his magic.

Besides Ralph Terry, another area resident was making his name about that same time with the Yankees. His name was Mickey Mantle (of Sandy Koufax curveball fame) and he hailed from Commerce, an hour's drive east of Dewey. Though I never got to see Mickey play in high school, I did get to watch him a time or two when he was in the Class D Kansas-Oklahoma-Missouri (KOM)

League made up of very small towns in those three states. The Bartlesville Pirates were one of the teams and Mickey played for the team from Independence, Kansas, a New York Yankee minor league farm club. As hard-core baseball fans might guess, The Mick did not last long in Class D ball, and the rest is baseball history.

A "Fearsome Foursome": All Stars Carl Trepagnier, Jimmy Williams, Bobby Shosty, and Yours Truly. Throughout my baseball days in Texas City, there were four players who were more or less interchangeable as leading hitters and all-around dominant players. Yours truly was one, and the others were Carl Trepagnier (phonetically Trapanya), Jimmy Williams, and Bobby Shosty.

Carl Trepagnier was pretty much full-grown as a twelve-year old and struck terror in the hearts of many a pitcher when in the batter's box and more than a few batters when on the mound. Carl was left-handed, fast, strong, talented, and a youth baseball phenom (and rumored to be a heck of a football player, too). After his senior year in high school, he turned down a nice signing bonus with one of the professional teams to play baseball at Southern Methodist University (SMU) in Dallas. Carl never made it in the professional ranks, and ultimately cast his lot with a career in dentistry.

Jimmy Williams also turned down a signing bonus, reportedly $75,000 which was off the top of the chart in those days, to play at SMU. As opposed to Carl, Jimmy was sun-dial slow but he could hit and he could field. I lost track of him after college, but like Carl, he did not play professionally. As an aside, when I was twelve, Jimmy's mother decided to play matchmaker, convinced that she was going to start a lifelong romantic relationship between yours truly and an absolutely drop-dead gorgeous young nubile, also twelve, by the name of Phyllis Borden. Phyllis was in the process of becoming a woman well in advance of me becoming even a semblance of a man, so the attempt to get us together was doomed from the start. Mrs. Williams set up a "date" one afternoon at her house, and Phyllis and I ate cookies, drank soft drinks, and talked. I was intimidated by her presence (or any female, for that matter) and undoubtedly earned a spot in the Guinness Book of World Records for most immature and inane comments uttered to a person of the opposite sex during a one-hour "date."

Phyllis was a dark-haired, dark-eyed, pre-teen beauty who got even more attractive with age. If my memory serves me right, she married a young physician and lived happily ever after, or at least I hope so. Our arranged "date" in the summer of 1950 constituted the sum total of my life interactions with Phyllis, but I do thank Mrs. Williams for giving it a shot. She meant well and was great at evaluating young female talent. However, she greatly underestimated my ability to enthrall a woman when I was twelve years old. Those who know me best would say not much has changed in the intervening seven decades!

As for Bobby Shosty, he could hit a baseball and was probably the best hitter in our group of four. Bobby bypassed college in favor of a brief minor league career that stretched out over five years. He divided his time between the D and C classifications from 1957 through 1961, though he did do a brief stint in AA in 1958 with Victoria in the Texas League. He had a career batting average over those five years of .296 with an On Base Percentage (OBP) of .326. His best year was his last in 1961 when he played in 134 games, hit .307 with eight home runs and sixty-eight runs batted in.

Bobby did not hit with a lot of power but he was tough to strike out, averaging only one per thirty at bats. He was flat-out a good baseball player and the best of us four, for sure!

As intimated a few paragraphs ago, I went on to play high school and American Legion baseball with some success, though I had by then very little interest in baseball. That is unfortunate because it probably was the one sport that offered me the most long-range potential. Because fast runners are in such short supply in baseball, I have been told by reliable sources on several occasions that pairing my modest baseball talent with my speed afoot would have gotten me a two-year look in professional baseball. I harbor no long-lasting illusions that I was going to make the major leagues, or "The Show" as it is known in baseball circles, but I do harbor mild regrets in moments of reverie about not knocking around in the low minor leagues for a few years, riding rickety buses through villages and bergs, and just hanging out with some pretty wild and crazy guys. Little did I know as a high school player that fifteen years later I would get out my old glove and dredge up, resurrect, and put those old baseball skills to good use in 7,500 games of slow-pitch softball over a thirty-five-year period.

I was good enough to hang with accomplished youth baseball performers like Carl Trepagnier, Jimmy Williams, and Bobby Shosty, and based on their subsequent college or professional achievements, I feel I could have played at their level as a collegian or professional. Perhaps I could have, perhaps it was not in the cards for me, and perhaps I made a mistake by not trying, but as stated several times elsewhere, I was not especially fond of the game by the time I graduated from high school. I did consider walking on in baseball as a college freshman but opted to cast my lot with track as we will see elsewhere in recounting my undergraduate days at Texas A&M University.

In January of 2017, I learned from a childhood friend that Jimmy Williams had passed on and Carl Trepagnier was still kicking about. I know nothing of the fate of Bobby Shosty. At last report, I was still alive, though there have been moments when I wondered.

TEENAGE LEAGUE

Junior High School

Talk About Life Transitions!

My life changed dramatically upon leaving the comfortable confines of elementary school and childhood. For one thing, the infusion (intrusion?) of adolescent hormones reared its ugly head, creating unfamiliar urges, perhaps contributing to unanticipated complexion problems, and fostering an attitude about school that was both immature and counterproductive. Girls took on new if guarded importance, at least for brief periods of time; teachers were to be endured or tolerated; athletics became the be-all and end-all for me.

Speaking of complexion problems, my face became the site of a major acne and pimples invasion. Though there was seldom any humor to be found in complexion problems, in moments of weakness (strength?) I would tell my friends, "If I had one more pimple, I'd have to carry it in my hand!" My face was an unholy mess for all of those adolescent years, only to clear up almost overnight, or so it seemed, in my first year of college. There really was little that could be done with regard to treating complexion problems in the days of my adolescence. The standard medical and parental advice was to avoid carbonated drinks, chocolate, and greasy foods; washing one's face with soapy water was another option. Yet another possible solution was Clearasil, a foul smelling, obnoxious ointment that actually did little to relieve the complexion problem but did allow you to cover up your acne with pastel or light brown goo that seemed to highlight more than minimize the blight. It is gratifying to know that advances have been made in treating acne, thus sparing young people the considerable psychic pain I experienced in those important, formative, and socially sensitive years.

Junior high school in the Dewey school structure was made up of the seventh, eighth, and ninth grades. Huge differences in size and strength were noted between us scrawny seventh graders and the hairy-legged guys that represented the meanest and toughest in the ninth grade. Most of us wimpy seventh graders made a conscious and, I think, judicious decision to forgo playing junior high football until the eighth grade. We thus spent most of our first fall in junior high playing impromptu flag or touch football games around the school or in the neighborhood lots while the junior high team grunted and slaved away at football practice, beating each other into submission on an almost daily basis.

JUNIOR HIGH FOOTBALL & BASKETBALL TEAMS WITH COACH CARL DAVIDSON

Ova Farrow Asks My Class to Redshirt

The junior high principal at that time was a likeable enough fellow with the unlikely name of Ova Farrow. He had once been a coach and had the physique and rugged good looks often associated with that profession, and became a principal ostensibly due to his organizational, leadership and people skills. How many times over the years has that scenario unfolded in our schools where a coach ascends to the throne of school administration?

One day, Mr. Farrow called a meeting of the seventh grade athletes and ran a proposal by us, hoping the kids and parents would view his idea as viable and worthy of consideration. He and other close observers of the local sports scene were of the opinion that our class was loaded with athletic talent and would most likely challenge for honors at the state level four or five years down the road. Mr. Farrow proposed that we, as a group, consider repeating the seventh grade, thus making us a year older than the competition in that critical last year of high school. I suppose this was early-day redshirting at the junior high level. Mr. Farrow seemed genuinely surprised when no one bought into his proposal. I prefer to think that down deep he knew it was a far-fetched, perhaps even cockamamie idea. In his defense, however, it did turn out five years later that the omniscient Mr. Farrow was correct in his assumption that this was indeed an athletically talented class. We were strong contenders for the state title in both football and basketball in 1955-1956, and yours truly represented good old DHS at the state track meet in 1956.

The Fearsome Mrs. Elva Myers

We boys staggered through the seventh grade, trying to get a grip on whom and what we were, where we were heading, and how the nettlesome, ever-annoying females fit into the scheme of things. For me, girls were more curious than compelling, and for the most part just got in the way of my first priority, sports. I also still liked school, but the spark that produced my previous classroom excellence was fizzling, and fast.

My favorite teacher that first junior high year was a highly eccentric woman by the name of Elva Myers who was stern, stern-looking, authoritarian, and exceedingly impatient with the average and below average students in her classes. Mrs. Myers (I think she was a Mrs.) wore blue jeans in an era when no teacher would dream of showing up at school in such apparel. As well, she held back her short, cropped, gray hair with a visor that had a green, reflective bill of the sort more associated with bookkeepers, professional gamblers, or card dealers. The combination of blue jeans and the green-billed visor served to accentuate her severity and sternness.

Mrs. Myers was undoubtedly guilty of coddling her best students of which I was one. She thought I might possess a modicum of intelligence worth nurturing, so I received lots of help and praise from her. She had a disconcerting habit of publicly ridiculing the poor students while using the better students to try to wheedle better performance out of the ne'er-do-wells. The better students were shoved down the throats of the poor ones, to the chagrin of both groups. I know it made me uncomfortable to be held up to the class as one of the virtuous golden boys, or someone she viewed as having a trace of neuronal electrical activity.

At some point that year or the next, our class took one of the standardized group intelligence tests, and a week or two later we walked into Mrs. Myers' classroom to see our IQ scores listed on the classroom blackboards in descending order from best to worst. I had the top score, followed by Russell Wilson. I would guess in retrospect, that Kenneth Rigdon who went on to earn a graduate degree in Geophysics from the University of Oklahoma also had to be high in the mix somewhere.

Rigdon spent the vast majority of his career as a Research Geophysicist with Phillips Petroleum there in Bartlesville. In any case, you can imagine the brouhaha and hubbub, not to mention the hurt feelings, generated by this public disclosure of IQ scores. Given my lofty status within the group, I was subconsciously pleased by the public revelation, and it certainly did not hurt my standing with Elva Myers any. In a bit of a disclaimer, I think it is fair to say that I was a big frog, IQ-wise, in a staggeringly small pond.

George "Chief" Tyner

Our high school principal at that time was named George "Chief" Tyner. He was middle-aged, a full-blood Cherokee Indian, and married to an elementary school teacher from his tribe. "Chief" Tyner was what we called him, and there was not a hint of disrespect intended. He was a good man, a just man, a bit intimidating, perhaps even scary because of his regal appearance, tribal chieftain demeanor, warrior ancestry, and esteemed position at the school.

"Chief" Tyner occasionally gave us glimpses of his childhood in the old Indian Territory prior to Oklahoma being granted statehood in 1907. He once told us as he was growing up, it was not unusual for newly-arrived white settlers who had never crossed paths with Indians to run away in terror when encountering them for the first time. As a young boy, Chief Tyner often rode a horse and would occasionally come across new settlers who seemed fearful of his presence though he obviously meant them no harm. He, like other tribesmen, was a victim of tall tales and unfounded stereotypes promoting the image of the fierce Red Man as a savage. This image was abetted and maintained by the existing folklore and decades of cowboy movies that took considerable literary license with the truth.

One could never escape the thought that deeply imbedded in "Chief" Tyner's psyche and soul were the pains and privations of his ancestors who survived the terrible marches from their homes in North Carolina when the Cherokees were forced westward in the 1830's to the Indian Territory. "Chief" Tyner's face resembled that of a SharPei, and it seemed plausible to me that every wrinkle was put there as a remembrance of the suffering of his ancestors.

The Cherokee Tribe, or the Tsalagi. The Cherokees, or *ah-ni-yv-wi-ya*, are native to North America and were originally situated mostly in the eastern and southeastern parts of the United States. They were 25,000 in number and held dominion over almost 150,000 square miles of land encompassing all or parts of eight southeastern states. With the increasing usurpation of their lands by white settlers around the time of the Revolutionary War, some Cherokees left their ancestral lands and settled in Missouri and Arkansas. Around 1800, a reservation was set up for the Cherokees in Arkansas, but tribal dissidents led by Chief Dragging Canoe fought against this white encroachment by raiding their settlements. This resistance, of course, was common among many of the other tribes intent on slowing or stopping the settling and subsequent pilfering of their lands by the "White Eyes."

CHEROKEE NATION SEAL

The most famous of all Cherokees was Sequoyah who, among other things, invented the 86-letter Cherokee alphabet in the 1820's, thus making his tribe one of the few to have its own formal system of letters. Sequoyah's alphabet was reputedly so efficient it could be learned in fewer than thirty days. Sequoyah's home still stands in Sallisaw, Oklahoma, in the southern part of the state.

The word "Cherokee" in Sequoyah's alphabet comes out as Tsalagi (pronounced Jah-la-gee or Cha-la-gee), and it is widely believed the word "Cherokee" evolved from the Portuguese *chalaque* to the French word *cheraqui* and finally the English word *Cherokee*. Modern Cherokees refer to themselves as either Cherokee or Tsalagi.

A dismal chapter in the treatment of Native Americans took place in the 1830's when the Cherokees in Georgia and the Carolinas were displaced by the white settlers and literally herded off to their new home in the Indian Territory. The forced march was 1,200 miles long, and lives in infamy as the "Trail of Tears." The trek was characterized by extreme hardship, with weather and disease extracting a fierce toll on the disenfranchised Cherokees. As a result, many were buried along the way, some properly and some not. It was a major violation of tribal custom not to be given a proper burial but the soldiers leading the march paid little attention to propriety when disposing of dead bodies. As a tribute to the fallen, the Cherokees sang "Amazing Grace" for those not receiving a proper burial, and the song came to symbolize the "Trail of Tears." "Amazing Grace" has been retained in the hearts and souls of the Cherokee people as their national anthem.

As a parting testimony to this dark chapter in American history, on November 4, 1838, Charles Hicks, a Tsalagi and Vice Chief on the Trail of Tears, wrote the following heartbreaking note which poignantly captured the mood of the unfortunate displacement of a noble people:

> "We are now about to take our leave and give kind farewell to our native land, the country that the Great Spirit gave our Fathers, we are on the eve of leaving that country that gave us birth…it is with sorrow

we are forced by the white man to quit the scenes of our childhood...we bid farewell to it and all we hold dear."

There was scattered resistance to the forced move in North Carolina, and some dissident Cherokees hid in nearby remote mountainous areas, thus escaping the forced deportation. Others were hidden by sympathetic white people or granted citizenship which exempted them from the forced trek to the west. Today, descendants of those who resisted deportation have their tribal headquarters in Cherokee County, North Carolina, and are known as the "Eastern Band of Cherokees." Those Cherokees who were forced to move to the Indian Territory, "The Cherokee Nation of Oklahoma", have their tribal headquarters in Tahlequah, Oklahoma, 115 miles southeast of Bartlesville and Dewey. Thus, there are now two viable Cherokee Nations, each with their own tribal councils, constitutions, and action agendas.

In the early 1840's, a Cherokee newspaper known as *The Phoenix* emerged and was distributed throughout the Indian Territory. It was printed using the Cherokee language created twenty years earlier by Sequoyah. Discriminatory ethnocentric practices prevented Cherokees from speaking their own language for many years, but some schools actually teach such courses now, and hearing the Tsalagi converse in their native tongue is still a fairly common occurrence in some places.

The Cherokee Nation of Oklahoma has 250,000 members and the Eastern Band of Cherokees around 10,000. Using a complex system of determining who in fact is Tsalagi, it is estimated the total of all people claiming some degree of Cherokee heritage is 730,000. The two major bands of Cherokees participate in a number of cooperative activities, and these gestures of mutual respect are known among them as *go-hi-yu-gi*. Both bands have active programs aimed at bettering the lives of their people through tribal council activities and political lobbying at the state and national level.

Prominent Americans who have laid claim to Cherokee heritage include tribal chief and one-time President of Phillips Petroleum W. W. Keeler, singer Rita Coolidge, actors Johnny Depp and Chuck Norris, guitarist Jimi Hendrix, and Vice President John Nance Garner. Other Cherokees mentioned elsewhere include humorist Will Rogers and politician, Indian affairs advocate, and tribal chief Wilma Mankiller.

"Chief" Tyner Provides an Unforgettable Civics Lesson. During the eighth grade year, "Chief" Tyner asked several of us if we would like to accompany him on a day-long pilgrimage over to far eastern Oklahoma, near the Arkansas border, maybe a 300-mile round trip all told. I think our entourage of would-be humanitarians was made up as best I can recall after all these years of Mr. Tyner, Glenn Wright, David Miller, Ed Davis, and yours truly. It is interesting in retrospect to note that all members of the party possessed some degree of Native American heritage except for yours truly. Makes you think "Chief" Tyner chose his participants with a scheme in mind. In any case, we took food baskets and other provisions to distribute to various tribes in and around Fort Gibson and Tahlequah, the capital of the Cherokee Nation and the home of Northeastern A&M College. I had been accustomed to an integrated, self-sufficient, and reasonably prosperous Native American population in Washington County, so I never knew such poor, down-and-out, destitute, and demoralized people existed until we made that memorable trip. None of us had ever encountered such profound destitution and utter despair. It was hard to imagine from our youthful, middle-class perspective that such conditions could exist in our orthogonal, neat, orderly world. These people were dirty, bedraggled, beaten down physically and psychologically, and unbelievably impoverished. I cannot remember seeing a smile that entire day, but I like to think our gifts of food made a slight dent in their deprivation and despair.

There was obviously a method to "Chief" Tyner's madness, involving us in his mission of mercy. I will always owe him a debt of gratitude for the humanitarianism he modeled for us on behalf of his less fortunate brothers and sisters, and his willingness to share a most teachable moment. One could sit through classroom lectures for a long time without learning as much as we did that long, sometimes depressing day. It was a classic example of a picture being worth a thousand words, and this life lesson of sixty-plus years ago still guides much of what I do with my college students of today, with my class field trips to prisons, juvenile delinquency facilities, mental hospitals, and state schools for mentally challenged adults.

Acne, Blindness, Hairy Palms, and Insanity: The Evils of Masturbation

Sex education if it existed at all, circa 1952, was a crude (pardon the pun) hodgepodge mishmash of misinformation, often ineptly presented, and almost always myopic and judgmental in tone. Our first organized dose of school-sponsored sex education took place during the eighth grade. All eighth-graders were gathered together for assembly one day and then split into two groups by gender. The girls went to one room where they were shown a movie on something they had probably started doing a year or two ago earlier. As for us guys, we got to listen to a hell fire and brimstone diatribe from a local Methodist minister on the evils of masturbation, that most heinous and degrading of human sexual behaviors. The purveyor of this message about the excesses and outcomes of onanism railed on for sixty, perhaps even ninety minutes, raving about hairy palms, bad complexions, total blindness, and almost certain mental illness, all end products of godless, unthinking, uncaring, self-polluting sexual profligacy.

Though consummately unworldly as an eighth grader (despite earlier attempts by my mentor on matters sexual, Earl Marshall, to relieve my ignorance), I was not persuaded of the veracity of the arguments put forth by the man of the cloth. Part of my skepticism was fueled by a few surreptitious sneaky peeks at the 1948 landmark book on sexual behavior authored by Alfred Kinsey and his associates entitled, *Sexual Behavior in the Human Male*. In that informative, ground-breaking, primer on sexuality, Kinsey reported that masturbation was a common human behavior, was not gender-specific, and probably had healthy consequences in most contexts. On the other hand, if Kinsey was correct in his assertions about the incidence of masturbation by gender and if our misguided preacher man was on target about the myriad afflictions arising from such behavior, then we should have an epidemic of blind or mentally ill men and women running around with hairy palms and pockmarked, scarred faces. Since that clearly was not the case, I figured there must be something wrong with the message, and by association, the messenger. I still today resent that pompous, sanctimonious, righteous fellow because of the potential damage that a man in such a position of power and prestige may have inflicted on vulnerable young people with his false prophecy.

Coaches have long seen sexual activity of any kind as the bane of excellence in sport performance, and male athletes have been warned since time immemorial that poor play would surely result from masturbation or, heaven forbid, an actual sexual relationship with a real live female. Floyd Patterson, the heavyweight boxing champion of the 1960's believed so much in the message he would move out of his home for six months before a fight so as to not give in to sexual desire that would dilute his pugilistic propensities.

What would our preacher friend and those of his ilk think about modern day openness to sexual mores? Could they have ever envisioned that things would deteriorate to the point that there would be a designated thirty-day period each year since 1995 designated as "National Masturbation Month?" And what would they think of the irreverent writer, film maker, and comedic Woody Allen's definition of masturbation as having "sex with someone I love?"

It seems strange that about all I remember about being an early teenager is athletics. Football was king! Between the eighth and ninth grades, my teammates and I would sit under the dim, almost eerie glow of the street light on Choctaw Street until late at night, trying to get a futuristic glimpse into our football fortunes for the upcoming fall. Playing positions were dissected at great length, and projections were made about how big, strong, and mean each player was going to be by the start of the season. We were convinced that each player would grow three inches and put on at least fifteen pounds of twisted blue steel sinew and muscle by late August.

Everyone was going through growth spurts, with some growing at a much greater rate than others. In my own case, I grew six inches and gained thirty-five pounds between the eighth and ninth grades. Though I did not know it at the time, I was pretty much full-grown. I was 5'9" and 155 pounds, shaved three times a week, and pretty much buffed in comparison with most of my age-mates. Coach Carl Davidson related a comment from his wife to the effect that she could never figure out how anyone with as many muscles as I had could possibly play basketball. Being a hormonal and impressionable adolescent male, I took her comment as high praise.

Alvin "Bear" Smith. As evidence for the tremendous variations in individual maturation, my friend Alvin Smith was 5'1" and maybe 105 pounds, hairless below his sideburns, and cursed, for the time being at least, with a very small penis. The guys in the football dressing room, that shrine to all that is masculine in the adolescent world, used to point at Alvin's undeveloped penis and laugh, derisively calling him "Diapers." In order to heap even more indignity on my friend, the guys tacked on a last name, so he became not just "Diapers" but "Diapers Lamont", stated with a lispy voice accompanied by the mock limp wrist, to further accentuate his failed masculinity. I never got into teasing people much as I absolutely hated being teased, and Alvin was spared my derision.

Events of the next few years clearly showed how wise, judicious, and insightful my decision not to tease Alvin had been. He hit a late growth spurt somewhere around his sophomore year, and by the time our senior season rolled around, he was 5'11" and 200 pounds. Hair oozed from virtually every follicle, and he looked like a giant, mobile, pyramid-shaped hairball in motion. As Alvin experienced the late-adolescent testosterone infusion, he got bigger, stronger, and meaner, which led him to systematically call out most of the guys who had so gleefully (and unwisely) called him "Diapers Lamont." His goal was to either scare the jeepers-creepers out of them or beat them to a pulp, or both in some cases. He eventually came to be known as "Bear" not "Diapers", a 180-degree turnaround on our loosely constructed, nebulous scale of assigned ferocity and masculinity. He was reputed to eat raw chickens for midnight snacks, though I never saw evidence of it. However, such apocryphal tales added to the legend of the "Bear". Alvin developed into an outstanding high school two-way lineman and later played junior college football in Coffeyville, Kansas. In all honesty, Alvin "Bear" Smith was a pretty kind soul without much larceny in his heart. He just did not appreciate being teased.

As stated several few pages ago, Sigmund Freud, the famous Viennese psychoanalyst, theorized that we are all driven by two opposing and powerful forces, a life wish, or *Eros*, and a death wish, or *Thanatos*. With regard to the latter of those two powerful forces, Freud would have loved Alvin Smith. As early as our high school days, "The Bear" had a preference for living on the edge by hanging around with or dating married women. He finally dated one too many and paid for the lapse in judgment with his life before his thirtieth birthday.

The tragic story goes something like this: Alvin left junior college, moved back to Dewey, and started an up-and-coming construction business. He forsook most of his waywardness, cut his beer consumption to a six-pack a day, and became a deacon (elder?) in his church. One day while working at a construction site, Alvin was confronted by the husband of a woman he had been seeing on a serious basis. The guy apparently had just been released from the mental hospital in Vinita, Oklahoma, and was bent on avenging his honor and that of his wife. He shot Alvin several times and ran back and forth over his dying body with "The Bear's" own pickup truck. Alvin "Bear" Smith met a very premature end, but perhaps he died when he most wanted to live, which is essentially what Freud would have predicted with his concept of Thanatos.

Politics, First Kisses and a Loser Husband

Three other events related to the junior high days merit mentioning. One was my acceptance from the kids at school. One index of my popularity was being elected class President for the seventh, eighth, and ninth grades. In the tenth grade, I was locked in a tie vote for the presidency with Russell Wilson. The teacher in charge of the election process whose name eludes me now decided that since I had been the class President three times, she would cast the tie-breaking vote and give the office to Russell. That decision put an end to my career as a politician. Lloyd Dunn got the position in the eleventh grade and Frank Ringo in the twelfth. Frank now holds the permanent position, and deservedly so. Frank is still involved with people in Dewey with whom we went to school, is highly respected among his peers, much more so than I, and for good reason; Frank is one damned decent human being!

Another event of some magnitude involved the Halloween festivities sponsored by the school. The celebration of that holiday was cause for a nice soiree at school, and one of the highlights was the election of a Halloween Carnival King and Queen. As it turned out, Ernavay "Erni" Balentine was named Queen and I was elected King. One of the requirements of that unlikely alliance was that we share a kiss on stage in front of the entire junior high. I cannot speak for Erni, but kissing the opposite sex was a totally new experience for me. Dread filled my every waking hour for days leading up to the big event, and the apprehension had nothing to do with Erni. My dread was of the unknown.

In any case, the big night went off well, I kissed Erni as required, and blushed for what seemed like the better part of two weeks. Thirty-five years later at a class reunion, Erni put one on me late in the midst of a beery evening (as least for me if not her) and asked, "Have I gotten better over the years?" She had indeed! Some years later, Erni struck up a relationship at one of the reunions with a one-time ninth grade boyfriend, and this inadvertent meeting of an old flame led her to eventually marry my good friend from Houston by way of Dewey, none other than Frank Ringo!

Hubert Hunt: Husband Number Three

An interesting though not remotely positive aspect of my junior high school days was my mother's marriage (and divorce) to her third husband, a consummately cruel man named Hubert Hunt. Husband number two was a man named Bill Berryhill and the marriage was brief and unspectacular, at least to me. About the only thing I remember about Mr. Berryhill was a rumor that he shot a toe or toes off to avoid having to serve in World War II. I have no idea of the veracity of this assertion which does not speak well of husband number two if it is true.

As for Hubert Hunt, he and my mother were married shortly after Grandfather Paul Richard died in 1948. Again, I cannot speak to the truth surrounding that unholy matrimony but there is abundant evidence in retrospect that the motive on his part was greed not love. My grandfather left my mother some money, how much I would not begin to guess, and Hubert Hunt saw her as a cash cow that would enable him to create a top-of-the-line farming operation on some country acreage near Dewey. As a result, I spent my eighth grade year as a "farmer", raising milking shorthorn cattle, Hampshire (Berkshire?) hogs, and Rhode Island Red chickens. One thing I learned from that experience is the work is NEVER done on a farm. I cannot remember a day off in that entire year; the cows have to be milked, the hogs slopped, and the chickens fed and the eggs gathered. None of the animals took a day off and neither did their human caretakers.

Hubert Hunt was reputed to be the strongest man in Dewey which is an informal accolade conferred by the local yokels who were impressed that he was reputed to be the only man in town who was strong enough to lift a keg of nails onto the bed of a pickup truck with only his thumb and forefinger. Hubert Hunt was also a giant of a man for that period, probably six feet four and well over two hundred pounds, sort of an early day reincarnation of the fictional giant, Jack Reacher, and he used every ounce of his weight and every inch of his height to be the meanest son-of-bitch I ever met. He drank excessively and would go on drunken tirades in which he obliterated anything that got is his way. He would beat up his younger brothers (and reportedly his school teacher sister), perhaps my mother, and occasionally my siblings and me. In my own case, he only hit me once and it was a slap to the right side of my head for whatever reason I do not remember that left my face stinging and my ears ringing for hours afterward. Our television set was destroyed and the refrigerator and other appliances all dented where he had kicked them in one of his many drunken sprees. It was said that a cow angered him one day and he proceeded to kick the poor beast to death with his sizeable and formidable boots. I cannot speak to the truth of that little story, but I witnessed many acts of cruelty he perpetrated against animals on our farm that year in hell.

In trying to get some sort of a fix on where all this anger and viciousness sprung, a popular hypothesis suggested his meanness was due in part to his prisoner of war (POW) experiences during World War II. My mother always said he was captured by the Germans in 1943 or 1944 and entered the POW camp at well over two hundred pounds; when the camp was liberated in 1945, he weighed slightly over one hundred pounds. Given that the Germans could not feed their own soldiers and civilians late in the war, it should come as no surprise the POW's got the short end of the nutritional stick. Those who knew Hubert Hunt prior to the war bought no part of the theory about the war making him mean; they said he was mean long before he ever served in the Army.

Out of all this human debris and pathos came my half-sister, Roberta Lee Hunt, better known almost from birth and to this day six-plus decades later merely as "Babe." Life was not easy for "Babe" as her father was a brute and her mother a hopeless alcoholic. He abandoned the family in "Babe's" first years of life after my mother wisely and courageously divorced him. Our mother died a few years later of nutritional deficiencies associated with chronic alcoholism just prior to "Babe" reaching adolescence. "Babe" survived her rugged childhood and teen-age years, was a successful businesswoman for many years, and celebrated her forty-fifth wedding anniversary with her husband, a good man named Doyle Gentry, on March 15, 2018. "Babe" and Doyle live near quite an assortment of children and grandchildren in the Dallas-Fort Worth area, or the "Metroplex."

One of the happiest days of my young life was when Hubert Hunt suddenly disappeared. He was a toxic man, a mean man, a vile man, and a cruel drunkard who hurt all who had the misfortune to cross his path. About the only good thing that came from my association with Hubert Hunt is I now have a very clear understanding of teenagers who kill men who are cruel to them and their mothers. Of course I would never condone murder but as a young boy I lived in fear of Hubert Hunt and just wanted the no-good bastard out of my life for what he did to my mother, me, and his other victims. In all honesty, though I am not proud to admit it, killing Hubert Hunt crossed my mind more than once. Fortunately, there were no guns at my disposal and I was armed with the good sense not to do anything stupid.

I think "Babe" saw him for the first time since her earliest years just prior to his death several decades ago. In retrospect, I am truly amazed as I think back on those days, that he did not kill my mother, us children, his siblings, or a combination thereof in some drunken haze. Or just out of sober meanness!

Carl E. Davidson: My First Lesson in Sport Psychology

A favorite recollection and one that has had a profound transformative effect on my life in the intervening years since its occurrence concerns the appointment of Carl Davidson to the position of junior high football coach. Little did I know at the time, but Mr. Davidson was to provide my first lesson about the relationship between psychology and sport performance as well as arming me with many tutorials, through both words and personal example, about being a good person.

The story about how he came to be the coach in the first place borders on the surreal. It seems that our school superintendent, Jack "Highpockets" Hay, (who acquired his nickname by using his belt to cinch up his trousers halfway between his navel and shoulders), had commissioned the junior high principal, Ova Farrow if I recall correctly, to select a football coach. After giving the edict some thought, Mr. Farrow decided Carl E. Davidson, our erstwhile high school biology, physics, and chemistry teacher, was the solution to his problem. He immediately called a meeting with the unsuspecting science teacher and soon-to-be heir to the coaching throne.

The ever-diligent, conscientious Mr. Davidson arrived for the meeting with Mr. Farrow precisely at the agreed upon time, which was his custom. He was in his early 30's, of average height and weight, nicely dressed in slacks, dress shirt, and tastefully matching sport coat. He wore black horned rim glasses but in no way looked the part of the stereotypical science geek. I think he might have actually been seen as handsome; his wife thought so anyway, and I agreed with her.

Mr. Davidson Becomes a Football Coach, If Unwillingly. The conversation that took place between Mr. Farrow and soon-to-be Coach Davidson is speculative on my part but is based on recollections reported by the man himself as he settled more comfortably into his role as coach. Bear with me as I try to reconstruct the dialogue between the two men.

"Come in Carl. I have something to discuss with you" said Mr. Farrow. "I know your schedule is full, what with teaching all those high school science classes. However, we are in need of a junior high football coach and I have appointed you to fill that job for this year and probably beyond. Unless you can come up with a compelling argument to change my mind, you are it."

"Ova, Ova, Ova" said Mr. Davidson, obviously shocked and a bit nonplussed by the news. "You do know you could not have made a worse choice. Believe it or not in this football crazy state, I have never thrown a football or been to a football game. I know absolutely nothing about the sport. You could not have made a worse choice for the kids. Is there someone else who would be a better coach?"

Sentimental Journey Home II (1938-1965)

ARNOLD LE UNES

MYRNA JO BROWN
Drum Major

FOOTBALL PICTURE, BASEBALL PICTURE, GIRL FRIEND
MYRNA JO BROWN, COACHES, MENTORS, ROLE MODELS
FROM L TO R-L. E. "HOOTER" BREWER, MARVIN LEON
BROWN, CARL E. DAVIDSON

"Not really" said Mr. Farrow. "In looking over my faculty roster and their teaching and extracurricular assignments, there is little choice in this matter. You are, in a word, "The Man."

Mr. Davidson replied, "I guess there is no use arguing with your decision any longer, so what do I do now? There are only three weeks to get ready for the start of fall practice and I am starting from a knowledge and experience base of zero."

"That seems like an accurate assessment of the situation, alright" said Mr. Farrow. "What I would suggest you do is get in touch with Glenn Wright and Arnold LeUnes and see if they can bring you up to speed on football. I know they are just kids, but both seem to have a modicum of intelligence, undoubtedly will be two of your best players, and they do know a little about the game."

At this point, Mr. Davidson left Mr. Farrow's office and headed home to break the news to his wife. She, like her husband, was taken aback. However, also like her husband, she eventually interpreted Mr. Farrow's decision as a challenge and the two of them started talking about some solutions to the unanticipated dilemma. After looking at a number of options, she said, "Carl, call those kids. What do you have to lose at this juncture? Maybe they can help get you to at least get started."

A little later, I received a phone call from Mr. Davidson. I figured it was one of the guys wanting me to go downtown to the Rexall drug store for cherry limeade and do some serious if fruitless flirting with Carol Sue Fielder or Dianne Kite or one of our other female classmates who might be on duty that night. I was surprised to hear Mr. Davidson's voice, and I frankly must admit that I barely knew who he was at that time. I soon discovered what the man was made of, however.

He said to me, "Arnold, Mr. Farrow suggested that I might talk to you about football since I have been appointed to be the new junior high coach for this season. I know nothing at all about the game, and would like to pick your brain a bit. I will also call Glenn Wright later, and maybe the three of us can get together over at my house for the next week or so or however long it takes for me to learn a bit about the game."

"Sounds great to me, Coach" I said, "though I don't think I know very much. I mean, what in the world does a fourteen-year-old know about anything? I have played a bit of football, listened to a few games on the radio, and read everything about sports that I can get from *Sport Magazine* and *The Sporting News*, for whatever all that is worth. Anyway, I will give it my best shot. Give me a day and time."

"We might as well get going" said Mr. Davidson. "Run by my place at seven this evening if you can and we will get this show on the road."

Pepsi, Peanuts, and Charles "Bud" Wilkinson. When Glenn and I reached the house, he let us in, introduced us to his lovely wife, and the three of us sat down at the dining room table with some pencils and writing pads, and a cold bottle of "pop", the term we Okies used for all soft drinks like Coca Cola and Root Beer. This label is in contrast to "soda" and "soda water" I had often heard the previous summer while visiting my father in Texas. We also called small bodies of water "ponds" in Oklahoma but they were "tanks" in Texas.

But back to the story: I said to Mr. Davidson, "If it is alright with you, I will take a Pepsi. I brought along a bag of peanuts to doctor it up a bit." My friends and I often poured peanuts into our Pepsi's. This strange, and to some, disgusting combination produced a delicacy that had often been used to carry us through a friendly game of dominoes over at Easy Ed "The Eager Beaver's" pool hall on Main Street. Mr. Davidson did not blink, but I couldn't help but sense that he thought us a bit strange.

I had also brought along my dog-eared copy of the football Bible by Charles "Bud" Wilkinson, the highly successful coach at the University of Oklahoma. OU had embarked on the aforementioned 47-game winning streak a few years earlier, and this unparalleled success had made a national football guru out of Coach Wilkinson. His book, *The Split-T Formation*, was a best-seller and his formulations and expostulations were absolute gospel for a whole generation of high school and college coaches.

Within a week, the three of us had digested all we could process from Coach Wilkinson's book. We coupled Wilkinson's considerable pigskin wisdom with a small dose of our own personal philosophies and experiences and came up with what masqueraded, more or less, as a philosophy and technology of football that would guide Mr. Davidson as he learned the many nuances of coaching. When we concluded our meetings which often went for four or five hours at a time, he said, "I can't thank you guys enough. I actually think I know enough about the game to at least fool a few 14-year olds. I am going to see if I can create a play book that is appropriate for junior high players."

Much of what he ultimately produced was straight from Coach Wilkinson, though Coach Davidson added a wrinkle or two catering to the particular talents he saw in his players. For instance, in addition to the usual handoff of the ball from the center to the quarterback that was part and parcel of the Split-T Formation, he created a wrinkle that seemed pretty hokey at the time but may actually have been prescient. His little variant was to have the center snap the ball through the legs of the quarterback directly to the tailback. Coach Davidson had unknowingly created a 1950's version of the shotgun formation so popular throughout all levels of football today.

Mr. Davidson was obviously a quick learner. He put together some productive, well-conceived practices where he was able to impart his offensive and defensive philosophies and, more importantly, his ability to motivate young people. Kids would literally run through the proverbial brick walls for him which is at least half the battle in football where merely wanting to succeed is such an important ingredient. Yes, you need ability to play the game, too, but I have always said that if you are fast and shifty and can outrun people or are big and ugly with a penchant for wrestling with hot, sweaty, hairy-legged guys, there is a place for you in football.

Mr. Davidson Reveals a Strange Quirk. Mr. Davidson had his idiosyncrasies like everyone else, but one we all found particularly disquieting. He was known to occasionally prowl the dressing room before or after practices or games, patting guys on the back, and exhorting them to greater heights of athletic excellence. Occasionally, he would randomly and unpredictably select a most unwilling and soon to be exceedingly uncomfortable, red-faced victim for his favorite question *de jour*: "Hey, _____, did you masturbate last night?" The standard answer throughout the team, always hurried and dismissive with eyes averted and delivered with the requisite red face borne of almost certain guilt, was: "Heck, no, Coach. Not me. I love football too much to squander my energy and talents that way." Coach Davidson would then walk away with a perverse grin on his face for he knew that he had just been bullshitted by a rank amateur!

I think he was capitalizing, probably sardonically, on fears that were widespread in the 1940's and 1950's about the evils of masturbation. As noted a few paragraphs earlier, preachers sermonized about its dark side, parents chimed in their two cents worth, and the media beat the topic to death (again, pardon my feeble pun). Acne, pimples, hairy palms, blindness, mental illness, and low intelligence were pretty much guaranteed if you did the unthinkable, the dastardly deed, and one had to be alert to its dangers so as to not uselessly squander important bodily fluids and pollute one's mind. Needless to say, the topic was a subject of some embarrassment to a bunch of scared adolescents, and no one needed to be reminded of it by their coach.

Gene Power, a former student, softball teammate, domino partner, and old friend from Marshall, Texas, used to relate a masturbation story about his high school basketball coach. Gene's mentor would urge his players to check out handcuffs after practice if they thought it would keep them from masturbating the night before a big game. He told them something to the effect: "If you guys can't keep your hands off that thing tonight, cuff your wrists to the bed posts so you will be ready for the big game tomorrow." According to Gene, the coach did not get too many takers for to do so would have been tantamount to confessing to thinking about or doing the unforgiveable.

Mr. Davidson Builds a Juggernaut. We proceeded to win all eight games Mr. Davidson's first year, most by a large margin. We had an extremely gifted athletic class as had been noted by Mr. Farrow a year earlier and reported elsewhere. Having excellent athletes most certainly aided Coach Davidson in his transition from neophyte coach to the big winner that he was to become. His teams lost something like five games in his eight-year coaching tenure, testimony to his ability to take on what appeared at first glance to be a hopeless task and do the necessary homework to make it happen. His technical expertise which became considerable was paired with an unbelievable ability to motivate young people to strive for team and individual excellence, and they were the cornerstones of his success. Almost without exception, we would have done anything Coach Davidson asked (except publicly confess to secretly "spanking the monkey").

A variant of this theme unfolded when my son, Lyndon, played junior high football fifteen years ago or so. He was a punt returner, and he and his teammates were instructed to yell "Peter! Peter" any time a punt might be hard to handle and thus likely to be fumbled. When the boys asked the coach why that particular terminology, they were told "You know, Peter, you wouldn't want to touch that thing, would you?"

Though I did not fully realize it at the time, Carl Davidson taught me my first lesson about the psychological side of sports performance. He showed us that there was a cerebral and a psychological side to football, a view that ran counter to the Darwinian "King of the Mountain" philosophy espoused by most coaches back then and even today. Psychology did matter; wanting it more than the other guy mattered, your teammates mattered, and giving your all each and every day mattered. There were football lessons in there but there were life lessons he imparted each and every day with his example, his teaching, and his positive attitude about young people and what could be accomplished with the help of a concerned, caring adult. Carl Davidson taught me a lot about football, taught me a lot about life, and perhaps most important of all, modeled for me the fundamentals of what a good man looked like. Carl E. Davidson, the coach, the teacher, and "The Man" remains one of my life heroes to this day.

The Freshman Year

Junior high football season rolled around in August, and Coach Davidson had become a fixture by then as our mentor and coach. I was a pretty decent-sized guy as junior high players went in those days, and he built his team around me as the featured tailback. I had won the district championship in the hundred- and 220-yard dashes the previous spring. My size (for a ninth grader) coupled with sprinter speed made me a reasonably formidable weapon, and Davidson capitalized on these qualities as you would expect any coach in his right mind to do. If you have a good horse, ride him into the ground was the operative philosophy, but I loved being the featured if sometimes sacrificial steed.

We ended up having an undefeated season, and generally romped on most of our opponents. The ghost that Mr. Farrow had envisioned two years earlier was starting to materialize and would emerge in full force three years later. I gained maybe 200 yards and scored two or three touchdowns per game, decent but not off the top of the chart numbers. Glenn Wright, Edwin Davis, Floyd Brown, Jimmy Dick Baker, Robert Bayne, David Miller, Bobby Thomson, Lloyd Dunn, Johnny Gutierrez, Raymond Gray, and an eighth grader, Jerry Jones, were key players in our successful running of the table that year. Each was to go on to a successful high school career.

H. L. "Goob" Arnold. The crowning achievement of the freshman year for me personally was being called up to the junior varsity by the high school football coach, H. L. "Goob" Arnold, to play against the Nowata Ironmen Jayvee team. I was the only ninth grader to get the call, and it was a real honor. Unfortunately, the game itself was a yawner, a 0-0 tie that was played almost entirely between the two forty-yard lines. It was an incredibly boring game for the players and one can only speculate how the fans felt. I suspect many in the sparse crowd were asleep by halftime. I rightfully interpreted this call-up as a sign that I had a bright future with the Bulldoggers for the next three years and, later on, with the Sooners of Bud Wilkinson. I guess the latter was a goal, though getting a scholarship and playing college football was remote in my thinking by junior high and drove little of my behavior on the field. I mainly played football because I was decent at it and liked the game well enough, and it was expected of you if you were an adolescent male growing up in Oklahoma. And, as an added extra, you got to hang out with your friends.

"Goob" Arnold, the high school coach, was memorable for several reasons. He was sober, tough, and more than just a bit mean. In fact, he was not only mean but looked even more menacing. Everyone ran scared of "Goob", and he terrified people into good performance as the price of making a mistake was too high. Psychologists would say that his coaching approach exemplified the concept of negative reinforcement. In the case of positive reinforcement in football, you increase the likelihood of any particular response through positive verbal comments, pats on the back, or decals on the helmet. In the case of negative reinforcement, the likelihood of good performance is increased by preventing, avoiding, or short-circuiting the wrath of the vengeful coach. The end result of the two approaches to reinforcement can often be the same, namely an increase in desirable athletic performance.

Apparently, terror worked wonders for "Goob" Arnold as he had previously won state championships in both football and basketball at other schools. I once saw "Goob" take a player aside at practice who made the mistake of making a mistake and throw a football to the ground with instructions to pick it up. Upon bending over to pick up the ball, the offender was kicked in the face, and we did not have face guards on our helmets in those days. On another occasion, I saw "Goob" run laps with two players who fought in practice, paddling them every step of the way with a barrel stave.

My personal favorite terror tactic of his, however, was one he used at basketball practice. "Goob" carried a classroom blackboard pointer which was designed to strike fear into people who dared depart from excellence by its liberal application. I do not know if there is such a thing as a blackboard pointer any more, but they were maybe three feet long and had a hard, bullet-shaped rubber object on one end for emphasizing important written material written on the blackboard. At the other end, there was a metal ring with which the pointer could be suspended for easy retrieval. Sometimes Coach Arnold's shot from the blackboard pointer would be across the back or the chest. If you really screwed up, he would pop you on one or both nipples with the rubber tip, a skill he had perfected to the nth degree. We quickly figured out the blackboard pointer, and most particularly its rubber tip, were to be avoided at all costs. Needless to say, it did not take us long to also start cutting down on our mistakes as the price for performing poorly was simply too high. Again, negative reinforcement at its best!

Speaking of basketball and negative reinforcement, I had a tall blonde in class in 1990 named Holly Hughes who had been a basketball player at Southwest Texas State (now Texas State University) prior to transferring to A&M. Holly had become increasingly disenchanted with being a college basketball player anyway, and an incident involving her coach, a male, put the final touches on her college athletic career. Apparently, she had made a mistake of some kind at practice one day, leading the coach to call her aside where he uttered the following sweet nothing in her ear, "Holly, if you ever do that again, I am going to cut your nipples off." Personally, if I was given the choice of playing better or losing my nipples, I would choose to perform more effectively. Or, better yet, transfer to Texas A&M.

I got my only school paddling in the eighth grade, and it was at the hands of "Goob" Arnold. One afternoon, "Ock" Davis and I cut class, opting instead to go fishing or picking pecans in the woods or something. We returned from our brief and restful hiatus in time for football practice, and "Goob" met us there to mete out the punishment for missing school. In our case, the penalty was ten licks with his specially made paddle. A lot of planning, and a modicum of malice, had gone into the creation of that instrument of torture, and one wrinkle he added was to drill holes in the wood so as to maximize pain. Ed and I later agreed that "Goob" packed a pretty good wallop!

"Goob" Arnold was dismissed from his coaching duties by the school administration and moved elsewhere after our ninth grade year. We heard that some of the more politically empowered parents were behind his removal, citing his harsh approach to motivating young people as the reason. Even in an era when you could pretty much say and do anything you wanted to an athlete, "Goob" Arnold probably overstepped the line. He was a very effective coach in terms of wins and losses but fun was certainly taken out of the game with his negativity and scare tactics. He was an object of great fear, and I still feel a gray cloud forming around me when I think of H. L. "Goob" Arnold. Occasionally, even after all these years, when I hear my name spoken, the word "Arnold" becomes a source of apprehension. It is sort of sad when one is conditioned to fear his own name!

Goober, Gonorrhea, and the Boys of Summer Go To High School

"No distance of place or lapse of time can lessen the friendship of those who are truly persuaded of each other's worth."

Robert Southey, 19th Century English Poet and Essayist

Nicknames

Thanks to the name similarity between the aforementioned H. L. "Goob" Arnold and yours truly, coupled with some circuitous mental gymnastics on the part of my friends, I became "Goob" to them. The reasoning went that if he was "Goob" Arnold, then I was Arnold "Goob".....it made perfect sense to them at the time. I was known as "Goob" and the unenviable "Goober", that symbol of being a southern rube, throughout the rest of my high school days.

Nicknames are such part of the zeitgeist of the adolescent years, and my crowd took to the task of assigning them with great gusto. Ed Davis was "Goat", supposedly the result of a failed attempt to transact a casual sexual relationship with a girl from some other city who, in the eyes of my running buddies, resembled a goat. Ed's parents called him "Ock" and "Ockey", and I have no idea from whence those family nicknames arose. Of course, the big guy, Alvin Smith had outgrown his aforementioned eighth grade humiliation as "Diapers" to become the "Bear." Frank Ringo, all 6'5" of him, was called "Johnny" Ringo after a legendary gunslinger reputed to be long and tall. In a moment of rare creativity, we were able to transmogrify Mike Rhea's last name (pronounced Ray) by pronouncing it like the Australian bird, the rhea, due to the obvious similarities in spelling. We then preceded Rhea with "Gonna" and produced "Gonna Rhea", a sobriquet hung on him no doubt in honor of the well-known venereal disease and our adolescent fascination with anything remotely sexual (I admit arriving at this pejorative nickname required some lapses in logic, but it was lots of fun and we had an abundance of time on our hands as teenagers to think about such inane things).

David Miller was known alternately as "Mole" because of his mole-like facial features, and as "Moth" or "Butterfly" in reference to his last name and its similarity to those flying insects. Glenn Wright took on the unseemly sobriquet of "Bonehead", but I do not remember if the nickname was

Arnold LeUnes

coined in reference to his general intelligence or his propensity to pull off some stupid bonehead moves in athletics.

THE BOYS OF SUMMER----L TO R
YOURS TRULY, FRANK RINGO
MIKE RHEA, ROBERT BAYNE, EDWIN DAVIS,
ALVIN SMITH, 1955-1956

Mike "Gonna" Rhea. In the Class Prophecy section of *The 1956 Bulldogger*, our school yearbook, it was opined that Mike would end up being "a between-the-acts comedian at a burlesque show." That event, of course, did not happen but Mike was and is one of the most unusual and interesting people I have ever met. He lived on the east side of Creek Street maybe a five-minute walk from my house. Mike's father was a traveling salesman and, according to Mike, a bit of a skirt chaser. His mother was a housewife who raised five children, four girls and Mike. He thus grew up surrounded by a house full of females and a largely absentee male role model. I am not sure how much that affected Mike psychologically, if at all, but it certainly made for a lot of armchair speculation as we were growing up.

Mike was an enthusiastic pretender when it came to sports but, bless his heart, did not have so much as one athletic bone in his body. As more than one sports sage has put it in reference to people like Mike, he made up for his lack of size and athleticism by being unbelievably small and slow. But he played football, basketball, and ran track, and gave it his all in every case. He played little but was a great teammate and constant companion.

Mike joined the U.S. Marine Corps right out of high school in 1956, and remains a devoted "jarhead" to this day. His enlistment went well for the most part, but he did have an unfortunate experience while stationed in Honolulu in the late 1950's. It seems that an Army enlisted man was manhandling a woman behind a local bar called George's Inn. Mike, in the spirit of being a Good Samaritan, made the mistake of intervening on behalf of the female victim. A fight broke out between Mike and his newly-acquired adversary, an Army Corporal from Schofield Barracks, who was armed with a knife. Mike was nicked in the cheek and stomach with two swipes of the knife but a third got an artery in his chest. A waitress at George's had the presence of mind to call Tripler General Hospital where emergency room personnel were eventually able to stanch the arterial bleeding, thus saving Mike's life. Apparently, the medical personnel were not so sure they could save him at first, and even after surgery, he was on the critical list. Back in Dewey, his mother received a telegram to the effect: "Don't come out. We'll send the body home."

Mike's assailant was later court-martialed, served time in the stockade, and eventually was cashiered out of the Army with a dishonorable discharge. Because of his injury at the hands of the knife-wielding Corporal, Mike spent the rest of his Marine active duty time on light duty. Today, one of the joys of his life is attending the annual Marine Corps national reunion held in different cities across the country.

Mike is a journalist by trade and disposition. When he got out of the Marine Corps in 1959, he began a long journalistic sojourn, initially serving as a cub reporter for the *Ponca City (Oklahoma) News*. Prior to starting my senior year in college, I was in Oklahoma and walked with Mike on his maiden journalistic voyage for the paper, covering a golf tournament in Edmond, near Oklahoma City. I had always wanted to be a sports reporter, so it was good to observe a future "pro" in the making.

Mike later moved to the *Daily Oklahoman*, Oklahoma City's largest newspaper, and the *Stillwater (Oklahoma) News Press* before becoming a crime reporter for the *Baltimore (Maryland) Sun*, a position he held for three years. From 1964 to 1970, he worked for the Associated Press in Baltimore and New York City, and then took a position as Writer, Editor, and Assistant News Director for WINS in New York. At that time, WINS was the third all-news radio station in the country and, as of 2013, the longest-running station of its kind with over forty-five years of providing the public with the latest in current events. He then spent twenty-one years in New York with Reuters News Service and retired after a ten-year gig in Washington, D.C. Not too shabby a resume' for a country boy from Dewey, Oklahoma.

Sometime in the early 1980's, Reuters asked Mike to cover the launching of a space capsule at the Johnson Space Center. Shortly after his arrival in Texas, Mike called to see if we could get together for a visit during his stay in Clear Lake City, near NASA. I was not very excited about the prospect of battling the five o'clock Friday Houston and Gulf Freeway traffic on my way from College Station, but the opportunity to join up with an old friend was too enticing to pass up. When I finally arrived at the hotel around nine that evening, Mike and I and a third party, also a journalist covering the launch, sauntered over to the hotel bar where we drank some beer. I'm not sure how many beers we actually quaffed, maybe two dozen between the three of us, but the table was completely covered with the "dead soldiers" (not us, the empty beer bottles) when we left the bar. Closing time caught up with us at 1 a.m., so Mike and I adjourned to his room to "kill off a bottle of vodka", as Mike put it. Vodka had no appeal for me as my only drug-related vice for the past forty years or so has been beer, so Mike disposed of the fifth by himself into the wee hours of the morning.

Around three a.m., Mike got a wild hair and started making phone calls to old and dear classmates. Over the next several hours, he rang up the Right Reverend Lloyd Whistler in Dewey, Robert Bayne in Baltimore, Frank Ringo in Houston, Dianne Kite Boultinghouse and Shirley Viles in Bartlesville, and perhaps one or two other classmates as well. The receptions he received to phone calls at three and four in the morning varied widely, with Dianne taking the dimmest view of the proceedings. Mike eventually succumbed to the twin effects of sheer fatigue and over-consumption of beer and vodka and called off his efforts to convene a class mini-reunion. As for me, I eventually passed out from fatigue, sleeping long enough to enable me to make it home by noon on Saturday, leaving Mike to cover the space adventure by his little lonesome.

A few days later, Mike confessed to pangs of guilt for the beer and vodka-driven phone calls by sending along a peace offering via a memo on Columbia University Graduate School of Journalism letterhead addressed to Frank, Robert, Lloyd, and Shirley with a cc to me. The memo subject line had an entry entitled: "Early morning calls, December 10, 1983." He went on to tell the group he would not be able to blame me for the inconvenience, and offered the following "doggerel in apology" (his words, not mine):

Treasured Times

If by chance, you should awake
Early one morning. For Friendship's sake
Do not condemn – hold back your scorn.
Remember the motive --an impulse born
Of memories of treasured times.

Too late the night – too long the years,
But distance cannot still the fears
of contact lost through time and fate.

Sentimental Journey Home II (1938-1965)

Returning from the mid-life state
Brings memories of treasured times.

Why the need to communicate
At a time considered much too late?
Professor LeUnes, too many beers,
talk and laughter rolled back the years
to memories of treasured times.

Pain and anger of those times past
Fade and wither, until at last
We look, learn and recognize
Appreciate and learn to prize
Those memories of treasured times.

No illusions of our lost youth,
With greater age comes greater truth.
Review with wisdom those old days
Of children headed a hundred ways
From memories of treasured times.

Decades passed; the fire went cold.
Could of any of us foretold
Of the friendliness and fun
Of our reunion in '81?
More memories of treasured times.

So grew a desire to regain
The sound of Ringo, Bayne,
Whistler and the fair Shirly.
Perhaps the time was somewhat early
For memories of treasured times.

But in truth and honesty,
Rhea cannot say he's sorry
For the calls that did awake.
The impulse occurred for the sake
Of memories of treasured times.

It is events like these, you see
That provide continuity

> For discussions sure to crown
> Visits to our old hometown
> And memories of treasured times.

While working as a newsman in New York, Mike earned an undergraduate degree in English and Philosophy from Queens College, a Master of Arts degree in Media Studies from The New School, a Master of Education degree from Teacher's College, Columbia University, and the greater part of a Doctor of Philosophy degree, also from Columbia. Mike gave up the latter endeavor in 2001, lacking only the completion of a dissertation. His educational attainments led him to accept adjunct professorships and other professorial assignments with a variety of institutions including Columbia University, Upsala College, William Paterson University, American University, American Military University, University of Maryland, and Wesley College. Again, not too shabby for an Okie boy!

Mike apparently got cross-wise with the administration while on the William Paterson faculty, probably for a number of reasons given his considerable quirks and idiosyncrasies, but one in particular may have been a big part of his undoing there. It seems that Mike had an annual tradition in his classes known as the "Wet Seminar." In this instance, Mike would help the students celebrate the end of his course by bringing a keg of beer to the last class meeting. The tradition was somewhat problematic from its inception, but got more so when the drinking law changed, thus making it illegal in New Jersey to buy or provide alcohol to people under the age of twenty-one; not all of his students were of legal age.

Other accomplishments that define Mike Rhea included authoring an unpublished book on the life of Martin Luther King entitled *Rebellion in Black*, the creation of a weekly television show known as "New Jersey Magazine", and holding several important positions with the National Press Club in Washington, DC. While Mike was Chair of the Forums Committee for the Press Club, he wangled an invitation for me to take part in a forum on youth sports there.

Mike has been married to his wife Paula for more years than I can recall. They had no children of their own though Paula had two from a first marriage, and Mike has had a good relationship with the stepchildren over the years. I still hear from Mike once or twice a month, meet up with him from time to time, and greatly value his friendship. He is one of those people who steadfastly refuses with all his might to let old friendships, or "memories of treasured times", die.

Frank "Johnny" Ringo. Interestingly, in doing research for this volume, I found out that no yearbook prophecy was made for Frank; he was strangely omitted from the list and I guess it was anticipated he would simply disappear into thin air. In any case, and as noted earlier, Frank Ringo was and is an absolute prince of a fellow. I spent a lot of time at his house in elementary and junior high school, and his mother often took me in and kept me fed. I think she believed me to be a quasi-orphan due to the disarrayed home life I had stemming from my mother's excessive drinking and the absence of a father figure in the home. Frank lived just east of the aforementioned cement plant, and I would often pedal my bicycle out to his house, a leisurely ride of maybe two or three miles.

Frank grew to be 6 feet 5 inches tall which no doubt contributed to his being a reasonably decent high school basketball player. After graduation from good old DHS, Frank went to Northeastern Junior College in Miami, Oklahoma, where he roomed with high school classmates Ed Davis the first year and the second with Robert Bayne. From there, Frank transferred to Northeastern State College in Tahlequah, the home of the Cherokee Nation mentioned earlier. The standing joke among the students was that once you learned to spell Tahlequah correctly, you were automatically awarded your bachelor's degree from Northeastern.

Frank married Bonnie Smith in 1960 and moved to Houston where job opportunities were more abundant than in sometimes economically moribund Oklahoma. Frank and Bonnie had three children, all of whom still reside in Houston. His first job there was as a juvenile probation officer, and he served seven years in that capacity before taking a position with Big Brothers of Houston. Frank eventually became Executive Director of that agency where he served for fifteen years, at which point he retired. Frank now does volunteer work with United Way and other organizations and agencies in the Houston area.

Many years ago during Frank's tenure with the Big Brothers organization, he called me out of the blue one day with an interesting if mostly rhetorical question. He wanted to know in my role as a psychologist if I knew of an assessment device that could identify and thus screen out the child molesters who sometimes applied to volunteer with his agency. He told me that pedophiles were a big problem, and the "cleaner" the volunteer was, the more likely he was to molest. He further related that some of his best volunteers were not squeaky clean at all, and sometimes had minor issues with alcohol- or drug-related offenses in their backgrounds. In the latter case, he was talking mostly about marijuana use, not hard drugs. His summary of his dilemma went something like this: "The cleaner they are, the more likely they are to molest. Give me a guy with a few hickeys on his record, you know, maybe a PI (Public Intoxication) or a misdemeanor marijuana offense. They are my best volunteers." Frank knew I possessed no magic pixie dust that would remedy his problem. He just wanted to vent a bit, I suspect.

Somewhere in the midst of all this, Frank and Bonnie divorced and he remarried a woman named Melanie. I was around Melanie a few times and found her to be very personable and an interesting conversationalist who was seemingly devoted to her husband. Their marriage lasted twenty-five years but also ended in divorce.

Frank and Melanie never had children, and her explanation for the decision to remain childless makes for an interesting story. It seems that Melanie did not want children, and a large part of her reluctance to become a mother had to do with spending her teenage years raising younger siblings. She felt that she had had enough of childrearing by the time she reached adulthood. Ironically, after taking birth control pills for much of her adult life, she underwent an examination in which it was determined that she had never had any ovaries and thus could have never gotten pregnant anyway.

That is a lot of years to take birth control pills and put up with all the attendant side effects when there was never any reason to do so.

Right after our fortieth class reunion in October of 1996, Melanie unexpectedly left Frank for another man. The irony of it all is the two of them were in attendance at the reunion just a month earlier and everything looked hunky-dory (peachy-creamy? lovey-dovey?). Certainly, Frank thought so. He never saw the left hook coming, and the blow of the divorce sent him into a temporary depressive funk. But life has a way of evening out, and Frank eventually reunited with a woman he dated in high school, the aforementioned Ernavay "Erni" Balentine of eighth grade Halloween King and Queen fame. They have been married for maybe twenty years.

Frank and I correspond by email pretty much once a week or more and occasionally visit over a meal at a restaurant in the Houston area. He has an incredible sense of humor, and we have a lot of laughs when we get together, mostly retelling old stories and making fun of life's endless ironies. They don't make people much nicer than Frank Ringo. I have been blessed by having him as a friend.

On a more somber note, Erni suffered a terrible fall in 2016 and spent a considerable amount of time in physical rehabilitation. To compound matters, Frank tells me Erni has been diagnosed with aphasia, with the attendant problematic speech and memory issues. When it rains, it pours, and getting old only adds to the fire. Ah, the wonders of the "Golden Years"…

Kenny "Red" Rigdon. Kenny's yearbook prophecy was pretty much right on target, suggesting that he had "given the world a new theory replacing Einstein's theory of relativity." He was the class brain and had no interest whatsoever in athletics. Kenny was nicknamed "Red" Rigdon in reference to his bright reddish-orange hair color. Unfortunately, Kenny had to endure that curse to which all red-heads I have met throughout my life regardless of locale are exposed, namely the gross and pejorative "I'd rather be dead like a knot on a log that red on the head like a dick on a dog." His obvious and duly warranted lack of appreciation for this ribbing is understandable.

Actually, Kenny was a nice guy, a low-key, solid sort, and seemed to handle the joshing pretty well. My suspicion is that Kenny Rigdon operated on a much higher mental and moral plane than we did, essentially writing us off as knuckle-dragging nitwits who were, *in toto*, incapable of thinking deep thoughts or making informed judgments about much of anything important. And he was not too far wrong, unfortunately. We never thought of what we were doing as bullying but the obscene nicknames and related nonsense would probably be labeled that way today. We owe you, Kenny!!

Kenny was a bit of an anomaly in our mostly carefree and sometimes shiftless world. He seldom came to town at night to hang out with us ne'er-do-wells, preferring instead to work after school, attending to his homework, saving some money for college, and generally being a good citizen. "Work ethic" was a largely alien concept to us and we always looked at Kenny with some suspicion or skepticism because he actually worked hard on his academic subjects and the after-school job at the ranch owned by the Frank Phillips family of aforementioned Phillips Petroleum fame.

FRANK AND ERNI RINGO, YOURS TRULY, IDAHO, 1999

We found out a couple of things after high school that lent new insights into Kenny, and we finally came to the realization that he actually led quite an interesting life. Strangely enough, he did so without including us in his activities or asking if his actions met with our approval! One awe-inspiring thing Kenny did prior to our senior year in high school was hitchhike to Canada and Alaska where he mined for gold, worked assorted odd jobs, and saw parts of the world that we only knew vaguely from school books or encyclopedias.

Another momentous event for Kenny, his fifteen minutes of fame if you will, took place after our senior year in high school. For whatever reason, Kenny was in Oklahoma City and had booked a hotel room adjacent to one reserved for the one and only Elvis Presley who was in the early stages of becoming an American musical icon. His adoring fans crowded into the hotel, pushing, shoving, jostling, shrieking like banshees, trying to touch or at least get a glimpse of "The King." The din and hubbub kept Kenny from getting his nightly beauty sleep so he went to Elvis' room to enlist his aid in muting the crowd noise. One thing led to another, and Kenny reportedly got into a shouting and shoving match with Elvis. Imagine the sudden escalation in status of a guy who had met and shoved Elvis Presley around. We did not find out until several years afterwards about the Alaska and Elvis adventures, but Kenny earned some additional if belated points with the boys when he finally fessed up about his secret celebrity life.

A few years ago, at a class reunion, I tried to get Kenny to substantiate and/or elaborate on these events of many years ago, but my requests went unanswered. At last report in 2010, Kenny had retired from Phillips and was working full-time in the geophysics business with a Pennsylvania oil company. The new job required that he be away from the Dewey-Bartlesville area for weeks at a time but he retained his home in Oklahoma where his semi-invalid wife resides.

Elvis the Pelvis, Janice Golden, Marilyn Ruthrauff, and "Stink." Speaking of Elvis, it was a constant source of adolescent amusement among my amigos to contemplate the ramifications of Elvis having a long-lost brother named Enis. At any rate, my first exposure to the music of Elvis the Pelvis came as an eighth or ninth grader. Janice Golden, a classmate, would occasionally have dances at her house, thanks to the largesse and forbearance of her gracious parents. On one occasion, Janice announced a party with the theme of introducing her peers to the music of an exciting new singer, a guy named Elvis Presley. Little did we know what life had in store for us (or Elvis)!

Janice always had us play games at her parties, things like Spin the Bottle and other kissing games. I could outlast the best of the girls who ended up on the porch with me, awaiting a kiss or hoping like hell to avoid one. I never knew which they preferred but I was not going to kiss the enemy anyway, no matter the degree of provocation!

One of my early infatuations was with a junior high classmate named Marilyn Ruthrauff who, if she shared my feelings, hid them extremely well. We were never remotely a serious item, but I did have feelings for her for a short time. She was a pretty girl, easily among the most attractive in our class. Marilyn lived in a two-story house near the high school, and it was hard to miss going by there on the way to town. Directly across from her house was a two-story home owned by a local physician which was cordoned off from the hoi polloi in town by a three-foot-high stone wall. My friends and I used to congregate on the low-set wall ever so often to gaze up at Marilyn's bedroom window in vain hopes of getting a glimpse of her striking a provocative pose. Absolutely nothing of interest ever transpired so far as I know. Marilyn was an absolute model of discretion, seemingly unaware or not caring we were sitting out there in a quasi-voyeuristic fog.

My short-lived non-romance with Marilyn ended when she took up with a two years older guy with quite a reputation as a lady's man. The new beau had acquired the nickname "Stink" or "Stinkfinger" because of his ways with the women and, I can only suppose, his prowess in manual sexual foreplay. I had no way of knowing his numbers, but "Stink" was a legend among the guys for his success with the women, or at least for his persistence.

"Stink" was also a player in one of my most mortifying adolescent experiences. It seems I had come home late one night my sophomore year, and overheard my mother having some sort of a dysfunctional sexual experience with him in her bedroom, and from the sound of things, it was not going well. My mother by that time in her life had become pretty much a hopeless drunk, and I guess sexual predators like "Stink" found down-and-out women like her to be easy pickings. The last words I heard between them occurred when he gave up trying to consummate the act, because my mother was, as he put it, "too dry." I never cared for the guy much, and that episode does little to alleviate my disdain for him and his predatory ways, even after six decades. There clearly is no honor among thieves.

High School Football: Coach Kester "Tractor" Trent

High school proved to be a roller coaster ride, emotionally. I had a great sophomore year in football, ran around with a bunch of funny and rambunctious guys, and encountered some interesting teachers and coaches. As well, I developed a really dismissive attitude about school, fell in love for the first time, and generally had some good moments mixed in with a few bad ones. The vast majority of the bad moments had to do with that first love affair with Myrna Jo Brown to be mentioned shortly.

But let us get off of women and talk about something of earthshaking significance, football. Prior to the start of our sophomore season, the authoritarian dictator H. L. "Goob" Arnold had been forced out of his coaching position and speculation was abundant about who would be our new guiding genius. As it turned out, we fell under the tutelage of one Kester "Tractor" Trent, a highly successful football coach at two cities in the southeast part of the state, Poteau and Heavener. "Tractor" acquired his nickname because of his propensity for running roughshod over would-be tacklers on the football field at Oklahoma A&M College (now Oklahoma State University) where he was a standout running back.

By his own admission, "Tractor" was not much of a student. On more than one occasion, he would remind us of his lack of academic prowess with the following: "I walked in the front door at Oklahoma A&M and out the back door four years later, and never opened a book." Anyone who ever talked with "Tractor" for any period of time could readily see that getting him in the same room with a book while he was in college had to have been a daunting challenge! You can also imagine what kind of History teacher he was, given his disdain for the learning process.

You could see that "Tractor" had been quite nice-looking as a young man but his face showed the effects of a lot of exposure to the sun and the inexorable effects of aging. He had wavy, brownish-gray hair that was thinning a bit, and a face and forehead so wrinkled he resembled a SharPei. He had that athletic look so common to members of his profession, and if you were to encounter "Tractor" on the streets you would say he had "Coach" written all over him. He had that trademark look and swagger.

When we first met him in 1953, "Tractor" was in his mid-forties, not a particularly big man, maybe 5'10" and 190 pounds, but appeared to be in magnificent shape for a guy his age. On occasion, he would boast that he had to quit suiting up with his previous teams while in his thirties because he hurt too many of his players; none of us ever doubted that he was a tough guy. "Tractor" played in the days before the availability of good helmets, face guards, mouthpieces, and other protective equipment. As a result, a number of his front teeth were missing, having been replaced by a set of false ones that were not particularly secure. Sometimes in the excitement of a game, "Tractor" would accidentally spit out his teeth. More often than not, they would end up buried lightly in the chalk dust marking the sideline. Without so much as a moment of hesitation, "Tractor" would reach down and reinsert the missing items in their proper place. "Tractor" also spit a lot when he talked, so players kept their distance when he beckoned, particularly if he was excited.

"Tractor" could be found at a couple of area hangouts just about any night of the week, smoking his unfiltered Camel (or was it Lucky Strikes?) cigarettes and slurping down copious amounts of bad, black, coffee at an all-night restaurant known, as best I remember, as the Tuxedo Cafe. We would occasionally pop in to say hello, and during one impromptu visit "Tractor" told us he drank two to three dozen cups of coffee a day. I have no idea how many cigarettes he smoked daily, but one was always near his beloved cup of coffee, burning away in the ash tray and polluting the air for all in close proximity. In those days, no one really thought much about the hazards of smoking, its nuisance value, and the effects of second-hand smoke. As one might well imagine, football injuries and the constant pairing of the twin demons of caffeine and nicotine left "Tractor" with markedly stained dentures.

"Tractor" was a decent coach, but one from the "old school" who unfortunately fully endorsed the time-honored coaching shibboleth that if a two-hour practice is good, then a four-hour one must be magnificent. Adherence to this philosophy cost the team dearly our junior year as we lost eleven starters for one game or more due to injuries sustained in practice. When your roster was as thin as ours, any injury is a big loss, but eleven of them are essentially fatal. Thank goodness, that philosophy was not operational the next year, and the positive effects of junking the long, arduous workouts became obvious as the season progressed, namely no practice-related injuries. More on why this transformation took place a bit later.

"Tractor" designated me as the starting varsity tailback as a sophomore, much to the chagrin of a surly Native American upperclassman with a chip on his shoulder by the name of Jake Scruggins. Jake constituted my main competition but was unhappy with the coach and, by association, me concerning what he deemed to be an unfair decision about playing time. As is too often the case with young guys, these disappointments are just cause for a fight. Jake felt that if he couldn't beat me out on the field, he could damn sure beat me up off of it. A near-fight ensued one night, but wiser heads intervened and the big event never came off. Jake quickly became a distant memory for me as the season unfolded.

COACHES CARL E. DAVIDSON, KESTER "TRACTOR"
TRENT, AND MARVIN LEON BROWN, CIRCA 1954

We won five games and lost six my sophomore year, and I started in ten of the eleven games. The only exception involved an early season non-district game with our arch-rival, the Bartlesville Wildcats. When I did not start, I figured "Tractor" was trying to either protect me from physical injury or damage to my potentially fragile sophomore psyche that might result from playing a physically talented team from a much larger school.

Athletic competition in Oklahoma at that time operated under a state classification system made up of 2-A, 1-A, B, and C schools. A new system has since emerged over the years starting with the larger schools in 6-A followed by smaller schools in 5-A, 4-A, 3-A, 2-A, and 1-A. In 1955, Bartlesville was 2-A and we were B, and they had a much larger student body from which to find players. As a result, they typically fielded bigger and better athletes, and generally beat us though not by huge margins.

The Kid Needs Seasoning. In his infinite wisdom, "Tractor" figured since I was a sophomore I could use some additional seasoning beyond what I would get playing for the varsity each Friday. To accomplish this goal, he put me on the junior varsity (JV) team as tailback and free safety. As a result of this decision, I started ten games with the varsity and seven with the junior varsity. The end result was that I played a game every Tuesday with the JV team and another every Friday with the varsity (except for the aforementioned Bartlesville game). I never knew or gave much thought to the notion that playing twice a week might violate the rules of the state athletic governing body though I had my suspicions that it was probably illegal. Also, it may not have been in my best interests, health-wise or injury-wise, to take on two games per week but I was young, enthusiastic, and gung-ho, and never gave it a second thought. Ours is not to reason why, ours is to do or die. Semper Fi!

Because of the talent deficits and lack of playing experience among the players on the various JV teams, I played offense only in the first three games and scored three or four or five touchdowns each time, almost all from long range. At that point, "Tractor" decided the seasoning I needed for the offensive side of the ball was being met by my varsity participation, so he switched me totally to defense where I played free safety for the last four JV games. It is noteworthy that many players in the 1950's and 1960's played both offense and defense, in stark contrast to today where everyone is a specialist on one side of the ball or the other.

I scored at least one touchdown on a pass interception, punt return, or kickoff return in each of those final four games, but was largely unspectacular in my role as free safety. I really did not have much of a nose for the football; I just liked outrunning the players from the other teams.

The "Oklahoma Jackrabbit" Breaks an Opponents' Neck. Caney, Kansas, lies sixteen miles due north of Dewey on State Highway 75, literally a few yards across the state line in Kansas. The city generated much of its income in the mid-1900's from a busy strip of liquor stores conveniently located to cater to Kansans and thirsty patrons from Oklahoma. My home state was legally dry, and the only alcoholic beverage sold in the taverns and beer joints was beer. If hard liquor was the drink of choice, Oklahomans motored to Caney to stock up. It was always interesting to see the near-gridlock as the luxury cars belonging to the Bartlesville power brokers at Phillips Petroleum made the Friday afternoon trek up Highway 75 from Bartlesville to the Kansas state line to replenish their liquor cabinets.

The liquor situation also gave rise to entrepreneurs known affectionately as "bootleggers", men who made their living selling hard liquor illegally out of the trunks of their automobiles. These guys were legendary, larger-than-life, much-admired characters for whom stories abounded about their run-ins with the law, their fast cars, and the high speed chases they were involved in while running from the highway patrol and local police. I am sure most of the stories were more apocryphal than real, but they made the bootleggers out to be modern day Robin Hoods as they provided the locals with taboo alcohol.

CAMPING OUT WITH FRANK RINGO, ED DAVIS, MIKE RHEA

One such character in Dewey was John Juby, and he drove a brand spanking new black Hudson Hornet that was weighted down in the rear end to make it more roadworthy and thus harder to apprehend. The Hudson Hornet and John Juby were common topics of admiring conversation among the local citizenry. It is hard not to like Robin Hood in whatever form he may take!

But let's get back to Caney, Kansas. Somehow, some way, I had picked up the nickname "The Oklahoma Jackrabbit" because of my speed in running with the football. In October of 1953, we were playing against our counterparts from Caney in what was to be the final JV game in which "Tractor" penciled me in to play on the offensive side of the ball.

As the fourth quarter rolled around, I had racked up five touchdowns against what turned out to be almost non-existent opposition. Shortly before the game ended, I broke through the line on the way to a sixth touchdown from about fifty yards out, and the only player blocking my progress was a decidedly undersized, gangly defensive back. For whatever reason, my thought processes at the time went something along the lines of this: "Hey, you have scored five touchdowns and the game is in the bag. Do I juke this guy, which would be easy, or do I teach the son-of-a-bitch a lesson and plow him under." The entire thought process took at most a nano-second, and I chose to go for the guy, fully expecting to break out of his tackle and score anyway. In preparing to hopefully ride me to the turf, the talent- and technique-deficient defender put his head down in an awkward position just before the two of us met in a helmet-to-helmet collision. The defender came out of the collision with a broken neck. Fortunately, as it turned out, the break involved a couple of vertebra and not the spinal cord.

Six years later, I accidentally found out the guy made a complete recovery from his misfortune. The way I found out was serendipitous, to say the least. The story goes like this: During my senior year at A&M, I decided to spend the Christmas holiday in Dewey, visiting with old high school friends and my alcoholic and increasingly sickly, nutritionally-deficient mother. On one occasion, as I was leaving to go out for the evening, my mother told me that I had a nice back. When I asked her what that meant, she said the only part of me she ever saw during the entire two weeks I was home was my back as I went out the door. No doubt, I should have made more time for her, but such is the way of youth, I suspect. We think parents are forever. And we, of course, are dead wrong…

On New Year's Eve, my football and pool hall buddies "Ock" Davis, "Bear" Smith, "Johnny" Ringo, "Gonna" Rhea, and yours truly ended up at a party in Coffeyville, Kansas, thirty-three miles northeast of Dewey. During the course of the evening, I struck up a conversation with a muscular, mesomorphic Marine who was home on Christmas leave. As we talked, he related an incident in which he had been injured in a high school football game in Caney, no less. And the opposition was Dewey! I was initially hesitant to reveal much to this buffed-up, killing-machine Marine (who had been the proverbial 98-pound weakling when we first crossed paths). I eventually confessed my complicity in the fiasco, and we had a good laugh about it all. He admitted to being undersized, under-equipped with an ill-fitting uniform and headgear, and totally under-coached, with minimal instruction about tackling technique. As he put it, "I should have never been on the field in the first place." We reached a mutual agreement that the incident was over with and done, best put behind us, and he and I parted ways on most amicable terms. It was reassuring to learn that an ugly story had such a happy ending, but I do not think I ever really enjoyed playing football near as much after that night in Caney, Kansas, in which our later-to-be Marine friend was grievously injured. To add to the legend, in another game a Caney running back broke loose and I eventually caught him maybe sixty yards downfield. In the process, he suffered a neck injury from the tackle, though not of the magnitude of my Marine friend. Such exploits added to my Caney mystique as the "Oklahoma Jackrabbit", however undeserved.

After many hours of drinking mostly cerveza with the Marine and others, we capped off our New Year's Eve spree in Coffeyville by killing off a bottle of sweet and sickening apricot brandy, most assuredly a recipe for disaster when paired with all the beer we had consumed. We somehow made it back to Dewey without killing ourselves or innocent bystanders and spent New Year's Day at "Ock's" house in an advanced state of nausea that ran well into the evening hours. We tried to watch the New Year's Day bowl games, but with little success due to the unending unease. Needless to say, I have not had the slightest urge in the past fifty years to have so much as a sip or even a sniff of apricot brandy!

Speaking of apricot brandy, I was in J. J.'s liquor store in College Station the evening of December 21, 2009, and happened to pass by a shelf containing the dreaded liquer. That sighting brought back a flood of memories of events that transpired exactly fifty New Year's Eves earlier almost to the minute. The *déjà vu* experience was a poignant reminder of the evils of apricot brandy as well as how fast five decades can pass. Unfortunately, nothing seems to totally erase those half-century-old memories of apricot brandy.

No Post-Season Honors for Me. In addition to my JV experiences, I had a nice varsity season that first year also, generally scoring in every game at least once and gaining between one hundred and maybe two hundred yards, in most of the games. I was the leader or among the leaders in the district in both scoring and yards gained, but received no post-season laurels. "Tractor" later told me there was a district policy preventing sophomores from being named to the all-district team, which was disappointing because I thought I clearly deserved it. As consolation, I told myself that my time would come as I expected to improve on my performance over the upcoming two years anyway.

In this connection, I remember talking to a player from the Hominy Bucks after our game with them. For whatever reason, the two teams shared a common dressing room arrangement, leading me to start a conversation with a Hominy player who congratulated me on a good game. In the course of our discussion, he indicated he thought I was a senior and most certainly deserving of all-state honors. When I told him I was only a sophomore with two more years to go, he was clearly taken aback. Though I did not know the guy by name, he was one of their best talents, and it was nice to think I might be an all-state caliber running back, at least in the eyes of one talented and admiring opponent.

Another memorable game was against the Cleveland Tigers, an important district game. I had done exceptionally well early on, gaining maybe two hundred yards and scoring a couple of touchdowns. I broke loose at one point on an 89-yard run, and suffered the ultimate humiliation for a sprinter posing as a running back of getting caught from behind by one of their defenders on the one-yard line. We failed to convert the opportunity into a score, and ended up losing the game by a margin of less than a touchdown. I must say it was the only time I ever got caught from behind in football, and the defender who made the tackle did finish second to me in the hundred-yard dash two years later at the district meet, so at least I did not get pulled down by a slowpoke.

In that same game, I received a shovel pass right behind our center but their middle linebacker was not deceived by our play call. After making the catch, I turned up field to hopefully gain some big yards or score, but all of a sudden the ball was missing. It seems the middle linebacker had anticipated the play, stolen the ball right out of my hands, and joyously scored a touchdown from twenty-five yards out. Clearly, there were mixed blessings in my performance against Cleveland, but it was a breakout game for me because I knew for the first time I could compete at the varsity level with other good players.

This abortive play was brought back to me in vivid color, literally a *déjà vu* experience, while watching the 2010 Rose Bowl national championship football game between the University of Alabama Crimson Tide and the University of Texas Longhorns. It seems that UT coach Mack Brown opted to try to score twenty seconds or so before half-time by using a shovel pass that went awry, leading to a big score by Alabama. I was a fan of Coach Brown but the explanation given to the media concerning the decision to go with that play because he had never seen it backfire, thus making it a safe call, seemed feeble to me. I could have told Coach Brown differently from personal experience!

In a mid-season game with the Hominy Bucks my junior season, I was playing wing back and took a shovel pass from the tailback hoping, of course, to break loose behind the center of our offensive line. The nose guard was knocked off balance by a block from one of our linemen, but was able to alertly reach up somehow while lying on the ground and grab my shoulder pads as I went through the designated hole. He twisted me to the turf, transforming me into a human pretzel, and I felt a searing sensation deep in the right side of my abdomen. I later learned I had a torn ureter and a bruised kidney. Grabbing my shoulder pads from behind, which caused my injury, is now known as the horse collar tackle and is banned in professional football due to its dangerousness. I can certainly attest to that fact!

After passing blood for the entire weekend and being unable to have a bowel movement, my mother and I decided Monday morning it was time for a hospital emergency room visit to get the problem diagnosed and treated. The medical staff put me in a room for a couple of nights for treatment and observation, and "Tractor" made his way up to the hospital, assuring me I should be ready to romp and stomp by Friday. The doctor informed Coach Trent he better start adjusting his starting lineup as I was done for the year.

I spent the rest of my junior year on the sideline with our water boy, the round, rotund, cherubic, and likeable Clyde "The Mole" Tucker, aka "Clyde the Molefucker." The fact that Tucker conveniently rhymed with fucker, coupled with Clyde's stocky, low-to-the-ground build and appearance, led an unknown source to drop the nickname on him. During timeouts, Clyde and I were primarily responsible for carrying water bottles to the gritty, grimy, and occasionally gory gladiators kneeling on the field during time outs. As well, we jockeyed to see who got to retrieve the kicking tees after kickoffs.

The water we dispensed was snugly ensconced in the individual receptacles built into Coca Cola crates. Because of his short, stocky body build, Clyde's center of gravity was quite low, and the weight of the crate and the full Coke bottles created an ever-increasing forward lean as he ran from the sideline to the huddle during those cherished time outs. Defying the forces of gravity, and to our utter amazement, Clyde always arrived at his destination one or two steps before falling flat on his face. We often bet amongst ourselves whether Clyde would make the huddle in a standing position or face down. Clyde Elmer Tucker, remembered by relatives and friends as a hard worker and respected family man, died in 2011.

A Final Tribute to Kester "Tractor" Trent. "Tractor" Trent is truly one of the most unforgettable people I have ever met, and his name surfaces almost without fail when Dewey Bulldoggers (Decimals?) of the 1950's get together. Almost instantaneously, someone will bring up a "Tractor" anecdote, and many years ago I tried to capture the essence of the man in a song. For a short time in the 1970's, I played guitar (barely) and sang (badly), sometimes solo and more often with friends, at minor venues around campus, and on one occasion I broke out for the first and only time publicly, *The Ballad of "Tractor" Trent*." The site of my breakout performance was The Basement, a hole-in-the-wall music venue in A&M's Memorial Student Center (MSC), which for a brief period served as an outlet for local amateur musicians such as yours truly. However, some talented performers who went on to bigger and better things showed up there. For example, Michael Martin Murphy of *Wildfire* fame also appeared there, and you could hear the man sing at The Basement for a dollar. Thirty years later, my wife and her father divvied up a mere $2,500 each to take part in a week-long ride in the Colorado Rockies with Mr. Murphy as host. Each night, the group would gather around the campfire and listen to the troubadour (now in his early seventies) hold forth with such hits as "*Wildfire*", "*Carolina Pines*", and "*What's Forever For*." Clearly, the price of "playing poker" with Michael Martin Murphy went up over the years.

In a brief brush with celebrity, or my fifteen minutes of fame, I received a standing ovation from The Basement crowd for my performance of *The Ballad of "Tractor" Trent*. I have since rejuvenated the old ditty, and would like to include it here as a tribute to a man who had such an interesting impact on my life, Kester "Tractor" Trent.

Arnold LeUnes

Ballad of "Tractor" Trent

Sittin' around home the other day
Wishin' we had a team that could really play
Hopin' we could win some game this fall
At that game, King Football
We need coaching genius "Tractor" Trent.

We said, "Tractor", "Tractor", we can't win."
He said, "Don't worry boys, I'm gonna make you grin."
"I'm gonna find me some boys who wanna' really play
We're gonna' win every Friday
Or my name ain't coaching genius, "Tractor" Trent."

His hat size was seven and seven-eights
His body was fashioned from old orange crates
His mind, it worked like a buzz saw
Ham hands and iron jaw
Bionic man, tough guy "Tractor" Trent.

"Tractor" took command on August One
He said, "From now on boys, there ain't gonna' be no fun
We're gonna' slave and we're gonna' work
At our duties, we will never shirk
Hard-workin', slave-drivin' martinet, coachin' genius "Tractor" Trent.

We had a back by the name of bad Joe Brown
He could really pick 'em up and lay 'em down
Bad Joe Brown was a real speed burner
He had more moves than Tina Turner
Twistin', turnin', slippery, speedy Joe Brown.

Go, go, go speedy Joe Brown
Pick 'em up and lay 'em down
"Tractor's countin' on you to go, go, go
Or he's gonna' call you a gutless so and so
Mean mother, coaching genius "Tractor" Trent.

Out at practice the other day
Speedy Joe Brown came around on an end sweep play
The crack could be heard for miles around

Ed Davis knocked Joe to the ground
His leg was broken, no longer slippery, speedy, he's gimpy Joe Brown.

"Tractor", "Tractor" came runnin' up
He said to slow Joe, "Run it off, you lazy pup
Run it off or get out of here
I ain't gonna' have players who show fear."
Run it off, slow, gimpy, no longer slippery Joe Brown.

"Coach, coach, you know I can't go
My leg, my leg, it hurts me so
As sure as my name is Bad Joe Brown
That fracture is obviously compound."
"Tractor said, "You're a chicken and a pussy, Joe Brown."

"Tractor" said. "Give me someone who wants to play
We gotta' big game with Cleveland Friday."
Jerry Jones stepped up and he said,
"Coach, coach, I'll play in Joe Brown's stead."
Opportunistic, Joltin' Jerry Jones.

Friday night came rollin' round
The Cleveland Tigers steamrolled into town
The sky was clear, the night was great
"Tractor" said, "Boys, let's operate."
Silver-tongued motivator, coachin' genius "Tractor" Trent.

Down in the north end zone,
The Bulldogger cheerleaders were getting' it on
Slappin' their hands and kickin' 'em high
Showin the crowd just a bit of the thigh
Including dirty old man, coaching genius "Tractor" Trent.

At halftime, the score it was tied
"Tractor" said, "Boys, I'm mortified.
If you guys wanna' play, you wanna' play for me
You're gonna' have to stop squattin' to pee."
Smooth talkin', team motivatin', sexist "Tractor" Trent

We went out and won the game
"Tractor" got elected to the Hall of Fame

Town folks said he was the greatest man alive
But we on the team weren't diggin' that jive
For we all knew the man who saved "Tractor's" ass
Was "Hooter" Brewer!!!

Pros in our Midst: Opponents Who Went on to Stardom in the NFL. My friends and I had the good fortune to compete against three outstanding high school football players who later distinguished themselves at both the collegiate and professional levels, and I would like to accord them proper homage with a few words. Two of these immensely talented players were from Bartlesville and the other played for Marquette High School, a private Catholic school in Tulsa.

Kester Trent

Word has been received that Kester "Tractor" Trent, 83, resident of Stone Mountain, Ga., and former Dewey resident, died Dec. 27 of cancer.

Funeral services were at Avondale First Baptist Church in Avondale Estates, Ga., on Dec. 30, 1993.

Mr. Trent has lived in Georgia since his retirement in 1976 from the Dewey public school system. Better known as "Tractor" since his college football days at Oklahoma A & M College (Oklahoma State University), his high school coaching and teaching career spanned more than 35 years in Oklahoma.

He was honored by the Oklahoma Coaches Association in 1973 when he was inducted into the Oklahoma High School Coaches Hall of Fame. During his years of coaching he compiled more than .700 winning percentage in all sports. While coaching at Stillwell, Wilburton, Heavener and Dewey, he taught youth the basics of football, basketball, track, baseball and the realities of winning, taking basketball and baseball teams to the state playoffs while at Stillwell and Dewey.

He began his honors prog while a student at Heavener when he garnered All State recognition as a fullback in 1930. While attending Oklahoma A & M on a football scholarship, he was named to the All Missouri Valley Conference team and received contract offers from the Los Angeles Rams and the Brooklyn Dodgers. His nickname "Tractor" came from an unknown sports writer when he was a sophomore at A & M and the name stayed with him a lifetime.

Following his retirement from coaching in 1960, he continued with his teaching of American history and industrial arts at Dewey High School and stayed involved with sports by officiating everything from football to basketball to baseball.

Survivors include his wife of 62 years, Oleta Trent, of the home; a daughter, Mrs. Tommye Kay Wilkerson, of Stone Mountain, Ga.; two granddaughters: Mrs. Stephanie Harp of Decatur, Ga., and Kerry Wilkerson of Stone Mountain, Ga.; and a sister, Mrs. Ada Ruth Scroggs, of Stillwater.

COACH KESTER "TRACTOR" TRENT OBITUARY

One of those Bartlesville Wildcats was a gifted all-around athlete named Bobby Joe Green (1936-1993). Among other things, Green ran the hundred-yard dash in 9.7 seconds at a time when the world record was only four-tenths of a second faster. His speed, of course, helped him become a state champion hurdler, an elusive All-State running back, and a more than passable basketball player. However, his real forte was punting the football, and he had no peers at the high school level and, later, precious few in the collegiate or professional ranks. His punts were not the usual wobbly high school sort, low, short, and often easy to return. Instead, they soared high above the lights which were generally pretty pathetic in most high school stadiums in Oklahoma in those days, and he averaged forty-five yards a pop. One year, we played Bartlesville in a driving rain and I drew the unenviable task of trying to catch and return his punts. Those long, high kicks rose well above the lights which gave his teammates plenty of time to get downfield with the goal of beheading the punt returner if they could. I managed to acquit myself well enough that night, mainly by not bobbling a kick.

Bobby Joe was recruited by the University of Oklahoma coaching staff, and immediately established himself as their punter of the future. However, something went awry in Norman, most likely that bugaboo for many athletes, grades. This temporary setback led Bobby Joe to transfer after his freshman year to perennial junior college powerhouse, Northeastern Oklahoma A&M, in Miami. Following a successful junior college season in which he was named to the All-American team as a running back and punter, Bobby Joe moved on to the University of Florida where he was one of the nation's premier collegiate punters for his last two years. As well, he was also a star running back and a top sprinter on the Gators track team. His 44.9 punting average in 1959 still stands as the Florida Gators record, and he was named to their All-Century team in 1999.

Bobby Joe capped off a most successful career as a punter in the National Football League (NFL), kicking for fourteen seasons, two with the Pittsburgh Steelers and twelve with the Chicago Bears. His best year as a punter was his second while with the Steelers; he punted seventy-three times for a 47.0 average which was second in the league that season. He was second in the league in punting distance three times and had the third highest average two other times. For his entire NFL career, he punted 970 times for a 42.6 average which put him at fifty-eighth on the all-time list. He was finally named to the Pro Bowl in 1971, a fitting tribute to the end of a career for an outstanding punter. He retired from the NFL in 1973, coached at his alma mater, the University of Florida, from 1979 to 1989, and after retiring from coaching, started a business in Gainesville, Bobby Joe Green Monogramming. He ran that operation for four years until his premature death due to a heart attack on May 29, 1993, at the age of fifty-seven. Bobby Joe Green was an outstanding all-around athlete, the best in my own personal experience through high school, and I only wish I had gotten to know him better.

Another memorable chap from Bartlesville who also had successful runs at both the college and professional levels was David Lee Baker (1937-2002). David Baker was movie star handsome and athletically gifted, so much so that he was named first team All-State in three sports, football, basketball, and baseball. His best sport was football where he was one heck of a player on both sides of the ball at quarterback and linebacker. When playing defense, he would line up over center, wanting to hit someone so badly tears streamed down his face. I found it remarkable that anyone could take the game of football so seriously. In the one game I played against him, Baker fixed his gaze firmly on me at a point slightly above the upraised shoulder pads and helmet of our center, Raymond Gray, and mouthed a very intimidating, "You're mine, LeUnes." All I could think of at that time was "Ease up, Dave! This is not World War III, Dave, it's just a football game." Looking back, I think it may have been war to David, and I just did not get it.

David was recruited to play football at the University of Oklahoma by the legendary coach Charles "Bud" Wilkinson, and he started his last three years at quarterback, running back, and defensive back. The Sooners compiled a 30-2 record during that time, and Coach Wilkinson paid him a huge compliment with which I have absolutely no argument: "Baker is the killer type." When his career at OU was over, David Baker was the fifth pick in the first round of the National Football League (NFL) draft by the San Francisco 49ers. He was an All-Pro performer his first season but played only three years before being drafted into the U.S. Army in 1962 as things starting heating up in Vietnam. Former NFL player and coach, Monte Clark, said Baker was the best and hardest hitting defensive back he encountered in his fifteen-year Hall of Fame playing career.

After a two-year stint in the Army, Baker was contacted by the President of Southern Nazarene University in Bethany, Oklahoma, just west of Oklahoma City, about starting an athletic program there. He decided that he could best serve society as the Athletic Director in a Christian environment as opposed to playing defensive back in professional football. He took the SNU job for the princely sum of $3,600, far below what a twenty-seven-year old All-Pro defensive back could command in the NFL, and served there for ten years. He died on September 4, 2002, in Norman, Oklahoma, home of his beloved Sooners.

Both of those Bartlesville boys graduated from high school two years ahead of me, so I only got to compete against them once, but it was memorable for a small town boy of modest talent to meet and play against such high caliber athletes who went on to bigger and better things.

The third player in this trilogy, Bob Scholtz, played at Tulsa's Marquette High, a Catholic school. Scholtz was 6'4" and 250 pounds, a center and linebacker, and an absolute giant of a man in an era where players were really quite small. It was extremely rare in those days to run across any 200-pounders, let alone someone as big as Scholtz, who towered over all of our players, none of whom weighed more than 185-190 pounds. Marquette defeated us 9-0 my sophomore year and we returned the favor two years later by beating them 19-0 on our run to the state quarterfinals. One of the highlights that victorious evening was having "Ock" Davis blast Scholtz into the nickel seats with a blind side block. I set out on a fifteen- or twenty-yard run that took me down the right sideline in front of the home town cheering section, and as Scholtz moved in for the tackle, I veered sharply to my left in an effort to avoid him. Scholtz simultaneously adjusted his path and as he turned back to his right to make the tackle, Ed caught him under the shoulder pads, lifted him off the ground a foot or two, rolled him out of bounds with a thud, and sent him careening into the fence surrounding our football field. It was one of those plays that offensive lineman dream about at night. Running backs like them a lot, too!

Scholtz went on to start at center for the Notre Dame Fighting Irish, and had a seven-year career in the NFL as a center, guard, and tackle with the Detroit Lions and New York Giants. I have not been able to find out more about Scholtz's life after football but the image of Ed Davis, at maybe 180 pounds, cutting the 250-pounder down to size on that one memorable play that September night in 1955 lingers.

Myrna Jo Brown, Princess of the Delaware Tribe

"Someone I loved once gave me a box full of darkness.
It took me years to understand that this too, was a gift."

Mary Oliver, Pulitzer Prize-Winning Poet

The most significant thing that transpired that sophomore year other than football was my first true love affair, and it involved a young woman named Myrna Jo Brown. Myrna was half Native American and Princess of the Delaware Tribe; her mother, Loyce, was a full blood member of the tribe but the father, Joe, was Anglo. The family had moved to Dewey from Electra, Texas, in the late summer before my sophomore year. The father worked in the oil business as a pumper and the mother was a housewife. Myrna's brother, Joe, was sixteen and a junior-to-be, and Myrna was fourteen and was to be a freshman that fall. The family seemed incredibly harmonious to me, though I had little practice in evaluating such things given my own family history.

The children were clearly adored by their parents, and they supported Joe and Myrna to the nth degree in all their activities. For a guy like me with little stability in family structure, it was comforting to be around the Browns because they represented what a family unit should be….a hardworking and supportive father, a beautiful and devoted mother, and two bright, attractive, and happy kids. The dad was a nice looking, outdoorsy, weather-beaten guy with the appearance of a man who worked in the elements every day, rousting about on an assortment of oil rigs in the area. He was a hard worker and a good family man who provided well for his wife and children. His wife was absolutely beautiful with long flowing black hair, sparkling dark eyes, and a sculpted Native American face accentuated by a prominent mouth full of bright and straight teeth. She took great pride in her Delaware heritage, and the ecstasy associated with moments of tribal glory and the pain of past suffering of her ancestors, like those of the Cherokees and "Chief" Tyner, were etched in her beautiful face. There was a real air of mystery about her, borne no doubt of her ancestral heritage.

The Delaware Indian Tribe, or the Lenni Lenape. These indigenous people got their name from the Delaware River where most of them lived before moving to the Indian Territory. The river itself got its name from Lord de la Warr, a governor of the Jamestown colony. The Delawares called themselves the Lenni Lenape (len-NAH-pay) which means something like "The People." Though they could be fierce warriors if provoked, the Lenni Lenape were generally known among the settlers in the original colonies to be peacemakers and settlers of disputes within or between the European settlers and various Indian tribes. The early Lenni Lenape were farmers, hunters, and artisans, and made pottery, beads, and objects used in both warfare and hunting. The tribe was divided at one time into three clans, "The Turtle," "The Wolf," and "The Turkey", and each division had its own chief. However, the overall leader came from the Turtle clan, a position that was passed on from generation to generation without question or argumentation.

DELAWARE TRIBAL SEAL

The Lenni Lenape were eventually forced westward from their native lands, though not as rapidly and inhumanely as the Cherokees on the infamous Trail of Tears. The process was less draconian, spread over more territory, and spaced over a greater time period, perhaps as much as 175 years. While most of the Lenni Lenape ended up in the Indian Territory, some found their way to the Ontario, Canada area and two reserves are still in existence today, and are known as the Delaware Nation at Moraviantown and the Munsee-Delaware Nation. Today, the headquarters of the Delaware Nation is in Bartlesville, Oklahoma, and there are some 10,000 members. My own personal familiarity with several members of the Lenni Lenape ran deep. Many were friends and acquaintances throughout my youth, and several have had a significant impact on the way my life has unfolded.

But let us get back to Myrna Brown and her family. The two parents passed on their good looks to the two children. Joe was tall and handsome, muscular, athletic, quite vain about his good looks, and was widely regarded as a "pretty boy" by classmates and football teammates. It always bothered Joe that he did not get his mother's genes which would have, among other things, left him largely free of facial hair. Young Joe was often seen before his bathroom mirror, armed with tweezers, trying to pluck away newly discovered whiskers in hopes he would eventually end up with a hairless face. Though the strategy was a failed one, it never stopped Joe from trying. Joe went out for the football team and immediately became a first team running back. He was pretty darn good at it but a compound lower leg fracture suffered in practice in mid-year put a premature end to his season. His football misfortunes were chronicled earlier in *"The Ballad of "Tractor" Trent."*

As for Myrna, she was named after the distinguished actress of the day, Myrna Loy. She was striking, inheriting features from her mother that were poignant reminders of her Delaware heritage, namely black hair, very dark eyes, and brown flawless skin. She also had a large mouth with white, straight teeth, and a body like the quintessential sex symbol of the era, Marilyn Monroe. She was a happy person and her sunny disposition was accentuated by a wide, radiant smile. Since contact lenses were unheard of at that time, Myrna was stuck with wearing glasses but she carried that off well enough by selecting tasteful, unobtrusive frames. The glasses were a part of her and no one really thought much about it.

As I got to know the family better, they introduced me to Indian powwows and ceremonial dances. Myrna was a champion war dancer and as stated earlier, the Princess of the Delaware Tribe. She was often a featured performer at the small area powwows as well as the mother soiree of them all, the American Indian Exposition, held the first week in August in Anadarko, Oklahoma. It was an annual ritual for the Browns to make a late summer pilgrimage to Anadarko for the various festivities associated with the Exposition. Myrna looked absolutely resplendent in her Indian powwow war dance costume made up of multi-colored feathers and ribbons and whatnot that blended so beautifully with her Native American personae; she made a heck of a fetching princess, if I do say so myself! She and her mother were working on a war dance costume for me at some point but that project, for whatever reason, never reached fruition.

I loved the powwows, the beat of the drums and the ceremonial, rhythmic dancing, and always looked forward to taking part in the old and time-honored Delaware traditions. On occasion, there would be hardheads at the powwows who would mutter under their breath or make verbal threats because I, "White Eyes", was a potential contributor to the pollution of the purity of the Delaware Indian Tribe. As those nights wore on, the discriminatory remarks would ratchet up in frequency and intensity, greatly fueled by the over-consumption of alcohol. The tensions generated from the comments made me uneasy from time to time perhaps, but I was never really afraid to attend and take part in the powwows. On more than one occasion when things looked potentially threatening, Myrna or her mother would quietly escort me off the premises.

The old Indians had a name for me that was pejorative and confined to Anglos who dated their women, "Sycamore Indian," or the Indian name for a white man. I have from time to time jokingly told people that I was from Oklahoma, and thanks to an informal edict from the elders of the Delaware Tribe dating back to the 1950's, I remain today a full-fledged and proud member of the Sycamore Indian tribe!

Sports for Women in the 1950's. Myrna was quite fit and athletic and could run extremely fast. I always suspected she could give brother Joe and me a good race for a short distance. In another era, she would have undoubtedly become an accomplished female athlete. I really believe she was more of an athlete than her brother, but there were virtually no sports outlets for females at that time other than cheerleading. Myrna followed the trend of the period as did most attractive and energetic young women, becoming a Bulldogger cheerleader (aka Pompom Person). As well, she was the Drum Majorette for the marching Bulldogger band. Academically, Myrna was blessed with an exceptional mind, and she generally made all A's on her report cards. I think school work was pretty easy for Myrna and I do not remember her having to study very much at all.

It is interesting to note that the women's movement had not reached much of mainstream America by the 1950's and Dewey was certainly no exception. Participation in sports was not seen as proper for females, with arguments to the effect that athletics put too much pressure on fragile female psyches and constituted a disruptive force with regard to the menstrual cycle which, in turn, threatened reproductive capacity.

Those opposed to women participating in sport cited the 1928 Olympic Games in Amsterdam, Netherlands, as proof positive that women could not handle the rigorous demands of competitive athletics. The 800-meter run was introduced for women at the 1928 Olympic Games and every contestant got sick, threw up, passed out, or otherwise was unable to finish the race. As a result, the 800-meter run for females was cancelled and reinstituted thirty-two years later at the 1960 Olympic Games in Rome. Looking at the modern competitive female and their times in such events as the 100-meter dash, the 800-meter run, or the marathon race, the scenario that unfolded in Amsterdam nine decades ago seems surreal.

Women's basketball in the middle part of the twentieth century was another interesting case in itself. The accepted dogma of the period was that women could not handle the physical rigors of the full-court game, so the court was divided in half, thus making the game essentially a half-court, three-on-three competition. Each team had three offensive and three defensive players, or a total of six, and none were allowed to cross the mid-court line. That six-on-six, half-court version of basketball was the woman's game during my high school years, but even then only in nearby small towns. The conventional wisdom was that it was not appropriate for girls of that era to sweat; you know the old adage: "Horses sweat, men perspire, and women glow!" If anyone had to sweat like a horse, it would be best if it was done by a country girl. Big city girls, those living in towns with a total population of 500 or more, did not have basketball teams; city girls simply were not allowed to sweat, at least publicly! The end result of these sexist notions was that many potentially talented females of that era, such as Myrna Brown, never got a chance to test their skills in the athletic arena.

The last two states to do away with the six-on-six, half-court game were Oklahoma and Iowa, both in 1991. Prior to that time, at least in Oklahoma, the superintendents of each school within the respective districts would meet once a year and decide if they wanted their female students to play five-on-five full court or six-on-six half court basketball.

I cannot remember exactly how Myrna and I became so fond of each other. I think it may have started with casual chatter at a school fund-raising project for one of the clubs, or some such thing. It was not long after we met that we became inseparable as many young couples are wont to be, and she consumed virtually all of my time and energy for nearly two years. After a period of six or seven months, we started a wonderful sexual relationship as a present for my sixteenth birthday that was to last for eighteen months. We agreed that April 16 would be a good time to move to another level in our relationship, and that is what we did, awkwardly fumbling our way through the whole process like the novices we were!

As was too often the case with teenagers and young adults in those years before the creation of the birth control pill, we gave little thought to the possibility of a teen-age pregnancy. Sweating out many a monthly period became the norm, but the anxiety did nothing to change our sexual behavior. Given that neither of us ever used any birth control measures, it was a miracle that conception never took place. As I understand it through the grapevine, Myrna never had any children while I have six, so I suspect our good fortune, as it turned out, was more a function of her reproductive shortcomings than mine. I am happy things turned out that way, of course, and one can only imagine how different life might have been for both of us had there been an unwanted, untimely pregnancy.

This situation is a poignant reminder that life takes twists and turns over which we are not always in total control, sometimes with potentially life-changing repercussions. I think it is human nature, if you will, to believe that we are indeed captains of our own ships and masters of our destinies, but there is ample evidence for chance factors also shaping our fates. I really do not like to invoke chance much as an explanatory mechanism for human behavior, but it is simply too compelling to ignore some times. Would I have gone to college, been in the U.S. Army, received a doctoral degree, become a professor at an outstanding university, married the women I did, and fathered these six children are epic questions, at least at the personal level. How different would life have been under other circumstances? The counter notion that I would have accomplished none of the above and ended up spending my life in Dewey in some menial job is even harder to conceive. But it could have just as easily turned out that way. Who knows?

As I became more wrapped up in the relationship, I lost interest in my friends, academics, and athletics. For over a year, I was a virtual stranger to the friends I had known all my life. It is hard to imagine that situation now, but young love can be quite compelling, as anyone who has been there can attest. And who among us has not been there at least once or twice?

I had been an A-B student throughout the early school years, but I completely lost interest in my studies by the end of my sophomore year. I only graduated because of a forgiving school administration that took me on as a charity case. I can honestly say that I did not turn in an assignment in any class during the last part of my junior year and the entire senior year. This is an example of social promotion at its finest/worst. During football season, I would sometimes be ruled ineligible on Monday only to find out that I had been returned to eligibility in time to play Friday night. Clearly, there was a double standard for disciplining athletes, and I quickly learned there were not any real consequences attached to my tardiness and school truancy.

As for athletics, I started at tailback again my junior year, but the effort and the interest were lagging behind, and then I suffered the season-ending kidney injury mentioned elsewhere. I had gotten into a funk about life, and could not get out. I poured every ounce of my existence into my relationship with Myrna, and that is about all I thought about. It did not help that I had little guidance and support from my steadily declining mother. As for my father, he was capable of wise counsel and unflagging support but was hundreds of miles away in Texas City, Texas. It was a lonely, confusing time in my life.

Our Relationship Goes South, and So Do I. I put everything into Myrna and that came back to bite me in the behind early in my senior year. For whatever reason, she decided that we should break up but I could not face that rejection, hoping against hope that she would want to ultimately rekindle the relationship. That wish was not to be, and I began to sink into a psychological abyss from which I could not extract myself.

Depression is a common outcome of breakups with significant others and almost everyone has to face this challenge at some point in their relationships. And you do not have to confine your conversation to lovesick adolescents; just look at the murder, mayhem, and misery caused by adults who cannot handle their romantic relationships at ages twenty-five or thirty-five or even fifty-five. In any case, I went into a depressive funk that lasted well past the first half of my senior year. My desire to play football waned to an asymptote of complete indifference, and I quit coming to school to avoid the pain of seeing Myrna there. I once calculated that I missed thirty full days of class and parts of sixty others my senior year. Talk about getting socially promoted out of high school!

There is absolutely no question that for a period of time I was by any definition a full-fledged stalker. Myrna could do nothing without me showing up. I would beg and plead for her to give me a second or third or fourth chance, always to no avail. One night I waited in the bushes near her garage until midnight, just to see what she was up to. When she arrived home, we talked for a while and it became obvious from assorted tell-tale signs that she had just had sexual activity with someone. She denied it, of course, but admitted she had been out with Raymond Gray, our star football center and linebacker. She convinced me nothing of a sexual nature had taken place and I naively took her word for it and left. Sometime later, I found out from Frank Ringo that I was suckered in on that deal. According to subsequent conversations my friends had with Raymond Gray, the sexual relationship had occurred and was consensual.

My depression over the breakup deepened and intensified, taking over every waking hour. When I could sleep, and sleep was fitful at best, I often kept a kitchen knife at my side, alternating between wanting to commit suicide or kill her. One night, I carried the knife to her house, and made weak threats against both our lives. Her dad intervened before things got completely out of hand, though I do think that better judgment on my part would have kicked in to defuse the situation anyway. I was not interested in really hurting anyone, I was simply making a grandstand play for her affection. She was resolute in her desire to break up with me, and the light finally went on in my head. I came to the realization that night that the affair was over. Though hardly comforting at the time, my awareness of the futility of trying to patch things up laid the groundwork for my ultimate recovery the following spring.

Myrna's father wisely called my mother over the incident, and shortly afterwards she contacted my father in Texas City. They worked out a deal where I was to spend the Christmas holidays with him and June, a move analogous to the behavioral treatment known as time out, I guess. The two-week "vacation" helped reduce the tensions a bit, and I returned to Dewey where I limped through the first part of the spring athletically and academically. I gave up basketball, a sport in which I had inordinately modest talent, and baseball at which by my own humble estimations I was actually quite decent.

Finally, the fog began to lift in the middle of the spring of that otherwise horrific senior year. For one thing, and a very important thing, I got to where the sight of Myrna or thinking about her generated little or no psychic pain. The funk began to slowly lift, I began coming to school more predictably, and most important I rekindled my friendships with the "boys of summer." Also, a great deal of the improvement in mood and spirit had to do with going out for the newly-formed track team, thanks to the encouragement of the coach, L. E. "Hooter" Brewer.

As for Myrna Jo Brown, she started dating a childhood neighbor and high school football teammate, Jerry Jones, and they got married shortly after high school. They had no children, and the marriage broke up after some time. The last time I ever saw Myrna was in the fall of 1959 when I was home from college for the Christmas holidays. She drove by my house, we went for a short ride, and talked for maybe thirty minutes about the past, the future, life, dreams, goals, and whatnot. The conversation was not at all heavy as I remember, and she shortly thereafter vanished from my life. In retrospect, I have no hard feelings about anything and I learned a lot about myself. I learned about the depths of hell, despair, all-consuming loneliness, and psychological pain and its fallout. I also learned about resilience, mental toughness, and getting up off the deck when you have been knocked down for the count. I was not aware of it at the time but I now know I had, unknowingly, received the gift mentioned so eloquently by Mary Oliver in the introduction to this segment.

The saddest part of the whole affair is that I actually remember little other than the painful part. Undoubtedly, there were infinitely more good times than bad, but I have virtually no recall of the positives in the relationship that had such a major impact on my life. One would think the experience would be etched indelibly into my brain, tiny neuronal detail by tiny neuronal detail, but that is not the case at all. I unfortunately remember too little. The last I heard, Myrna had married a fellow, I think with a military background, and was living in the state of Illinois. I have tried unsuccessfully on a couple of occasions over the years to track her down via social media; it would be interesting to know how her life has unfolded.

The Senior Year

Doing Dumb Stuff

My final year of high school began in September of 1956 and started off with a bang. The very first day, my partners in crime, "Ock", "Bear", "Gonna", and I joined forces in cutting class shortly after lunch. Knowing our habits to a tee, the principal showed up at the Eager Edgar the Eager Beaver's pool hall and unceremoniously escorted us back to school. He knew from experience where we would be or, alternatively, was tipped off by a do-gooder informant of which there are many in small towns. Having your whereabouts monitored informally 24-7 was pretty much the norm in small towns like Dewey; not much went unobserved and unreported.

Ed Bishop and Easy Ed

The two pool halls and the three drug stores were pretty much our every night hangouts throughout high school. Literally, our world view as 1950's small town teenagers was largely limited to events that took place in or near those five business establishments. The sad things is for some people in this so-called civilized world, their life horizons are that limited. For whatever reasons, many of us escaped, and I cannot help but think we were lucky ones.

The pool halls were owned by Ed Bishop and Ed Avery. We did not spend much time in Ed Bishop's place as it seemed to cater more to adults who were hard-core drinkers and serious gamblers. The place had an aura of mystery and darkness about it, deserved or not, and was pretty menacing on the whole. Bishop himself had a reputation as a tough guy and he looked every bit the part, with a quasi-Humphrey Bogart presence about him. He would disappear from time to time, and the rumors had it he was in Alaska testing his gambling skills against the best card players and pool sharks in the frozen tundra. However apocryphal, the aura associated with the Alaska gig, coupled with his tough-guy Bogey-esque look and demeanor, lent an air of foreboding to Ed Bishop.

As for Ed Avery, he was fondly known as "Easy Ed" or "Eager Edgar the Eager Beaver." Easy Ed was round and had a dissipated look about him. He was maybe 55- or 60-years old, and seemed a bit doddering, confused, and sort of hapless. But, then, we were prone to think that all people over fifty seemed doddering, confused, and hapless.

We spent many an afternoon and evening hanging out in Easy Ed's place, shooting pool or playing snooker which was our preferred game. Snooker was apparently invented by British soldiers stationed in India in the latter half of the nineteenth century. The game is played with a white cue ball, fifteen red balls worth a point apiece, and seven balls of different colors which must be sunk in order from yellow (the two ball worth two points) to black (the black ball worth seven points). The object in snooker is to alternate between sinking a red ball and a colored one in one of the six pockets, with scores being determined by how many of each is sunk. When all red balls are gone, then the remaining colored balls are dispatched in numerical order. The game can be played one-on-one or with two-person teams. In the latter case, the teammates take turns trying to sink the appropriate balls. When all balls are off the table, the person or team with the most points wins.

We far preferred snooker to pool because it took so much more skill. In snooker, the pockets are smaller and a more precise touch is required to sink the balls. Seldom is a player rewarded in snooker for just blasting away, a strategy that often pays off in pool with its larger and more forgiving pockets. Also, the strategy in snooker was much complex, given the nature of the rules of the game. Getting favorable position to make shots is at a premium in snooker.

Straight pool, or "rotation" as it was more properly known, was not as much fun though "eight ball" could be challenging. In rotation, balls are simply sunk in order and whoever scores the most points wins. In eight-ball, each player in singles or each team in doubles is responsible for sinking seven balls, either the "solids" (balls one through seven) or the "stripes" (balls nine through fifteen). The player or team that sinks their seven balls first can then win the game by sinking the eight ball. In seriously competitive eight-ball, the one and the fifteen balls must be sunk in opposing middle pockets designated before the game starts. If they are sunk elsewhere, they must be spotted back on the table for later disposition in the appropriate, preselected middle pocket. If at any time someone accidentally sinks the eight ball, the game is over. If all balls have been run off the table in proper sequence, then the eight ball must be sunk but the shooter must designate the pocket for the final shot. Again, sinking the ball in a pocket other than the designated one ends the game. The skill required in eight ball is an improvement over straight pool but it is still quite a bit less sophisticated than snooker.

The best pool and snooker players I ever saw in my hometown were Cecil Magana and Leroy Leaf, though my brother John Phillip, aka "Bub", came along six or seven years later and certainly deserved to be in the conversation. Cecil was one of my first idols. He was four, maybe five years older than me, an unbelievably talented multi-sport athlete, incredibly handsome, and one of those fortunate men who looked like a million dollars dressed in something as simple as a pair of Levi's, a football jersey, and Indian moccasins. In the case of moccasins, they were made popular, of course, by the presence of so many Native Americans in Dewey. For full social acceptance, the jeans had to be Levi's. Lee's might work as a secondary option but other off-brands simply did not make the cut. Outcast status was your fate if caught wearing something other than Levi's or Lee's

I remember a time a year or two after Cecil graduated when he came to one of our football practices and threw a few balls to the backs and wide receivers. Every pass I had caught up to that time had a rainbow arc, and almost anyone can run under a ball that has that much air under it and make the catch. Cecil's throws were laser-like, and literally went through my near-scorched hands almost untouched. I had never seen such velocity on a thrown football, but I learned that day the difference between pretenders and real quarterbacks. I also found out there are people with good hands and people who can simply run under a football. The former become wide receivers and the latter defensive backs! Simply put, a defensive back is nothing more than a wide receiver with bad hands!

Cecil was a quarterback and basketball star at Dewey High and signed a football scholarship with the University of Tulsa. For whatever reason, Cecil left the Golden Hurricane football program early on and moved over to Oklahoma City University where he cast his lot with basketball. He played at OCU for the legendary Abe Lemons who was immensely successful at OCU, Pan American College (now University of Texas Rio-Grande), and The University of Texas. Abe Lemons' took his teams to two National Invitational Tournament (NIT) berths and seven NCAA Tournament appearances in his eighteen years at OCU. All told, his teams won 599 games and lost 343 in thirty-four years of coaching at those three schools.

Cecil was a starter and played a big role in the success of those first national-caliber OCU teams in the mid-1950's. He later married a daughter of the exceedingly wealthy and politically powerful Senator Robert Kerr of Oklahoma who, in addition to his seat in the U.S. Senate, was also a founder of Kerr-McGee Oil Company and Oklahoma's first Native-American Governor. The couple eventually divorced, so I am told and, as of 2014, Cecil was living in Dewey and working in the oil business there.

HIGH SCHOOL BASKETBALL TEAM, 1955-1956 SEASON

Abe Lemons was an exceptional coach, and had a reputation for also being a first-class humorist. One of my favorite Abe Lemons stories concerns a game his Texas Longhorns played against Howard Payne University in the small west Texas town of Brownwood. The Longhorns were prohibitive favorites to win the game against a lesser opponent but had played poorly in a narrow win. Upon being queried by a sportswriter about whether or not the team had been punished for their lackadaisical performance, Abe said: "Doggone right I did. I made them stay out past nine pm in Brownwood!"

Other famous quotes and comments attributed to Abe Lemons included:

*"You may be big in New York, but in Walters, Oklahoma (Lemons' birthplace) you're nobody."

*Comment made to the famous sports announcer Howard Cosell: "How hard is it to coach track? Tell 'em to stay to the left and get there as fast as you can."

*Comment after Athletic Director and former track coach Deloss Dodds fired him as coach at the University of Texas: "What am I going to do with all those orange clothes I bought?"

*When asked how to stop illegal recruiting, Abe said, "Just give every coach the same amount of money and tell them they can keep what's left over."

*"Finish last in your league and they call you 'Idiot'. Finish last in medical school and they call you 'Doctor'.

*"Doctors bury their mistakes, but mine are all on scholarship."

*"I hope they notice the mistletoe tied to my coattails as I leave town."

*"We ran all over Texas-Arlington last season, 84-83. Ozie and Rich scored 71 points for us. After the game a reporter asked me how I thought we would have done without them. I said, "Figure it out for yourself. We'da got beat 83-13."

*"We went to Alaska once and they made us honorary Alaskans. Then we went to Hawaii and they made us honorary Hawaiians. We're going to the Virgin Islands this year."

But let us return to our discussion of pool and snooker. Another great pool and snooker player, in addition to Cecil and my brother, Bub, was the aforementioned Leroy Leaf, a full-blood Native American (Delaware tribe, I think). I was never sure who was the best among the older two guys, Cecil or Leroy, and I cannot remember them ever meeting face to face though they probably did. Leroy was right up there with Cecil Magana, for sure.

Another thing I remember about Leroy Leaf was prowess with his fists. He was as good a fighter as he was a snooker shark, and no one messed with him. The aforementioned Jake Scruggins who the reader may recall once tried to take my starting position on the high school football team by force via a fistfight. Jake smarted off to Leroy one night and absorbed a positively fierce ass-whipping in which he was finally deposited into an excavation where a building had once been. Fortunately, Jake was not badly hurt but he never got in Leroy's path again. I have no earthly idea what became of Leroy Leaf. Nor Jake Scruggins, for that matter.

When my friends and I were not shooting pool or snooker, we played a lot of dominos. Sometimes we played straight dominos but variations such as moon and 42 were mixed in for variety from time to time. Our standard modus operandi when preparing to play dominos was to load up a bottle of Pepsi Cola with a bag of shelled and salted peanuts a la our meetings with Carl Davidson when he first became the junior high football coach. We would sometimes get bored with dominos and playing tricks on "Eager Edgar the Eager Beaver" broke the monotony. One of our favorite ploys after we finished a game, and one that never failed to torch "Eager", was to load all the dominos in the box save one. That final domino would be surreptitiously deposited in the nearest spittoon as we were departing the premises. It goes without saying that fishing missing dominos out of a spittoon did not please Ed.

Our domino caper at "Eager Edgar's" reminds me of a spittoon joke we used to tell in those days. It goes as follows: A long, tall Texan with his big hat, shiny cowboy boots, and big belt buckle walks into a bar, surveys his surroundings, takes a good look at the crowd, and orders a beer. After chugging several beers and engaging in some casual conversation, the long, lanky stranger challenges anyone in the bar to take a drink out of a nearby spittoon, offering anyone who would step forth and answer the call twenty dollars. A dumbass Okie walks up and calls him out on the bet. The unsuspecting victim turns up the spittoon and ends up chug-a-lugging the entire contents of the vile vessel. The amazed Texan says, "Hey, podnuh, you only had to take one drink in order to win the bet." The dazed Okie replies: "I know but I couldn't stop. It was all in one string!"

A couple of years after I left Dewey for college, "Easy Ed" was charged by the police with beating John Fugate to death with a two-by-four. Fugate was the uncle of my childhood friend and high school classmate, Jimmy Dick Baker, and widely known as the town drunk. I do not think I ever saw John Fugate draw a sober breath; he looked every bit the part of the stereotypical bleary-eyed, slack-jawed, stumbling, mumbling, town drunk.

Apparently John Fugate was trying to force his way into the pool hall via the back entrance of Ed's Place at 1:30 am, long after the business had been locked up for the evening, no doubt to cadge a drink. He interrupted a high stakes poker game with Ed and some other "upstanding" Dewey citizens, and apparently his entry made Ed mad. "Not So Easy" Edgar proceeded to attack poor old John with the piece of lumber, and ended up killing him. A court later decided that John Fugate had broken into Ed's place illegally, and thus placed himself in harm's way. Believing they had no real case against Easy Ed, the court let him go free. John Fugate was seventy years old at the time of his untimely death. I cannot imagine how he lived that long with his affinity for alcohol, but he deserved a better fate than dying at the wrong end of a two-by-four in the hands of Ed Avery.

The Drug Stores

POPKESS PHARMACY, DEWEY MAIN STREET

When we were not in one of the pool halls playing snooker, shaking some dominos, consuming the delightful peanuts and Pepsi concoction, or jacking with Eager Edgar, we could probably be found in one of the three downtown drug stores. One of the establishments was known as William and Sally's, more or less on the west end of Main Street. A second hangout was The Popkess Pharmacy located at the east end of Dewey's Main Street. It was not a welcoming place, too business-like, and was remote (if anything in our quaint village could be called remote) from most of the evening action. Thus, it seldom got factored into our busy social agendas. On the other hand, the Rexall Drug Store owned by the DeShazo family and located maybe fifty yards to the east of William and Sally's, was high on the list of places to be. For one thing, we got to flirt nightly with classmates Carolyn Nelson, Dianne Kite, and Carol Sue Fielder who worked there as what were then known as "soda jerks." Also, we were able, on rare occasions, to beat one of our lovely lady friends out of a free cherry limeade, cherry phosphate, or chocolate root beer. For the uninitiated, a cherry phosphate drink was made of cherry juice and acid phosphate, a compound no longer in production. There are Internet rumors that cherry phosphate drinks can still be found in Minnesota, Kansas, and Oklahoma, most particularly in Pauls Valley just south of Oklahoma City (home of my esteemed high school football and track coach and life mentor, L. E. "Hooter" Brewer to be discussed in fond detail elsewhere). Again, since acid phosphate is no longer produced, citric acid or lemon juice suffices as a substitute. To the purist, this would not really be a cherry phosphate, but then most of the purists are of my vintage and thus deceased or in their dotage.

Carolyn Nelson was a real cutie, short, petite, pretty much your prototypical small town girl-next-door type. Carolyn was a cheerleader at school, and aptly fit the bubbly, bouncy, energetic, and endlessly upbeat and enthusiastic pompom person stereotype. As for Dianne Kite who lived a few houses down from me, she was always at the center of social activities in our grade. She was blond, pretty, lean, and, I thought, sexy. I had one date with her in the eighth grade for a hayride but she ended up being escorted home by the more aggressive Raymond Gray. While I was dwelling on whether it would be proper to put an arm around Dianne, Raymond was on the other side of her, thinking darker thoughts and apparently doing things I would not have thought possible in my wildest dreams. It has been my lot in life to be what my friend John Badgett of Slippery Rock University calls a "green-ass", or the guy who is eternally behind the curve when it comes to sizing up the motives of women.

In any case, I liked Dianne a lot and we remained friends up to her death several years ago. She fought cancer valiantly for years, the "The Big C", that dreaded scourge which has claimed the lives of so many of my high school and college classmates. Ed Davis and his absolutely off-the-top-of-the-chart, consummately sexy sister June, Raymond Gray, Donny Bible, Floyd Brown; the list goes on and on among the high school group. Cancer has also been the cause of death for many of my college friends and acquaintances who have passed away thus far, as well as a number of other friends and university colleagues. Almost makes you think there was something in the Dewey water, the walls of our college dormitory, or in the air in the hallowed halls of the Academic Building or Nagle Hall at Texas A&M University. Perhaps a clinical study of these environments might be revealing. There is so much folklore out there, linking cancer to all kinds of absurd correlational factors. Virtually everything we do or eat at one time or another has been linked to cancer, and I do not think we are even close to unraveling that mystery. I would love, of course, to be wrong.

The third member of the soda jerk triumvirate was Carol Sue Fielder, a wholesome and attractive brunette who went on to bigger and better things as an adult, achieving some regional notoriety, along with her husband, as gospel singers. I somehow talked Carol Sue into a date one time in high school and went home to make sure the family vehicle would be available for the much anticipated big event.

I had acquired my driver's license two years earlier, though not without incident. Being able to drive legally is one of the crowning achievements of adolescence, signaling the opening of all kinds of opportunities for independence and exploration. In those days, the license meant you might get to drive the family car on special occasions, in stark contrast to today where it is part of the rite of adolescent passage to have your own vehicle at age sixteen. Parents are now expected to pony up the cash to have a brand new car sitting in the front driveway coincidental with the granting of the license or, at the very latest, upon receiving the high school diploma.

Becoming legal at the wheel was not without anxiety and psychic pain. Studying for the written portion of the driving license examination, learning to parallel-park, and becoming familiar with the endless nuances of driving were sources of endless angst. In my own case, I went to the designated site to take the written examination and driving test, and things seemed to be going quite well in my estimation. My grade on the written portion was acceptable. I parallel parked proficiently enough, and seemed to be pretty much in control of my fate. At the end of fifteen or twenty minutes (though it seemed an eternity), the state trooper conducting the test announced that I had done pretty well overall, but he was not going to be able to give me a passing grade. It seems that speeding in a school zone is unacceptable and grounds for flunking an applicant. Unbeknownst to me, I had gone through a school zone at nine miles an hour over the posted speed limit of twenty. Twenty-nine in a twenty! I was mortified, but was able to take the exam a week or two later, passing all portions in flying colors. And you can bet your sweet bippy I was driving at the correct speed when I went through the school zone the second time!

Now I know some of you are curious about the term "sweet bippy"; there is no definitive answer and some say that it means whatever you want it to mean. Others say it has no meaning at all. In the opinion of the *Random House Historical Dictionary of American Slang, Volume* 1 published in 1994, it is most likely a jocular term for one's derriere popularized by comedians Dan Rowan and Dick Martin on their television comedy program, "Laugh In", which ran for well over one hundred episodes from 1968 to 1973. The following exchange between the two comedians may shed some light on how "sweet bippy" became a part of the daily lexicon for a period of time some forty years ago:

> Dick: May the Good Fairy sprinkle stardust on your bippy.
> Dan: Just a minute now. I've been meaning to ask you; what's a bippy?
> Dick: It's a baby bip.
> Dan: Then what's a bip?
> Dick: It's a big bippy.
> Dan: Are you sure?
> Dick: You bet your sweet bippy, I'm sure!

Heaven forbid that we bog down having so much fun, so let us return our attention to the storm clouds brewing with regard to the impending Carol Sue Fielder fiasco. In response to my request to reserve some time with the family car, my mother said that she had other plans for it that evening. This turn of events set me off in an incendiary adolescent snit, so I stomped out of the house, ripped off my nice, fairly new watch, and bounced it off the sidewalk at point blank range. Predictably, wheels and cogs and dials and hands went everywhere, dancing about and eventually settling serenely on the cement walkway. I marched into the house, called Carol Sue, and cancelled the date, not knowing that my last opportunity to win over the affections of such a handsome woman had passed. But one good thing came out of this teenage tempest in a teapot; I will go to my grave knowing in my heart of hearts that I taught my mother an important lesson about the consequences of saying no to me! Say no to me, I destroy my most treasured possessions! I guess I showed her!

When we weren't flirting with the girls, thinking of ways to mess with the mind of the man who owned William and Sally's was a major passion of ours. His name, strangely enough, was William. I am not sure I ever saw Sally and remember absolutely nothing about her, but William was a tall, cadaverous, bespectacled, Ichabod Crane-like fellow with an obsessive-compulsive anxiety disorder (though we had no familiarity with such official psychiatric nomenclature at that time). He also appeared to have an addiction to coke syrup, a demon he assuaged by surreptitiously nipping on the languid liquid off and on all day long.

We tortured William with petty tricks and hijinks, and his aversion to us was both visibly unmistakable and deservedly pronounced. One night when things were slow and not much was happening, my guys and I caught William at a busy time and while he was distracted, being the well-oiled machine that we were, we set a couple dozen of his displayed alarm clocks to go off at various times but within a few minutes of each other. We then camped outside the store to watch the results of our absolutely brilliant tomfoolery. A few minutes after our departure, the alarms started going at random times off all over the shop. It was a source of pure, unadulterated joy to watch William run from point A to point B, furiously trying to find and stifle the noisy clocks. It was this sort of never-ending nonsense that earned us his eternal enmity. Is it any wonder?

Another highlight, and an index of just how little there was to do in Dewey and how easily we could be entertained, was watching William close up his store each night. He would turn out the lights, carefully lock the door, shake it a few times, and walk to his car parked nearby. Within thirty to sixty seconds or thereabouts, he would return and give the door a good shaking to make sure it was locked. It was not unusual for him to shake the door three or four separate times before departing for home. It was also not unheard of for poor tortured William to return from his home after an hour or two to once again go through the obligatory door-shaking ritual.

As I said earlier, we knew nothing of Obsessive Compulsive Disorder (OCD) at that time, and I am not even sure it was an entry in the initial 1952 *Diagnostic and Statistical Manual*, the system developed by the American Psychiatric Association for classifying mental disorders. But in retrospect, our friendly drug store owner certainly displayed many of the salient identifying clinical signs.

Beyond the pool halls and the drug stores, our horizons were pretty limited. We often rode around in Ed Davis' green 1952 Buick which was modeled after a World War II Sherman tank and weighed approximately the same. With a bit of effort, we could cram four people in the front seat and shoe-spoon (shoe-horn?) four more in the back to make our nightly run up and down the main drag in Dewey to see who was out and about. If the excitement level in our village was low, we might mosey over to booming, bustling Bartlesville to see how things were going there, and maybe check up on our beloved football coach, "Tractor" Trent, at one of the all-night restaurants. We knew he would most likely be indulging his highly predictable evening cigarette-and-coffee ritual at the Tuxedo Café, just to the south of the Caney River Bridge.

Occasionally, we would put a .22 rifle or two in the Buick and go shoot rabbits along the country roads north of town. Two people might shoot sprawled across the front fenders while others would try to pick off a rabbit from a side window. None of us were really into killing animals, were not really very good at it, and pretty much abandoned the practice after a few uneventful forays. We were probably lucky no one got shot accidentally, what with several weapons and too many "marksmen" aboard (or riding a fender).

During the winter, when snow had accumulated from one of the occasional storms, we might make a run to the school playground, rev up the old Buick's powerful engine, and cut some figure eight's, slipping and sliding about as if we were riding a breath-taking amusement park ride. The playground was big enough to allow us to cut our didoes without too much danger to us or damage to the playground structures; we always tried to make sure the snow was deep enough to avoid harming the turf hibernating for the winter beneath the mostly pristine blanket of white.

From time to time, someone would have a date, but mostly we hung around in our group of six or eight guys, just acting silly and enjoying the male bonding. I would say that of all our assorted activities, male bonding was pretty much what we did best! I was to perfect that trait at the Terrace Drive-In in Texas City on off weekends during my undergraduate days or in the boarding house watching TV westerns with my friends at UNT in Denton some five years later while working on my master's degree.

Memorable High School Teachers

There were a number of teachers known for their valiant efforts to mold our minds and win our hearts, and I would be remiss in not mentioning them. Some were dear to our hearts and others memorable for other reasons. By and large, these people were inordinately humane and endured a lot from us as we were not very serious about school. We played pranks on the teachers almost daily, and spent most of our spare time trying to figure out how to laugh it up, do as little as possible, and generally flaunt the system.

Marvin Leon Brown. Mr. Brown was ruggedly handsome, a big man by 1950's standards, maybe 6'2" or 6'3" and a bit over two hundred pounds. He had a good-natured, self-deprecating manner, and was exceedingly gentle and kind to his students in the classroom and his players on the football field. Mr. Brown was our high school mathematics teacher, though in all honesty, he was not very good at it. He once told us that he had taken eighteen hours of college mathematics, and never made a grade above D. It showed.

Because Mr. Brown was mathematically-challenged, we often solved the practice problems in the textbook during class through a collaborative effort. Between Mr. Brown's lack of knowledge of his subject matter and my almost incalculable indifference to the task at hand, I graduated from high school with huge gaps in my mathematics skills. I should have anticipated this gap in my academic background would come back to haunt me in my freshman algebra class in college.

Mr. Brown was much admired among the boys for the way he dressed. He typically wore black or dark brown suits, often set off nicely by a red shirt and tastefully chosen tie. From time to time he would dispense with the tie but always cut a truly dashing swath through the school landscape with his imposing size and spiffy sartorial splendor. When my thoughts wander back to those, in some ways, halcyon days, it is hard to get past the image of Mr. Brown dressed resplendently in his dark suits and tastefully chosen red dress shirts.

I also have fond memories of his almost boundless patience, tolerance, forbearance, and sense of humor. He was always upbeat, positive, and happy, and we absolutely adored him. Like everyone else, however, even Marvin Leon Brown could have an occasional bad day. For reasons he never revealed, Mr. Brown came to class late one morning with an unusually surly, biting attitude, something we had pretty much never seen before. After some careful thought and quiet conferral, several of us took matters in our own devious hands to see if we could bring some joy to his day. "Ock" Davis carefully crafted a terse note and folded it with tender loving care. He then tapped Mike Rhea on the shoulder and forwarded the missive to him. Mike, in turn, forwarded it to Frank Ringo who sent it to Robert Bayne who finally handed it to me on the front row. In his infinite wisdom and awareness of our capacity for minor mayhem, Mr. Brown had assigned us seats in single file to cut down on chicanery and nonsense, and the system worked most of the time. But not always…

Clearly, by geographical proximity to the teacher's desk if nothing else, I became the designated spokesperson for our clandestine cabal. Thus, I said, "Coach, the guys asked me to hand you this note. They thought you ought to see it." Mr. Brown unfolded the note, read its contents, interlocked the fingers of his left and right hands, and put his hands on the desk with the knuckles up for just a few seconds. He then placed his forehead on his upturned knuckles, staying in that position for a few moments. He then raised his head, and with his usual crooked grin, he said, "You guys are impossible. You won't even let a guy have a bad day." The note initiated by Ed Davis and passed on by his henchmen read: "Mr. Brown. If you got any last night, smile!" The fact that he could see humor in the well-intended, admittedly goofy contents of our juvenile note says a lot about Mr. Brown.

At some point after graduation, my classmates designated/elected Frank Ringo to be the permanent class President, a role he still fulfills when occasions call for his leadership. In that role, he came up with the idea of getting Mr. Brown to serve as the keynote speaker at our 40th class reunion in 1996. In trying to make contact with him, we learned that our beloved mathematics mentor and erstwhile football coach had passed away earlier that same year. That news cast a pall over the proceedings as Marvin Leon Brown was dearly loved, greatly admired, and highly respected. He was truly a prince of a fellow.

The most enduring thing Marvin Brown taught me is the teacher can often transcend the subject matter in terms of long-term impact. That lesson has guided much of my teaching philosophy over the years and manifests itself in my enduring belief that anything that takes the teacher out of the classroom is misguided. I am not opposed to technology, but Marvin Brown and a long list of subsequent teachers and professors have only reinforced my belief about the importance of the teacher in the classroom. You can supplement good teaching with strategic use of technology but it is a disservice to the educational process if technology is allowed to completely replace the professor. Learning is best facilitated not by technology but through live, interactive, caring, and informed professors in the classroom. In the process of crafting this brief diatribe, I suppose I have tipped off the reader as to my feelings about much of what passes for on-line education!

Marvin Leon Brown was a gentle giant who was a role model for a bunch of adolescent males who were sometimes at loose ends with life, yours truly included. For me, he was a substitute father figure for the biological one I only saw three months a year in Texas. He truly was not much of a mathematics teacher, but he more than compensated for that deficiency by being a supremely fabulous human being.

Ralph Peck. Another interesting teacher, though not remotely as warm and fuzzy as Coach Brown, was Ralph Peck, our Future Farmers of America (FFA) sponsor and Agriculture teacher. The guys and I enrolled for his classes because they got us out of something more distasteful or onerous, namely the dreaded industrial arts or "shop" class. I think our avoidance of shop class was somehow grounded in the fear that we might, heaven forbid, actually learn something we could use for the rest of our lives, valuable skills such as carpentry or welding. But learning things that were useful took purposeful effort and squandered time better spent on our top priority, goofing off.

Mr. Peck was fortyish, thin, with salt and pepper gray hair and afflicted with a pronounced stutter. His speech defect opened up all kinds of avenues for beating up on poor Mr. Peck, or Mr. P-P-P-P-P-P-P-P-P-Peck as we always addressed him when we weren't using his alternate name, Ralph Pecker (pronounced P-P-P-P-P-P-P-P-Pecker), a rather obvious reference to things sexual, that enduring obsession of adolescent boys. P's gave Mr. Peck a lot of p-p-p-p-p-p-p-p-problems, and it is not a good thing when you introduce yourself the first day of class as Peck and it comes out as Mr. Ralph P-P-P-P-P-P-P-P-P-P-Peck.

Mr. Peck was actually a good teacher, and got us involved in some valuable learning experiences via our FFA projects. My project one year was to raise a shorthorn calf, and that went well enough. I eventually showed the calf at the county fair and sold it for about what I had in it, money-wise. I think most of us hoped to at least recoup our investment but the top animals in each category could earn some real money when they were auctioned off during the fair.

Clearly, we were small potatoes in comparison with the top prizes available in something like the Houston Livestock Show and Rodeo. I have no idea what a top steer or pen of broiler chicken was worth in Dewey, Oklahoma, in 1956, but the steer auction in Houston, Texas, 2010 brought in nearly $3,000,000 for those participants. A year later in Houston, a market pen of broiler chickens shown by thirteen-year-old Colton Russell from Beeville, Texas, was auctioned off to seven bidders for the tidy sum of $120,000. The world record in that category is $210,000 and was set in 2007.

The next year, I became a star member of the Dewey FFA seed judging team. Mr. Peck would take us to area competitions where we would look at plates full of seeds and make our best guess as to which, if planted, would produce the best crop. I actually was passably decent at judging seeds but if asked to assess a cow or a coop of chickens, the results were disastrous. You could have mixed a herd of cows with a diplodocus or a coop of chickens with a pterodactyl and I probably would not have known the difference. Judging animals was definitely not my thing!

My last two FFA projects involved raising pigs to show at the fat stock show in nearby Bartlesville. I have not been able to locate where the term "Fat Stock Show" originated but the terminology has changed in the last twenty years. For examples, livestock shows in two Texas cities, Fort Worth and Houston, have changed their names; Fort Worth now sports a Stock Show and Rodeo and the Houston soiree is now known as the Livestock Show and Rodeo. My hunch is that the word "fat" never really was descriptive of the animals in question and its demise was probably hastened by the political correctness movement that takes great umbrage at the word "fat."

I raised a pig my junior year and he developed normally enough for a while, but took a turn for the worse somewhere between the time of I bought him and the stock show. He started shrinking and developed a noticeable arch along his nose. The physical deterioration and the visibly different nose led a veterinarian to diagnose my pig as having Atrophic Rhinitis, a fatal disease in swine. Atrophic rhinitis was also called "Roman Nose", undoubtedly due to the wrinkling, twisting, and shortening that produced the distorted snout. The poor fellow lost his appetite, withered away to almost nothing, and probably suffered unnecessarily before being euthanized by a local veterinarian.

The next year, I raised a Hampshire piglet, and by stock show time he weighed about 250 pounds. I trained him to march and turn obediently to the touch of a knee or a small stick, and on show day, gave him a bath, glitzed him up with a coat of baby oil, marched him around the arena for a time, and sold him for a decent profit. Events such as this and my other FFA enterprises were actually very valuable as they gave me glimpses of what responsibility looked like, something I was not particularly attuned to at the time.

A funny thing took place one morning while my friends and I were feeding our animals. It seems that "Ock" Davis's pig surreptitiously deposited the digested contents of his breakfast into the cuff of "Ock's" rolled-up Levi's. Later in the day during Mrs. Cearley's English class, the tell-tale odor generated by the pig's peristaltic presentation led to its discovery in "Ock's" cuff. Of course, "Ock" received plenty of good-natured ribbing for quite a long time as a result of that petite piggy present.

The classroom part of FFA was okay but the upkeep and care of the animals was more fun. It was also outdoors, hands-on, and active, which I liked. Looking back, I suspect we got a lot more out of Mr. Ralph P-P-P-P-P-P-P-P-P-P-Peck's classes than we wanted to admit to at the time. All things considered, Ralph Peck was a good guy and an effective teacher.

Muriel Cearley. Another notable person was our English teacher, Muriel Cearley. Mrs. Cearley was divorced (I think), middle-aged (I know), a bit on the frumpy (and grumpy) side, and the mother of an overindulged, overprotected, somewhat overweight, geeky fourth-grader named Wilbur D. She taught English, sponsored the pep squad known as the Larriettes, and oversaw the production of the school plays. On the whole, she was a decent woman who meant well and I think for the most part did good things for her students. She was just one of many dedicated classroom teachers saddled with partial responsibility for reining in the misdirected energies of a bunch of guys who could care less about diagramming a sentence, memorizing some passages from Beowulf, or properly reciting our lines in the play *de jour*. We did what we had to do to keep her off our backs, but English class was pretty much a nuisance.

I had actually become pretty damn proficient at diagramming sentences thanks to Elva Myers, my aforementioned mentor in the seventh and eighth grades, so English was not all that arduous for me personally. I actually liked the subject a lot for deep down I knew I wanted to be a writer, and thought I was pretty good at it until I took my first university course where the professor politely, firmly, and continually pointed out my numerous shortcomings. It was not that I did not know English; I had just gotten sloppy at applying it properly, primarily due to disuse. It is my fondest hope that those of you reading this document will think my English has improved since that first college experience.

A classroom incident may capture the essence of our not-so-harmonious relationship with Mrs. Cearley. One afternoon during our junior year, Mike "Gonna" Rhea and I were supposedly working on an in-class project but were really talking and laughing about things unrelated to anything academic, probably sports or girls, our primary fascinations at the time. Mrs. Cearley got wind of our dalliance and departure from decorum and came over to see what it was that we thought was so hilarious. She said, "Mike Rhea. I know you are not taking your work seriously, and you are disturbing the rest of the class. You really need to tone it down a bit." In response, Mike said: "Actually, Mrs. Cearley, I was just telling Arnold some dirty Larriette jokes." Since Mrs. Cearley was the faculty sponsor of the Lariettes, Mike's mirthful meanderings hit a sore spot. In our wildest imagination, we could have never anticipated Mrs. Cearley's response to Mike's silliness.

Mrs. Cearley, perhaps middle-aged crazy and most likely menopausal, started hitting Mike on his upper arms and shoulders with her not particularly imposing fists; Mrs. Cearley was no Marvin Brown, so thank goodness for small favors! After pummeling Mike for a moment, she broke into tears, and blurted out, "I hate you, Mike Rhea. I hate you." I know deep down she did not mean those words, but Mike certainly received a lot of kudos from the guys for provoking such an outburst on her part. Today, Mrs. Cearley would almost certainly be removed from her teaching position and led blindfolded to be stoned on the playground, hanged in the gymnasium, or eviscerated at a PTA meeting for such unprofessional behavior.

That same year, Mrs. Cearley directed the junior class play and I got to play the role of "Flint Buckner", a dark, brooding, badass character straight out of the wild, wild west. My part was relatively minor, but I cherished the role of getting to play the bad guy in black. I sometimes wish I had gotten more serious about being a thespian as I really liked my brief foray into acting. However, in the code of the west that operated with us self-appointed macho guys, plays were really for sissies, pansies, and others who are thought in some quarters to be of the limp-wristed persuasion, and taking such fluff too seriously was just a touch too unmanly. At least I was a bad guy in that play which bought me a measure of forgiveness from the guys for going temporarily thespian.

When there was a lull at play practice and things were quiet, certain members of the cast plotted ways to torture Wilbur D. Abusing Wilbur D. came easy because he was such a great target, overweight, whiny, and most important, available. Racism, ethnocentrism, and bullying are based in part on the availability of a vulnerable and physically identifiable target. Wilbur D. fit the bill perfectly. Looking back in retrospect, we should all apologize for bullying poor Wilbur D., but it was fun at the time.

Stupid adolescent tricks are not new and seldom terribly inventive, but two that we directed at Mrs. Cearley were pretty hot stuff in our estimation. One night we "broke" into the school, wandered about, and decided that it would really be cool to engage in group urination using Mrs. Cearley's classroom trash basket. The next day, we waited eagerly to see her obvious revulsion; we knew it would be an absolutely exhilarating event to behold. And it was!

A second prank involved filching an unused kotex napkin from a personal products dispensing machine in the building and suspending it from a string about ten feet above Mrs. Cearley's desk. Students smiled, smirked, and guffawed for a couple of class periods before she finally looked up and figured out what it was that was evoking so much interest. She was duly offended, and naturally the miscreant Mike Rhea was grilled thoroughly as a "person of interest". After much intense interrogation, Mike was subsequently released even though we knew for certain he was guilty as charged. The other perpetrators were never brought to trial and went unpunished for their juvenile caper.

Jack "High Pockets" Hay. Another teacher, though less memorable than Marvin Leon Brown, Ralph P-P-P-P-P-P-P-P-P-Peck, and Muriel Cearley, was not really a teacher at all. He was the superintendent of schools and his name was Jack Hay. Mr. Hay was middle-aged, graying, fairly tall and slim, a bit foppish, nerdy to the nth degree, and best known among the student body, as noted earlier, for wearing his pants tightly cinched several inches above his navel. He was quickly dubbed "High Pockets" Hay by some observant soul with a flair for alliteration. "High Pockets" taught us history for a semester but the demands of being a school superintendent made it difficult for him to show up for class on anything approximating a regular basis. We hardly ever saw "High Pockets" and learned little history from an endless succession of substitute teachers.

Miss/Mrs. Fry. Miss or Mrs. Fry (Yvonne, I think) was not really one of my teachers. Rather, I got to know her briefly in her role as study hall supervisor when I was in junior high school. We students were allowed one period a day to study for our academic courses during the school day, and the teachers mutually shared the responsibility for supervising that activity.

Miss Fry is memorable because of a personal idiosyncrasy that was the topic of considerable conversation among my friends (and ultimately among the school administrators, so it seems). Miss Fry was maybe in her late thirties or early forties, nice-looking and well-dressed, a bit taller than average, and something of a mystery to us naïve, inexperienced guys. Miss Fry was known to prowl around the study hall, looking for what I thought at first were slackers not doing their homework. I soon learned what she was really looking for were unwitting victims for her affections, however misplaced.

On several occasions, I was the designated "victim" of these displays of affection. Miss Fry would make her way over to the table where I was "studying" and put her arms around my neck. She would then place her lovely head next to mine and wiggle her tongue strategically around the rim of my ear. Her breathing would become heavy and rhythmic as she ran her tongue around and around in my ear, slowly and erotically. I suppose sexual excitement would be an expected response to her advances, but I think I was mostly confused and embarrassed. I had no idea how to respond to such behavior from a mature adult woman whose experience I knew for certain had to have far outstripped mine. Come to think of it, if she had any experience at all, she had me beat hands down.

Miss Fry vanished in the middle of the school year, and rumors, however apocryphal, had it that she had gone beyond heavy breathing and the kissing of ears to more advanced acts with one or more or the older students in an out-of-the-way cloakroom. Several names, Gary Schooler and Gilbert Edmiston among them, came up as persons of interest in relation to the supposed cloakroom caper. Neither the caper(s) nor the names of students were ever officially confirmed, but Miss Fry suddenly disappeared without warning or fanfare, which was cause for some interesting speculation on our part.

Postmortem on our Teachers. Capable, conscientious, and caring teachers have an immeasurable impact on the lives of young people, and it is an indictment of both me and perhaps to a lesser extent the teaching profession that I can remember so few of my teachers after all these years. I suppose most of them really were forgettable and had minimal impact on learning or the development of a sense of "I" and a viable philosophy of life. In all fairness, however, it is impossible to put a price tag on the impact teachers such as Ida Allen, Elva Myers, and Ralph Peck, and coaches like Carl Davidson, H. L. (Goob) Arnold, Kester "Tractor" Trent, Edd Hill, and L. E. "Hooter" Brewer have made on my life. I love each of them dearly to this day!

In some way or another, I owe each and every one of these valiant people an enormous debt of gratitude for believing in me and helping me through school, particularly during those turbulent, troubled and trying teenage years. In almost every case, these people unselfishly gave a lot more to me than I gave back, and for their kindness I am at once both grateful and apologetic. They cared, forgave my foibles, misdeeds and idiosyncrasies, and convinced me there was a glimmering of potential buried beneath all the mental and emotional debris. I certainly had assiduously done my best to hide my native ability and work ethic from them (and me). The worst part is that most if not all of these mentors are now deceased. The kind words and the beautiful flowers should have been forthcoming while they could still hear the compliments and smell the roses. That omission is a source of considerable sadness for me. Perhaps the famous physician, philosopher, and clergyman, Albert Schweitzer, said it best: "When I look back upon my early days I am stirred by the thought of the number of people whom I have to thank for what they gave me or what they were to me. At the same time, I am haunted by an oppressive consciousness of the little gratitude I really showed them while I was young. How many of them have said farewell to life without having made clear to them what it meant to me to receive from them so much kindness or so much care! Many a time have I, with a feeling of shame, said quietly to myself over a grave the words which my mouth ought to have spoken to the departed, while he was still in the flesh." So elegantly stated, Dr. Schweitzer!

As partial repayment for the glaring and unforgivable omissions with regard to my own mentors, I have written letters of appreciation to several of my children's teachers over the years when I felt they had measured up to their Dewey predecessors. The fact that these letters on more than one occasion brought tears to the eyes of the readers tells me teachers richly deserve and greatly appreciate a pat on the back. I think Ida, Elva, Marvin, and Ralph P-P-P-P-P-P-P-P-P-Peck would approve of my feeble but well-intentioned attempts at redemption!

Racial Integration, "Hooter", Two-a-Days, and Our Final Season of Football

There were several issues, one societal and three others football-related, that exerted a significant impact as we headed into our senior year and final season of football. One most important event with both local and societal implications was the racial integration of public schools in the state of Oklahoma in 1955. Secondly, a new assistant coach had been hired by "Tractor" Trent and he harbored some revolutionary ideas about how to run a football program. We were soon to reap the benefits of his insights, though we were not aware of it at the time. A third issue had to do with surviving the dreaded two-a-days, the bane of all football players. Finally, a most successful regular season was capped off as the Bulldoggers went two rounds deep in the state playoffs, highlighting our final foray into football.

Racial Integration Comes to Oklahoma

Prior to 1955, there were separate schools for blacks and whites in Dewey and Bartlesville. Blacks in the two cities attended Douglass High School in Bartlesville, named for the famous nineteenth century abolitionist, orator, writer, and civil rights advocate, Frederick Douglass (circa 1818-1895). The Douglass Dragons, as they were known, never played against the white schools in the area, and we knew virtually nothing about them. Even the newspaper coverage of their accomplishments was minimal.

One of the stipulations of the integration policy put in place in 1955 afforded black students and athletes from the ninth grade on up the freedom to finish high school at a school of their choice. Most chose to stay at Douglass High until the last class graduated a few years later, at which time the school was to be permanently closed. Others elected to attend either the white high school in Bartlesville or ours in Dewey, and we inherited three football players as a result. Our new teammates, all juniors by grade in school, were Robert Mundine, his brother Vastine, and Kenneth Daniels. Of the three "recruits", Daniels turned out to be by far the best player. The Mundines were tall and slim and modestly talented whereas Daniels was short, agile, muscular, and, as we were to find out later, a dynamic player.

"Tractor" initially underestimated how valuable the new guy was going to be to our team, but it did not take long for Daniels to win over his teammates. At one of the practices during two-a-days, "Tractor" asked Daniels to take a turn at tailback, the same position I played. I instantly (and rightfully) viewed Daniels as a threat to my position and playing time, but "Tractor" remained unconvinced, at least in the beginning.

While the scrimmage was going on and Daniels was trying to assert himself, "Tractor" came up to me in his pigeon-toed shuffle, put a friendly arm around my shoulders, and asked: "What do you think of the nigger, Lee?" "Tractor" could not say LeUnes without ejecting his dentures, so he always called me "Lee." Actually my name came out more like "Wee" because he also had difficulties pronouncing his L's. To his query about Daniels, I replied, "Coach, he looks pretty good to me. I think he is a real player." In response to my assessment of Daniels, "Tractor" said, "I am not sure you are right but we will keep the nigger around for laughs."

That "nigger" kid went on to share playing time with me that season, and made second team all-state at the end of the following season. Not bad for a "nigger" who was kept around "for laughs!" In fairness to "Tractor" Trent, such racist sentiments and references were commonplace during that time and not necessarily borne of virulent racism. It was, simply put, the way things were in 1955 in Oklahoma, the south, and in reality, the northern US, though Yankees liked to smugly deny their own brand of often virulent racism.

It eventually dawned on "Tractor" that he had a real talent in Kenneth Daniels. Though he was short, maybe 5'5" and weighed around 160, Daniels was muscular, strong, shifty, agile, and elusive. He was also blessed with unusually large hands that enabled him to become a passably proficient thrower out of the single wing formation "Tractor" had installed when he took over the coaching reins in Dewey.

"Tractor" soon figured out he had a tailback "controversy" on his hands, and his solution to the problem was to play Daniels and yours truly in alternating quarters during each game. I was not especially pleased with that arrangement and I suspect Daniels was not either, but the strategy kept peace and harmony in the football family. From my perspective, it was not like I was being benched my senior year in favor of an inferior player or a player with politically favored parents as was sometimes the case with children of Phillips 66 employees. If anything, Daniels had absolutely no political clout, given his race and low socioeconomic status. But I thought we made a nice tandem, and there was little if any drop off in talent when either of us was on the field. We each had our own talents, mine being speed and his strength and agility, but he beat me badly in the dedication domain. Daniels was a heck of a talent, plus football was more important to him than it was to me.

After breaking the neck of the guy in Caney as a sophomore, getting my own urinary system scrambled my junior year, and being emotionally consumed by the breakup of my adolescent romance my senior year, football for me had lost most of its fascination and had become quite secondary in importance. By the Picher game in the quarterfinals of the state playoffs, I was pretty much reduced to spectator status, though I did show occasional flashes of the old "brilliance" from time to time when re-inserted into the lineup. Overall, I had a great sophomore year, one of all-state proportions in the minds of some, a good junior year prior to my season-ending injury, and an absolutely non-descript, washout, blah senior year; I did not go out with a bang, but with a whimper. But the second it was over, it was over for me. I never once considered playing football again except for a nano-second my sophomore year in college, which will be discussed later in this humble document.

Lester E. "Hooter" Brewer. One of the best things that ever happened to me, a true life-altering or transformative event, was the hiring of L. E. "Hooter" Brewer as assistant football coach. "Hooter" was actually the only assistant, so he and "Tractor" constituted the entire coaching staff. Just think of the high schools today, particularly the large ones where the head coach often also serves as the Athletic Director, is paid over $100,000 annually, and has no teaching responsibilities. His staff may include an offensive coordinator, a defensive coordinator, and six or seven position coaches. I do not think anyone could envision such an explosion of coaching positions over the years. We were thankful just to have "Hooter" out there, serving as a buffer between us and old-school "Tractor."

"Hooter", like the aforementioned Marvin Brown, was a graduate of Central State College (now the University of Central Oklahoma) in Edmond, a suburb of Oklahoma City, where he was a stellar running back in football and a top sprinter in track. "Hooter" grew up in Pauls Valley, about an hour south of Oklahoma City, and had been quite a star athlete there. Among his achievements in track was running the hundred-yard dash in 9.6 seconds which was three-tenths of a second off the world record in the 1950's. That world record was set by American sprinter Mel Patton in 1948 and eventually lowered to 9.1 seconds in 1964 by "Bullet Bob" Hayes, sprinter *par excellence* and Hall of Fame wide receiver with the Dallas Cowboys.

In "Hooter's" day, and mine as well, we ran one hundred yards rather than meters which is the norm today. One hundred yards is roughly equivalent to 109 meters, and to get an estimate of equivalency across the two events, one would add .9 seconds to a time in the hundred yard dash. Thus, a time of 9.5 seconds in the 100-yard race would translate to 10.4 seconds in the 100-meter event. Of course, track and field fans of today are familiar with the now-retired Jamaican sprinter, Usain "Lightning" Bolt, who obliterated those seemingly modest times of Patton and Hayes. Bolt's world record of 9.58 seconds in the hundred-meter dash translates to 8.68 seconds in terms of yards, an almost unfathomable accomplishment.

In his day, "Hooter" was right up there with the best. The athletic pedigree of their coaches is very important to high school boys, and knowing "Tractor" had been a standout player at Oklahoma A&M and "Hooter" a stellar running back and national class sprinter at Central State held a lot of sway with us.

In a stroke of football genius, "Hooter" somehow convinced "Tractor" to take a different approach to practice our senior year, and I give him much of the credit for our success that season. How in the world he was able to convince old-school, hard-ass, intractable "Tractor" to go easy on us at practice is still a source of amazement to me, but he somehow sold his plan. I would have loved to have been the proverbial fly on the wall during the deliberations that led "Tractor" to acquiesce.

It is obvious that a football team in a small town with an inherently limited roster can ill afford injuries. In that regard, we lost most of our starters for one game or more due to practice-related injuries my junior year, a fatal blow to the hopes of almost any team, but certainly to one with limited talent and a small roster. "Hooter" was able to convince "Tractor" to move away from the time-honored notion that grueling practices (1) fostered an environment conducive to honing their skills and maximizing their talents, and (2) whetted their appetites for committing mayhem on Friday night. Fortunately, "Hooter" did not believe that long, grueling practices accomplished either of the two goals despite their time-honored reverential status among football coaches. The conventional wisdom was that if a grueling two-hour practice is good then an even more arduous four-hour practice must be twice as good. "Tractor" dragged us through many drudgery-laden practices our junior year, and we had the fatigue-induced injuries to prove it.

Thanks to "Hooter's" genius as both salesman and football philosopher, we never held a full-scale scrimmage after two-a-days except on one or two occasions where "Tractor" thought putting on the pads and knocking each other about would be just punishment for past or anticipated sins. All practices were brief, maybe ninety minutes, and the uniform of the day was shoes, helmets, shoulder pads, and shorts. Emphasis throughout was on timing and conditioning, and drudgery became a distant memory. Practices were almost always fun, and it was nice to actually look forward to football practice. Also, practice-related injuries were non-existent, and we were fortunate enough not to incur any game-related injuries that entire season either.

Another remarkable thing that transpired was disconfirmation of the coaching mantra, "If you don't hit in practice on Tuesday, you won't hit in the game on Friday." If I have heard that coaching shibboleth once, I have heard it a thousand times, and never once believed it to be true. No one to my knowledge had ever tried an alternate approach to see what would happen, but "Hooter" dared to be different! He convinced "Tractor" to put the hypothesis to a season-long test and "Hooter" won! We scored lots of points and held the opposition in most cases to none. It seemed to me that if the opponents are not scoring, there must be some substantial hitting taking place during Friday games.

More recently, John Gagliardi was an immensely successful coach who seemingly borrowed a page from "Hooter's" playbook, or vice versa, though it is actually quite unlikely the two ever met or heard of each other. I do wonder in retrospect if "Hooter" had somehow learned of Gagliardi and his revolutionary approach to coaching by the time he got to Dewey in 1955. Given that Gagliardi was just beginning his hugely successful run in the early 1950's, it seems possible though unlikely that word of Gagliardi's coaching success had spread from Minnesota as far south as Oklahoma.

Gagliardi was the long-time coach of perennial Division III powerhouse, St. John's University, in Minnesota. Now well past his eightieth year and finally in retirement, Gagliardi coached for fifty-seven years. His teams won 565 games, five national championships, ten national runners-up trophies, and twenty-seven conference championships. The Gagliardi Trophy awarded each year to the top Division III football player bears his name, and was begun in his honor in 1993. Also, Gagliardi was inducted into the College Football Hall of Fame in 2005.

One unique features of Gagliardi's coaching philosophy (known as "Coaching by No's") is he asked to be called John by his players; no "Coach" or "Mr. Gagliardi", just John. Another unusual thing is that you never saw a tackling dummy or blocking sled on his practice field. No one wore pads, and seldom did a practice ever last more than ninety minutes. Lifting weights was not required or even encouraged, and no scholarships were offered at St. John's consistent with the policy of all Division III athletic programs. Coach Gagliardi (John) had a disdain for the coaching mentality which says you live and breathe football in eighty-hour per week chunks as is the wont of so many members of that profession. He, like "Hooter", knew that football could be taught in ways that did away with most of the drudgery, thus returning fun to the game. Fun is what high school and college football should be about anyway. I know! I know! I know! I am being a Pollyanna, thinking that the real purpose of football is to have fun. Let me cling to my childish notions.

I am convinced the philosophy espoused by these two revolutionaries, John Gagliardi and L. E. "Hooter" Brewer, would work at any level, but its tenets run counter to the "no pain, no gain", "If players don't hit in practice, they won't hit in the game" zeitgeist of big-time football. Thus, there are probably not many Gagliardi/Brewer disciples among their tradition-bound peers in the coaching fraternity, though it does seem there is a gradual shift taking place in coaching philosophy at the big-time level. Coaches are figuring out that players who are injured in drudgery practices and thus standing beside them on the sidelines during actual games do them little good when it comes to the Holy Grail of wins and losses.

Gagliardi said it was never his intent to convert other coaches to his ways of thinking, preferring instead to do things his way and carve his niche at St. John's. Though "John" was not interested in winning converts, I count myself as a member of that small fraternity of true believers. "Coaching by no's actually works! I am thrilled that I got to see and experience "Hooter" Brewer's version of John Gagliardi's philosophy up close and personal; "Hooter" may well have been my first fraternity big brother!

The Dreaded "Two-a-Days." I have several enduring memories of my five football seasons, not the least of which is the phenomenon known throughout football at all levels as "two-a-days." "Two-a-days" refers to the two-week period prior to the start of the season where teams work out twice a day. In order to beat the August heat in Oklahoma, the first practice was held early in the morning, maybe 0700 or 0800 hours. In reality, there was no way to beat the heat for either workout but particularly number two, for no matter what time the practice was held, the temperature hovered around one hundred degrees.

There is nothing like "two-a-days" anywhere in athletics. The mere mention of those words will cause ex-football players at all levels from high school through professional to break into a cold sweat. It does not matter how long the player has been away from the sport, the mere mention of "two-a-days" generates feelings of dread. "Two-a-days" means being so sore for ten days you can hardly move. "Two-a-days" means suffering through morning practice, showering and dressing, throwing your tired, beaten body down in the shade outside the gym, and waiting there as your muscles lock up from fatigue and lactate accumulation until the second practice of the day comes around. "Two-a-days" means dragging yourself up for that second practice, entering the stinking dressing room to reluctantly put on pads, jerseys, and pants that are still cold and sweaty from the morning workout. "Two-a-days" also means wearing filthy, foul-smelling gear for several weeks, at least in small schools where laundry budgets and capabilities were limited. You might end up wearing the same jersey for several days or even a week without it being laundered. "Two-a-days" means that after a few practices, your pants, jersey, and pads are streaked with random, rainbow-colored sweat lines. "Two-a-days" means there is no need to hang your gear up in the locker; the uniform stands on its own. If one is remotely imaginative (or delusional), depending on one's perspective, the dirty, stiff uniform stands alone, faintly reminiscent of gladiatorial armor worn by the early Romans prior to doing combat in the Coliseum. "Two-a-days" means that the perspiration generated by those long, hot, arduous workouts in hundred-degree heat seeps irretrievably into your shoulder and hip pads, rendering them both odoriferous and cold upon first contact prior to practice. It is hard to describe the feeling generated when that cold, stinking uniform makes first contact with one's warm skin. There is simply not sufficient time for anything to dry in your dark, dank locker. "Two-a-days" means teammates hurt all over, and the smell of liniment is both pervasive and offensive. Bandages, the ever-present aroma of Ben Gay, ankle wraps, and analgesic balm are the order of the day, ever-present reminders of the frailty of bones, joints, and skin. The whirlpool works overtime, trying to wash away strains, sprains, and muscle pulls.

In our day, there was no such thing as a trainer, so taking care of injuries was pretty much an individual thing. If you needed a bandage, you bandaged the injury yourself. If you thought a whirlpool treatment might help, you turned on the water and jumped in. If you were seriously hurt, you pleaded your case with the coaches, though most of our players fully endorsed the theory that if there were no bones sticking through the flesh, you must not be hurt. No blood, no foul!

"Two-a-days" means that coaches roam the locker rooms looking for the weak, hoping beyond hope to find a weakling, sissy, or a "girl" to use as an example for the rest of the team. Any suggestion that one was weak or slightly effeminate and girlish would give the coaches license to heap all kinds of indignities on the guilty party or parties, all in the name of inspiring the other, more masculine, testosterone-driven types to maim and kill their opponents.

Speaking of pansies and wimps, one of the things we had learned during "Tractor's" first two years, words of wisdom we knew we could count on, eternal verities, if you will, was his favorite half-time speech. He used it during virtually every game, no matter the circumstance or score, and we knew it was coming early on in his half-time diatribe just as surely as the sun was going to rise in the east the next morning. We could be up 30-0 or down 7-6 and the litany remained pretty much the same. His opening words at halftime went something like this, "You guys are a bunch of quitters. On top of that, you are sissies. In fact, you're a bunch of pansy-asses. There's no passion, no character, no toughness, no nothing. It makes me sick to have to come in this dressing room and look at you girls." We knew from experience that "Tractor" was building up to the ultimate humiliation which he invoked as a plea to commit mayhem in the name of good old Dewey High: "You guys have to squat to pee." How much more humiliating can it get than that? "Tractor" thought likening us to females who had to squat to pee would jumpstart our testosterone-driven, football-loving bodies and pea-sized brains into a feverish, fanatical frenzy. If there ever was a call to commit mayhem on the football field, "Tractor" had found it! Cheer, cheer for old Dewey High!!

"Two-a-days" meant that water was taboo and not permitted anywhere near the practice field. Games, yes, but practice, absolutely not! Occasionally, "Tractor" would use water or orange slices as motivational ploys, but getting to drink water during practice was a two- or three-times-a-season event at best. I remember a couple of practices where, as usual, no water was available but we were allowed to run nearly a quarter of a mile during a practice break to the nearby basketball gymnasium to drink from a water hose. The run was equivalent to four times the length of a football field, over and back, and the time allowed was short, so it seldom seemed worth the effort to seek hydration. Looking back, I am flabbergasted that coaches of that era did not, with their disdain for hydration during practices, kill more young men than they did.

"Two-a-days" in mid-August meant practicing in temperatures of one hundred, 105, or even 110 degrees. To describe the conditions as oppressive does an injustice to the word. In what can only be called a grandstand or "hot dog" move, I practiced one entire season in a black jersey even though the school colors were red and white. I think I was trying to promote the "bad guy in black image", sort of an early precursor of the Oakland Raiders in their heyday. That black jersey, despite its macho appeal, was the only one of its kind in stock. And it had a huge downside in that it soaked up those hot August sun rays like a sponge. Thus, I suffered somewhat more than I might have had I chosen a lighter colored jersey. I paid a sweaty and richly deserved price for my ill-chosen grandstanding.

The 1955 Starting Lineup. Apart from the trials and tribulations of "two-a-days", the final year of high school football was memorable for a number of other reasons. One was we lived up to our Principal Ova Farrow's prediction made five years earlier about the athletic potential of the class of 1956. We were ranked second in the state in our classification for most of the year, and won the majority of our games by outlandish margins. Some of the most memorable people I have ever met played on that team, guys whose memories are still with me every day. At least six of the twelve starters have passed through the golden gates of that vast gridiron in the great beyond, and hardly a day passes when I do not think of one or more of them.

We ran a popular formation of the day, the Single Wing, with an unbalanced line to the right (four players on the right side of the center and two to his left). The starting lineup was made up of all seniors save Jerry Jones (not THE Jerry Jones of Dallas Cowboy fame!) and Kenneth Daniels, and read like an Anglo Who's Who, though four or five had some degree of Native American ancestry. Jimmy Dick Baker, Lloyd Dunn, Bobby Thomason, Robert Bayne, Raymond Gray (Center), Ed Davis, and David Miller made up the offensive line from end to end. The backfield was composed of Glenn Wright at blocking back, Jerry Jones at wingback, Floyd Brown at fullback. Kenneth Daniels and yours truly shared the featured tailback position. All things considered, those twelve names are about as vanilla as they get. How did someone with a Greek name such as LeUnes get in that mix?

Almost everyone played both ways and thus generally played the entire game. Ten of the eleven starters on offense also played on the defensive side of the ball. The only exception was Johnny Gutierrez who would come in to play safety in lieu of Daniels or me. "Tractor" viewed Johnny Gutierrez as a more than adequate replacement for either of us. Also, he wanted to protect his two tailbacks and lower the risk of either of us getting injured. As the post-season unfolded, our woeful lack of depth played a big role in the heartbreaking loss to Picher in the second round of the state playoffs to be discussed shortly.

Right end. My best friend starting in the second or third grade and continuing through maybe the fifth or sixth grade was a guy named Jimmy Dick Baker. As is the case with most childhood friendships, it had a lot to do with neighborhood geography. Jimmy Dick lived maybe a half mile down Creek Street on the same side of the tree-lined street as me, and we visited back and forth a lot as small boys. You could get to his house by biking or by walking the alley from my house to his. The biggest impediment to getting to his house by bicycle was his next door neighbor's seemingly vicious bulldog. I cannot count the number of times I went to Jimmy Dick's along the east side of the street to avoid the Creek Street version of the Hound of the Baskervilles who was always lurking menacingly on the west side. Occasionally, I would push the risk-taking envelope, generating as much speed as I could, put my feet up on the handlebars, and sail by the unsuspecting mutt before he could react and rip off one of my legs. In what turned out to be a fortuitous turn of events, the bulldog actually caught up with me one day and clamped down on my calf. He had no teeth! He had no frigging teeth! From that moment on, I declared open season on the offensive little bastard. I taunted and terrorized that miserable mutt every way I could short of animal cruelty as a payback for all the grief he had caused me.

As for the alley, I often went on foot to Jimmy Dick's via that route. I seldom went barefoot, which made me a real anomaly among country kids in in the 1950's. I just did not like going without shoes. On one of the rare days when I did eschew shoes, I stepped on a nail protruding from an old two-by-four lying about in the alley. When I told my mother about what had happened, she did the good parent thing and took me down to Dr. Van Zandt's office for the treatment of choice for stepping on rusty nails, the always enjoyable tetanus shot.

Jimmy Dick and I spent many a winter afternoon for a year or two playing a table football game his parents had given him to occupy his time and energy when it was too cold or rainy to go outside and play. The game was played on a lighted reflective surface, and one player would first superimpose an offensive play and the other player would counter with an overlay designed to throttle the offensive effort. It is hard to describe without seeing or doing it, but the two of us whiled away many a cold afternoon with that game, imagining ourselves to be the next Knute Rockne of

Notre Dame fame or his legendary successor in coaching, Oklahoma University's Charles "Bud" Wilkinson.

Jimmy Dick's father, Jesse, was known to be a heavy drinker and hell-raiser on occasion, and those unenviable traits caused some family problems of which I was only minimally aware, given my youthful unfamiliarity with marital matters. Jimmy Dick had a brother named Joe who we largely ignored, mostly because he was quite a bit younger than the two of us. Today, Joe Baker is a noted Native American artist last known to reside in that famous New Mexico artist colony, Santa Fe. I have tried without success to contact him on several occasions as I would like to renew old acquaintances and visit with him about his wonderful career as a talented artist. Given my monumental talent deficiencies in the art department, I am always in awe of those with a flair for it. In any case, my suspicion is that Joe, like so many people who grow up hardscrabble in small towns and have gone on to perform on a larger stage, would rather not be reminded of those not-so-halcyon days. Joe's fascination with Native American art no doubt grew out of the fact that he and Jimmy Dick were half Lenni Lenape Delaware Indians. Their dad, Jesse, was a full-blood Delaware.

Jimmy Dick had a real nose for fighting and occasionally got in some scrapes at school, but was able to keep his nascent antisocial tendencies sufficiently in check long enough to play football and ultimately graduate from high school. He joined the Army shortly after graduation and, according to reports that filtered back to Dewey later on, was named the Soldier of the Quarter in his command in Hawaii the same month he was arrested for robbing a bank. He supposedly was dishonorably discharged from the Army for that offense after serving time in a military prison. In retrospect, it is interesting to note that the school yearbook prophecy for Jimmy Dick read: "Jim Baker is now doing twenty years for burning the school house down."

The last time I saw the inimitable Mr. Baker was when he made an unanticipated and largely unwanted appearance at our thirtieth class reunion. He showed up at the reunion hotel in an advanced state of inebriation that had turned his mood quite foul. Needless to say, his dark, confrontational demeanor fueled by alcohol was the source of consternation, ultimately causing several female classmates to complain he was scaring them. Jimmy Dick was eventually ushered off the site by security people before any real trouble broke out.

Prior to his unceremonious expulsion from the premises, several of my female friends, for reasons unbeknownst, chose me to serve as their protector. Though they may not have been aware of it, I was an extremely poor choice for that role, and frankly was not looking forward to taking on a drunk and surly Jimmy Dick Baker. A smallish, sober coward is seldom a good match for a big, mean, surly drunk! My friendship with Jimmy Dick Baker never flourished beyond elementary school and completely disappeared before our high school days were over. We played football together but seldom ran in the same circles otherwise.

Strong tackle. Lloyd Dunn manned this position. Somewhere along the line, perhaps late in high school, Lloyd fell in love with Dorothy Sue Butts, the daughter of the First Christian Church minister, the Right Reverend Eugene Earl Butts. This fortuitous event (for him, at least) led Lloyd to also enter the calling. He and Dorothy Sue eventually married and raised five children before she died of cancer just before our twenty-fifth class reunion in 1981. Lloyd later remarried and forsook his ministerial calling in favor of building homes and churches. Lloyd had a good run of popularity in high school, once being elected to the class presidency. However, he had a reputation as a bully and that trait did not serve him well with his constituency. He asked my wife at the twenty-fifth why so many of his classmates were standoffish or unfriendly. She, or course, had no way of knowing the answer so she asked me what I thought. I told her that Lloyd was perceived in high school to be an opportunistic high-roller and a bully, a sanctimonious one at that, and apparently not much had transpired in the intervening twenty-five years to alter that perception among some of his classmates. The "high-roller" image was given additional life at the reunion when Lloyd showed up in a rented Lincoln Continental with our lovely classmate, Shirley Adams Viles, on his arm. His grand entry was perceived widely among his peers as a grandstand move by a life-long grandstander!

Weak tackle. Bobby Thomason had a physique that could only be achieved these days with heavy duty weightlifting or the use of performance-enhancing steroid compounds, or both. In our high school days, steroids and weights were both pretty much unknown, thought there were rumbling to the effect that the Russians were using banned substances for the first time in the 1956 Olympics in Melbourne, Australia. Needless to say, we were light years away geographically and pharmaceutically from Melbourne. And the first time I ever saw a set of weights was during the Christmas holidays my senior year when Jerry Miller's sister, Carolyn, briefly dated a cadet from the United States Military Academy, otherwise known as West Point. While visiting Dewey over Christmas, the cadet opened up the trunk of his car to show off a small set of weights. None of us had ever seen such a thing and they were a source of genuine wonderment! So was the cadet who, given our provincial perspective on the world, might as well been from Mars. Our imaginations were simply not robust enough to imagine a scenario whereby a West Pointer could be spotted in rural Oklahoma!

Bobby got his enormous muscles by working every morning before school at a slaughterhouse, throwing around animal carcasses weighing more than he did. Thankfully, Bobby had an even disposition except on the football field where he was an absolute monster. He married a Dewey girl, Virginia Murguia, and they celebrated their fiftieth anniversary in 2008. Bobby retired from the local gas company as well as the volunteer fire department, and lived in Dewey at last report. I visited with him briefly at the fiftieth class reunion in 2006 and he looked like he could still toss around a heavy animal carcass or manhandle a wimpy running back.

Right guard. Robert Bayne held down this position, and did it well despite his lack of size, speed, and athleticism. My friendship with Robert Bayne is difficult to explain, with Robert much more close to Frank Ringo than me. We were often thrown together socially during our elementary and high school days because of our mutual association with Ringo and others, but seldom did Robert and I actually pal around together as a duo.

Robert was not a particularly imposing physical specimen. Sopping wet, Robert spread a scant 165 pounds over his 5'11" frame, and in addition to being somewhat slight he was slow and not especially athletic either. A few years ago, Robert and Ringo came to College Station along with their wives, Joan and Ernavay, to visit and tour the George Bush Library. I suspect that Robert's politics were similar in sentiment to those of our forty-first President, though we never discussed that issue.

During the course of our visit in College Station, I introduced my then twelve-year old son, Lyndon, to Ringo and Bayne. When the two of them departed for Ringo's home in Houston, Lyndon expressed utter amazement that these two fellows could have possibly ever cleared a path for me on the football field. He was not aware that Ringo did not play football but I had to agree that even with the passage of fifty-five years, it was hard to imagine that Robert Bayne was any kind of a force in opening holes in a defensive line. Robert was a good example of what I have always believed about football. The game, as I have stated elsewhere, really does not take much talent if you (1) are willing to run through brick walls on command, (2) are fast on your feet, (3) can catch or throw a football, or (4) like to wrestle with big, ugly, foul-smelling, sweaty guys.

Speed was most certainly not Robert's strong suit. I remember a time when some of the guys trumped up a race between the two of us, though everyone knew full well it would not be close. I think the real issue in everyone's mind was how bad I would beat Robert, since we were most likely the bookends on speed on the football team. The race was held on our football field and one of the concessions I made in an effort to keep the race mildly competitive was to grant Robert a huge head start, maybe as much as fifteen or twenty yards. I won by at least ten yards, thus dashing any hopes that Robert may have entertained about becoming a tailback or running a leg on our four by one hundred relay team! Actually, Robert was pretty much a realist and I doubt he ever daydreamed about being a sprinter. He knew who and what he was.

Robert graduated from Northeastern Oklahoma University in Tahlequah, as did our good friend Ringo. From there, Robert went on to a successful career in the business world in several cities across the country, finally settling in 1988 in the Phoenix, Arizona, area. For a while following his retirement, Bob and his wife Joan embarked on a dog-sitting operation where the two of them would live in peoples' homes and tend to the family pets while the owners were away. It did not matter to Bob and Joan whether the absence was for a weekend or for an extended time; they were there for the duration. For the life of me, I cannot imagine dog-sitting for fun or money, but they seemed to really love it.

Bob fought a seemingly endless series of painful and near-fatal battles with cancer beginning in 1994. His first diagnosis was for cancer of the prostate gland, and the required surgery left him pretty much bladder incontinent for the rest of his life. After going into remission for a time, he was diagnosed in 2004 with bladder and lung cancer. His cancer once again went into remission, but returned in 2008. This time tumors were found in multiple organ systems, and an extremely rare malignancy of the penis was detected. He went into a short period of remission but in 2010, the cancer returned once again and spread to the bones in his pelvis. Bob underwent chemotherapy, radiation, and experimental treatment in fighting each of these flare-ups, and suffered numerous debilitating side-effects from each of these procedures. I admired him more than I can express for he fought a tough, resolute, and positive fight for many years. In addition to the repeated bouts with cancer, he had a quintuple bypass heart operation and dealt with the effects of diabetes for some time, too.

I cannot imagine what Joan went through with Bob's repeated bouts with the dreaded cancer. I remember an email I got from her on June 14, 2006, in which she related that Bob was set to have his 68th birthday the following day. To celebrate, they were motoring from Phoenix to Harrah's in Las Vegas, fully intending to enjoy a good meal and ostensibly spend an enjoyable, relaxing evening together celebrating life and its blessings. However, before they could get away from Phoenix, Bob had a relapse and ended up in a hospital emergency room. His white blood cell count was dangerously low, so they spent his birthday in the oncology treatment unit of the hospital. I could sense the dismay for Bob (and for Joan) in reading about events of that evening which had started out with such promise. They both so richly deserved a brief respite from their collective and recurrent nightmare.

Bob finally succumbed to cancer in 2010. It is trite to say, of course, but Bob's trials and tribulations and his unbelievably courageous response to them clearly demonstrate that life can be damned unfair!

Center. Raymond Gray was named to the All-State football team after our senior season and was invited to play in the Oil Bowl, that annual tribute to the best high school football players in Oklahoma and Texas. The game took place each summer in Wichita Falls, Texas, and the Texas team almost always won for reasons that are obvious; simply put, there are football players galore in Texas and scant few in sparsely populated Oklahoma. After high school, Raymond bounced around from job to job and ended up tending bar in California. He died of cancer in 1996. Once again, as was the case with Jimmy Dick Baker and others, it is interesting to note how perspicacious our high school yearbook staff was in making their prophecies for the future of our various class members. The yearbook staff prophecy read: "Raymond Gray is a bouncer at the Starlight Club (a local night club in Bartlesville)."

A great proportion of the fortieth class reunion in 1996 was spent engaging in a maudlin memorial service devoted to glorifying Raymond. The morbid fascination my classmates shared with his life and death finally eventually got to me so I left the reunion, and as reported elsewhere, participated in the Tom Mix five-kilometer run which was being held as part of an annual celebration of the life of the famous silent movie star and former town marshal in Dewey. After the run, I watched a high school softball tournament, and headed back to Texas a day earlier than planned.

During a Friday night get-together at that same reunion, one of Raymond's sons related to me that it was most thoughtful of our class to remember his father so fondly. I was taken aback at a comment he then made which went roughly as follows: "He wasn't really much of a father but we do appreciate your classmates caring so much about him." "He wasn't much of a father" does not strike me as a highly-coveted epitaph. Raymond and I, for whatever reason, had never been very close throughout our childhood, and I was especially not fond of Raymond for his opportunistic and short-lived "romantic" involvement with my old high school girlfriend, Myrna Brown, at a time when it particularly painful to me.

Left guard. Ed "Ock" Davis was my best friend, a perhaps pre-ordained bond forged as a result of his checking in late in the evening on April 15, 1938, some six hours before I made my grand entry. "Ock" was an extrovert *par excellence*, a great guy with an incredibly infectious sense of humor, and I cannot count the number of fabulous, fun-filled times we had together. After high school, "Ock" went on to play football at Northeastern A&M Junior College in Miami, Oklahoma. He later joined the army and, upon his discharge, moved back to Dewey. There, he pursued a number of entrepreneurial enterprises including constructing and operating several bowling alleys, running an air charter service, teaching flying lessons, dusting crops from his airplane, raising cattle, and dabbling for several years in the oil production business.

"Ock" Davis married for the first time in 1982 at the age of forty-four (to Elizabeth "Betty" Barrett), and died quietly of cancer six years later (1988) at the age of fifty. I never even knew he was ill until his obituary came out in the Bartlesville newspaper. I have since used his death as a didactic device to generate a discussion with my college students about the nuances of friendship. I ask them: "Is it the ultimate act of friendship to die without informing your best friend beforehand of your illness, or is it a major act of rejection?" I take the former position and my students more often than not the latter, which I think is a natural artifact of their youth, lack of experience with both life and death, and their misguided belief that friendships (and to some extent, life) are eternal.

The last time I saw "Ock" Davis was in 1981 at the twenty-fifth class reunion. Though he lived in Dewey, he chose not to take part in the festivities. Noting his glaring absence, some of my classmates petitioned me to intervene with a phone call and see if I could convince him to at least join us for a while. He reluctantly agreed to my repeated entreaties, and our enjoyment of the evening was greatly enhanced by his presence. I had no way of knowing at the time I would never see him again. Fortunately, we shared enough laughs to last several lifetimes and I still miss his fun-loving personality. His death (cancer), that of my college roommate of three years, Dorsey Blue (effects of old age), and the premature and unfortunate demise of my best faculty friend of thirty-five years, Jack Nation (alcoholism), have wiped out my best compadres from three periods in my life, high school, college, and beyond.

Left end. David Miller. David was variously nicknamed the "The Mole" for his sharp, almost rat-like facial features, and "Moth" and "Butterfly" for the similarity between those two flying insects and his surname. I spent many a sleepover at his house in the early 1950's, our early adolescence days, and really enjoyed his friendship. It was impossible to imagine at that time that he would lead such an interesting life after high school. For that matter, it was beyond our comprehension that any of us would ever lead interesting lives. Dewey, in some ways seemed like a death sentence, albeit a slow and not particularly painful one, but one from which there appeared to be no reprieve.

David volunteered for military service right out of high school and spent most of his time at army bases in Korea and Japan. Upon discharge from the service, he joined a geophysical firm which for the next ten years led him all over the United States and most of the countries in South America. While in South America, he married an Argentine woman and they had one child. The relationship dissolved after twelve years, and he married his second wife, Irene, in 1978, the same year he signed on as a Geophysical Operations Consultant with Occidental Petroleum. That job took him to even more distant points, and by the time David retired in 2001, he reckoned his business travels had taken him to forty-two countries in every continent save Australia. David lived his last years in Tulsa and died a slow and at times agonizing death in 2010 of complications from a myriad of health problems.

Blocking back. This position was held by Glenn Wright, aka "Bonehead" or "Bones." Glenn lived down the street from Diane Kite, David Miller, and me, and I also spent a lot of time in his home, too. He had an enchanting older sister, Lassetta, and just getting a glimpse of her gorgeous face and tempting torso made the walk to Glenn's house well worth it. Any day in which one got a long look (leer?) at the lithesome, no doubt libidinous Lassetta was indeed a memorable one. Glenn lived with his father and mother who were separated but living in the same house, perhaps to save a few dollars while also saving face with the community, I suppose. Mr. Wright traveled a lot with his job and his wife was seldom at home for whatever reason, so the house was often ours.

After high school graduation, Glenn went off to sample fraternity life at the University of Oklahoma where he quickly became, for lack of a better term, a casualty of that very lifestyle. He transferred to and eventually graduated from Southwestern State University in Weatherford, Oklahoma, and followed in his father's footsteps as a pharmaceutical salesman. In 1973, he got involved in the oil business which led him to spend several years in Iran. His tenure there took place prior to the revolution in 1979 in which the Muslim cleric, the Ayatolluh Khomeini, deposed the reigning dictator, Reza Pahlevi, the Shah of Iran (a topic addressed in considerable detail in my companion volume). As a result of the revolution, the Iranian people essentially traded one form of despotic dictatorship for another even more oppressive one.

Glenn returned to the US and retired at age fifty-one (or so he reported at our fiftieth class reunion in 2006). He also estimated that he had been in even more foreign countries than David Miller, perhaps as many as forty-eight. At last report (2006), Glenn's wife Glennis was a freelance writer and business owner, and they had four children, all of whom were college graduates. The daughters are, respectively, a nurse, Certified Public Accountant, and flight attendant, and the son is a computer programmer. Not too bad a run for a Dewey guy nicknamed "Bonehead." Perhaps the success of his children is a testimony to marrying well and wisely.

Wing back. Jerry Jones, one of only two juniors in the starting lineup, occupied the wingback position. He was a good player, and his older brother Jack was a monster linebacker who played on earlier, less successful Dewey Bulldogger teams prior to his graduation. Jack hated offense because you could not hit people as hard as he liked to on that side of the ball. Naturally, a guy like him would love defense, and he was way ahead of his time, technique-wise, as a tackler. We were pretty much instructed in those days to latch on and drag ball carriers to the ground, but Jack preferred burying his helmet in your sternum. Few players tackled that way in the 1950's, and I always looked forward to the actual games, knowing that no one on the opposing teams would hit with the ferocity of Jack Jones. He only weighed 165 pounds but he was a true kamikaze with no regard for the welfare of his own body or that of any running back he chose to obliterate.

When we were growing up, the fiercest fights I ever saw were between the three Jones boys, Jimmy, Jack, and Jerry. To put it in the vernacular, the boys would literally "beat the shit" out of each other, and their father was their biggest cheerleader at those random but seemingly daily events. Jerry was the youngest and least violent and fearsome of the three boys, but still a pretty tough guy. I know absolutely nothing about his later life other than that he was married to my old high school girlfriend, Myrna Brown, for a short time after high school. They later divorced.

Full back. Floyd Brown made all-state in two sports, football and basketball, and represented our biggest threat on the offensive side of the ball. He was 6'2" and 175 pounds, and all sinew and bones. Despite Floyd's lack of bulk and real running back speed, it was painful to tackle him because all you got were elbows, forearms, knees, and most of the other two hundred bones in the human body. He was a very good player, but possessed of atrocious training habits. He started smoking early in high school and trained on cigarettes, carbonated drinks, candy, and hamburgers. His disregard for training was legendary among his peers and a source of wonderment given his outstanding production on the football field and in the basketball arena.

Floyd was also "Tractor's" pet, and that issue came back to bite us in a big way during preparations for the Picher High School game in the second round of the state playoffs in 1955. Floyd threw a temper tantrum at practice one day, and "Tractor" wrongly, in the opinion of his teammates, sided with our oft-indulged star. There was widespread sentiment throughout the team that Floyd was being pampered when disciplinary action for his temperamental snit seemed more appropriate. This coaching faux pas created a lot of dissension and team morale took a major hit at a most inopportune time. For all practical purposes, Tractor had lost the locker room, to put it in the sports vernacular. Mike "Gonna" Rhea, waxing poetic as only he could, pretty much captured the attitude of Floyd's relationship with "Tractor" when he said: "Floyd could shit on "Tractor's" desk and he would say it smelled like roses." I do not know much about Floyd's life after graduation other than he died shortly before our fiftieth class reunion of heart and respiratory complications no doubt traceable to his lifelong relationship with the nicotine monster. His wife, Phyllis, also a classmate (but not teammate), died of cancer in September of 2017.

Tail back. As noted elsewhere, the schools in Dewey and Bartlesville were integrated our senior year and we picked up one really fine player as a result, the aforementioned "Let's keep the nigger around for laughs" guy, Kenneth Daniels. Daniels and I eventually split the tailback position for most of the year until "Tractor" benched me for lack of dedication, a decision that I thought then and now was fair, just, appropriate, and long overdue. For a variety of reasons that are neither here nor there, football was no longer among my priorities. On the other hand, football was terribly important to Daniels and he was an electric player as evidenced by the all-state recognition he received at the end of his senior season. Unfortunately, I have heard nary a word about Ken Daniels since high school graduation.

The Regular Season

We beat Tulsa Marquette, the defending state champions among Catholic schools, in the season opener and then lost 13-7 to Bartlesville, one of those so-called "moral victories" where a school in a much lower classification plays a close game against one in a higher division. It was David versus Goliath, with us in the B classification and Bartlesville two classes up in 2-A. Unfortunately in this case, Goliath put a slight drubbing on David. However, losing to a much bigger school was not a disgrace and we gave it a valiant effort, thus reassuring us of our potential to have a good season.

The next pre-conference game was against the Oklahoma Military Academy (OMA) team from Claremore, and it was a joke, a real laugher. We were up 50-0 at half, and despite the lopsided score, we got the predicted "squat to pee" speech from "Tractor" at half time. The first unit played one series in the second half, pretty much sitting out the rest of the game which ended up 76-8. In that one second half series, I scored from fifty yards out. As an indicator of just how overmatched the OMA team was, the handoff that led to that touchdown run was so poorly executed that I had to come to a complete stop at the line of scrimmage, secure the ball, and take off again from what amounted to a standing start. I scored untouched, just one index among many of the fecklessness of the OMA defense.

We were undefeated in district after six games, steamrolling the teams from Drumright, Newkirk, Shidler, Cleveland, Hominy, and Fairfax by a combined margin of 168 points to 12. We then headed into the ninth game of the year, a non-conference game with the Nowata Ironmen, a state-ranked 1-A team. "Tractor" warned us not to take the Ironmen lightly, and we knew his admonition was spot on, for they were a very good team. However, throughout our game preparation that week, it seemed a pall or dark cloud had settled over the entire team. Prosperity had become an enemy of preparation. No matter what "Tractor" and "Hooter" did, we could not shake the doldrums; we were a logy, listless, and uninspired lot. Though we had no name for it at the time, I now know we were experiencing what sport psychologists call staleness or burnout, the bane of athletes, coaches, sports teams, and even business executives. I have studied the phenomenon fairly extensively, and it remains largely a mystery to coaches, players, and sport psychologists. None of these "experts" have found an effective answer to combat the multidimensional monster known as staleness.

The extent of this mental and physical lethargy was poignantly brought to our attention on the very first play of the game with the Ironmen. We won the pregame coin flip and chose to receive the ball, so they kicked off to get the festivities going. The kick was not a very good one, spinning feebly just inside the east sideline around our 35-yard line. As was the case with most if not all of my teammates, I was in some sort of a funky trance. I watched the ball tumble about right in front of me, almost in awe of the more alert Nowata player who fell on the ball to make the recovery. The ball was live, and I knew it, but I just could not pull the trigger and fall on it myself. Nowata went on to thrash us 34-0, thanks to a total team meltdown that had started immediately after the previous game. I think it was inevitable that we were not going to play well that night irrespective of my own personal misadventure which ignited the firestorm collapse. We were in a zone alright, but not a good one.

The richly-deserved pounding administered by the Nowata Ironmen, or what our coaches more accurately described as a "major league ass-kicking", fortunately was a blessing in disguise for it forced us to refocus our attention on the final game of the regular season with the Pawnee Indians. Since the winner of the Dewey-Pawnee game would advance to the state playoffs, much was at stake in that matchup. Thanks to the wakeup call we got from being beaten into absolute submission by the Ironmen of Nowata, we were prepared for Pawnee, convincingly defeating the Indians 34-7. That lopsided win allowed us to move on to the first round of the playoffs.

For our season-long string of successes, we ended up being ranked second in the state, right behind the Lindsay Leopards from south central Oklahoma. It was our goal to get to the Lindsay game, and the bracket was drawn in such a way that if we both stayed undefeated, the two top-ranked teams in our classification would meet four weeks later for all the marbles, the coveted state championship.

The State Playoffs

Our first game was with the team from Bixby, a small town a few miles due south of Tulsa. Bixby started off like a house afire, with their star tailback scoring on the very first play of the game from sixty-five yards out. Things did not look good at that point, but our defense stiffened, the offense got in high gear, and we closed out Bixby by the score of 32-12.

Our next game was in the quarterfinals round with the Picher Eagles. Picher is located in the far northeastern corner of Oklahoma, a couple of miles from both the Missouri and Kansas state lines and only five miles or so from Commerce, the hometown of Hall of Fame baseball player Mickey Mantle, his twin brothers Roy and Ray, and cousin Max. The younger Mantles were a three or four years older than us and were decent athletes. In my humble opinion, after watching Roy and Ray play basketball and baseball (never saw them play football), I am convinced the all-state accolades they received in those three sports were much more a function of their older brother's fame than their own athletic talents and accomplishments. My circle of friends agreed with me that Cousin Max was the best athlete of the three.

I have no words at my disposal capable of capturing the essence of just how cold it was the night of the Picher game. On occasion, Oklahoma can get quite frigid in the winter, and "beyond Arctic" is the only way I know to describe that December night in 1955. The coldest temperature I ever remember experiencing in Dewey prior to that night was a minus nine degrees. I was then an eighth grader and lived on a farm, and can remember carrying a bucket to water the pigs and spilled some of the near-frozen liquid on my jeans. The water froze so fast it did not even soak through; the creases in my Levis were literally frozen in place.

It was that same kind of night when we played Picher. I do not know if I ever heard the actual temperature, but we estimated the wind chill factor to be zero to maybe even ten or fifteen degrees below. To partially combat the wind chill, both teams were provided with wood-burning stoves on the sidelines, admittedly a nice (warm?) gesture but they only slightly mitigated the effects of the bone-chilling cold.

Perhaps someone from the distant past in Picher knows the actual truth about this happenstance, but something took place just before the game that seemed a bit fishy or suspicious. It seems that once the allotted time for pre-game preparations was over, the stadium lights suddenly went out. When it became apparent that the lights were not coming back on any time soon, we retreated to our dressing room where the temperature hovered somewhere in the vicinity of freezing. We sat on the benches in that frigid dressing room, shivering in the cold and getting stiff, while Picher waited cozily in what we later found out was a heated dressing room.

Once the lights came back on some thirty minutes later, the game commenced and, despite the inauspicious beginning, we were able to forge a 12-0 lead by the end of the third quarter. However, the failure to get those two vital extra points and our utter lack of any depth on the bench bit us on the posterior throughout the fourth quarter. As noted earlier, our players almost without exception had to play both offense and defense for the entire game, and we were hamstrung by our small roster and so little backup talent. Fatigue became a huge factor in that ill-fated fourth quarter and the cold only exacerbated the bone-weariness. It was equally cold and miserable for both teams, but the Eagles seemed to have something left in their tanks in that fourth quarter and we did not.

What Picher had really had in their tank that we did not was a big, bruising, banger of a back by the name of Larry Carnes. Their coaches wisely decided to put the game in his hands in the fourth quarter. The Picher quarterback handed the ball to Carnes play after play after seemingly unending play and he became a ground-gobbling, clock-killing juggernaut. Carnes took one handoff after another, plowing over our guys in five- and ten-yard chunks each and every time he touched the ball. First down after inexorable, clock-eating first down piled up for Picher. On the rare occasion when we did get the ball back, our offense sputtered, failing to keep the ball away from Carnes and his maniacal teammates who repeatedly opened gaping holes in our defensive front. The Eagles eventually rode that big horse Carnes all the way to the barn, and forged ahead late in the game by a score of 13-12. After they scored the go-ahead touchdown, we had a few minutes to try to get one last score, but were unable to mount even a modest challenge to their fourth quarter onslaught. The clock ran out and we suffered a heartbreaking loss by that one critical point. Thus, the 1955 season and my football career came to screeching, simultaneous halts.

Picher went on the next weekend to take Holdenville apart in the state semi-finals, prevailing by the score of 34 to 0. The Holdenville win set up the coveted match with the undefeated Lindsay Leopards in the state finals. We knew that if we could get by Picher, the Holdenville game would be pretty much a slam dunk barring overconfidence or another bout of Nowata Ironmen-type staleness, which was unlikely. The only enemy we would have had to contend with in a game with Holdenville would have been "Us", as they say in the Pogo comic strip. The thrashing administered to Holdenville by Picher pretty much substantiated our thoughts about them, though those ruminations were of little consolation as we sat at home that Friday night.

Picher gave it a good shot for a while in the state championship game, but they were no match for the mighty Leopards from Lindsay. I have forgotten the score but I know Lindsay won fairly convincingly after a slow start. I am not sure we would have matched up well with Lindsay either, but it would have been nice to get opportunity to test ourselves against the best. They were ranked number one in the state from game one through game fourteen, while we pretty much held on to the second spot for the preponderance of the season. The Leopards obviously deserved their lofty status in the polls; they were without a doubt the best team in our classification that year. However, old teammates who have passed on to the golden gridiron in the great beyond died believing the Dewey Bulldoggers (aka the Decimals) should have been in that championship game with the vaunted Leopards from Lindsay. Those of us fortunate enough to still be above ground agree with their assessment.

As an addendum to the season, local businessmen in many communities have been known to jump on the bandwagon when their high school teams are winning, and our situation was no exception. One of the interesting things that happened, or did not happen actually, was a promise the boosters made to us that they were going to take us to Dallas for the Cotton Bowl as a reward for having such an outstanding year. The thought of going all the way to Dallas, Texas, and watching some college teams in the Cotton Bowl generated much excitement among the troops. However, no mention was made of any trip anywhere, even to Copan to watch the chickens cluck and scratch and the pigs pick among the pebbles, after the heartbreaking loss to Picher. The fair weather nature of our boosters did not go unnoticed: "As long as you guys are winning, we are with you, but please do not lose. Our enthusiasm is shallow and ephemeral" seemed to be the message we got from the adults.

Track and Field, Graduation, and Goodbye to Dewey, Oklahoma

Track and Field

A retired colleague in the Department of Health and Kinesiology, Dr. Jerry Elledge, is fond of reminding me that "the only thing more boring than track is field." The majority of Americans seem to share his dim view of the sport, and about the only time Americans get serious about watching the sport is during the Olympic Games. The Europeans, on the other hand, take their track and field, or what they call "Athletics", very seriously, and a fair number of American athletes have made a good living competing "across the pond."

Speaking of my esteemed colleague, Dr. Elledge, he is from the city of Brownwood. BHS produced one of the notable powerhouse football programs in Texas for many years, and much of their success was due to the coaching acumen of Gordon Wood, a legend virtually without parallel in the annals of Texas football. Jerry played football for Brownwood High just before Gordon Wood took over the reins there and was a member of the football team at Texas A&M University coached by another legendary coaching figure, Paul "Bear" Bryant. After graduation, Jerry coached and served as athletic trainer at several public schools prior to becoming a professor at A&M.

One of Elledge's more interesting quirks, and he has many, is his disdain for exercise. Despite a life-long association with sports and fitness as player, coach, trainer, and professor of health and physical education, Elledge does not believe in exercise because, as he puts it, "You are randomly allocated a finite quota of heartbeats at birth, and that number is unique to each of you. If you exercise, you use up these heartbeats at an inordinate rate, thus shortening your life. Since one never knows how many heartbeats are in their preordained allotment, exercise then becomes not an ally of longevity but the enemy and should thus be avoided." I have always thought my curmudgeonly friend was advancing his theory in a tongue-in-cheek manner, but I am not so sure any more. I have known Elledge for many years, and the closest I have ever seen him get to exercise is when he hits golf balls off his backyard deck. He has constructed a nice green that sits maybe sixty yards from his house and, when visiting, it is fun to take aim at the flag from time to time. In Jerry's defense, he has always worked hard around his place and stayed in decent shape by doing those myriad things essential to keeping a house and small acreage nice and attractive. Do you suppose hard work uses up heartbeats at an inordinate rate, too?

But back to track (and not so much field). "Hooter" Brewer volunteered to be our track coach in the spring, and I soon developed an abiding fondness for him both as a mentor and person. He had been a bit of a distant figure in football, but his presence in my track life was both considerable and invaluable.

My joining the track team my senior year was actually somewhat serendipitous. It seems that early one mild late winter day, I was walking from the main school building which was separated from the gymnasium by a wrought-iron fence. "Hooter" happened to be in the area and watched me hurdle the fence with relative ease. He then approached me, saying what he had observed actually bore some resemblance to the hurdling event, and asked if I had ever thought about running track. I had once won the hundred-yard dash at the county track meet as an eighth grader, beating a heavily favored speedster named Bob Bogle who everyone thought was invincible. I later won the district championship in the hundred-yard dash in the ninth grade, but had not given track any thought other than on those two occasions. Our school had never had a track, a track coach, or a track program, so not thinking about track came fairly easy.

Speaking of the hundred-yard dash, and as noted briefly earlier, races were run in yards not meters so our distances in the 1950's and 1960's were the hundred, 220, 440, 880, mile, and two-mile. It was not until the 1970's that the track world embraced the metric system, thus creating the 100-, 200-, 400-, and 800-meter races as well as the metric mile, metric two mile, and beyond.

"Hooter" told me he was creating a track program and asked if I would be willing to take part in the upcoming tryouts. Going out for track at Dewey in 1956 was an adventure for at least two reasons. To start with, as I said, we had no track which is a major problem! In order to have a practice area, "Hooter" took his measuring tape out to a grassy plot which was, in reality, a section of the football practice field and using chalk dust, marked off the starting line and finish of a hundred-yard track. That primitive beginning epitomized the state of the sport of track and field in Dewey, Oklahoma, in 1956. Compounding "Hooter's" problems in instituting the new program was the fact that we were almost totally devoid of track talent at good old Dewey High.

"Hooter" let me know early on and in no uncertain terms that he harbored reservations about my dedication and mental toughness because of my lackluster approach to football the previous fall. Despite being impressed with my earlier impromptu hurdling demonstration, he told me he did not think I was mentally and physically tough enough to excel. However, as the season wore on, he told me my dedication to being a physically fit and mentally tough track competitor had caused him to reassess and reject his initial evaluation. I was pleased, of course, as I greatly admired "Hooter" and wanted his approval and support.

"Hooter" devoted some time to the other guys, but as the season wore on, he evolved into my own *de facto* personal trainer because I was his only track talent other than "Ock" Davis who was mildly competitive in the weight events. It is amazing in retrospect to think we had such a good football team the previous fall considering the glaring absence of individual and collective team speed. As noted elsewhere on several occasions, toughness, dedication, and good physical conditioning in the absence of any meaningful speed can sometimes carry you a long way in football, particularly when coupled with the burning desire to wrestle people to the ground!

At the first practice "Hooter" organized a race to get some preliminary idea of who might be his sprinters. Our immensely pampered and almost always out of shape All-State fullback Floyd Brown was among those who tried out. His tenure with the team was brief, however, most likely tied to the fact that I beat him by six or eight yards in our first attempt at the hundred. I do not think Floyd could handle coming in second, and the idea of working at something so arduous and lonely as track did not have much appeal for him. His cigarette habit, disdain for proper diet, and aversion to hard work were serious impediments to success in that admittedly non-glamorous, lonely sport.

Floyd's dissipative habits and absence of work ethic apparently did him no favors in the eyes of football recruiters, either. Scuttlebutt circulating about among the guys had it that the legendary University of Oklahoma coach Charles "Bud" Wilkinson was in the stands at one of our games to take a serious gander at Floyd. For whatever reason, after watching him for that one game, Coach Wilkinson reportedly wrote him off as a prospect for his team. Again, this report is apocryphal but does fit with the facts of the case of Floyd Brown. Looking back, I have some reservations about the entire episode simply because an appearance in little old Dewey by someone of the luminary status of Bud Wilkinson would not have gone unnoticed by the locals.

I Tie the World Record in the Hundred-Yard Dash (Almost). One of the more humorous and, at the same time, exciting things that happened during track practice was the day I tied the world record in the hundred-yard dash, or so it seemed for a few minutes. I had been laid up for about a week early on in training due to a pulled groin muscle, and "Hooter" limited me to running six-minute miles for about a week. As I came off the "too-injured-to-perform", list "Hooter" decided to put the balky groin to the test. He lined me up for my first crack at the hundred and when I got to the finish line, "Hooter's" time piece showed 9.3 seconds which was the world record for that distance in 1956. For a fleeting moment, "Hooter" thought he had found the ultimate prodigy. He and I both knew I was reasonably fast, but 9.3 was a mind-boggling time! Of course, none of us could believe it, and "Hooter's" skepticism as well as my own turned out to be warranted.

After considering all possible explanations for my apparent record-setting performance, none of which made any plausible sense, "Hooter" got out his measuring tape and determined that the track was maybe three yards shy of the prescribed one hundred. While "Hooter" was measuring the length of the track, I basked in the brief glory of being a world record holder for those few precious minutes. We all shared a good laugh about the whole fiasco and I went back to running more pedestrian hundred-yard times of 9.8 and 9.9 seconds (10.7 or 10.8 in meters). World-class American sprinters of that era, guys like Dave Sime of Duke, Bobby Morrow of Abilene Christian, Thane Baker of Kansas State, and J. W. Mashburn of Oklahoma A&M could now rest easy; their spots on the 1956 Olympic team were not in jeopardy after all!

Though not remarkable by standards set by the aforementioned Usain "Lightning" Bolt, the incomparable Jamaican world record holder in the sprints, those times propelled me to the state meet that year and, later, a spot on the freshman team in college. My sprint times fifty-plus years later would still earn a spot in the top six places in the Texas state high school track meet in Austin in every class except 6A, 5A, and, occasionally, 4A. While blazing speed is in abundance at the national and world class levels, the number of people with decent high school speed similar to what I possessed a half century ago has not changed much over the past six decades. The same can be said concerning horse racing's premiere event, the Kentucky Derby, where winning times are essentially unchanged since 1950 despite major advancements in equine genetics and breeding, diet, and training.

Speaking of Thane Baker, he was a top sprinter at Kansas State University who made the Olympic track teams in 1952 and 1956. Though he was one of the top sprinters in the world as a youth, in my mind the most remarkable thing about him occurred thirty years later. By then, Baker had become a successful Dallas businessman who also stayed active in track, so involved in fact that, as a 51-year old, he was able to run hundred yards in 10.1 seconds at a meet held at Southern Methodist University in Dallas. While this time was not a threat to the top sprinters of the world in the 1980's, it did remind me of the validity of the old adage, "If you use it, you don't lose it." Of course, Baker had lost a step or two in the thirty years since his Olympic days, but a man in his fifties who can run hundred yards in ten seconds is "cheeking it", as my friend Jack Nation was so fond of saying.

My hat also goes off to Thane Baker for providing me with an anti-ageism anecdote. It is sad to see people succumb to ageism because of pre-determined societal expectancies that with age comes infirmity and decrepitude. My feelings about ageism are summed up in the words of the old major league pitcher and erstwhile folksy philosopher, Satchel Paige, who once said: "If you didn't know how old you wuz, how old would you be?" Go Satchel!

Speaking of anecdotes, my good friend and track teammate, Mike "Gonna" Rhea, provided the team with a good laugh at one of the workouts. The incident in question involved Mike and yours truly. It seems that I was blessed with an iron stomach and was never prone to nausea and vomiting from sport workouts. On the other hand, for Mike vomiting during or after a workout was almost a daily occurrence throughout his entire athletic career. His propensity to upchuck became legendary and a source of mild amusement among his football and track teammates. One day after running a particularly grueling series of 100s, 220s, 440s, and 660s under "Hooter's" watchful eye, I lost it for one of the few times ever. As this inadvertence was taking place, Mike was coincidentally celebrating the fact that he had made it through an entire workout without losing his lunch. However, when he saw me throw up, he immediately followed suit. Mike has never let me forget I cost him that one vomit-free workout!

Our team participated in meets here and there as March and April passed. Our first competitive meet was in Cleveland, an hour or so from Dewey. I was relatively new to track competition and my inexperience showed. To wit, prior to my first competitive hundred-yard dash of the year, I was hanging out near the starting line, taking in the pre-race banter among the various sprinters. I was clearly intimidated after hearing these guys talk about their best times and accomplishments. I immediately sought out "Hooter" to get his input about their chatter which bordered on braggadocio. He assured me that the talk was all hyperbole (my word, not his) and that I should ignore it and just run my race. Their bravado, as he put it, were borne of insecurity and chutzpah (my words, not his) in roughly equal parts. I ran my race as he suggested, and was fortunate enough to win in a decent time despite stumbling over a soft spot as I came out of the starting blocks.

In a decidedly non-"Hooter" moment that same day, he suggested *sotto voce* that I might gain an edge in the 220-yard dash by cutting across a lane or two on the first curve, thus shortening the distance to the finish line by a few steps. The race was run on a curve, with the starting line on one side of the oval track and the finish line on the other, with the final 150 yards or so run on the straightaway. Judges who were to police cheating on the curves were often lax and inattentive, or even non-existent in small meets, and cutting across lanes was relatively easy to get away with if one were not flagrant about it. I did as "Hooter" suggested and won the 220 handily, though I do not think our collective bending of the rules really made the difference. I never cut across on the curves again nor was I asked to do so.

One of the competitors in that event was the star running back on the Pawnee Indians football team whose name unfortunately eludes me. He was the first black sprinter I ever ran against, something that was novel and exciting. At that time, the folklore about black sprinter superiority was not widespread and pervasive as it is today, and white sprinters were not handicapped by believing they were doomed to lose races because of their own racial inferiority. It never dawned on me that the guy had an edge on me because of his skin color, and I do not think I ever lost a race to a black sprinter that entire year. I was not aware that the "Honky" was supposed to lose! For the uninitiated, "Honky" is a racial epithet attached to white people, and is also sometimes spelled as "Honkie" and "Honkey".

Racial Folklore. There was plenty of raced-based folklore to go around in the 1950's (as well as before and after!). The sexual prowess of the well-endowed black male when in the company of the super-responsive black female was legendary and most certainly blown all out of proportion. No one, it was said, was endowed like the black male and no white female could possibly compete with a black woman when it came to enthusiasm and talent for sex. The prevailing wisdom suggested that black people got sex down to a science on the slave plantations, and that prowess was thus passed on from generation to generation.

Another piece of folklore had to do with swimming. The conventional view was that blacks were afraid of water, and thus unable to learn how to swim. As one of my female contemporaries in the elementary school days put it so eloquently; "Niggers have hypherdogia, you know, they are afraid of water." I have always assumed that my classmate's term "hypherdogia" was a neologistic version of hydrophobia. The fact that swimming facilities were almost never available to blacks prior to the Civil Rights Movement was seldom used to explain their futility in the pool. It seemed to me that if one never had access to a pool, it would be difficult to learn how to swim!

Good old "Tractor", bless his heart, added his own dose of racial folklore to the mix one fall afternoon while viewing some film prior to an impending football game. While waxing eloquent about black football players and their idiosyncrasies, "Tractor" said, "Men, let me tell you something about niggers. Niggers don't like to have their shins hit. Dive for their shins with the tops of your helmets. If you hit them hard on the shins, niggers will quit." He then instructed our offensive and defensive lineman to spend the first few minutes of the upcoming game aiming their helmets squarely at the shins of our black opponents to soften them up. "Tractor" said there would be a brief, counter-productive performance decrement but the long-range goal of getting the black players to give up would produce a rout in the long run.

As he talked, I could not help but hark back to personal baseball experiences in which I had taken some shots off my own shins. How many of you baseball/softball players have fouled a ball off your shins while batting? Or how many of you shortstops have taken one off the shins while fielding a ground ball? Or barked your shins while falling up or down a flight of stairs? I knew from personal experience that tender shins were not race-specific. I also wondered what the Mundine boys and Kenneth Daniels thought of such racial rhetoric. "Tractor" talked to our team as if those three black players were invisible and not in the room. They must have thought it all to be a bit ludicrous. I know I did, and I was not black!

The Track Season Continues. We next had a meet in Barnsdall, a very small community maybe thirty miles southwest of Dewey. I remember little about my performance there other than the weather turned quite cold as the evening wore on. A late spring cold front moved through with a vengeance, and by the time the penultimate event, the 220-yard dash, was run, the temperature was in the high thirties and the wind chill in the low twenties or teens. I never did really get warm enough to run the 220, let alone win the race. Track was not meant to be run in twenty-degree weather!

Another memorable moment, however unpleasant, took place at a competition held in Tonkawa, ninety miles west of Dewey. This meet, the Northwest Relays, featured many of the top track and field athletes in northern Oklahoma. To do well there was considered to be a major achievement and predictive of future success at the state level. Unfortunately, the wind was fierce that day, a not unusual occurrence in Oklahoma in the spring, and the hundred-yard dash was run straight into the teeth of the gale. I got a big lead right out of the blocks, so much so I could not even see anyone in my peripheral vision, an unheard of occurrence in such a short race. At the ninety-yard mark I had a substantial lead and one of my teammates standing nearby yelled something to the effect, "You got it! You got it." For whatever reason I cannot begin to explain, I let up, assuming from my teammates comments that I had broken the finish line tape though I had not felt it. As I slowed, the other runners blew by me at full speed, thus creating the visual illusion that I had finished last in the race. As a result of the confusion at the finish, there was a big brouhaha, with "Hooter" and my teammates assuring the meet officials that I had actually won though it did not appear that way. I also had burn marks on my neck from hitting the tape (actually twine), and "Hooter" used that fact to further argue my case, stating that if I had not finished first, there would be no tell-tale burn marks. Ultimately, the judges decided that I might have won since there was circumstantial evidence to support "Hooter's" assertion, but they nevertheless gave the gold, silver, and bronze medals to other runners. I still to this day do not know if I won or not, but it had to be one of my more stupid moments in sports. How could you possibly not know whether or not you had hit the tape? And why would you listen to a teammate in lieu of hitting the tape and letting that determine your fate?

Ironically enough, this exact same thing happened in one of the sprint races at the 2011 NCAA Track and Field Championships. A female sprinter thought she had completed the hundred meters and let up at ninety-five, thus losing the race as well as valuable points toward the team championship. It was somewhat reassuring to note that I had some company in the bonehead department, even if it took fifty-five years for a repeat performance.

Lest one think the NCAA sprinter and yours truly are the only dummies out there, a year after my fiasco in Tonkawa, the famous jockey Bill Shoemaker pretty much duplicated our scenario while competing in the highly prestigious Kentucky Derby, the horse racing equivalent of the World Series or the Super Bowl. It seems that Mr. Shoemaker, the winner of 8,833 horse races in his career, was leading the Derby on Gallant Man in 1957 when he mistook a furlong post for the finish line. He pulled up prematurely, and Iron Liege blew past him for the win. At least I did not pull my moronic stunt where millions of dollars were at stake.

We all know that jockeys tend to be diminutive, and Shoemaker may take the cake in this regard, at least in terms of birth size. It is said that he weighed two-and-a-half pounds at birth and was 10.5 inches long. One story, however apocryphal, has it that Shoemaker was kept alive his first night by being placed in a shoebox near an oven to keep him warm. He grew to be "gargantuan" as jockeys go, finally tipping the scales at a hefty one hundred pounds.

The District, Regional, and State Track Meets. At the district meet, I won the hundred and placed second in the 220 which qualified me in both events for the regional meet to be held in Tulsa the following week. As I prepared for the hundred that Saturday at Regionals, I went through my usual routine of physically removing myself from the distractions of the maddening hubbub while getting into my mental cocoon to visualize and meditate about the upcoming race.

As the time for the race neared, I felt sufficiently mentally prepared so I joined my teammates to relax, kibitz, and stretch out a bit to stay warm and loose. In the process, I lost track of time. My reverie was interrupted when an announcement was made over the public address system: "Attention all competitors. We are getting ready to run the hundred-yard dash and contestant LeUnes from Dewey is missing. You have already missed the final call for the race, so you better get over to the starting line immediately if you want to run." Needless to say, I beat a hasty trail to the starting line, and may have actually broken the hallowed 9.3 seconds barrier getting there. Clearly, I had no time to go through my final mental and physical pre-race preparations at that point, but what do you do under the circumstances? You run! You simply line up and take your chances. To make a long story short, I finished second which qualified me for the state meet the next weekend.

I lost the race by the thinnest of margins to an exceptional athlete from Grove named Jimmy Beauchamp (pronounced BEE-chum) who was one year my junior in school. Beauchamp was a legend in northeastern Oklahoma for his prodigious football accomplishments, and unbeknownst to me at that time, he was an even more accomplished baseball player. The reason I was not aware of his prowess in baseball is pretty simple really; high school football received lots of newspaper coverage and "America's Pastime" as played at the high school level was accorded little or none, particularly if you were from a very small town, and Grove more than qualified as small.

Beauchamp was a big guy for that era; at his athletic peak, he stood six feet two inches tall and weighed 205 pounds. He competed at the lowest level in the state at the time, Class C, and ran roughshod over and around the football competition every Friday night for four years. Every Saturday morning, the *Tulsa World* sports page would report that Jimmy Beauchamp had scored three, four, five, and sometimes six touchdowns, mostly from long-range, the night before. At his size and speed, he was truly a man among boys in Class C competition.

I had never met Beauchamp until the regional meet and, as stated earlier, was not aware he could play some baseball, too. He actually committed himself to that sport after high school and went on to spend ten years in the major leagues from 1963 to 1973 with five different National League teams, including the Astros and the Cardinals. He played in the outfield initially, and ended his playing days as a decent pinch hitter and occasional first baseman. Beauchamp's career batting average was a modest .231, but there is no denying he made the "big show", the major leagues, and had a nice career. After retiring as a player, Beauchamp went into coaching where he was bench coach for several years for Manager Bobby Cox of the Atlanta Braves. Jimmy Beauchamp passed away on Christmas Day, 2007, at the age of sixty-eight.

But back to the regional meet. I took inexcusable advantage of "Hooter's" good nature by opting out of the 220-yard dash, and I still occasionally think about what it said about me at the time, both as a person and competitor. As stated earlier, I had placed second in the 220-yard dash in the district meet which had qualified me to move on to the next level. When it came time to run the 220 at regional's, I balked, coming up with some feeble excuses about how I wanted to concentrate exclusively on the hundred or some such nonsense. "Hooter" lodged a mild protest and I could see the hurt in his eyes, though he said nothing. I wished then and now that I could take that decision back, for the man had invested a great deal of time and emotion in me and I repaid him for his kindness by engaging in my best horseshit impersonation of a prima donna athlete. Prima donna athletes are pretty unlikeable people and I am not very fond of myself when I think of this incident.

There is no denying that one's ego must be huge to handle the stress of the short sprints for pre-race tensions run high and there is so little margin for error. Unless, of course, you are the latest genetic anomaly in the world of sports, Usain Bolt of Jamaica. By referring to Bolt as a genetic anomaly, I am in no way, shape, or form trying to downplay the hard work that goes into becoming a world champion. Simply put, however, Mr. Bolt and his counterpart in swimming, the American phenom Michael Phelps, both got a huge head start on the competition in their respective sports as a function of the genetic crapshoot from whence they sprang.

The week of preparation for the state track meet which was held in the Oklahoma City suburb of Edmond turned out to be a nightmare. It rained cats and dogs that entire week, negating the possibility of any outdoor workouts. In an effort to maintain some degree of physical conditioning and mental focus, I worked out daily inside our gymnasium, running on the boards and up and down the gym steps.

I did not make it through the preliminary round in the state meet, and I am convinced to this day that my poor performance was due in great part to dead legs brought on by training all week in the gym instead of on our makeshift track, however primitive it might have been. The obvious counter to my contention about leg fatigue, of course, is that I simply was not fast enough to compete with the better runners at the state level. This supposition may well have an element of truth to it, but I had beaten a number of those same competitors in other meets. My legs were lifeless, and I did not make it out of the time trials, thus ending my high school track career. I take some consolation in the fact that I could run below ten seconds in the hundred-yard dash, admittedly modest by world class standards today but a time still unattainable by the vast majority of the male population.

In the final analysis, it was the patient, firm, and sincere encouragement from "Hooter" Brewer that made my modest successes possible at the district, regional, state, and later at the collegiate level. Over the years, I have tried to track "Hooter" down, but to no avail. He would be well past eighty by now if alive, and I regret never telling him how much he meant to me as a seventeen-year old. Inspirational people like L. E. "Hooter" Brewer are precious commodities and are few and far between. He has been a lifelong hero and inspiration for me.

High School Baseball

In addition to running high school track, I did dual duty in baseball. I typically worked out for track for as long as "Hooter" wanted and then went over to the baseball field for what remained of practice there. "Tractor" Trent had the baseball team but seldom did any real coaching, living up to the stereotype of the coach who rolls out the ball, takes a seat, snoozes a bit, and lets the boys play. To their credit, "Hooter" and "Tractor" were simpatico with me doing both sports concurrently which made my sporting life easy.

Throughout my six years in "organized" baseball (i.e., Little League, Teen-Age League. American Legion, high school), I played first base. I was a pretty decent fielder with a good glove and I saved my infielders from many a miscue by digging errant throws out of the dirt. On the other hand, I could not throw a lick. I never was much of a thrower, but during my sophomore year I developed a sore throwing arm after working out in 35-degree weather shortly after receiving a tetanus shot. My arm was swollen when I went to that practice and though I do not remember hurting it, I never threw very well after that. Fortunately, I could hit a bit, and with some power, particularly to the outfield gaps. With my sprinter's speed, I could easily stretch singles to doubles and doubles to triples, and I could also steal bases, almost totally on speed alone. No one ever taught me how to slide, and I never learned how to do it correctly. It seemed wasteful to me at the time to handicap a player with my speed by not teaching him proper sliding techniques. Perhaps I should have taken more personal responsibility for that weakness in my game but I generally outran my sliding inadequacies.

In stark contrast, my 29-year old son has pretty much the same speed as his old man, but in one of his first Little League games, he executed a perfect pop-up slide. After the game, I asked him where he learned to do that, and he told me he had seen it done on television so he executed the slide just like the major leaguer did. Oh, to have had that pop-up slide in my bag of tricks! And also that ability to see something once and be able to execute it perfectly without instruction!

Good old Dewey High went nowhere that year in terms of the playoffs and the baseball career came to a screeching halt. As stated elsewhere, I do harbor minor regrets I never gave baseball a better shot for the game, in retrospect, probably was my best sport. Unfortunately, I liked it the least. The cold spring seasons, the nagging dust storms, and seemingly incessant wind took all the fun out of baseball. On top of that, we had no baseball field at our school. We took a page from Hooter's book and created a field just as he did in track, namely by taking a tape measure and some chalk dust and marking off a venue in which to play. When I look at the softball, baseball, and track facilities in Dewey today, I can only wish we had had the same opportunities and caliber of facilities.

My friends who played minor league baseball have always told me I would have gotten a look for a year or two in professional baseball because I had reasonably decent baseball skills and unusual (for baseball, at least) foot speed. Speed is so scarce in baseball that having any will get you a good look if you can hit and field a bit, so they say.

When I was sixteen, I was highly tempted to attend a St. Louis Cardinals tryout camp being held in Texas City. Unfortunately, I never got there. I really do not know if baseball was not that important to me or if I just lacked the confidence to put my talents on display in front of a critical audience composed of baseball scouts. In the jargon of my profession of Psychology, I was suffering from "evaluative apprehension", or the fear of being evaluated by others. In retrospect, I wish I had given baseball a better shot, but I harbor no illusions about possessing the talent to make much more out of it than a year or two in the minor leagues.

Graduation and Goodbye

Despite my considerable academic shortcomings, graduation day finally rolled around and I received a diploma or, more accurately, I sort of received it. I was in arrears on a small library debt to the school and had been growing a beard, too, and both offenses were deemed sufficient to warrant withholding my "sheepskin." I shaved off the beard and my dad paid my library debt, thus allowing me to participate in the graduation ceremony. However, none of these acts of contrition took place soon enough for me to get the diploma at the scheduled graduation ceremonies. I received my "sheepskin" in the mail a week or two later.

Looking back in retrospect, I am in awe of how well the lives of many of my classmates turned out. Virtually none of us came from homes where the parents attended college and few were apprised of the value of an education. At school, it was rare for a teacher to talk about college with us, and there was no such thing as a guidance counselor in those days, at least not at good old Dewey High. The fact that any of us went on to college and had productive and rewarding careers is miraculous to me.

At our fiftieth class reunion in 2006, many of my classmates provided brief biographies that were reproduced in a booklet. It was fascinating to read about the adventures and occasional misadventures of these people with whom I had grown up. Their accomplishments in many cases were astonishing. There were a fair number of college degrees, some exceptional career paths, a lot of national and international business and leisure travel, and what appear to be highly rewarding family lives in almost every case. I marvel at the educational, career, and personal achievements of my peers when I think of the backgrounds from which most of them came. Perhaps their stories were repeated every day in the 1940's and 1950's in small-town America though I cannot help but wonder if there was something a bit unusual about this group. Their accomplishments and attainments far outstrip what anyone would have predicted. I salute my classmates. They have done well for themselves.

Prior to the graduation ceremonies, my father let me know in no uncertain terms it was time to abandon my deadbeat days and wastrel ways, put good old Dewey behind me, and look to the future. He further informed me that he was driving up from Texas City for graduation and the two of us were turning around that same night and motoring back to his home on the Texas Gulf Coast. His plan, however draconian it may have seemed at the time, meant I had to miss the after-graduation party held at nearby Lake Pawhuska. It saddened me greatly to think I was not going to get to say a proper goodbye to my friends of the preceding eleven years, but that is exactly what happened. I missed the party and, strangely enough, the sun came up the next day and the world continued to spin on its axis. However, I would have bet a million dollars that Armageddon was imminent. I was peeved at my dad, but deep down, I knew he was right. It was time to get on with life with a fresh start in the land of opportunity, the great state of Texas. I was to learn he had fallen in love with the Agricultural and Mechanical College of Texas (now Texas A&M University) and had plans for me to become an Aggie. There was no way, of course, to know what the future held in store for me at A&M and beyond. In retrospect, it has been a fascinating ride and I owe much of my success, such as it is, to the great experiences as sort of a full-time Okie and part-time Texan in the years from 1938 to 1956.

Undergraduate Days, Graduate School, and the United States Army

The Agricultural and Mechanical College of Texas

As noted previously, I grew up mostly in the northeastern part of Oklahoma in a small city called Dewey, with summer stints from ages ten through eighteen in Texas City, Texas, on the Gulf Coast near Galveston. My parents were divorced when I was seven, and my brother John (aka "Bub"), sister Paula (aka "Jo"), and I spent the majority of our childhood with our mother in Dewey. However, at age ten, we three kiddos started spending summers in Texas City with our father who, as stated elsewhere, was a labor union organizer, arbitrator, and business agent for the International Union of Operating Engineers, Local 347. I greatly enjoyed having two homes, two sets of friends, and the wonderful association with my father and his second wife, our "wicked" stepmother, June, who was anything but evil. She was an absolutely delightful woman, the antithesis of Cruella de Ville.

In the summer before my senior year of high school, the topic of college attendance took on major importance and some decisions had to be made about my educational future. My favorite high school coach, L. E. "Hooter" Brewer, and I had talked cursorily about the possibility of me playing football and running track at his alma mater, Central State College (now Central Oklahoma University) in Edmond, Oklahoma. However, those deliberations were doomed to failure from the onset because of my deeply-rooted aversion to hitting and being hit. Such a mindset makes football a bad option, and I was not talented enough in track to warrant any kind of significant scholarship assistance. Thus, my father and I agreed on an alternate plan which he essentially phrased as follows: "You can go anywhere you want for college, but I will only pay for it if you go to Texas A&M." The decision about where I was going to school was, as they say, a no-brainer! Though I was almost totally naïve as to what was about to take place in my life, I knew that I would be in College Station for the fall semester of 1956. I was going to be a Texas Aggie, of all things!

I spent a forgettable summer prior to moving to College Station doing absolutely nothing of interest other than watching the movies *de jour* at the various theaters in Texas City and Galveston. I had gone through some turbulent times those last two years of high school, and looking back, was probably in a mild depressive funk for the entire summer of 1956. I did not have a job, avoided contact with pretty much every other human being other than my immediate family, and essentially buried my lingering sorrows from the good old high school days in an endless diet of movies. When that largely forgettable summer came to a close in late August, my father packed me up and dropped me off in College Station at what was known then as the Agricultural and Mechanical College of Texas.

The college had been created under provisions of landmark legislation known as the Morrill Act which was passed by the U.S. Congress and signed into law by President Abraham Lincoln in 1862. In all, seventy-eight universities owe their origins to the Morrill Act, including such stellar bastions of higher learning as The Ohio State University, Purdue University, the University of Florida, and, of course, our own little beacon of light here in College Station. In order to comply with the mandates of the Morrill Act, on June 20, 1871, the citizens of College Station set aside 2,416 acres on which the college was to be built. A&M officially opened its doors five years later, in 1876.

Interestingly, in the fall of 2015, I had a student in my Sport Psychology class named Zach Lawrence, and his great-great-grandfather, John Archibald McIver, is generally believed to be the first Aggie. Legend has it that McIver rode his horse from nearby Caldwell to College Station, a distance of twenty-five miles, only to find out he was a day early for registration. He and his equine companion apparently found a spot in some nearby trees and spent the night there. The next morning, bright and early on October 4, 1876, McIver registered for class and thus became the first Aggie.

As for young Zach Lawrence, he was a campus leader and occupied the prestigious position of Head Yell Leader for the 2015-2016 school year. Zach hails from Shiner, Texas, home of Spoetzl Brewing Company which, among other things, brews Shiner Bock which is easily the best beer in the entire United States bar none (its only rival is 1554, a beer brewed in Fort Collins, Colorado). The Lawrence family are fifth generation Aggies; Zach's great-great grandfather (McIver), great-grandfather, grandfather, and father were all members of the Corps of Cadets and graduated from A&M. Also, older brother Ryan graduated from A&M in 2015 and his sister, Lindsay, was an Aggie, too.

The original intent of the Morrill Act was to provide instruction in agriculture, military science, mechanical arts, and classical studies for young people from working-class families. As such, these universities have traditionally been thought of as "Ag Schools" though many have outgrown that reputation with the emergence of new and exciting areas of inquiry in science, engineering, and technology and the morphing of agriculture into new, more mechanized, and technologically advanced forms.

In 1963, the words "Agricultural" and "Mechanical" were abbreviated to just A&M (sometimes alleged by the more cynical critics of the university to stand for "Texas Athletic and Military College"), and the Texas legislature officially changed the name of the institution to what it is today, Texas A&M University (TAMU). Looking back, it is strange to think I had watched the football game between A&M and the University of Texas on Turkey Day of 1955 with my old high school chums in Oklahoma and rooted for the Longhorns. Nine months later, there I was, a Texas Aggie!

To put my arrival in the wilds of central Texas in some historical context, 1956 was the same year Fidel Castro launched the Cuban revolution by overthrowing the Fulgencio Batista regime; John Lennon and Paul McCartney met for the first time and performed at a church dinner; Martin Luther King organized a boycott of buses in Montgomery, Alabama; "As the World Turns" made its television debut; undefeated heavyweight champion boxer Rocky Marciano retired; Elvis Presley's "Don't Be Cruel" and "Hound Dog" were the number one hit songs on the charts for eleven weeks; the tuition at Harvard was $800 per year; bread was 18 cents a loaf; a new car cost $2000; boxer "Sugar" Ray Leonard, actor Mel Gibson, and professional football star quarterback Joe Montana were born; and the life expectancy was 69.6 years.

Bryan and College Station, Brazos County, and Texas A&M University

Brazos County, the cities of Bryan and College Station, and the Agricultural and Mechanical College of Texas were small, provincial, I would even say "backward" entities in 1956. According to the 1950 census, the county population was 38,390, and the cities of Bryan and College Station had 18,102 and 7,925 citizens respectively. There were no chain hotels or restaurants, and the few establishments that did exist were locally owned, often "Mom and Pop" operations. There is only one restaurant from the 1950's still serving food today, and that is Martin's on College Avenue. Another well-known eatery from that era, Zarape's, closed in 2009. No alcoholic beverages were sold at North Gate, the well-known student hangout area of today, but a few bars in Bryan and College Station did serve beer. No mixed drinks were available anywhere in the county, and those who preferred their alcohol to pack a bit more wallop had to transport it from out of town or drive out Highway 60 past the School of Veterinary Medicine ("The Vet School", in the vernacular of the locals) to "Whiskey Bridge", located just a few yards off of the west bank of the Brazos River near Snook, to buy their beverage of choice. Our favorite hangout that did cater to beer drinkers was Uncle Jimmy's, located on Texas Avenue in College Station somewhere between the Mexican restaurant, On the Border, and another popular eatery of today, Chili's. I apologize for my vagueness concerning the location of Uncle Jimmy's, but far too many years have passed and many new businesses have opened in the area, thus obscuring all my old landmarks.

Goodbye to the Good Life

I remember that first fateful August day at A&M as unbelievably hot and humid, a typical Central Texas summer scorcher. You could literally see the streets and sidewalks reflecting the radiated sun rays back toward the heavens. My dad and I had made the three-hour trip from Texas City to the campus without incident and when we pulled up to a parking area near the Corps of Cadets dormitories, he, minus any pomp and circumstance, pronounced me ready to serve and he drove away, leaving me to my fate. No long lectures, no motivational pep talks, no advice about how to survive in a hostile environment, nothing, just a quick goodbye! If he looked back in his rear view mirror, he probably saw me being greeted by a young man who was to dominate many aspects of my life for the next two years, our unit First Sergeant, Richard Whitmire. I will have more to say about Richard Whitmire shortly.

The entire experience was a jolt to my system because I knew next to nothing about A&M except a few tidbits gleaned from casual conversations with my father and his friend, Frank "Skip" Simmen, of LaMarque, Texas, a city located a few miles from my "second" hometown of Texas City. As mentioned cursorily earlier (and in considerable detail later), I lived nine months a year in Oklahoma with my mother, and my familiarity with institutions of higher learning was largely confined to the University of Oklahoma, Oklahoma A&M College (now Oklahoma State University), University of Tulsa, Central State College (now Central Oklahoma University), Northeastern State College in Tahlequah, and a couple of area junior colleges, Northeastern Oklahoma A&M JC in Miami, and Coffeyville JC in Kansas. Local (i. e., Dewey) or area athletes, such as high school classmates Alvin Smith and Ed Davis, who went off to play junior college football almost always ended up at one of these two schools.

My dad's friend, Frank Simmen, was a successful insurance executive and a member of the A&M class of 1951 who to this day, sixty-seven years later, still bleeds maroon in profusion. Frank was the catalyst for piquing my dad's interest in getting me to attend A&M in the first place, so I guess I owe him although I am not sure what. Thirty-eight years after I first enrolled at A&M, I was fortunate enough to have Frank's son, Will, in my Psychology of Adjustment class in the fall of 1994. Will became a successful businessman in our community.

I last talked to Will in August of 2010 when he hailed me down as I was leaving Wings and More, a popular restaurant in south College Station founded and owned by former A&M and Miami Dolphin NFL standout, Mark Dennard. Will indicated at that time that his father and mother were hale and hearty and doing great. Frank is in his late-eighties and Henny Sue comes from parents who lived well into their nineties, so longevity abounds in the Simmen family.

After saying goodbye to my father on what I would describe as a physically bright but psychologically bleak August day, it was obvious that I was in strange surroundings, definitely in over my head, minus a safety net. I had the sinking feeling I was in deep doodoo up to my diaphragm. My apprehensions were considerable, to put it mildly. I found myself, a young, naïve, unworldly Oklahoma country boy, lost in the wilds of central Texas in what seemed to me at that time to be a huge and intimidating major college campus. It did not help that I knew next to nothing about A&M and its academic, military, and athletic traditions, nor could I name one other person who was attending the school. As it turned out, I actually did know some guys from Texas City and LaMarque from my previous summers on the Gulf Coast, and they surfaced here and there on campus as the school year unfolded and several went on to become close friends.

First-year cadets expressing a preference for the Army were assigned to Armor, Artillery (Anti-Aircraft and Field), Chemical, Engineering, Infantry, Ordnance, Signal, and Transportation units. Students who wanted to be pilots or navigators and such were assigned to an appropriate Air Force wing. Cadets who earned Army contracts after their sophomore year generally ended up in the military branch corresponding to their A&M Corps assignment. A contract was not guaranteed by mere participation in the Corps; rather it was an agreement between the cadet and the U.S. military made possible if the student had met certain academic, character, and military training standards by the end of the sophomore year. This agreement specified that the student would have to continue to maintain high standards of conduct, attend summer training at the end of the junior year at a nearby military installation, and serve a specified number of years of active and reserve duty, depending on whether one was Army of Air Force. In the case of most of us Army types, we did our obligatory six weeks of summer training at Fort Hood in Killeen, Texas. Our contract agreements guaranteed us a stipend of $29 per month for those last two years of college. Though perhaps difficult to believe in 2012, we could actually make that $29 stretch as spending money from one month to the next fairly well. With beer costing roughly a dollar a six pack and Mexican food a dollar a heaping plate, $29 would go quite a ways in those days. Thanks to inflation, that $29 dollars would be roughly the equivalent of $210 a month today. Isn't inflation strange and just a bit scary at the same time?

My unit assignment rested in the hands of the authorities in the Trigon, the military headquarters for the university, and I ended up (I assume randomly) in B Armor, aka "B Jocks." The unit nickname came from the old Cavalry or horse units common to the military in the nineteenth and early twentieth centuries but non-existent in the modern army. The cadets in the three Armor units (A, B, and C) who had military contracts were referred to as "tank jockeys" those who had military contracts were typically assigned to tank divisions when they began fulfilling their active duty obligations. My affiliation with B Jocks led me to inherit a new nickname, one that was to stick with me throughout my undergraduate days. Through guilt by association, I became known as "Jock" to most of my friends on campus and in Texas City.

These 1956 unit designations were changed in the fall of 1958, my junior year, to a generic A-1, B-1, C-1, A-2, B-2, C-2 system minus any reference to branch affiliations. Though it was not required by the new system, most of my friends who were under military contract maintained their allegiances to the old system and ended up serving as Armor officers during their government-mandated active duty period. Frankly speaking, I had no desire to motor around in one of those cramped, claustrophobic, mobile coffins for two years so I requested and received an appointment to the Adjutant General's Corps (AGC). The AGC designation meant I would be either a postal, personnel, or special services (sports and recreation) officer when I went on active duty. As will be noted later, I ended up serving as a special services officer for the First Armored Division at Fort Hood, Texas, which dovetailed nicely with my background in athletics.

Participation in the Corps of Cadets was mandatory in the 1950's except for students who: (1) had served in the Second World War or Korean conflict; (2) were physically handicapped and thus not able to withstand the rigors of Corps life; (3) were graduate students; or (4) were international or foreign students. Also, athletes were exempt from Corps life if they chose not to participate. A few star football players, most notably Dennis Goehring and Jack Pardee, were exceptions. Goehring went on after fulfilling his military obligation to become a successful businessman in Bryan-College Station, and Pardee made his name as a player and coach in the National Football League (NFL). Jack Pardee passed away in 2013.

As mentioned earlier, my first acquaintance at A&M was the First Sergeant of B Armor, Richard Whitmire, a country boy from Edgewood, Texas, population a thousand or two. Richard had a fair complexion and tended ever so slightly toward the pudgy side, but he was an intense and resolute leader, generally a take-charge kind of guy. To his credit, Richard also brought this same intensity to his studies, and as a result he excelled in the classroom.

In the next few minutes after that first meeting, which seemed more like days or weeks, Richard Whitmire let me know in no uncertain terms that my ass was grass and he was going to be my self-appointed, up-close-and-personal lawnmower for the duration of his tenure at the university. Actually what I think Whitmire really said was that my ass was firmly ensconced in his foot locker and was thus no longer in my possession. And things went precipitously downhill from there! There were many times over the next several days and weeks when I more clearly understood how it felt to be the last wildebeest crossing a river full of ravenous, marauding crocodiles.

Whitmire walked me over to Dormitory Two, or Kiest Hall, and introduced me to several of my already frightened, woefully downtrodden, and obviously bewildered (depressed?) peers who had been put through the wringer by a handful of Whitmire's henchmen (i. e., the other upperclassmen) who had reported back to school early. Whitmire and a couple of other juniors taught us the rudiments of lining up, marching, polishing brass, spit-shining boots and shoes, and pressing uniforms. We also soon learned, without any tutoring from Mr. Whitmire, how to artfully dodge the upperclassmen who were constantly on the prowl for a freshman in obvious need of hazing.

We were likewise introduced to some of the basic nomenclature that became an integral part of our existence for the rest of our days at A&M, terminology still in use in the Corps of Cadets even today. For example, we were told that we were not freshmen, but rather "fish", and were so named because we "…were lower than the lowest pile of whale shit on the bottom of the ocean." Sophomores were called "pissheads", I suppose because their job was to make life as pissy and miserable for the "fish" as they possibly could. If the "pissheads" failed in their malevolent, misanthropic mission to manufacture misery, then the juniors (i. e.,"sergebutts") would, in turn, would make them miserable. Juniors were allowed to wear serge uniforms in addition to their khakis, hence the term "sergebutts."

As for the seniors, they were pretty much non-factors in the grand scheme of things. They reveled in their status as Corps elder statesmen and their approach to things going on around them seemed to vary from mild amusement to total indifference. For the most part, they came and they went, exerting little day-to-day impact on our lives. They were into their studies, starting the application process for graduate or professional schools, preparing to enter the world of work, going into the Army or Air Force to fulfill their previously agreed upon military obligation or, in some cases, working on becoming a career officer in one of the military branches. It struck me that the seniors had experienced enough of the happy, happy horseshit that passed for daily life in the Corps after three-plus years, and had pretty much given it up for Lent (or maybe longer!).

In addition to learning the basic survival skills that first week, we picked up our uniforms from the supply depot, bought some supplemental shirts and khaki pants, and registered for classes. Everything was rush, rush, rush at a pace far beyond pell-mell. We had to learn what seemed to be a thousand new things in an incredibly compressed time frame, and the pressure was mindboggling. As opposed to the "relative calm" of the first week, the second one was unadulterated hell. The upperclassmen, most notably the sophomores, were all back on campus and they screamed at us "fish" every waking moment of every long, miserable, terror-filled day.

Indiscretions, real or imaginary, were met with what psychologists would call non-contingent punishment. If the brass was shiny, the polish on the shoes was not good enough; if the shine on the brass and the shoes passed muster, the uniform was not properly pressed; if the shoes were shined, the brass polished, and the uniform immaculately tailored and pressed, then the shave was not close enough; if you showed up capable of passing even the most stringent of inspections, there was a problem with the way your bed had been made that morning. You could never win; the upperclassmen were going to find something wrong so that they could dole out non-contingent punishment. Most often, the price for sloppiness or carelessness, or just being alive really, was seemingly endless pushups. Boy, did those sophomores adore pushups (though not for themselves, strangely enough). If not performed properly the first time, another round was tacked on. If you did them well but could not complete the required number, then a cadet who was seen as more fit would find them tacked onto his allotment. In my own case, I could do pushups until the crows congregated in Capistrano, so it became the norm to tack on all uncompleted pushups for the other "fish" to my ledger. It was not unusual for me to do 300-500 pushups a day, and I will say I was in pretty good shape, upper body-wise, within a short time. It is a sad commentary that I can barely do one pushup today, and I am considered to be in decent shape for someone in his dotage.

As everyone who has ever been to Texas in the late summer can readily attest, it is excruciatingly hot and unbearably humid, the latter more of a problem in the southern half of the state which is where we most certainly were located. I really do not think the Grand Planner in the Sky intended for humans to live in this part of the world. I guess the same can be said for the winters in North Dakota where the temperatures are almost always beyond frigid. In any case, the heat and humidity were overwhelming, and the new khaki uniforms were absolutely stifling. They were heavy, hot, not especially well-ventilated, and the thickness of the shirt and pants kept the heat inside and near the body, sort of like a sweat suit. On really hot days, the heat held in by the uniforms was tailor-made for inducing a near-nausea state. To compound the problem, there was no air conditioning in the dorms and classrooms, so there simply was no relief from the never-ending August heat.

As if dying of heat prostration were not enough, the hazing was relentless, and the pell-mell pace did little to lessen the effects of the ever-soaring summer temperature. The heat and the hazing took their toll, and it did not take long for the pressures to build, tempers to flare, and resolve to weaken. On the third or fourth day of our tenure as cadets, a fellow "fish" was alertly retrieved by several of his peers as he prepared to jump out of a fourth story window in Dorm Two, our appointed palatial palace away from home. Another "fish" was sent packing in the middle of the second week, refusing to come out of his room, or "hole" as they were called, for days at a time. His withdrawal reached the point where he refused to come out even to eat. He sat in his darkened room for several days, his anger, fear, hostility, and who knows what other emotions silently festering. He just sat in a wooden chair near the lone window, repeatedly throwing a hunting knife at what I can only guess were some formidable enemies inside or just beyond his door. There was something very eerie and ominous about the repeated, almost syncopated thumping as the knife struck the door for hours at a time. It was eventually determined that our fish friend was psychologically unfit to continue as a student at the university. At that time, dismissal from the Corps also meant removal from school because, as noted earlier, participation in the Corps of Cadets was mandatory. Thus, our friendly knife-throwing "fish" buddy was dismissed and sent home.

A third incident, one far less life-threatening than the two above, thank goodness, involved a "fish" from Lewisville whose name I still remember but will not repeat here. It seems that our "fish" friend was entering rooms at times convenient for him and inconvenient for us and taking off with items he regarded to be of interest. Our miscreant fish buddy was dismissed from the university shortly thereafter, disappearing into what seemed like thin air as was the case with so many of our peers that first semester…there one day, mysteriously gone the next.

These stress-related casualties take on considerable significance if you assume that our unit was a microcosm for what was transpiring on the rest of the campus. To wit, there were perhaps forty units (companies if in the Army ROTC and wings if you were in the Air Force program) in operation at that time. If you then multiply that figure of forty by one, two, or maybe even three psychological casualties per unit, you get somewhere between forty to well over a hundred possible victims during that fateful first couple of weeks. The prevailing Corps zeitgeist was that it is preferable that these people be broken down in the relatively innocuous context of college student life as opposed to falling apart in the more volatile combat or prisoner of war environment where your life and/or that of fellow soldiers may be on the line. One fault with this flawed line of reasoning was that the "fish" in my class as well as thousands of others to follow who chose to serve on active military duty were increasingly in the minority.

Things Begin to Settle Down

Once we survived the trauma of the first couple of weeks, things settled into something resembling a routine. Routine may not be the proper term, for I found in moments of respite and calm, you always had the feeling the other shoe was getting ready to drop. An air of ominous apprehension permeated our mental and emotional lives. For the majority of that first year, I found cadet life to be analogous to navigating your way across an LA Freeway on foot during rush hour. There were classes to attend, rules of cadet life to learn, campusology facts to digest and regurgitate on command, upper classmen to kowtow to, endless marching, incessant hazing, and constant unease about the next moment, next hour, and the next night where terror might reign. It was truly a physically and psychologically "wear-them-out and break-them-down" brainwashing exercise.

The campusology stuff was a mishmash assortment of Aggie mores, folkways, traditions, facts, figures, and history that "fish" were expected to recall on command to avoid the wrath of the ever-present and almost always malicious upperclassmen. We also had to learn the yells for yell practice, an event that took place prior to each week's upcoming football game. Each home game required that we also draw and color or paint a picture or story on someone's bed sheet with a theme symbolizing the ass-kicking A&M presumably was going to inflict on an opponent on Saturday of each week. Once completed, these signs were draped from the upper windows of each dormitory, and automatically entered into competition with those from the other units for a small weekly monetary prize. It is a sad commentary on life at A&M during this time that these pieces of crudely constituted art actually dressed up a campus that, all things considered, added new meaning to the phrase "drab and dreary." As the trite saying goes, if you looked up "drab and dreary" in a dictionary or encyclopedia, there would be a 1956 photo of Texas A&M (and the two Brazos County cities, for that matter) prominently displayed alongside the verbiage!

One sanity-saving event that helped maintain stability and allay anxiety for all "fish" during that early adjustment period was the impromptu flag or touch football games held several afternoons a week. These contests took place in grassy areas adjacent to the various dorms, and provided precious moments largely devoid of hazing. For that hour or so, everyone was pretty much an equal, freshmen and upperclassmen alike, and those with athletic inclinations got to show off a bit. I immediately caught the eyes of my peers and the older guys because of my sprinter speed (Remember: I had made it to the high school state meet in the 100-yard dash earlier that year), and it did not take long before they were urging me to talk to the A&M coaches about walking on with the football team. It was at once amusing and mildly flattering to have their misguided admiration, but they greatly overestimated both my ability and intestinal fortitude, particularly the latter.

However, while walking on in football was never given any serious thought, those impromptu dorm games did get me to thinking about resurrecting my sports career in the spring semester by walking on in either baseball or track. As stated elsewhere, I was mildly successful in both sports in high school, and I decided to give baseball a shot first. Thus, I sat in the bleachers and watched the team go through their paces once the pre-season workouts started in February. After a good deal of back-and-forth about walking on in baseball, I decided track might be a better fit. I then started watching the team work out on the track which at that time encircled the football field in the old Kyle Field stadium. After a week or so of watching from afar, I worked up the courage to approach the assistant coach, one Ray Putnam who, in addition to his duties as assistant track and field coach, served as a half-time professor in the Department of Economics. Coach Putnam was reputed to have been quite a distance runner in college and his biases about sprinters versus distance runners was to become an obstacle to my own personal success and, ultimately, with that of the entire team.

I laid out my background and track credentials to Mr. Putnam and he told me to report to the head coach on the following Monday for confirmation of my status on the team. The gentleman in charge was a coaching legend in the US, and his name was Frank G. "Andy" Anderson, otherwise and more popularly known as "Colonel Andy." Rumors among the guys suggested Colonel Andy had been a coach with the U.S. Olympic team in 1952 (and possibly 1948, I am not sure), and thus was viewed with a certain amount of reverence in the world of track and field. In addition to his track accomplishments, Colonel Andy had been one of those relatively rare soldiers who saw combat duty in both World War I and World War II. He was probably in his sixties, a nice man with a kind face and grandfatherly demeanor, and he agreed if I has passed the vetting of Mr. Putnam, then he would be happy to have me aboard.

In what was to become one of the strangest moments in my life in sports, Colonel Andy asked me what size shoes I wore. I replied that I wore size eleven, and he handed me a pair of what I quickly figured out were nines. I called this to his attention, assuming it was a lapse in attention on his part. To my disbelief, he replied that he wanted me to wear shoes two sizes too small for practices so that when I competed in actual meets, I would get this gigantic leap of confidence, or the competitive edge, by putting on spikes that actually fit my feet. Being young and naïve to the ways of the track world, I trusted his judgment and wore the size nines to practice for a few days. Unfortunately, the shoes pushed my big toenails back into the quick, the two toenails turned pitch black, raised up like drawbridges, and fell off. The end result was I was barely able to walk and totally unable to run for several weeks. When I recovered, I took a razor blade and conveniently cut openings in each shoe at a point where my big toenails would ordinarily be, and I was able to resume workouts with a modicum of comfort. When I report this set of circumstances to my classes today, I am met with considerable skepticism which I think is pretty natural given the bizarre nature of the episode. But it has been said on numerous occasions that sometimes truth is stranger than fiction, and it was certainly so in this instance.

To compound the problem, Coach Putnam absolutely detested sprinters and never missed a chance to let us know how he felt about us. Prior to our first workout, he told us we were gutless and if we had any guts we would be out running to hell and back with his scrawny, chicken-chested, oxygen-converting distance runners. But to his way of thinking, it went without saying that we were gutless because we were sprinters; the two went hand in hand, as natural as the first breath of a baby. More often than not, Coach Putnam refused to post workout schedules for us sprinters, thus leaving our workouts pretty much up to our own discretion. There is an inherent problem with this strategy (or lack of one) for no matter how dedicated one might be, it is easy to slack off in your workouts if no one is there to push you along. Some athletes are so driven, I suppose, that they are autonomous but I was not one of them nor were most of my associates. We ran a bit but we kibitzed, joked, and lollygagged around a lot.

In those days and as noted elsewhere with regard to other athletic teams at A&M there were two squads in every sport, one for the freshmen and one for the other three classes. I quickly found myself thrown in with a bunch of guys, most of whom were posing as sprinters, but I was seldom used in actual meets, I suppose because I was a walk-on. I actually got to run in only one competition that whole season, a dual meet on the Kyle Field track with the University of Houston. In the one-hundred-yard dash, my only event, I was the top Aggie finisher but lost to one of the Cougar runners by a hair.

I never did figure out why I was never allowed to run the sprints and the relay teams for I consistently beat all the other freshmen sprinters in practice as well as in that one meet except for a teammate by the name of Ernesto Uribe who was faster than me but academically ineligible due to his fall semester grades. I sort of concluded maybe life isn't always fair and hung up my spikes for good at the end of the season. I did have a lot of fun at workouts, met some nice guys, and would not trade for the experience. I now have season tickets to all the indoor track meets at A&M and have often wished I had the equipment and facilities the track guys and girls enjoy today. As well, the track athletes receive some tremendous coaching from the legendary Pat Henry who has won literally dozens of national indoor and outdoor championships at A&M as well as Louisiana State University where he coached for many years.

As an aside, Ernesto Uribe, a native of Laredo, Texas, went on to graduate from A&M and spent thirty-three years in the U.S. Foreign Service, mostly in South America where he worked in seven different countries. Prior to his death in 2015, Ernesto penned a memoir in which, among other things, he discusses his A&M track experiences which parallel my own in many ways. It is nice to know my recollections are not too far off the mark.

Sports has a way of being the great social, racial, and ethnic equalizer, and my sandlot football "prowess" and modest accomplishments with the freshman track team earned me some points with the upperclassmen and helped lessen the frequency and severity of the hazing aimed in my direction. Being able to pass and catch a football, coupled with the possession of a modicum of foot speed, worked partial wonders for me as the year played out. Thanks to these traits, I earned a degree of forgiveness from the upperclassmen for both my countless actual and perceived sins.

Speaking of walking on in football, there was at least one other person who urged me to do so, though almost a year later. These events transpired roughly as follows: I had gone back to my roots in Oklahoma in August of 1957 just prior to returning to A&M for my sophomore year. While there, I drove over from Dewey to Miami (Oklahoma, not Florida) roughly sixty miles to the east toward the Arkansas state line, to watch my old childhood chum, Edwin "Ock" Davis, and his Northeastern A&M Junior College teammates begin fall practice in preparation for the upcoming season. My aforementioned compadre from Bartlesville, Bobby Joe Green, was also playing at Northeastern that season after spending his freshman year at the University of Oklahoma. As noted elsewhere, Bobby Joe was an instant junior college star, and he went on from Northeastern to the University of Florida where he was a punter and running back as well as sprinter on the Gator track team for two years. Upon completing his college eligibility, Bobby Joe punted for several National Football League (NFL) teams for fourteen years.

"Ock" Davis, serving as an intermediary, told me that Bobby Joe had talked to the Northeastern coaching staff about me walking on to their team even though I had not played football since graduating from high school fifteen months earlier. Green also indicated through "Ock" that he had expressed shock upon learning I had not walked on at A&M my freshman year.

A big limitation for me resurrecting my football career after the year-plus hiatus was my deep-rooted aversion to playing defense and there was no place for someone like me in that era where players had to play both offense and defense, or what was known as "two-way" football. I just could not see myself, as a decidedly undersized running back or defensive back with low motivation and an unabashed fear of hitting and getting hit, walking on to play football with those Korean War veterans, quasi-hooligans, and others at Northeastern. Or the larger and much faster beasts at A&M, the likes of John David Crow, Jack Pardee, Charlie Krueger, and my tough, tenacious, but under-sized friend Loyd Taylor!

I appreciated Bobby Joe Green's vote of confidence but I viewed myself as marginally talented and not remotely tough enough to play for Texas A&M, let alone Northeastern A&M! That violent game is best left to guys like Green's Bartlesville High School classmate, David Baker, the man who shed crocodile tears before each snap of the ball because he wanted to hit someone so badly.

The "Bear", John David, and "The Sugar Land Express"

Speaking of A&M football, the team was coached from 1954 through 1957 by the larger-than-life legend, Paul "Bear" Bryant, who loaded up on good players to make a run at the national title in 1956 and 1957. The talent he had amassed was a curious collection of young men from cities like New Orleans, Philadelphia, Albuquerque, and Spring Hill (LA). Players from Alabama and other cities and states with most unlikely ties to a conservative and backward cow college (i.e., A&M) situated in a small, lazy, backwater Texas village (i. e., Bryan-College Station) suddenly (and strangely) started showing up on campus.

In this regard, a prominent long-time college coach, an acknowledged defensive coaching genius with years of experience at A&M and many other Division One programs once told me the most illegal team ever put together in the history of college football was the one "Bear" Bryant fielded in 1957, his last year at A&M. When one considers the well-documented propensities of college coaches to cheat, it says something that our 1957 team, in the eyes of at least one knowledgeable and experienced observer, could have been the most illegal team ever assembled at the college level.

Prominent players that year included Heisman Trophy winner John David Crow, Charlie Krueger, Jack Pardee, Kenneth Hall, Loyd Taylor, and Bobby Joe Conrad. Each of these players other than the undersized but infinitely gritty and gutsy Taylor went on to play professionally. Crow, Krueger, and Pardee had particularly distinguished careers in the NFL and have been enshrined in the College Football Hall of Fame. Charlie Krueger, at the age of 77, was inducted into the Texas Sports Hall of Fame in February, 2014.

Football players in the 1950's played both offense and defense (i.e., "two-way" football), often for the entire sixty minutes, and games were grueling, gladiatorial challenges to stamina, fitness, will, grit, and determination. The rules dictated that if a player were substituted for or came out of the game due to an injury he had to sit out the remainder of the quarter in which he exited. As you would guess, substitutions were minimal and faking of injuries was rare. A huge premium was placed on being able to play defense first and scores were generally low as a result of the stacked defenses. For example, John David Crow won the 1957 Heisman Trophy with fewer than 600 yards of total offense. However, he was a bone-crushing defender, and the combination of his modest offense and sterling defense earned him collegiate football's highest individual award. The sixty-minute gladiator of that era could never have imagined the game as it is played today where specialists are numerous and wide receivers with track sprinter speed and mobile, rifle-armed quarterbacks dominate. Defense, for all practical purposes, has become an afterthought.

Sadly, the inimitable John David Crow, truly a local icon of major proportions, died at the age of seventy-nine on June 17, 2015. The image I will carry forth for the foreseeable future of John David, other than his prodigious accomplishments on the gridiron at A&M in the 1950's, is that of elder statesman holding forth at McDonald's on Rock Prairie in College Station. It was not unusual to see the legend visiting there with five or six of the local yokels, no doubt enthralled by his war stories from A&M and the NFL days. John David truly loved A&M, and the university and community were better off for having him here for so many years.

Of the many standout players of that era, Kenneth Hall, was perhaps the most enigmatic. Hall was known as the "Sugar Land Express" and to this day remains the all-time leading career rusher in Texas high school football history. His home town, Sugar Land, from whence his nickname arose, was a small country town in the 1950's and got its name from the town's leading industry, a sugar production facility. As nearby Houston has expanded its geographical reach over the past fifty years, Sugar Land has become an upscale suburb that has been swallowed up by the ever-expanding urban sprawl.

During his high school career from 1950 through 1953, Hall gained 11,232 yards and scored 899 points or the equivalent of 150 touchdowns. 395 of those 899 points were scored during his senior year, or roughly sixty-six touchdowns. Unfortunately, Hall did not measure up to Coach Bryant's standards as a defensive player, and never played much during his A&M career. Hall did go on to play for a couple of years, almost exclusively as a kickoff specialist, for the Houston Oilers of the now-defunct American Football League (AFL). Hall is now retired in the Sugar Land area, and his status as a Texas high school football icon is etched in stone. In an interesting postscript to the preceding, the aforementioned Dennis Goehring, in the course of a casual conversation with yours truly at a local political rally in 2012, said that Coach Bryant reluctantly admitted late in life that one of his worst coaching mistakes was his mishandling of Kenneth Hall.

In the 1950's, the football team lived in Walton Hall on the northwest edge of campus and the other athletes resided in Hart Hall, near the newly-renovated and luxurious, lap-of-luxury, state-of-the-art Memorial Student Center (MSC) and the Taj Mahal of all athletic arenas at the time, G. Rollie White Coliseum which was razed in 2013 to make way for the half billion (actually a measly 485 million) dollar expansion of Kyle Field. The new facility is both a monument to the excesses of college football and a veritable Roman Coliseum disguised as a football stadium. I was convinced there would be a magnificent half-time show at the opening home game in which hundreds of exotic animals would be slain, legions of gladiators would fight to the death, and dozens of virgins would be eviscerated. I fully expected to see some Christians or Corps of Cadet members, both of which exist in profusion and are thus expendable, fed to a pack of ravenous lions. And all of these events were to be presided over by the most recent Roman magistrate (aka head coach), none other than Kevinus Sumlinus. Though none of these events have come to fruition, I am convinced there are ongoing discussions about hosting such events in the future, particularly if A&M ever plays the dreaded Longhorns from the hippie haven in Austin known as "tu" or the University of Texas again.

Many a friend shed tears as they watched the old arena and classroom building being demolished. I had most of my undergraduate classes in G. Rollie, hid out in one of its numerous restrooms to avoid working on the bonfire my sophomore year, attended graduation ceremonies there, and took in a handful of musical concerts in that old acoustics-challenged structure. I was also a spectator at hundreds of basketball games in the "Holler House", as G. Rollie came to be known, in the halcyon days of A&M basketball during the late 1970's and early 1980's. Those teams were astutely led by Coach Shelby Metcalf whose tenure ran from 1963 to 1990.

The two athletic dorms, Walton Hall and Hart Hall, were places to be reckoned with in my day because you never knew what craziness might emanate from the high-spirited and occasionally out-of-control athletes living in those two facilities. One caper that stands out involved the "minor sport" athletes (i. e., any sport other than football) who were housed in Hart Hall. The front of their dorm faced the campus auditorium, the long-ago demolished Guion Hall, some forty or fifty yards to the south. The custom at Guion was to show a movie each evening, and the cost of a ticket was nominal, maybe ten or twelve cents. From time to time, to break the everyday monotony, the Hart Hall jocks would line up *en masse* after the evening meal, at which time they would carry out their best charge of the Light Brigade imitation, descending on Guion Hall in unison. The noise, confusion, and general chaos created by the stampede allowed most if not all of the jocks to get into Guion Hall without paying. It was not so much a matter of money that drove them to storm the ramparts as it was the thrill of competition. Just seeing the Guion Hall personnel scurrying about, trying to figure out who had paid and who had crashed the gate, was worth the price of admission.

The 1956 Aggie football team went 9-0-1 with the one blemish on their record coming at the hands of the University of Houston Cougars, affectionately known among the A&M student body as "Cougar High", an obvious slam at what Aggies have long loved to view as the inferior academic experience provided by that institution. A&M's 1957 team was undefeated and ranked number one nationally going into the ninth game with Texas Christian University (TCU), but in a move that proved to be catastrophic for local football fortunes, Coach Bryant dropped a bomb on everyone by announcing he was returning to his alma mater, the University of Alabama, at the conclusion of the 1957 season. The Aggies proceeded to lose their number one national ranking, falling 7-6 to TCU, 9-7 to the Texas Longhorns, and 3-0 to the Tennessee Volunteers. The vaunted Vols were led by All-American running back, Johnny Majors, and he and John David Crow were the main protagonists in what has become a major slice of Sugar Bowl folklore in which the two players collided helmet to helmet, rendering both gladiators simultaneously unconscious at mid-field.

Everyday Life in the Corps

But let us return to the daily life in the Corps of Cadets. One of the recurring and stressful daily events was eating in one of the two University dining halls, Duncan and Sbisa (probably correctly pronounced "Speeza" but known among the students and faculty then and today as "Sa Beesa"). That dining hall, built in 1911, was named after Bernard Sbisa, an Austrian chef who worked at A&M in 1879 (and did not pronounce his name "SaBeesa"!).

The troops would fall out in front of the dorms, get into formation, and stand at attention or parade rest until time came to march to the appropriate dining hall which was determined by where one lived on campus; south side you delighted in the delicacies of Duncan, north side you dined on the elegant, savory "SaBeesa" cuisine. These ten- or fifteen-minute periods in front of the dorms were almost always viewed by the upperclassmen as occasions to declare open season on hazing freshmen. Once the time came to march to the mess hall, it was not unusual at all for the first sergeant or his designated stand-in to lead what are known as Jodie (Jody) cadences or Jodie Calls. These calls are rituals engaged in by military units when running or marching, and are used to bolster morale and liven up what are inherently mundane or exhausting tasks.

Jodie Calls. Jodies were apparently brought to the military by black enlisted soldiers in World War II, and as desegregation continued in the 1950's, these cadence songs spread slowly throughout the army and all other branches of the service. Some Jodies were tame and others a bit on the raunchy side. An example of a relatively tame Jodie might sound something like this:

>Jody, Jody, six feet four
>Jody never had his ass kicked before.
>I'm gonna take a three-day pass
>And really slap a beating on Jody's ass.
>Sound off, 1-2; Sound off, 3-4.
>Cadence count, 1-2-3-4; 1-2-long pause-3-4.

Perhaps the raunchiest one in my memory is the following grotesquerie which I heard on more than one occasion while marching to Duncan Hall:

>I had a girl, she was tall and thin.
>Fucked herself with a fountain pen.
>The ink pen broke, the ink ran wild.
>She gave birth to a blue baby child.
>Sound-off, 1-2; Sound-off, 3-4.
>Cadence count, 1-2-3-4; 1-2-long pause-3-4.

Once finished with marching and the Jodie calls, we entered the mess hall and went to our assigned tables. The seating arrangement at each table typically included a liberal sprinkling of freshmen and upperclassmen, thus creating a veritable hazing mine field for freshmen but a treasure trove for the sophomores who would enjoy a field day haranguing and harassing the poor freshmen. The seniors were often the exception to this rule; they tended to congregate together at one end of the table or the other, staying above the fray and leaving the upholding of traditions in the grubby hands of the other two upper classes. "Fish" had to sit on the front edge of their chairs, erect with both feet on the floor and one hand in the lap. Whether a freshman ate or not was almost totally dependent on how things were going that day for the upperclassman and his ability to handle the never-ending campusology questions.

Fortunately, we were able to eat in some degree of peace for a few minutes at the end of almost every meal because the upperclassmen typically left the table earlier than the "fish" did. The mess hall food was actually quite good and there was always plenty to eat if you were patient and willing to outwait the upperclassmen (which most of us were). In my own case, I gained about twenty pounds that first year, so there must have been ample opportunities to eat.

Another feature of daily life at A&M was study hall, or what was technically known as Call to Quarters (CQ). CQ was mandatory and took place each night Sunday through Thursday from 1930 to 2230 hours, or for the civilians out there, from 7:30 pm to 10:30 pm. We were expected to be sitting at our desks, with both feet flat on the floor and both elbows on the table, and in a serious study mode. It was not permissible to lie down on the bed to study and breaks for any reason were rare. If one of the upperclassmen poked his ugly head in your room, you had better be following the correct protocol and have a textbook right there if front of you. Roommates were mirror image reflections of each other, sitting at the two desks near the window, with one cadet facing the south wall and the other facing north or east and west as the case may be in some dorms, with the two chairs nearly touching back-to-back.

It was not unusual at all for a cadet to be staring at the same page at the end of CQ as he had been at the start three hours earlier. Alternately, a cadet could navigate his way through ten or twenty or thirty pages of a textbook during CQ and remember absolutely nothing because of the interference produced by out-and-out, drop-dead, bone-weary physical fatigue compounded by the psychic effects of sleeplessness, mental torment, and fear.

The fun for the evening often began when CQ ended at 2230 hours, as the fish were once again fair game for some additional hazing. The sophomores were pretty much free to do anything they chose, particularly if a fish had committed a real or imaginary "unpardonable" violation of protocol during the day. If for some reason a lapse had not been called to one's attention during the day, you could bet the farm it would be on a sophomore's post-CQ menu. The after-CQ hazing was sometimes unrelenting, and could take almost any form the upperclassmen chose and for as long as they desired. At times, the entire freshman class would be required to wax the halls and the rooms of the upperclassmen, or taken to the room of a sophomore where everyone would be required to sit with their legs pulled up with chins resting on the knees. Can you imagine fifteen or twenty humans ripe with the smell of sweat and fear crammed into maybe a one-hundred square foot room?

Other hazing tactics included doing pushups to the point of collapse or sitting on an imaginary "pink stool", the latter a form of torture that involved placing your back against a wall and assuming a sitting position, arms out in front with palms down, butt even with the knees, and nothing underneath to support your weight. The musculo-skeletal misery produced by the pink stool set in rapidly and became excruciatingly painful as the muscles tightened and tetanied. Another biggie was forcing the fish to smoke cigarettes under a trashcan to the point of dizziness, nausea, or unconsciousness. An even more vicious hazing variant involved requiring a "fish" that departed from orthodoxy to sit for hours or, in some cases, the entire night under some sophomore's sink, thus reducing the victim to something resembling a human pretzel. The forced immobility would eventually cause your neck, spine, and kidneys to scream out in agony.

Middle-of-the-night raids to steal benches were commonplace events, too. Stealing benches was mostly done for the convenience of the seniors, for they seldom stood while we waited in formation for meals or other marching events. It was their privilege, and theirs alone, to occupy a bench while waiting, and there was hell to pay if one was not available when one of the prima donna seniors wanted to sit down. Seniors, as noted earlier did not have much to say, but there damned well better be benches around the dorm at formation time! If benches were not there, the juniors would hear about it, which meant the sophomores would more forcefully hear about it, which meant our happy little freshmen asses were going to be in a proverbial sling in a manner of minutes!

A once-or twice-a-year event, with an element of malice attached, was to steal bikes from the racks around the dorm area and throw them into random five-or ten-foot stacks of intermingled and tangled pedals, handle bars, and wheels. Minor or major damage to the bikes was almost a certainty, but that never deterred the upperclassmen from requiring our participation in this nonsensical misdemeanor destructive act.

As a result of these various nocturnal activities and forays, getting a good night's sleep was a rarity, with resultant dozing off in class and counterproductive lapses in attention during CQ. The last thing you wanted to do, or perhaps could do, after these almost nightly sleep interruptions was study. Fortunately, there were periodic breaks in the hazing, particularly during weeks when upperclassmen had several examinations and/or other classroom obligations. Another respite occurred on weekends, as the upperclassmen often went out for the evening on Friday or Saturday. Also, it was not unusual for them to go home or to another college campus on weekends to see friends or seek female companionship which was sparse at best on or near the A&M campus. The war on our psyches and souls abated sufficiently during these lulls in the action, thus allowing us to rest and regroup for the hazing sessions certain to begin Sunday night or Monday morning when things returned to "normal."

Earning Their Master's Degrees in Hazing. Hazing was a huge part of everyday life in the Corps, most of it tolerable but some of it downright sadistic. When it comes to the latter variety, several individuals stand out in my memory, even after a half-century. The two most sadistic sophomores were "Ray Royster" and "Heinz Ernst" (not their real names; they deserve to be exposed but I have chosen to protect their families who may view them in a more favorable light than I do, even after sixty years).

Royster was dark-haired, a bit pudgy and soft-looking, maybe 5 feet 9 inches tall and 190 pounds, but what distinguished him most was his willingness to inflict physical or psychic pain on freshmen with minimal provocation and maximal joy. As for Ernst, he was blond, wiry, 5 feet 7 or 8, 145 pounds, and a most willing and skilled practitioner of the art of hazing. I always had a difficult time getting past the Germanic nature of his name and the specter it raised about Nazi terror tactics. Hitler would have absolutely adored the guy!

Royster and Ernst took the university-condoned mandate to haze to a level unprecedented in my four-year Corps experience. These two partners in crime must have spent many an hour during their freshmen year and the summer prior to becoming a sophomore (i.e., "pisshead"), conjuring up creative ways to inflict physical and emotional pain on other young men. It is an interesting psychological puzzle, trying to explain what it is in the psyche of a 19-year old sophomore that would make him turn on a powerless, vulnerable 18-year old freshman, so willing to go way beyond the hazing norm with such joyful malice. Psychological researchers have been trying to answer this question since World War II ended in 1945. Of special interest in this regard is the research on Nazism, fascism, and the authoritarian personality to be discussed shortly.

The dreaded duo, Royster and Ernst, stayed away from me for the most part, giving me only minimal hell. They preferred instead to prey on those freshmen they perceived to be physically weaker or psychologically more vulnerable and thus less likely to defend themselves by fighting back. One of their favorite hazing tactics was requiring freshmen to come to their rooms every hour on the hour from midnight to 0600 hours in full dress uniform to sign in on a sheet of paper attached to the door. After signing in, the cadets were expected to return to their rooms, undress, and hopefully grab a few winks before the next sign-in period an hour hence. For some selected victims, this ritual was carried out three, four or even five nights in a row, and sometimes continued week after week with only occasional relief. The nice thing about this practice from the standpoint of the two instigators was the poor freshmen were punished without ever interrupting their own "beauty sleep." A variant of the preceding theme was to have a freshman report to their rooms where they would be required to sleep all night under their sinks, usually in full military dress uniform.

You can imagine how much studying these poor fish did, how attentive they were in class, and what their psychological state must have been. Sleep deprivation is often used widely as a tool for breaking people down in brainwashing or interrogation sessions, and it was used most liberally and effectively by Royster and Ernst.

There were occasional breaks in their hazing, and the respites were dictated more by fatigue on the part of the two perpetrators than the mental or physical distress of the victims. Is it any wonder that of the twenty-nine freshmen who started in my unit, only fifteen returned to A&M for their second year? And by the junior year, we were down to eight of the original twenty-nine who started the adventure in the fall of 1956. In this connection, I read a September 2017 obituary for E. L.

"Spur" Walker, a member of the class of 1953, in which it was reported he was one of only three among an original group of thirty-five "fish" in "A" Engineers to make it to graduation. I have some reservations about the accuracy of the reporting in the obituary but the numbers reported are not too far off. I can only describe those data as shameful!

It has been six decades since these events took place, and I can remember them almost as vividly as if they happened today. Royster and Ernst are permanently etched in my psyche, not for what they did to me but for the cruelty the two of them inflicted on people they knew could not or would not fight back.

As a footnote to the current discussion, I was listening to a book on tape recently which was based on a novel by one of the top mystery authors of the period, though the name of the book and the author elude me at this time. The relevance of the book on tape in question to the current discussion is that it was set in the United States Air Force Academy in Colorado Springs, and there is a segment devoted to hazing within that hallowed institution. It turns out that the main character in the book had a younger brother who attended the academy and later killed himself because of hazing on the part of one especially sadistic upperclassman. The parallel between the fictional characters at the Air Force Academy and the real-life people from my own personal experience at A&M was absolutely eerie. If I did not know better, I would swear the unidentified author had been a fly on the wall in Ray Royster's and Heinz Ernst's rooms in Dormitory Two at A&M during the 1956-1957 school year.

I would be remiss if I did not pay homage to two other upper classmen with special and memorable malice in their hearts, Bobby "Smut" Sullivan and Will Elias (their real names). Sullivan, a senior from Marshall, Texas, was a dark, simian-like, irascible and reclusive senior who occasionally departed a bit from the unconcerned and uninvolved norm characteristic of his class. Sullivan was particularly known for sending randomly selected freshmen (i.e., the ones unfortunate enough to be in the hall when Sullivan came out of his cave) out on midnight missions to steal things for his room. One night, he sent a couple of us unfortunate souls out to pilfer some decorative plants which required us to break into and burglarize the horticulture greenhouse located just north of the Corps area. You could have never convinced me otherwise, but I suspect we were probably not in much danger of getting caught in our little caper, thanks to the hugely understaffed, occasionally inept, and oft-comical campus security force at that time in A&M's history.

On another occasion, Sullivan's favorite chair suffered a broken spring so he ordered me to break into the office of Major Hugh Williams to procure a replacement part from the Major's chair. Major Williams was a full-time university employee and the officer in charge of our dormitory area, what we called a "bull." Sullivan targeted the office of Major Williams because he had earlier spotted a chair containing the identical spring mechanism needed to repair his own. Sullivan regarded freshmen pretty much as toys and seldom had anything to do with us unless he needed a decoration or doodad for his room. Fortunately, he seldom ever left his room except to go to class. Sullivan eventually attained the rank of Lieutenant Colonel in the army and died shortly before Christmas in 2013.

As for Elias, he was a native of Eagle Pass, Texas, a junior, swarthy and dark-skinned, with a heart that more than matched his skin color. Malice toward freshmen was irretrievably buried in the deepest, darkest recesses of his reptilian brain and primitive, mean-spirited soul. Though Elias was not in my unit, his reputation on campus as a person to be wary of was widespread and the news circulated early on among the freshmen to avoid him at all costs. The antithesis of Will Rogers, Will Elias never met a person, or at least a freshmen, he did not dislike. And I never met a freshman that liked Will Elias, either. For that matter, I do not remember ever meeting anyone who liked the man.

The incident that permanently imbedded Will Elias in my psyche took place at the very first home football game I ever attended at Kyle Field, the A&M football stadium. I forgot who we were playing that day and it really does not matter anyway. The temperature at game time was near the century mark, our military uniforms as noted earlier were heavy and oppressive, unbelievably inappropriate for the late summer 100-degree Texas heat, and everyone was sweat-soaked and miserable. To compound our misery, the student body stood for the entire game, a gesture of support which is still the norm at A&M games. We were located on the east side of Kyle Field which forced us to face that brutal late summer sun for three miserable hours as it settled over the top of the stadium in the west as the game drew to a close.

I do not know that Will Elias planned it this way, but he ended up standing right in front of me at that game. Immediately after the opening kickoff, he turned his back on the field and proceeded to blow rancid, stifling cigar smoke in my face for most of the afternoon. I was sunburned, nauseated, and so furious I seriously contemplated punching him out before the afternoon mercifully ended. My father picked me up after the game to grab a bite to eat and I told him that I was quitting A&M and getting away from people like Will Elias and his ilk. I did not know what I would do and could have cared less at that moment, but I was going to put some distance between Royster, Ernst, Sullivan, Elias, and yours truly. I had had it with A&M, particularly the surly, sadistic sophomores with spite in their sordid souls. My dad, ever the rational listener and advisor, patiently let me engage in my tirade, calmed me down, and essentially convinced me that you cannot let people like the ones I mentioned here beat you into submission. His advice reminded me of a pencil of which he was most fond that bore the words "Illegitimus non carborundum." Roughly translated, the message on the pencil said "Don't let the bastards wear you down." I took that message about fighting back and not letting the bastards wear me down to heart, and those words, along with some decent food, caused my anger to subside and I rejoined my friends in Dorm Two later that evening.

What these people, the Royster's, the Ernst's, the Sullivan's, and the Elias'es of the world did to their peers turned out in a perverse way to be a blessing in disguise. The glaring absence of an inspirational academic climate, mandatory Corps participation and incessant, out-of-control, institutionally-condoned hazing resulting in huge attrition numbers, and the absence of female students and competent faculty members coalesced over time to force those in positions of governance at the university and state level to face some cold, hard facts about the future of the Agricultural and Mechanical College of Texas. To put it mildly and succinctly, the place was in real trouble across a number of critical dimensions.

The Authoritarian Personality. To understand the mentality that was all too prevalent in the Corps at that time (and hopefully is not the case today), an analysis of the work of social scientists at the University of California-Berkeley is most instructive. In their classic 1950 book entitled *The Authoritarian Personality*, psychologists T. W. Adorno, Else Frenkel-Brunswik, Daniel J. Levinson, and R. Nevitt Sanford thoroughly described the relationship between deep-rooted personality predispositions and racial and ethnic prejudice. Their work focused on gaining an understanding of the roots of fascism, authoritarianism, and ethnocentrism, and was closely linked to an analysis of people and events in Nazi Germany during the period from 1933 when Hitler ascended to absolute power to the end of World War II and his death in 1945.

Essentially, the Berkeley research team, mostly expatriate Jews who fled Nazi Germany in the 1930's prior to the Holocaust, attempted to isolate the psychological variables that led to the inhumanities inflicted by Hitler and his henchmen on homosexuals, labor union leaders, Communists, Catholic priests, gypsies, and most particularly the Jews of Europe. Some of the questions the research team asked were: What kind of person would order the extermination of an entire race of people? What kind of person would discriminate against others perceived to be unlike them? What kind of person would strip another person of his livelihood and dignity, and do it with fanatical fervor? And what kind of person would gleefully devise new and creative ways to inflict pain, suffering, and death on others?

The end result of the Berkeley research was a description of the authoritarian personality, or the type of person who willingly discriminates against others perceived to be different from the norm in color, gender, racial characteristics, sexual preference, or political persuasion. This so-called authoritarian personality is made up of nine descriptors and they are:

1. **Conventionalism**: Rigid adherence to middle class values.
2. **Authoritarian Submission**: Submissive, uncritical attitudes toward authority of the in-group.
3. **Authoritarian Aggression**: Tendency to be on the lookout for, and to condemn, reject, and punish people who violate conventional values.
4. **Anti-Intraception**: Opposition to the subjective, the imaginative, and the tender-minded.
5. **Superstition & Stereotypy**: A belief in mystical determinants of fate; the disposition to think in rigid categories.
6. **Power & Toughness**: Preoccupation with the dominance-submission, strong-weak, leader-follower dimension; exaggerated assertion of strength and power.
7. **Destructiveness & Cynicism**: Generalized hostility and vilification of the human.

8. **Projectivity**: The disposition to believe that wild and dangerous things go on in the world; the projection outwards of unconscious emotional impulses.
9. **Sex**: Exaggerated concern with sexual 'goings-on.'

The parallels between the behavior of the Nazi leaders and those of the theoretical authoritarian personality are striking. Adherence to traditional German/Aryan values was of paramount importance. At the same time, the typical sycophantic martinet Nazi was extremely deferential to authority but gleefully inflicted pain and suffering on others perceived to be less powerful. When one dealt with a Jew or another perceived to be an enemy of the Reich, it was important to harm and humiliate. Why walk someone out of a business or a synagogue or a school when you could punch them, throw them down a flight of stairs, and kick them all the way to a truck waiting to deport them to a concentration or extermination camp. Blind devotion to the mystical and cultist environment created and promulgated by Adolf Hitler served to bind his henchmen to him. Also, the vilification factor was huge with the Nazi's, thus allowing them to discriminate against Jews with a total absence of humanity.

Hitler was a master at brainwashing, the consummate propagandist, and was able to capitalize on the authoritarians in his midst. They made good, loyal, obedient, conventional, Hitler-fearing storm troopers, bodyguards, secret police, and soldiers. These same individuals were also well-suited to serve as administrators and guards in the extermination camps because of their conventionality, blind obedience to authority, open willingness to aggress against those without power, essential meanness, propensity to see the Jews as vermin in need of extermination, and the blind adherence to Hitler's mystical cultism.

Applying the preceding discussion to events that transpired during my undergraduate days is an interesting intellectual exercise. The hazing and brainwashing that took place from 1956 to 1960, and I assume for many years before and after, was tacitly condoned by the institution (and to this day still defended and glorified by many former students of that era). At the same time, a fair portion of the mistreatment was mean-spirited, dehumanizing, and carried out in some cases by true authoritarian personalities straight from the Berkeley fascism primer.

The accepted local party line was that the Corps was "making men out of boys" when, in reality, it was breaking some of them down, and for what? It is a given that the Corps had as one of its major missions the creation of future military leaders, so conventional wisdom suggested that young Aggie Corps members were being physically, psychologically, and militarily prepared to be good soldiers and leaders, warriors who would not break if captured and subjected to unmentionable inhumanities at the hands of the enemy forces. The problem was that many cadets wanted to be students and nothing more, never wanting or expecting to be in the Army of Air Force because they were not under contract with the U.S. government to serve in the military upon graduation. One then has to ask what they were being prepared for by all the hazing and negativity. Remember: "Give only your name, rank, and serial number only! Semper Fi!"

As has been amply documented, the implementation of this warrior-building regimen was placed in the hands of the upper classmen, most particularly the sophomores. The majority of sophomores hazed freshmen because it was "the system" and they did it to avoid getting into trouble with the juniors and seniors. Unfortunately, however, there were always a handful who did so because they were inherently mean and sadistic and derived great pleasure from hurting people who were essentially powerless to fight back. Hitler would have adored a small handful of our sophomores for their zeal; they were the same sort of men the Fuhrer sought for his terror units, the SA, SS, and Gestapo.

The SA ("Storm-Abteilung"), also known as the "Brownshirts" for their uniform colors, was Hitler's private army. The SS ("Schutz-Staffel") were Hitler's personal body guards and operated the concentration and extermination camps. The Gestapo, or "Geheime Staatspolizei", were the regime's secret police headed up by one of the more heinous of Hitler's henchmen, Heinrich Himmler.

Our friends Royster and Ernst particularly come to mind in relation to this discussion because they unfortunately possessed most if not all of the defining characteristics of the authoritarian personality. Twenty years earlier, if living in Germany, they would have easily found a place of leadership among the Nazi terror groups. As I said earlier, Adolf Hitler would have loved those two sadists.

The Brain Drain. Another thing that bothered me in moments of reflection (there were not many of these moments for freshmen!) was the huge brain drain taking place at A&M in the 1950's. I looked around in January as the second semester of my freshman year started and noted the three guys in my unit with the highest grade point averages were MIA, or missing in action; all had transferred to other universities. They endured the hazing and harassment for the fall semester so they would not lose any credit hours, and then opted for greener pastures at other universities for the spring semester and beyond. If one assumes my experience was not an outlier and the same thing was repeated in most or all of the other forty Corps units, and I am almost certain it was, then it follows that an indefensible number of the top one hundred students left the university after one semester. Universities spend a lot of money recruiting and nurturing the best minds, and none can afford the brain drain that most assuredly was taking place at A&M in the 1950's.

In addition to the top students, others of more modest academic standing fell by the wayside in huge numbers. Again, if one extrapolates from my unit which suffered fifty percent attrition from the first to second year and seventy percent by the start of the third year, it seems logical to assume that total university enrollment suffered a major hit. I was once told that the picture was so bad with the class of 1961, or the freshman class after my own, that forty-eight percent of them had quit the university by Thanksgiving. I now know those numbers were somewhat inaccurate but they do provide a subjective index of the seriousness of the attrition problem at that critical time in the evolution of the university. My class learned to haze well, but then we had some masterful mentors to mimic! As a postscript, a report in a recent edition of the Texas Aggie, the magazine read by many former students, indicated that the graduation rate of the Class of 1961 was forty-five percent, an egregious statistic this university administration reluctantly confronted and would, thank goodness, find indefensible today.

First Semester Grades. Speaking of students of modest academic standing, my first semester grades were, as they say, nothing to write home about. The university administration must have concurred with my assessment for a mid-semester grade report was sent to my father confirming what I was already figuring out on my own, namely I was totally unprepared to survive academically in a university environment unless some radical changes were made. I had been pretty much a straight-A student during my early school years, but high school was a totally different issue. I was a total goof-off and got by on personality and athletic achievements. My grades, such as they were, were pretty much handed to me. I do not remember ever turning in so much as one homework assignment the last two years of high school, but I do recall being absent from school for all or parts of half of the required 180 days during my senior year. Hardly the stuff of college preparation and academic excellence!

HUMBLING MID-SEMESTE GRADE REPORT, FIRST SEMESTER, 1956

The end result of this indifference to the task at hand led me to enter A&M with nary a study skill. I did not have the foggiest notion of what it took to succeed, let alone excel, on papers and examinations. One saving grace was that I liked going to class, a total reversal of my lackadaisical, irresponsible, and reprehensible approach to high school attendance. I attended my college classes almost without fail and occasionally sought help from professors. Nevertheless, I struggled mightily at first, just trying to stay afloat, grade-wise.

At mid-semester of the freshman year, my father, bless his heart, received the aforementioned grade report from the university administration which read:

    Biology 101, C   Rural Sociology 205, D

    Military Science 121, C   History 105, D

    English 103, 67 (F)   Mathematics 101, 42 (F)

By way of summary, I was enrolled in sixteen hours of course credit and had a grand total of eight grade points, or a 0.50 grade point ratio (1.00 was a C average on the three-point system in place at A&M at that time). The grade report was accompanied by a terse letter from a Dean strongly suggesting that I would not be invited back for the spring semester unless there was dramatic improvement in my performance.

I took the low grades and the draconian warning from the Dean to heart and by semester's end, I was able to improve my grades by one letter in Sociology and History, thus raising my GPA to 0.875 (or what would be a 1.875 in today's 4-point scheme). This modest improvement allowed me to come back to school in the spring, though on academic probation. Getting accustomed to the rigors of college coursework was a tough transition, but I never had any trouble with my grades after that most challenging first semester, even making the Dean's List on occasion.

Somehow, somewhere, the university administration, the A&M Board of Regents, and the Texas legislature figured out that A&M was not retaining its best students nor keeping its overall enrollment numbers up and was in need of serious triage. The school was figuratively bleeding from the mouth, ears, nose, and a host of other pertinent orifices. As a result of critical examination and soul-searching at the highest levels of the university administration and state government, it was decided to reduce the influence of the Corps by making it an option rather than a requirement, add depth and breadth to the curricular offerings, and permit women to enroll which is a story of its own discussed elsewhere. It seemed to me, even as an unsophisticated and uninformed youngster, that Texas A&M University was in danger of impaling itself on its own sword of misdeeds in the 1950's. Change was sorely needed!

At some point in our senior year of 1959-1960, I had an informal chat with Bill Heye, the Corps Commander, and told him the enemy had been spotted and, a la Pogo, the enemy was us! For one thing, the steadfast refusal of the Corps of Cadets to change its counterproductive ways was exacting a huge toll. Also, there was rigid clinging to traditions and behaviors that simply did not serve the university and Corps of Cadets well. Unfortunately, many of these traditions were supported (and still are) by the legions of "Old Ags" who fought to maintain the status quo. Many Aggies of my generation still get chills when they think of the way things used to be, those hallowed days of what has come to be known as "Old Army", those good old days when bodies were symbolically stacked up like cordwood because of horrific hazing and failing grades.

As I told Bill Heye, the forces holding the university back were hazing, negativity, non-contingent use of punishment, a noticeable absence of positive incentives for good behavior, and a deep-rooted institutionally-condoned unwillingness to treat people with dignity. The prevailing attitude of most cadets was: "I caught hell from the class ahead of me and I am going to exact retribution from the one behind me." It was not clear to me that the authorities were really trying to break the cycle of retribution and negativity while concomitantly instilling and reinforcing a climate in which people thrived.

The Bonfire. Another major source of stress for the "fish" was the Aggie Bonfire, a tradition that has been discontinued as a university-sponsored event due to an unforgiveable lack of oversight on the part of the A&M administration. It seems that the building of the bonfire had become increasingly placed in the hands of the student leaders, and oversight by professionals and administrators became lax. The combination of student inexperience, zeal to get the job done at any cost, a youthful and cavalier attitude about safety issues, and negligence regarding adult oversight on the part of university leaders laid the groundwork for calamity. Years of institutional negligence culminated in the death of twelve students in November of 1999.

In my day, if a freshman had an hour off from classes, he was required to be at the stacking area, wrestling heavy logs on to the stack located behind Duncan Mess Hall. If he had two or more hours off, trucks transported him and others to the cutting area to chop down and load logs. This regimen went on for the better part of a month, rain or shine, hot weather or cold, in sickness and in health, in good times or bad, till death do us part. And there was no real relief at night because you were assigned to guard the bonfire should some ornery students from that fearsome frat-rat playground in Austin try to prematurely ignite the damn thing. Thus, the bonfire was pretty much our entire life for at least thirty long, sometimes wet, often cold, bone-weary days. We were almost always overwhelmed by mental and physical fatigue, and studying and preparing for class were of necessity or expediency relegated to the far back burner.

People often talk about the rare deaths or occasional serious injuries associated with the bonfire prior to the calamity in 1999. The usual lamentations were in reference to occasional broken bones or serious strains, sprains, and abrasions that are almost certain to take place when thousands of young people worked at an arduous and what ultimately proved to be a dangerous, life-threatening task. Something that has both intrigued and perplexed me for all these years is I have never heard anyone mention the academic casualties associated with the building of the Bonfire. Many of my so-called "fish" buddies were on the brink of flunking out of school by the first of November, and for quite a number the bonfire was the *coup de grace*, the final nail in the coffin. Not getting to engage in serious, productive study for essentially a month was absolutely fatal to those students who were hanging on by a thread. How many people have had their lives altered by flunking out of school? And what kind of price tag can we attach to such events? There is no doubt in my mind that hundreds and probably thousands of former students can trace their academic demise to what amounted to a month-long hiatus from the books in the name of erecting and burning a bunch of logs.

My own take on the bonfire, academic issues aside, was enmity at first sight; my dislike for the whole enterprise was evident from the moment the two of us first met. I detested the rainy, cold, windy, miserable November weather and the long tours of duty in the cutting area for what seemed deep down to me to be a task of monumental, unfathomable inanity. Guarding that monstrosity at night was an absolutely abhorrent task, particularly since there was no way in heaven a group of rank amateur fraternity brothers from that Austin Playboy Club on the Colorado River could have lit the thing on fire anyway. I personally thought it ludicrous that Aggies really believed a ragtag collection of UT miscreants out on an alcohol-fueled lark could carry around the necessary thousands of gallons of jet fuel required to torch our beloved bonfire.

I also did not like the time away from the books. As noted earlier, I was in serious academic trouble by bonfire time and needed to concentrate on my studies. One of the steps I took to survive academically was to hide out in the most unlikely of places, a restroom stall in the recently-razed G. Rollie White Coliseum. I knew in my heart of hearts that if my ruse had been uncovered, even the most red-ass of sophomores could understand a guy having to use the crapper. I spent many an hour in G. Rollie that November, sitting in my favorite "study carrel", fighting for my academic life.

This anecdote reminds me of Aggies who are always showing up on campus to relive their undergraduate experiences and to regale family members with stories of the "good old days." I practiced my own brand of reminiscing not too long ago by visiting G. Rollie for the last time, as it became a victim to the wrecker's ball in the summer of 2013 to make way for the expansion of our aforementioned Roman Coliseum posing as a football stadium, Kyle Field. As stated earlier, G. Rollie is full of great memories for me; most of my undergraduate classes were held there and I am a loyal fan of Aggie basketball where the home games were played for most of my years at A&M. I also graduated in that old building and enjoyed quite a number of concerts held there despite rather dismal acoustics. Perhaps most importantly, the G. Rollie crapper stall visits during the construction of the bonfire in 1956 may well have been my academic salvation, of which I am most thankful.

In an attempt to raise a few shekels for the athletic department while appealing to those of a sentimental persuasion, the university announced on September 24, 2013 that it would be possible to order an exterior brick from the demolished structure for $25 plus sales tax plus $11 shipping charges. Purchases came with a caveat that each brick would be considered a separate order. Also, each brick was guaranteed to be whole but with some variation in terms of blemishes and amount of attached mortar.

After my freshman year, I pretty much found other subterfuges to get out of working on the bonfire, and honestly do not think I touched a log the last three years. I never got near the bonfire site except to watch it burn. By now, you must have some sense of how I feel about the renegade bonfire a handful of misguided students have thrown together off campus of late. Succinctly put, the twelve people who died in 1999 deserve better from their fellow Aggies!

I was not a bonfire guy and am thrilled that it is dead as an institutionally-sponsored event, given the risks and the astronomical insurance tab it would take to reinstitute it. I grant that the bonfire was spectacular in scope and served as a great public relations tool for the university. However, those pluses pale badly when you consider the human toll the bonfire has exacted over the years. I am convinced that school spirit is quite high among the legions of Aggies, present and past, and will continue to thrive, even if no logs get incinerated on campus each Thanksgiving.

Positive Things, Good People. It is only fair to say there were far more positives than negatives about being a member of the Corps and a student at A&M. First and foremost, it is the people you meet who determine your happiness in most situations, and my A&M experience was no exception. For one thing, I met people I never knew existed….Czechs, Poles, Italians, Germans, Mexicans, Catholics, Jews, New Yorkers, you name it. I came from a sheltered life in Oklahoma and as will be noted in pages that follow later, my friends and acquaintances were Indians with names like Longbone, Horsechief, or Wahnee on one hand, or Anglos named Jones, Smith, Brown, Davis, Wright, Miller, and Gray on the other. We had a few Hispanic families in our town, a Jew of two, and one Greek family (the only Anglo Catholics I ever knew until I came to the Lone Star State), so Texas was a source of amazement with its ethnic and religious diversity. I was suddenly surrounded by classmates with names like Papacek, Warzecha, Janak, Murski, Ortiz, Saenz, and Stufflebeme. I visited cities with squares, an architectural phenomenon pretty much unheard of in Oklahoma. I learned that Catholics were numerous and mostly plain old ordinary people, not the mystical, secretive cultists we perceived them to be when I was growing up in rural Oklahoma. It was reassuring to learn that Catholics, or at least the majority of them, did not have two heads and one eye!

Charlie Janak was the first Catholic I really got to know well. He was from Smithville, near Austin, and the two of us would occasionally hitchhike to his home on weekends, particularly in the spring semester of our freshman year. We were able to get away fairly regularly by then as the hazing had eased up some and the rules governing our comings and goings on weekends were relaxed. We could see for the first time the glimmer of light at the end of the hazing tunnel!

While in Smithville one weekend, I attended my first Czech wedding and the first Catholic Mass, both totally new experiences. Charlie also fixed me up with a blind date another weekend with a lovely young woman by the name of Dianne McClure (I heard ten years ago that she still lived in Smithville) and we had a couple of dates and exchanged a letter or two after that. As is often the case with long distance relationships, this one lacked inspiration and it died a quick and painless death.

I had never even seen a Catholic priest before, let alone met one, until one showed up at Charlie Janak's home. It seems that during one of our weekends visits, Charlie's family invited the priest from their church over to the house for lunch after Mass one Sunday. I remember he was rather young and tall and dashing in appearance, with black cowboy boots and a big black hat fleshing out his more priestly attire. To add to the effect, he also drove a brand new pitch-black 1956 Mercury fitted with loud mufflers, fancy tail pipes, glitzy hubcaps, and a lowered rear end.

At one point during the meal, the unimaginable happened; the priest actually drank a couple of beers with Charlie's parents! This "blasphemy" destroyed my youthful and naïve image of the clergy in one fell swoop; the dress, demeanor, and dolled-up car all flew in the face of my uninformed stereotype of what any man of the cloth, let alone a Catholic priest, would be like. When lunch was over, the priest said his goodbyes, got into his vehicle, racked back the mufflers, and sped away, leaving a trail of simmering rubber and swirling dust in his swashbuckling wake.

Somewhere along the line, Charlie and I separated ways, and the last I heard he had been a Navy Seal. Undoubtedly, if what I had heard is indeed true, he would be long retired by now. I do owe Charlie Janak a pat on the back for providing a woefully deprived Okie with an enlightening if brief first exposure to Catholicism, Catholic priests, Czech culture, and, however briefly, Dianne McClure. Females were virtually non-existent at A&M and it was wonderful to just look at one of them in real life.

Thumbing a Ride. Speaking of hitchhiking, it was our main mode of transportation my freshman year at A&M. While hitching rides was interesting, I am thrilled to say that I did precious little of it during the rest of my college days. Having your own car at school was uncommon in those days, in stark contrast to today when getting a car on your sixteenth birthday is a rite of passage not a privilege. Cars were not permitted for freshmen (and, I think, sophomores), so the main mode of travel for most of us if we wanted to go somewhere was thus hitchhiking. I cannot remember anyone who had a car on a permanent basis that first year, so on those rare weekends when we were granted a little freedom, several of us would hitchhike somewhere, usually home or, in my case, to Smithville with Charlie Janak.

The year before I started A&M, a cadet named Ronald E. Menter was murdered while hitching a ride with David Broderick, a man he had met on New Year's Eve in an El Paso bar. As a result of this tragedy, the university administration urged students to travel in pairs or trios and to be smart when getting into a car with strangers. I do not recall ever feeling like my life was in danger at the hands of a homicidal fiend, but I did meet some strange, quirky people while "riding my thumb."

Once I got picked up by a middle-aged man who introduced himself as Tom X, an employee of the university's Agriculture Extension Service. Tom Terrific, as I preferred to call him, was traveling to Houston on business and had an Asian student driver, Korean I think, so he asked if I would read the Bible to them as we motored along. I was not keen on the idea, and if this were to happen to me today, I would bail in a nano-second in order to avoid being subjected to such presumption. However, I was young and naïve and rides were not easy to come by, so I politely took my place in the back seat and proceeded to read Bible passages Mr. X. had selected for our impromptu daily devotional. The evangelical spirit of the moment was apparently overwhelming for the man and he quickly shifted into his heavy duty, heavy breathing proselytizing mode. Feeling the spirit of the moment, he made frequent references to how many people he had converted to Christ in the back seat of his car, and urged me to join that select group. I know it was perverse of me but all I could think as he gyrated and gesticulated were some more secular back seat "conversions" my friends and I had attempted or consummated with willing females in high school or college. Eventually, we reached his Houston destination and I hastily got out of the car, thrilled at the prospect of being released from the verbal bondage he had imposed. For the next year or two, when the man spotted me on campus, he would stop and hand out daily devotionals and religious tracts. Some ten years later, give or take, his daughter enrolled in one of my classes but I had the tact to never broach the topic of my near-conversion experience at the hands of her religious zealot father.

One another occasion, I had hitched my way from College Station to the northwest side of Houston where an older couple in their fifties or sixties offered a ride. They seemed nice enough and all went well until all of a sudden, the man called his wife an ugly name or two and backhanded her across the front seat. At this point, they decided it might be best to resolve their differences alone, and I could not have been happier when they dropped me off to fend for myself right in the middle of big old Houston. I made it home unharmed, though bloodied and bowed a bit by the events of the day.

Another time, some friends and I were making our way along the Gulf Freeway near Main Street in the company of a member of the Houston Police Department who was kind enough to pick us up as he made his way home after work. Again, all was going well until the minion of the law suddenly swerved violently to his left, nearly running the car adjacent to us off the freeway. This maneuver was repeated a couple of times, accompanied by some random verbalizations to the effect: "Fucking niggers. Don't you just hate those bastards, always getting in the fucking way of white people?" Such malevolence on the part of a man commissioned to uphold the law for all races and creeds was both a shock and a revelation for this naïve country kid. I can only imagine what it must have been like to be black if this guy decided you had done something really wrong! And I'll bet he was not terribly different in his racial perspective than a fair number of his colleagues in 1957.

A final hitchhiking memory occurred near the Gulf Freeway fairly close to Alvin. I was riding my thumb alone, which was often the case despite the university admonitions to the contrary, and had managed in a short time to get from College Station to the southeast part of Houston where a large, pleasant-looking, tousle-haired, dark-skinned man offered me a ride. He did give me a warning before I joined him that he was going to Alvin via Highway 6 as opposed to taking the Gulf Freeway which was the more direct route to Texas City. I thought" "What the hell. I have time on my hands and I can probably get there about as fast going through Alvin. It's only a few miles out of the way." Wrong!! Another beautiful hypothesis shot down; I think it ended up taking three or four hours to make what at most was a one-hour trip from Houston to Texas City on the freeway.

The fellow who gave me the ride was Andy Hillhouse, an A&M football star of the late 1940's who played end. Hillhouse was drafted by the New York Yankees of the National Football League in 1950, the 146th player out of 391 selected. He would have been maybe seven or eight years older than me at the time we met. It was clear when I got in the car he had over-imbibed and was pretty much on a "crying drunk." As we made our way to Alvin, Hillhouse lamented the personal difficulties he had experienced and was currently experiencing, problems he had encountered in coming to grips with a drinking problem, and whatever else came to mind. It was sad to see him down and out, depressed, and crying in his beer, so to speak. Fortunately I never thought my life was on the line with him at the wheel though he was clearly not in total control and most certainly would have been given a DWI if he had been pulled over by the gendarmerie. I can state unequivocally, however, I was quite happy to get out of the car to catch a ride from Alvin to Texas City with someone of greater sobriety. I never heard of Andy Hillhouse again.

There were other hitchhiking episodes less memorable than the ones described here but I now know that people who picked up hitchhikers, at least in those days, were often a different breed; lonely, depressed, down-and-out, and often in need of someone to talk to about their desperate lives.

Outstanding Cadets.

A big plus associated with attending A&M and being a member of the Corps of Cadets was the bonding that took place among those fortunate enough to make it through the first year. For many people, a lifelong attachment to the university and to each other was forged from what can only be described as a survival experience. The guys you met and with whom you overcame adversity were a constant source of support and inspiration and, despite what I perceive to be the brain drain and overall student attrition mentioned earlier, there were many good, bright, and talented young men who stuck it out and became immensely successful. There is a virtually endless list of extremely accomplished people who have walked through these hallowed halls at A&M on their way to a lifetime of excellence in a variety of endeavors.

Some have gone on to distinguish themselves via military service, including seven World War II recipients of the Medal of Honor. Another 20,000 Aggie served in that war, 14,000 of whom were commissioned officers. The total number of officers from A&M was greater in World War II than the combined total produced in that same time period by the United States Military and Naval Academies. Additionally, over 250 Aggies have attained the rank of General in the Army or Admiral in the Navy. One of these generals was Earl Rudder, mentioned at some length elsewhere in this treatise, who led the charge up Pointe du Hoc on Normandy Beach in France on D-Day, the sixth of June, 1944. Rudder later served as President of his alma mater for a little over a decade prior to his untimely death in 1970. Two other Generals, Horace Carswell, Jr. and Bernard Schriever, have had air force bases named after them.

Other notables include actors Ty Hardin and Rip Torn, actress Martha Madison, and playwright Tim McCanlies who wrote the screenplay for the legendary movie, *Giant*, starring the iconic James Dean (not an Aggie!). Of these various thespians and writers, Martha Madison stands out for me as I was fortunate enough to get to know her reasonably well during her undergraduate days. Martha was a Psychology major, captain of the Texas Aggie Dance team, a 1999 A&M graduate, and later a graduate of the American Musical and Dramatic Academy in New York. Perhaps prescient about her ultimate destination in the limelight as an actress or dancer, Martha changed her name from Buttersworth to Madison at some point, I am assuming in her adolescence. There is something about the name Buttersworth that just does not resonate if one is a famous actress, but the alliterative "Martha Madison" has a ring of celebrity to it.

Injuries forced Martha to retire from dancing after two years and she moved to California to take a shot at film and television acting. She eventually made her name as an actress by playing Belle Black Brady on the immensely popular soap opera, *Days of Our Lives*, a role she held from 2004 to 2008 and again starting in 2015 after an absence of seven years. Martha has also appeared in films or televisions series such as *Kate and Leopold, Law and Order: Criminal Intent*, and *General Hospital*, and currently performs in California and New York. She married A. J. Gilbert in 2007, and they became the proud parents of Charley Elizabeth Gilbert on November 3, 2013. Martha and I have exchanged an email or two a year or visited on Facebook since her graduation in 1999, so I have been able to keep tabs on her life and career reasonably closely. I must confess I have never seen *Days of Our Lives*, so I know nothing of Belle Black Brady.

Country and western musicians Robert Earl Keen, Lyle Lovett, and Rick Trevino called Aggieland home for a few years. Despite a relatively short history as students at A&M, seven Aggie females have won ten beauty pageants including Miss USA, Miss Texas, Miss Teen Texas, Miss Louisiana USA, and Miss Texas USA. One of these women, Kim Tomes was Miss USA in 1976 and, later, a finalist in the Miss Universe competition.

In the business sector, Aggies have served as Chairman, President, or Chief Executive Officer of corporations such as Saudi Aramco, Honeywell, Gulf Oil, Rockwell International, Arrowhead Mills, Pier 1 Imports, Clear Channel Communications, Mitchell Energy, Zachry Construction, and jewelry giant Zale's.

Dozens and dozens of Aggies have served as college presidents, ambassadors, politicians at the state and national level, heads of state (Bolivia and Panama), cabinet secretaries, federal judges, mayors of Texas cities (Abilene, Austin, Dallas, and San Antonio), attorneys, medical doctors, and college professors. The university truly does have an impressive array of former students who are stars in their chosen professions and endeavors.

I still remember seeing cadets on campus when I was an undergraduate who I thought stood out from the crowd, young men I believed would go on to major accomplishments in life. These cadets cast a big shadow in their undergraduate days and have gone on to achieve imminence, partially validating the process whereby leaders at the highest levels in the Corps were selected. The predictive validity, as the statisticians and methodologists are wont to say, was quite high between leadership in the late 1950's and prominence more than a half century later. Among the most memorable cadets were:

Jack Lunsford, Class of 1957. Lunsford had a most visible presence in his position as Corps Commander for 1956-57. He went on to receive a PhD in Chemistry from Rice University in 1962 and held faculty positions at the Universities of Idaho and Texas. Lunsford became a member of the A&M faculty in 1971 and retired as Distinguished Professor Emeritus of Chemistry.

Thomas W. Adair III, Class of 1957. I knew Tom Adair only slightly as an undergraduate, but always thought he was a pretty classy guy, serving as one of the Brigade Commanders, a top leadership position in the Corps. Tom was a Physics major who went on to receive a PhD from Rice University in 1965. He joined the faculty in Physics at A&M in 1966. He has also been on the Athletic Council of the University and served as its head for many years. Though Tom retired in 2017, I still see him and his wife, Carolyn, here and there about town. The Adair's were featured a couple of years ago in the *Houston Chronicle* for the olive oil they produce at their second home in the Tuscany region of Italy.

Jon L. Hagler, Class of 1958. A native of Bastrop, near Austin, Hagler probably did more justice to the Corps uniform than anyone I can remember. He was the Corps Commander my sophomore year, and cut a most imposing swath as he moved about the campus. Hagler was handsome, with an aquiline jaw and a lean, wiry, muscular build. He oozed confidence and control, and his uniforms were tailored to show off his strapping physique. I seldom saw him on campus when he was not wearing his signature senior boots. Jon Hagler looked like he had arrived the day of his birth sporting leather.

In addition to his commanding physical presence, Hagler was an outstanding student and a most impressive leader. Following graduation, he spent the obligatory years in the Army before going on to graduate school at Harvard where he received an MBA in 1963. Post-Harvard, he held a number of important leadership positions with an assortment of investment and mutual funds companies, and served as President of the highly-prestigious Ford Foundation in New York for five years.

As is often the case with many prominent former students, Hagler has been generous to the university with his time and money. For his loyalty, he has been the recipient of numerous honors from his alma mater, and the Hagler Building on campus bears his name. He has also been instrumental in shaping the future of the university by serving on the prestigious 2020 commission which has its goal bringing A&M on par with the older, more established American public universities. Hagler's most recent act of largesse was to provide his alma mater with $20 million to endow the Hagler Institute for Advanced Study, an initiative designed to attract the best and brightest scholars from all over the world to spend time at A&M. In 2015, Hagler was awarded an honorary doctorate, making him one of only seventy people who have received this prestigious service recognition over the past 140 years.

A few years ago, Hagler took a strong stand against the Texas Public Policy Foundation (TPPF), an organization with designs on implementing draconian right-wing, conservative educational policies in several universities in Texas. The TPPF policies are at once asinine, naïve, and dangerous. The organization has contributed substantial amounts of money to the political coffers of former student and one-time Texas governor Rick Perry and thus had his unwavering support. For several years, Perry and the TPPF did their best to drag A&M back in time to the mediocre cow college it was when I was a student. Hagler is one of a number of prominent former students who went on record publically voicing opposition to Perry and TPPF. In 2011, Hagler joined 200 other prominent Texans in forming the Texas Coalition for Excellence in Higher Education which was created with the goal of protecting those tangibles and intangibles that make for excellence in Tier One research universities.

The Texas Coalition was formed in the wake of Governor Perry's relationship with the TPPF. It is too bad that Governor Perry, now Secretary of the Department of Energy in the Trump cabinet, does not love his alma mater in positive and productive ways as has been the case with Aggie coalition members Jon Hagler, Ray Bowen, Melbern Glasscock, Artie McFerrin, Jerry Cox, Arno Krebs, Jack Little, Weldon Kruger, Rod Stepp, and countless others.

It saddens me greatly that, at one time several years ago, the A&M administration actually considered removing itself from the Southern Association of Colleges and Schools (SACS). At about the same time, the leadership thumbed its nose at the President of the highly prestigious Association of American Universities (AAU), that august, by-invitation-only collection of sixty-two top US research universities, which has expressed great concern about the intrusion of TPPF-like initiatives into the affairs of the university. My own view is that it was a blatant attempt on the part of religious, right wing, ultra-conservatives to take over the running of Texas A&M. Losing SACS accreditation and forfeiting membership in the AAU would have been tantamount to creating two community colleges in Bryan-College Station, a small one with 12,000 students known as Blinn College and a gargantuan one with 65,000 students, Texas A&M Junior College.

I actually had a Hagler sighting not too many years ago while eating out with my family. I spied him with an associate dining on the elegant high cuisine served at the Chicken Oil Company in Bryan. He looked older, of course, but sufficiently like the 1950's version for me to make a quick identification.

L TO R – CORPS COMMANDER JON HAGLER AND
DEPUTY COMMANDER RAY BOWEN, 1957-1958

Ray Bowen, Class of 1958. I do remember Dr. Ray Bowen, hometown Fort Worth, from the old days but only slightly. Ray served as Hagler's Deputy Corps Commander, and received his bachelor's degree in Mechanical Engineering in 1958. He went on from A&M to earn a master's degree from California Institute of Technology in 1959 and the PhD from the old alma mater in 1961. Among his other achievements, Dr. Bowen served as Vice President of Oklahoma State University and was Interim President there for a year prior to taking the Presidency of A&M, a position he held from 1994 to 2002. Though retired from the Presidency at A&M, he is still a member of the faculty in Mechanical Engineering and I see him occasionally at basketball games on campus.

Like his classmate Hagler, Bowen was also vocal in his opposition to the Perry-backed TPPF political meddling. Bowen has been a voice of reason for his alma mater, and is also a member of the Texas Coalition for Excellence in Higher Education.

Donald Cloud, Class of 1959. Don Cloud was from Kerens in deep east Texas and not especially memorable for me other than the fact that he was Corps Commander. Though he did not have the eye-catching physical presence of a Lunsford or a Hagler, Cloud was reputed to be a most capable leader with a keen intellect. Behind the red faced, ruddy complexion, and small town upbringing was a first-class mind.

I am not sure how he felt upon sober reflection as he aged, but Don Cloud made quite a stir on campus with his involvement in a caper which unfolded at the SMU football game in November of 1958. *SI Vault*, the archival branch of Sports Illustrated carried the following excerpt from the A&M-SMU game:

> "A Texas record is established as a boy and girl meet at halftime in the middle of the Cotton Bowl and in front of 53,000 patient fans, kiss for one minute and 45.8 seconds. The stalwart lad is Texas A&M ROTC Commander, Don Cloud; the stalwart lass is Aggie Sweetheart Millie Rowland. The big smooch is a traditional ceremony, and the ceremony has become more everlasting each year. This time the kiss was so protracted that the 240-piece A&M military band marched off the field leaving the couple as lonesome as a pair of lonesome ends. Not to be outdone, Southern Methodist, A&M's rivals, set an endurance record of their own; their doughty band played Peruna, the SMU fight song, 382 times."

A classmate reported in late 2013 that Don Cloud was receiving treatment for cancer, and he apparently succumbed to the illness on November 17, 2013, at the age of seventy-six, though his obituary in the local paper did not specifically make mention of the cause of his demise. In a recent email to me, Tom Adair said Don Cloud had been receiving cancer treatment for several years prior to his death.

Melbern G. Glasscock, Class of 1959. Mel Glasscock was right up there with Jon Hagler in my memory as one of the spiffiest dressers in the Corps. He was nice-looking, clean-cut, slender, and his uniforms always looked as if they had just been plucked fresh from the dry cleaners. Glasscock, like Hagler before him, was enamored with his senior boots. I always sort of figured the two of them may have taken the boots off long enough to study in the evening but slipped them back on in order to get a good night's sleep. Glasscock majored in Mechanical Engineering as an undergraduate, and later founded and became chief executive officer of a petrochemical marketing company in Houston with annual sales of $400 million dollars. His business success allowed him, in conjunction with his wife Susanne's interest in the humanities, to create the Susanne M. Glasscock School for Continuing Studies at Rice University and the Glasscock Center for the Humanities at A&M. A building on our campus now bears his name and serves as the home of the Center for the Humanities. The Center was first directed by Dr. James Rosenheim of the History faculty, and Jim turned over the Glasscock Center reins to Dr. Joseph Golsan from European and Classical Languages and Cultures in 2011.

You could see success written all over Melbern Glasscock as a young man, and he has lived up to that expectation in both his engineering career and in promoting the humanities, a marriage of perspectives that Glasscock would like to see become more common among engineers. As he said in an interview in 2005: "Engineers learn a lot about how to do things, but they do not get lessons on whether or not they should do them. Classes like history and other humanities can give students those kinds of lessons." Glasscock was another prominent member of the Texas Coalition for Excellence in Higher Education. He, like Hagler and Bowen, fought to protect the university he has so benevolently supported from the malevolence of Rick Perry and the TPPF.

William B. Heye, Class of 1960. Bill Heye always struck me as a good guy, and I thought he handled the affairs of the Corps well in a period of transition from what might be called "Old Army" to "New Army" as the university changed from mandatory Corps participation to a less restrictive and more voluntary student commitment. Bill served in the U.S. Air Force for three years, earned an MBA from Harvard, and held a number of important national and international corporate positions. He has also won a number of awards from his alma mater and has served on a number of important boards for the university. He was named a Distinguished Alumnus in 1991, and is the proud father of four children, all of whom have degrees from A&M. In light of my high regard for Bill Heye, it was an honor and my distinct pleasure to have the opportunity to teach one of his daughters, Kathy, in my Psychology of Adjustment class in the spring of 1984. She graduated three years later.

In addition to the good people you meet, there were many other positive features of A&M. The football march-ins, the street parades during Corps trips to Houston, Dallas, or Austin, Aggie Muster, the Elephant Walk, Parent's Day, Final Review, the Thanksgiving Day football game with the University of Texas, or "tu", the Ring Dance, and perhaps most significant of all, Silver Taps, that Tuesday night ceremony honoring Aggies who have died recently are all precious memories for anyone who has been an Aggie. For most Aggies, hearing the Fighting Texas Aggie Band fire up to play the War Hymn always raises the hair on the back of your neck. Overall, there was far more to like about A&M than there was to dislike. It is a unique school with fascinating traditions and incredible loyalty on the part of the student body and its 400,000 former students.

That First Miserable Semester Comes to an End at Christmas, Sort Of

After that rather Raggedy Andy (Raggedy-Ass?) start in the classroom, I figured out how the game was played and made decent grades for the last seven semesters, even shocking myself by making the Dean's List, I think three times. My sophomore year, I completed twenty-two hours in the fall and nineteen in the spring, and those were my two best semesters, grade-wise, at A&M. At that stage of my life, I thought I wanted to coach football and frankly A&M offered a limited number of majors of interest to me, so I chose Physical Education (now known as Kinesiology). The longer I stayed in the major, however, the less I wanted to coach. For one thing, I did not have the big athletic name so important to landing a relatively prestigious coaching position, and the thought of laboring for years as a junior high school coach and physical education teacher was unpalatable to me.

Christmas finally arrived, and it was great to go home for two weeks of rest, relaxation, and good food. We freshmen endured a lot of good-natured ribbing from our peers from other schools about what they perceived to be a dreadful choice of university, as well as our freakish shaved heads. Even if people did not know you personally, everyone in town could tell you were an Aggie by that telltale shaved head. But it sure was great to sit down to eat without some sophomore with male premenstrual tension screaming at you at the top of his leathery lungs simply because you did not know the name of some statue on campus or the score of the A&M-Texas football game in 1929.

One wrong-headed practice in place at A&M when I started was the policy of completing the semester not at Christmas but three weeks later in January. Thus, when students headed home for the holidays it was certain there would a round of exams in each course prior to finals, the last theme in English would be hanging over your head, and the much-dreaded term paper in History almost certainly would not write itself in your absence from campus. Most everyone took a load of books home, carefully placed them on a small table beside the front door, and retrieved them, untouched and a bit dusty, from that same spot two weeks later just prior to heading back to campus for the final three weeks of academic and Corps-related torture. The intention to study over the holiday was honorable but the practice, for me at least, never matched the theory. As my father was fond of saying, "Son, the road to hell is paved with good intentions." I am not completely sure about my intentions but I sure as hell did not dishonor the Yuletide holidays by cracking a book during those two weeks!

As a result of letting dust collect on the good old books during the holidays, it was crunch time when we got back to school in early January. One of the best things the A&M administration ever did was institute a policy whereby finals exams were completed prior to Christmas, thus making the holiday season, or winter solstice to be politically correct, a true break for faculty, staff, and students alike. With that overdue and welcomed change, there was no longer any need to feel guilty about letting the books collect dust during Christmas.

Another interesting and wrongheaded policy at that time was Saturday classes. The typical class pattern in those days was Monday, Wednesday, and Friday, and Tuesday, Thursday, and Saturday, though classes mercifully did stop at noon on Saturday. Few students can even imagine having any 8 o'clock class, let along one at that time on Saturday morning! Again, the university did away with this practice after my first year, thus laying the groundwork for the now familiar hour and fifteen minutes course offerings on Tuesdays and Thursdays. I think all would agree the new approach is far better than the old.

Freshmen Come and Go

As the thought of being allowed to return to good old Aggieland for the sophomore year became a reality, I reflected on the events of the freshman year with a mix of joy and melancholy. At the freshman orientation the preceding August, we made our choice of major and enrolled for our first set of courses. A top A&M administrator held forth in Sbisa Hall and gave us a "Rah-Rah" talk about campus life. At the same time, he offered a somber reminder that we should all look to our left and then to our right because only one of the three of us would be around for the sophomore year. Those numbers were not altogether accurate, but they were not very far off. As I listened to his dire prediction of gloom and doom, I had the sinking feeling we were a herd of wildebeests and two-thirds of us were going to be picked off by ravenous crocodiles as we crossed the (Brazos?) river. There were crocodiles out there alright, but not in the river; they were of the human variety and were called upperclassmen and professors!

As predicted, freshmen came and went; my first roommate, Robert Martin from Premont, Texas, flunked out after one semester. My second roommate, Bob Warzecha, a Cuero Gobbler, was more fortunate; he made it back for year two and beyond. Bob and I were never close at all but he was a nice guy who graduated at the same time I did. I noticed recently in the Texas Aggie that Bob has passed away, which as noted elsewhere is the case with many of my college friends and acquaintances.

A particularly gratifying aspect of my freshmen year was re-establishing relations with friends from Texas City who I knew to varying degrees as a result of spending summers there from age ten until I started college. Since I did not go to high school in Texas City, the base of continuity so essential to cementing these relationships was missing. I more or less started over every summer, and the same was certainly true for my first year at A&M.

Mostly, the Texas City relationships were based on summer baseball, limited exposure at an adolescent hangout called the Teen Age Club, and miscellaneous random social interactions. During those first months at A&M, I got to recapture and nurture friendships with guys like Jack Cooper, Earl Yarbrough, Tommy Moore, and others. Later on, I developed a close relationship with a handsome chap named Joe Saunders after he transferred from the University of Texas to A&M, an unimaginable occurrence in those days. As a result of these renewals, I had a solid base of friends to hang out with during Christmas and when school ended in May. The summer following the freshman year was spent working construction at one of the refineries and just hanging out with these rediscovered old friends as well as guys from other universities such as Jimmy (Monk) Martin, Johnny Garton, Richard (Crow) Koehler, and Jimmy Welch.

Betty Grey Brightens the Day

Another highly significant person in my life that summer of 1957 was a lovely young woman by the name of Betty Grey McDuffie. I do not recall exactly how the two of us met but we were inseparable that summer and into a fair portion of the next school year. Betty McDuffie was an attractive, brown-eyed brunette with a lovely smile, a fetching full-body physique, and a much-appreciated if misguided fondness for me. I remember feeling some reluctance about approaching her initially because she had been dating a local tough-guy football hero with a reputation for scaring away potential suitors. For whatever reason, the transfer of her affection from Brutus to me went smoothly and the two of us never locked horns. Had we tangled, he was a lion and I was bait, and I owe a debt of gratitude to the great poobah in the sky for conferring that much-needed protection.

My first date with Ms. McDuffie was a bit tense as she was widely regarded in Texas City to be a major catch, and I wanted to impress her with what a warm, witty, wise, and gay guy I was (Isn't it interesting how the word "gay" has changed in connotation?). A major obstacle in getting to know my newly discovered friend was her mother who ran a tight ship when it came to the comings and goings of her three children, particularly the daughters, Betty Grey and Edna Earle.

Girls in those days often had curfews and Betty Grey was no exception. I do not remember what we did that first night, probably the obligatory first date movie, but we failed to make the 10:45 curfew by fifteen or twenty minutes. Even though the hour was late and the sky dark, I could see The Iron Maiden perched on the porch as we approached. Mrs. McDuffie was polite but grim-face and firm, spelling it out in no uncertain terms that if this blatant disrespect for her rules of conduct were to continue, it might be best if I start looking for another girlfriend. She threw in an added zinger, intimating that she should have expected this sort of misbehavior from the son of George LeUnes. I heard this sort of rhetoric on more than occasion as my father was a controversial figure locally because of his involvement in labor union business and the emotion such an affiliation evoked in a city with divided feelings about organized labor in the 1950's. When I let my father in on the barb from Mrs. McDuffie, he indicated he had heard it before and suggested I would no doubt hear it again. We shared a good laugh, and neither of us lost any sleep over her comment.

There were actually a couple of times, usually blind dates, when parents of girls I was dating for the first time would not allow them to go out with me when they ascertained my relationship to George LeUnes. I once showed up at the house of a cute little blonde whose name eludes me after all these years (could it have been Sharon Ricketson?) and immediately upon being introduced, was asked by the father to evacuate the premises. If I remember correctly, the father in this instance was a "scab", the term of endearment used by labor bosses and union members to refer to men who crossed picket lines to go to work during labor strikes. This was the first but not the only time I was to experience such negativity, and I know it was due to the aforementioned volatility of my father's labor union affiliation. Labor unions in the petrochemical industry along the Gulf Coast in the 1940's and 1950's created strong allegiances and some equally fierce animosities, and I felt the sting of those prejudices on more than one occasion. Actually, the whole thing lent an air of excitement to first dates that most of my friends never got to experience.

The Sophomore Year

Old Blue

It felt unbelievably good to have survived the freshman year, and I was excited to be shed of my gritty, grimy summer job as a laborer in the refinery and head back to school for the sophomore campaign. When I arrived on campus in late August, I was attired in Hawaiian shorts, a colorful tee shirt, a pair of ugly but comfortable flip-flops, or what we called thongs in those days (as is the case with the word "gay", the meaning of "thongs" has changed, also, has it not?), and a multi-colored, resplendent beret which matched nothing and barely kept my long, curly (wavy?), dark brown hair in place. I entered Dorm 2, went immediately to my assigned room, and met for the first time the guy who, unbeknownst to both of us, was destined to be my roommate for the next three years. I think my appearance scared the hell out of him; he was not sure what to make of the wild man who had just walked into his room. I could tell at a glance this good old ultra-conservative country boy was having trouble digesting the presence of what he must have perceived to be a real-life, wild-eyed, Gulf Coast, hippie liberal.

The new roommate was named Dorsey Dwain Blue, and he hailed from the small ultra-conservative and unapologetically racist, central Texas community of Hamilton. As one index of just how racist the city and area were in the 1950's, legend had it that there were warning signs posted all over the county stating: "Niggers, you can pass through but don't let the sun set on your black ass in Hamilton County, Texas." I do not remember for sure if I actually saw such a message posted anywhere, but there is a vague memory trace that tells me I did on one or two occasions. Without a doubt, the sentiment expressed therein was widely endorsed among whites in the area. It is interesting to note that according to 2010 census figures, blacks made up only seven-tenths of one percent of the county population. If my mathematics skills haven't abandoned me in my dotage, with a population of just over 7,000 people, I figure that a grand total of four dozen black people resided in Hamilton County as of that 2010 census. That may say a lot about a racist past (and present?).

Arnold LeUnes

DORSEY BLUE, EXECUTIVE OFFICER, COMPANY C-1, 1959-1960

Dorsey was diminutive, maybe 5 feet 4 and 110 pounds, nice looking, brown-eyed, with closely cropped, meticulously coiffed brown hair. He was also an immaculate dresser which greatly contrasted with the would-be hippie he had inherited as a roommate. Meeting Dorsey was the highlight of the year and without a doubt my entire stay at A&M. We roomed together for three years and enjoyed being around each other immensely. If you saw one of us, you inevitably saw the other. I think Dorsey and I had an exchange of angry words for fifteen minutes once, but that was about the only negative experience I can remember. His bullshit meter was finely tuned and his tolerance for such stuff was high, so he was thus able to tolerate my numerous idiosyncrasies.

Dorsey's father was a salesman with the Ford dealership in Hamilton for most of his adult life, and absolutely everyone in the city knew Clancy Blue. Dorsey's mother, Edna, was a housewife, a very nice, intelligent, straight-laced woman who doted on her baby boy, one of only two male children on either side of the family for several generations. Dorsey, or "Dwainy" to his mother (much to his chagrin) always wore tailored uniforms that might evoke envy on the part of the aforementioned cadets, Hagler and Glasscock. Dorsey Blue was in their league, at least sartorially, for sure. His mother was a master seamstress and it was important to her that Dorsey look good in his uniforms and, to Edna's credit, he always did.

Dorsey's parents were members of the local Church of Christ and, as was the case with Charlie Janak and his Catholic cohorts in Smithville, I had never known anyone from that denomination until I met my new roommate and attended church services with him. It struck me as odd that hymns in the Church of Christ were not accompanied by instrumental music; every other church group in my experience made liberal use of the time-honored, omnipresent church organ or, occasionally, the guitar.

On weekends when I went to Hamilton with Dorsey, his mother made sure we purged our sinful souls of lascivious thoughts and dastardly deeds by attending church services. To pass the time while the preacher droned on with his seemingly endless messages of gloom and doom about the human species, Dorsey would point out different holier-than-thou types in the congregation, an assortment of hypocrites, womanizers, philanderers, income tax cheats, and the like. While this elaboration made for interesting conversation, I strong suspected the local Church of Christ in Hamilton County, Texas, had not cornered the market on these kinds of people.

Dorsey once fixed me up with a lovely Baylor coed from Hamilton by the name of Doris Lengefeld. She was a beauty, slim with dark hair and eyes, but the relationship never amounted to much. I think time and distance and the 9 pm curfew imposed by her parents were factors in its demise. You can get in trouble before 2100 hours in the evening but I suppose it does reduce the likelihood some. I am reminded at this point of a student I had in class some years ago from Manor, just outside Austin. He told me his fifteen-year old sister had been dating a nineteen-year old and because of his age, obvious worldliness and attendant suave sophistication, her parents would only allow the two of them to be alone for an hour of two every fortnight. Ironically enough, it did not take long for little sis to turn up pregnant despite the strictures put in place by the well-meaning but misguided parents. This is another case study in support of my contention that consummation of the sex act takes little prior planning, often requires a minimal amount of time, and has few space requirements. What was it they said about the old Volkswagen beetle? "If you're good enough, it's big enough!" Maybe that old shibboleth should be amended to read, "If you're dedicated enough, an hour is quite long enough!"

There was another lovely Hamilton woman with whom Dorsey was always trying to get me a date, but to no avail. Her name was Carolyn Groves and she was, according to Blue, a rising new star on Broadway. It sounded absolutely enchanting to have a friendly relationship or romance with a beautiful and accomplished young woman from Hamilton County, Texas, who was a budding starlet in the Big Apple. Nothing ever came of it, however, because Carolyn was seldom in town, and never when I was there. Actually, there were few available women in such a small town, so I spent a lot of my time in Hamilton sitting around the town on Saturday night, square kibitzing with the locals while waiting for Dorsey to say goodnight to different girls he dated over the years. It was not as if Dorsey did not try to fix me up with dates; there simply were few women from which to choose. The odds were not good in Hamilton, Texas, and what goods there were, with a few exceptions, seemed odd in my humble estimation.

The true-blue highlight of my occasional weekend trips to Hamilton with Dorsey was the Sunday night stops at a dance hall in Rogers, Texas, on our way back to campus. Our honky-tonk of choice was a modest wooden structure with a large sliding door at one end which came in handy if a fight broke out. The management would open the sliding doors and use the crowd to slowly force the combatants out of the building. The same band played there every Sunday night, led by a country and western singer/guitarist by the name of "Dink" Kelly. Our favorite part of those stops, other than the beer, was getting to dance with a young, attractive, one-eyed girl we only knew as Margaret. She was friendly, easy on the eyes for those of us with two of them, possessed a nice, shapely body that was fun to hold while dancing, and she greatly enjoyed having a never-ending assortment of partners with which to do the Texas two-step. None of us ever found out what caused her to lose sight in the blind eye. I guess we were too polite to ask. Or maybe it simply was none of our business. But I have to admit, I have not known too many one-eyed girls in my life. Right now, I can only think of one…Margaret.

Dorsey Blue was actually a member of the class of '59 but the academic affairs people at the university had politely requested he cool his heels for the academic year 1956-1957 to see if he could acquire some firmer resolve about his studies. Perhaps a more parsimonious way to say the same thing is: Dorsey flunked out and was given a year to think about what he wanted to do with the rest of his life! While sitting out of school that year, he worked full-time and used the hard-earned money to buy a flashy black 1957 Ford Fairlane, an ultra-sporty model for that day and time. As stated earlier, few of us had our own transportation in those days, so Dorsey was unique in that regard. From time to time, some of our parents would let us drive a family clunker back to campus for a week or two, which occasioned considerable celebration. Perhaps no one was happier about these events than Dorsey for it provided him with temporary respite from his chauffeuring duties which at times were undoubtedly onerous. You have a lot of friends when you have the only car, I guess.

Dorsey had a penchant for fast driving which led him to acquire enough speeding tickets in the year he sat out of school to be threatened with suspension of his driver's license should he continue his wayward ways behind the wheel. Actually, Dorsey drove exceptionally fast but he was always in control. I often told him he had missed his calling; he should have been a race driver on the NASCAR circuit.

Dorsey's fascination with speed nearly did him in one weekend, though he apparently was not at fault. He and two hometown buddies, the Streger twins, Raymond and Rayburn, decided to go to Hamilton for the weekend. Fortunately, I decided to stay in town for whatever reason. On the way to their hometown, Dorsey was speeding as usual and came up over a hill on one of those country roads, I think Highway 485, in Milam County, northwest of Bryan-College Station. As he crested the hill and looked down, he spotted a farmer driving a pickup and pulling a trailer inexorably executing a slow U-turn at the bottom of the rise. In order to avoid a collision, Dorsey hit the ditch, lost control, flipped over, and ended up totaling his beloved Ford Fairlane. Fortunately, no one was hurt in the incident; a few minor nicks from flying glass were the extent of the injuries to Dorsey and the twins.

The Streger twins were good guys….classic Germanic, light skinned, blue-eyed blondes. They were identical twins, so much so I could only tell them apart because Raymond had a small mole on the side of his nose….I used the mnemonic "Raymole" to separate him from Rayburn who had no tell-tale identifying mark. Both guys ended up teaching school in the College Station Independent School District for a while after graduation and eventually migrated back to Hamilton area where they both currently reside so I am told.

It was not until months after Dorsey and I met that he felt comfortable enough to express his initial apprehensions about me that first day we met in the dorm. We hit it off pretty much from the start, however. He was a good guy and fun to be around….good sense of humor, emotionally stable, clean and orderly in his habits, though not an obsessive neat freak. If you drew up the ideal roommate for me, old Blue was the gold standard.

All of us have our quirks and Blue had one that always struck my running mates and me as hilarious, and it had to do with oral sex and his abiding belief that it was somehow tied to homosexual behavior. As might be expected with a dorm full of young males, a favorite topic of discussion focused on the many manifestations of human sexuality, and the topic of oral sex would come up from time to time. When such discussions took place, Blue always offered up his predictable "If you'll eat a hole, you'll eat a pole" dictum. I always found the notion to be comical but it did capture in a few words the misgivings some people had about oral sex and the homophobia so ingrained in young males at that time.

In an interesting postscript to this anecdote, Blue fell in love with a young waitress in a family-owned restaurant at North Gate in College Station whom he later married. As the two of them became more intimate, Dorsey proffered late one night over beer that he had softened his stance a bit on the "Eat a hole, eat a pole" idea. Hmmm….sort of made me wonder about my man Blue!

Another interesting postscript to the Blue saga took place in early April of 2017 when I received a phone call from Dorsey's son, Shawn, who was on campus showing his own son, Robert, around. He asked if I would be up for a visit, and a chance to catch up with their lives and that of my old cherished roommate was most welcomed. The three of us laughed and told stories, mostly about Dorsey, for the better part of two hours. In the process of our deliberations, I also learned how impressive young Robert Blue is…three-sport athlete, number two in his class academically, class President, President of the National Honor Society, member (President?) of the Future Farmers of America (FFA), band member who played a wind instrument but also taught himself to play the piano. One of his sports accomplishments involved tennis, a sport he taught himself as a high school freshman. From that inauspicious start, he earned a spot in the state tennis tournament in College Station both his junior and senior years. Robert's accomplishments are numerous and impressive and I am sure Dorsey would be immensely proud of the young man Robert has become. Robert is presently a freshman Honors student majoring in Psychology so I look forward to seeing him around for the next several years.

As for Dorsey, he worked for Bell Helicopter in Fort Worth when he got out of the army in the mid-1960's and retired from there when he was around eighty. Upon retirement, he spent a good deal of time in Hamilton hanging out with the Streger twins and other associates from his youth. As noted elsewhere, he died in 2015 and I miss my old roommate and regret that we grew apart over the years.

Hong Kong Flu Decimates the Student Body

The second and third weeks of school brought the world-wide influenza epidemic of 1957 up close and personal for us Aggies. Dorsey and I and maybe Leroy Becker from New Braunfels or Joe Watson from Webster, I cannot remember for sure, headed off to Dallas on a Friday to take in an A&M football game in the Cotton Bowl where we played the University of Maryland Terrapins (the Aggies won 21-13). There was nothing particularly memorable about the game or the weekend other than I started feeling absolutely miserable mid-Saturday and things went rapidly downhill from there. I was feverish, flushed, lethargic, drowsy beyond belief, completely out of sorts, and borderline delirious. All I wanted to do was lie down in the back seat of the car and go to sleep. At times, I felt it would have been perfectly fine if I did not even wake up, I was so sick. Little did I know this episode was to be repeated with a huge segment of the student body for the better part of the next week. We were totally oblivious to the fact that literally thousands of us were becoming statistics in one of the three largest influenza epidemics of the twentieth century.

In a recent historical review, the United States Department of Health and Human Services indicated there were three pandemics influenza outbreaks and several occurrences of "pandemic flu scares" in the 1900's. The first of these three major pandemic events occurred in 1918 and was known as the Spanish Flu. It is estimated 20-40% of the world's population was stricken with the flu between September of 1918 and April of 1919, and an estimated twenty million people died as a result. There were a half million deaths in the US alone.

As an interesting side note, one woman who reportedly contracted the Spanish flu but survived was Rosemary Kennedy (1918-2005), a member of the immensely wealthy and politically powerful Massachusetts Kennedy family. Unfortunately, Rosemary was left intellectually disabled as a result of her illness but because of the Kennedy wealth and their strong family bonds, she was provided with a relatively normal childhood given her intellectual limitations. At the age of twenty-one, she became troublesome and unmanageable, overly aggressive, ran away from school and home, and generally caused the family a lot of consternation. In their desperation, the Kennedy's sought help from some of the leading physicians in the country and, somewhere in the search, became convinced of the efficacy of a new and promising medical procedure to alleviate Rosemary's problems. This revolutionary and "promising" medical innovation was known as the prefrontal lobotomy, and the family consented to have the operation performed on Rosemary. Though Rosemary had done reasonably well physically and intellectually prior to the surgery, she spent the remainder of her final sixty-five years in a treatment facility in far worse shape than she had been prior to the soon-to-be scandal-ridden medical intervention. She was perhaps the more famous of an estimated 100,000 victims of a procedure for which its creator, Dr. Egas Moniz of Portugal, was awarded the 1949 Nobel Prize in Medicine. In an interesting and ironic side note, Dr. Moniz was shot by one of his patients and spent the last years of his life in a wheelchair.

The second pandemic event, one we would call our very own, was the Asian flu which took place between September 1957 and March 1958. It was preceded by small outbreaks in the summer of 1957 as the virus spread from the Far East to the US. Before the siege was over in 1958, approximately 70,000 US citizens had died. Fortunately, because of our youth and relative fitness, there were no fatalities associated with the Asian flu at A&M.

It is fascinating in retrospect to think that probably a third to half of the A&M students had the flu and were tended to, fed, and nurtured back to health by those cadets who had been spared the affliction. Headlines in *The Battalion* on September 20, 1957, read: "Influenza hits 450 Aggies; College Hospital Overflows." It was further reported that the staff there treated a student a minute for quite a period of time. Later headlines from September 24 stated: "Flu hits 1500 Ags in 5 Days: Hospital Received 600 Yesterday." A day later, it was reported that "Aggieland Stays Open Despite Mounting Flu: Campus Cases up to 1600 Tuesday." In addition to those who had been hospitalized, a number of Aggies went home to ride out the epidemic. It would be interesting to know why so many of us were flu victims and a relative few were spared the malady. After a week or so, the flu symptoms subsided, things returned to normal, and life went on pretty much as before.

After the siege ended, the juniors and seniors decided discipline had become a distant memory, largely ignored during the week of the epidemic. The discipline lapse pretty much meant the place was going to hell in a handbasket. We sophomores, of course, were held accountable by the juniors for this dastardly departure from decorum. As a result, all upperclassmen vowed vengeance on our sophomoric souls for our dereliction of duty, and the price we paid for our neglectful ways was being "allowed" to wax the dormitory hallways and rooms of each of the juniors and seniors for the next three nights. And since shit almost always runs downhill, you can imagine what life was like that week for the poor unsuspecting freshmen. Their short tenure at A&M and the ravages of the flu were not regarded as acceptable excuses for their negligent, undisciplined ways; hazing of fish (and us sophomores) went on in earnest.

The third pandemic event was the Hong Kong Flu of 1968 which was the mildest of the three sieges, with "only" 35,000 deaths. The three pandemic events were followed by the Swine flu scares in 1976 (and 2009), the Russian flu scare of 1977, and the Avian flu scare of 1997, all of which were less dramatic in impact.

Gerald Avery

My second year went quite well academically as I had learned how to play the game, choosing my courses and professors wisely, better managing my time, and allocating the necessary study resources to do well. I took twenty-two hours in the fall and made a 3.33 grade point average, which was my highest average ever at A&M. In the spring, I decided to take it easy and cut back to a nineteen-hour load where I recorded a 3.00 GPA. Students today view fifteen hours as pushing the upper limit, with twelve the norm. Maybe A&M was easier in those days, or perhaps the students of today are a bit softer. Or maybe the spiraling cost of a college education today forces people to work more and take reduced course loads. One thing is for sure; the cost of a college education is high, with typical student debt variously reported in the range of $10,000 to $25,000. It is both fascinating and a bit frightening to think the cost of college tuition has increased five-fold in the last two decades while inflation rose slightly over 100%.

The person who played this course overload provision to unparalleled extremes was a chap in our unit by the name of Gerald Avery. Gerald, from Paris, Texas, was in the class of 1959, and an academic wunderkind. Gerald took twenty-four hours each semester for six semesters, or 144 hours, at which time he was awarded his double degree in Chemistry and Chemical Engineering. He had a grade point average around 3.90 and, as best I remember, was awarded a lucrative scholarship to continue his graduate studies at Columbia University in New York.

Gerald was a bit on the reclusive side and deadly serious about his grades, so I did not get to know him especially well; I do not think anyone else did either. One poignant memory I have of Gerald concerned Economics 203, a course we took together due more to luck of the draw than design. The professor was a master's degree graduate of Harvard, and the kindest assessment of his personality and demeanor I can conjure up is that he was a really odd duck. He had a deadly monotonous lecture style and absolutely no regard for time or our class schedules. His lectures were scheduled to last for fifty minutes but it was not at all out of the ordinary for him to run ten, twenty, or even thirty minutes over his allotted time. He was totally oblivious to the fact that some of us had classes or other obligations immediately following his lectures, and thanks to his inconsideration, some of us were often late for the next class or had to miss it altogether.

Where I had a choice, I always sat in the back of the classroom in all my classes so I could see what everyone was up to, and this one course was no exception. As for Gerald Avery, he was the opposite, preferring to sit front and center, right under the nose of the professor. Gerald would walk in right before the lecture began each class period, take his seat, spread his homework across several nearby desks, and spend the entire period doing Chemistry problems and, I suppose, listening with one ear to the numerous and no doubt utterly fascinating nuances of Economics 203. As for me, by sitting in the back, I pretty much got to watch two dozen guys sleep while Gerald did his chemistry problems, totally free from interference from his somnolent peers and the man who was inducing the soporific state for the huddled masses in the room. Typically, the only three people who were awake during the class the professor, two students, Gerald Avery and yours truly.

Several of my more observant and perhaps perverse classmates noted that our ritual-bound (obsessive-compulsive disorder?) professor was enamored with placing his class lecture notes on the lightweight, wooden podium resting on a small table at the front of the room. As well, he kept a generous supply of chalk which he used to illustrate the many arcane nuances of supply and demand and the gross national product. I can say with absolute certainty being able to say those six words, "supply and demand" and "gross national product", represent the sum total of all I know about Economics to this day. And to add insult to injury, economists have done away with nearly half of my economics vocabulary by junking "gross national product" in favor of the current "gross domestic product." I have joked over the years with my own students if I had been required to take one more course in Economics, I would still be an undergraduate. The same can probably be said for Mathematics, Political Science, and Military Science!

But let's get back to my Economics 203 classmates. One day before class, several of them hatched a plan to see what would happen if the professor's beloved podium and chalk were no longer at his disposal. The miscreants figured they would disrupt his predictably obsessive-compulsive routine by removing his rusty trusty teaching aids from the room. To put their theory to the acid test, the culprits arrived early one day and set the cherished didactic devices on a ledge just outside the south window of the classroom located on the second story of Nagle Hall. To further ensure the missing objects would not be spotted, the perps then walked the podium and chalk around the corner to the west side of Nagle, resting them safely out of sight. When the professor walked in for the day's lecture, he noticed his dearly beloved academic accoutrements were nowhere to be found. He immediately went into a panic state, eyes darting back and forth, pacing and muttering and muttering and pacing, trying to come up with a solution to the didactic dilemma. After pondering the situation for a bit, he walked out, went down the hall, and retrieved some chalk from another classroom. He then retraced his steps and created a makeshift podium by placing a chair on the table at the front of the classroom. In order to have a resting place for his copious notes, he turned the chair around with its back side facing the class. He then situated his notes on the chair seat, not noticing or perhaps not caring that we could only see bits and pieces of him through the rungs of the chair. The lecture lasted for thirty minutes beyond the allocated time and he missed nary a lick, apparently oblivious to the fact that he was mostly invisible and largely inaudible to his audience.

My final recollection of the class is that it was the only time in my 297 hours of college credit that I attempted to cheat. I am not sure what prompted that inanity other than retaliation or desperation, or perhaps the novelty and intrigue of seeing if I was any good at the art of cheating. It was sort of an "Everyone else is doing it, so why not me?" type of experience. While preparing for an impending exam, I more or less figured out what topics would be most likely to show up and then wrote out a detailed answer to those anticipated questions and stuck them in my class binder. At an opportune time where it seemed to be a good fit, I slipped a prepared answer to one essay question into the rest of the exam. I do remember it had to be a rough fit grammatically since the verbiage on the exam paper and my pre-determined answer did not completely jive. I guess the professor did not notice, and I made a C on the exam which is probably what I would have made anyway. I then decided cheating was just not for me. It was not necessary and I did not like myself much when I tried it, so I took a novel approach to the rest of my classes…..I studied!

I got involved with Gerald Avery in another situation, this time involving Chemistry 106, or what was known as "Cowboy Chemistry." It was ostensibly a crib course created for non-science majors, not the demanding Chemistry real men like Avery took. I rocked along with an A after a couple of examinations, no doubt due in large part to a Chemistry gene I surely must have inherited from my maternal grandfather, P. R. Chamberlain and, through guilt by association, his son, P. G., themselves Chemistry graduates of Case Institute and the University of Oklahoma respectively.

At the end of one of his lectures, the professor announced the grades were entirely too high and he was going to remedy that problem on the third exam. He gave us several homework problems which were to be a major part of the upcoming exam, and one was so difficult I sought Avery's wise counsel and enlightened expertise. After several hours of deep thought about the problem, Gerald was equally confused, so I knew I was in deep doodoo. Sure enough, that unsolvable problem constituted half of our exam grade and almost everyone in the class made a D or an F. The net effect was I ended up with a C in the course and a poor attitude about what the professor had done to us. I am not sure I had notions at the time of ever becoming a college professor, but I promised myself right then and there if I ever was one, I would find a fairer, more equitable way to deal with potential grade inflation.

Toward the end of the spring semester, I was designated to become the Sergeant Major of the First Brigade in the Corps of Cadets for the junior year. This nomination places a student directly in line to at least become the Brigade Commander, with an outside chance of becoming the Corps Commander or Deputy Corps Commander the following year. Though deeply honored to have received the nomination, I came to realize during the first couple of weeks of my junior year the Brigade Sergeant Major appointment was just not me, plain and simple. More on this issue shortly.

Another Summer in Texas City

Once again, I went back to Texas City for the summer of 1958 where I divided my time working as a lifeguard and tumbling tutor for tiny tots. My father was on the advisory board of the Texas City Department of Parks and Recreation and persuaded the Director, Dubba Dooley (Isn't that a great name?), to hire me for the summer. I was assigned to work mornings teaching things like tumbling to three- and four-year olds, or maybe some basketball to eight-year olds, and just hanging out at the gym, shooting baskets and doing whatever needed to be done. In the afternoons or evenings, I served as a lifeguard at the city pool. I learned one thing from this summer experience; I did not want to spend the rest of my life ministering to children as a career. The kids that came to the swimming pool were very often a pain, and several were dropped off just as we opened in the morning and picked up, strangely enough, at the end of the day when their mothers' got off work; they clearly viewed the pool as out-and-out free babysitting. I was tempted to say glorified babysitting but there was nothing glorious about the job.

I had been a terrible swimmer all my life, and to this day remain pretty much a sinker. Completing the lifeguard training and passing the examination with such a huge handicap took some doing. As it turned out, the Cox twins, Harla and Darla, were classmates at A&M as well as Water Safety Instructors (WSI's). The Cox twins took me under their inordinately generous protective wings and nursed me through the lifeguard certification process. I would not have asked them to get involved if being able to REALLY swim had been an issue. I knew deep down if genuine swimming skill was required for the lifeguard job, I would be a liability, a veritable death sentence for some drowning person (or me). If a kid got in trouble in the water, I would surely drown and the constituency would no doubt follow suit. But the pool in Texas City was shallow from end to end and the diving area relatively small and not especially deep, so legitimate swimming skill was never a real issue. You could walk from one end of the pool to the other and not encounter water deeper than six feet, and one could pretty much reach across the diving area with a safety net.

On unfortunately rare instances, girls our age or nearly so would show up at the pool, thus making the job somewhat more bearable. Music from the public address system also helped, though I must say if I ever hear Donald and Philip, the Everly Brothers, sing "Bye Bye Love" or "Wake Up Little Susie" again, I may commit mayhem against a random gaggle of brats. When my case went to trial for murder, I would try to win pity points with the jury by using Post-Traumatic Stress Disorder (PTSD) involving out-of-control pre-teens, the overpowering aroma of chlorine, and "Wake Up Little Suzie" circulating about in my brain as my defense. Surely, no jury would condemn a man to death under those mitigating circumstances.

My good friend, Earl Yarbrough, was also a lifeguard as was a guy named Lanny Landtroop, so the three of us hung out together at the pool a lot. Earl Yarbrough had been an All-Galveston County football player in high school, and was an all-around good guy. He was one of the biggest flirts I ever knew and he could launch a lecherous leer at the ladies with the best of them (which was part of the reason he came to be known among his peers as "Dirty Earl"). He also was inordinately fond of a standing joke or repartee he used at least a thousand times in a variety of settings. Every time the two of us were together and Earl found a new audience, or one he thought might be uninitiated, he would use me as a pawn in his predictable prank by asking: "Hey, Arnold, does your dick ever burn after intercourse?" In order to play out the ruse, I would promptly reply in a serious tone and with a straight face: "I don't know, Earl, I never tried to light it." Yikes and egad!!! I do not think Earl ever tired of that bit of tomfoolery.

Lanny was a bit of a poolside anomaly because of his red hair and even redder complexion. He simply was not predisposed genetically to handle prolonged exposure to the sun. Watching him turn lobster-red in the sun, accompanied by an exponential increase in the size and number of freckles on his exposed body, was painful. However, Lanny loved the water and the job. After graduating from college, he became one of the most successful coaches in the annals of Texas high school swimming at Clear Creek High School on the Gulf Coast where his boys and girls teams won nine state championships between 1976 and 1994. Lanny later plied his coaching skills at Humble Kingwood High School and won four more state titles before retiring.

Julia Catherine Jacobson Wins, Breaks My Heart. Of utmost importance, however was a wonderful relationship that developed at the onset of summer involving a beautiful woman of Scandinavian descent by the name of Julia Catherine Jacobson, aka Judy, who remains to this day one of my most highly cherished memories. She was sweet sixteen (I was twenty and obviously "robbing the cradle"), blond and blue-eyed, with predictably fair Scandinavian complexion and the physique of a runway model. She was one of those fortunate women who would appear chic and elegant wearing a gunny sack, so she always looked great no matter the attire. Judy and I were inseparable for that summer, literally dancing the night away from June through August. We hung out virtually every night anywhere there was a band or jukebox and got to be pretty fair at the jitterbug which was the dancing rage in the 1950's.

Not surprisingly, given our age and stage, she and I developed a strong physical attraction though she remained a virgin for the duration of our relationship. Perhaps the closest we came to sexual consummation was at my parents' house late one afternoon while my dad, stepmother June, and my two youngest siblings, Nancy and George Wayne, were ostensibly away on vacation. As fate would have it, the family came home from their trip a day early and caught the two of us in bed in the midst of a passionate embrace, if you will. After taking a moment to gather our wits (and a few clothes), we rounded up our things and I took her home. As was my father's typical low-key style in dealing with matters of discipline, he pulled me aside when I returned from dropping Judy off, and we calmly discussed, among other things, his belief that my (mis)behavior was setting a bad example for my siblings. As well, we discussed the even more salient unwanted consequences of an unplanned pregnancy. I convinced him that pregnancy was unlikely, and to get this episode behind us, I talked Judy into coming over the following weekend for Sunday lunch. Things went well, the air was cleared, and, miraculously enough, the sun arose in the east the following morning.

Summer ended, I went back to A&M, and Judy returned to start her junior year of high school. Long distance relationships often do not pan out, and ours was unfortunately no exception. Judy dumped me unceremoniously in October, opting for a budding young rock singer named Dean who, according to rumors was not nearly as protective of her virginity as I had been. The break was quite painful as Judy Jacobson had been the third real love of my life after my high school heart throb, Myrna Jo Brown, and the aforementioned Betty Grey McDuffie. Unfortunately, the dissolution of a romantic relationship is seldom painless. In the words of an anonymous source, "Sometimes I wish I was a little kid again: skinned knees are easier to fix than broken hearts." Julia Catherine Jacobson broke my heart.

Several years later, in the fall of 1961 and long after recovering from the dissolution of our relationship, I was sitting in the bleachers at a University of North Texas Mean Green football game and felt a tap on my shoulder just before the opening kickoff. The "tapper" was none other than Judy Jacobson. We chatted briefly, and this was to be the final time I saw or heard from her. I hope life has been good; she was a beautiful woman and a wonderful person who afforded me some great companionship (and a couple of fancy dance steps) for one memorable summer.

My Final Two Years at A&M

The Junior Year

The junior year got off to a rocky start, largely because I was so unhappy with my role as First Brigade Sergeant Major. From the moment I first assumed what was widely perceived as a prestigious position, one coveted by more than a few of my peers, I had second doubts about my decision. This, in turn, caused me considerable consternation as well as difficulty in concentrating on my studies. In one fell swoop, my quality of life had plummeted to depths I could not have foreseen when I accepted the Sergeant Major position at the end of the spring semester of 1958. All I could think was: What have I done to myself and how can I rectify this mistake? I almost never saw my friends and could not imagine going through two more years of college making the First Brigade and the Corps of Cadets my life, not being able to hang out and experience the camaraderie of Blue and my other friends.

The position of Sergeant Major, however prestigious, was primarily an administrative one with considerable inherent paper-shuffling and pomp and circumstance, and it just was not me. It took two weeks of painful soul-searching to figure out I had made a major mistake by accepting the position. I finally mustered up the courage to visit with the military powers-that-be in the Trigon (ROTC Headquarters) to inform them I was resigning to return to my old unit. As I recall and to their credit, there was no real argumentation or wringing of hands on their part, and I returned to my unit without fanfare. I was awarded no rank upon rejoining my old company, and for a junior with a military contract to have no sergeant stripes on the uniform sleeves was unusual.

By then, B Armor had become C-1 in the Corps reorganization scheme, but my personal support framework had not changed. The guys I ran around with were still there, and it was great to be home, so to speak. As stated above, leaving the Sergeant Major position meant I would be a junior with no rank, but that was of no importance to me. I did not care; I was where I wanted to be, and honestly cannot imagine a scenario even today in which I could have made it through my last two years in a Brigade or higher level position. I simply was not cut out for that sort of life. I was a people person, not a pomp and circumstance, pencil-and-paper pusher.

Things rocked along well academically and otherwise, other than the breakup of my summer affair with the consummately lovely Judy Jacobson, and the year ended with me being interviewed for the position of Corps Commander. I was honored to be one of only eight people interviewed though I could have never have taken the position if it was offered for the same reason I could never fulfill my Brigade Sergeant Major obligations. It was comforting throughout the interview process to know in my heart-of-hearts the best I could do in the eight-man lineup was finish dead last. I had the lowest overall grade point ratio of any of the candidates and most certainly the lowest grades in Military Science, both highly important requirements for the position. I think my major strength and the one that got me the interview was my savvy with the underclassmen. I had a reputation for relating to the troops in ways some others did not, but I came up far short of the other candidates on most of the standards by which Corps Commanders are selected. The position was eventually offered to the aforementioned Bill Heye, and it was hard to argue with his selection. He was a great student and held positions of leadership that made him uniquely qualified for the position of Corps Commander.

ROTC Summer Camp at Fort Hood.

One of the more interesting aspects of Corps life if you were awarded an Army or Air Force ROTC contract was attending summer camp after the junior year. Having such an obligation hanging over your head made it difficult to find work that particular summer, but I found some piddling jobs to keep me busy and made a shekel or two here and there before camp started.

Summer camp for us Army types was held at Fort Hood, a massive, sprawling training base in the Central Texas town of Killeen. Because of its geographic isolation, large size and relatively flat terrain, Fort Hood was particularly well-suited for conducting mock artillery, infantry, and tank warfare. When I returned there three years later as a full-fledged second lieutenant in the Adjutant General's Corps, it was home to the First ("Old Ironsides") and Second ("Hell on Wheels") Armored Divisions as well as Headquarters, Third Army Corps.

Audie Murphy I Ain't. The six weeks I spent in summer camp reminded me in some ways of the freshman year in the Corps. We were treated as raw recruits to familiarize us what it was like to be at the bottom of the military barrel. The entire enterprise was clearly designed to help us better understand the troops in our command when we entered active military duty as officers, and I thought it accomplished that goal quite effectively. Essentially, what we experienced was a reasonably close facsimile of army basic training. We went to bed early, got up early, marched a lot, ran our butts off, fired weapons, and generally learned as best we could how to be real soldiers. We worked menial jobs in the mess hall, known as KP (Kitchen Police) duty, and spent some time on guard duty protecting the Fort Hood from hobgoblins and things that go thump in the night. We learned to read a compass, fire M-1's, machine guns, and rocket launchers, pitch a tent, and dig a slit trench so the troops would have a proper place to placate their peristaltic passions.

On one unfortunate occasion, I became more familiar with digging slit trenches than I wanted, thanks to a major lapse in judgment during mock combat training. If our Drill Sergeants told us once, they told us a thousand times not to ever let our M-1 rifles out of our sight, and I committed that cardinal sin late one afternoon after a long, arduous hike. We were in full battle gear and had marched for miles in the hot Fort Hood boondocks in search of a place to bivouac. At some point, the Drill Sergeants gave us a short break and in the process of catching my breath, I did not pay proper attention to the location of my M-1 which had been deposited on a nearby log. The next thing I knew, the drill sergeant was yelling at the top of his lungs, waving a rifle around, and searching for its rightful owner. Guess what? That poor, sheepish, unfortunate soldier was me! That lapse cost me a major league ass-chewing plus I got to devote an hour or two to digging a slit trench for my friends.

Another un-Audie Murphy lapse with negative personal consequences occurred during hand grenade training. The session started with a brief lecture on how to properly grasp a grenade, pull the pin, and throw it. Fortunately, those training grenades were dummies packed with a powder charge which ignited when the pin was pulled. Once thrown in the general direction of a target, a mild explosion ensued and it got the point across about how grenades really work without putting any lives or limbs in jeopardy.

As part of the training session, the instructor showed us how to reload the dummy grenades once they had been detonated so they would be ready for use by the next group of trainees. As was often the case in things military, I did not pay much attention to what the instructor was saying about how to safely reload the dummy grenade. Being a bit of a maverick, and a wise-ass to boot, I thought I had figured out a better plan to accomplish what seemed to be a very mundane task. In the process of implementing what I thought was a beautiful alternative reloading plan, the relative serenity of the moment was broken by a loud explosion. The grenade went off, burning the hair off my hands and lower right arm and blackening ever so slightly the right sleeve of my fatigue jacket. As might be expected, when the dummy grenade charge exploded, a number of startled onlookers turned to see what had happened.

A nano-second after the detonation, I picked up in my peripheral vision the presence of several knees at eye level. Two of those four by then airborne appendages belonged to the post commander, a three-star General, and the other pair were attached to the torso of an even higher ranking officer, a four-star General whose name was General Bruce Clarke if my memory serves me correctly (or was it General Mark Clark?). At that time, General Clark (or Clarke) was visiting Fort Hood as part of his duties as Commander in Chief of the United States Continental Command.

When the two "bulls" recovered from being startled shitless, they lit into me in unison with all the authority invested in those collective seven stars. They wanted to know what ancestry could produce such an utterly stupid bastard, if I really was a college student or just some fucking outrageous impostor, and what kind of institution would admit such a dumb shit as me and still have the chutzpah to call itself a goddamn university. Their expressions and salty language led me to believe they were not happy campers, to put it mildly!

This episode and others of lesser significance piled up over the summer and led me to be ranked in the lower quarter of all participants on the final camp evaluation. Four years later, I ended up in exactly the same position on my first active duty evaluation at Fort Benjamin Harrison. As I said, I was no Audie Murphy! But I always had the undying loyalty of the men under my command, and that fact bought me a certain amount of reprieve with the system.

The Ku Klux Klan Comes to Summer Camp. Unfortunately, before camp ended, there was an ugly incident in which a young black man in our ranks was confronted by "peers" outfitted in Ku Klux Klan (KKK) paraphernalia. The target of the consummately stupid and misguided terroristic stunt was Prentice Gautt, a football star at the University of Oklahoma, that school's first-ever black player.

Gautt was born in Oklahoma City in 1938 (nine weeks before yours truly) and was an all-star running back at Douglass High School in the city of his birth. His considerable ball-toting skills, outstanding academic credentials, and sterling character brought him to the attention of the highly-revered coaching legend, Charles "Bud" Wilkinson, who felt the time had come to integrate sports at the University of Oklahoma in Norman. He thus offered Gautt an athletic scholarship to attend OU in the fall of 1956. However, powerful politicians and influential alumni of obviously racist persuasions pressured Wilkinson into revoking the offer. Undaunted, a group of prominent black physicians and other professionals in Oklahoma City raised enough money to replace the rescinded athletic scholarship and Gautt thus became OU's first black football player. Interestingly, Wilkinson offered Gautt an athletic scholarship at the end of his freshman year and the money raised by his earlier benefactors was used thereafter to underwrite the education of black students at OU who were not collegiate athletes.

Not everyone on the OU team was pleased with Gautt's debut, and his presence was the source of much unrest. However, one player who chose to rise above the fray in accepting Gautt was then-running back and now-prominent wealthy Texas oilman, Jakie Sandefer. Sandefer stood up for Gautt when others did not, and the two of them were roommates for their final two years. When Prentice Gautt was inducted into the Oklahoma Sports Hall of Fame in 2000, Sandefer was chosen to speak on his behalf. In response to a question about whether there was something different about his roommate, Jakie Sandefer said, "Was Prentice different? Yeah, Prentice was different. He had more class than the rest of us, and he was a better student."

Gautt was a novelty at Fort Hood in 1958 because integration was in its infancy at most universities, particularly those in the south. For example, A&M was five years removed from admitting its first blacks (and first degree-seeking females) so most of us had little familiarity with black athletes or black students of any kind, for that matter. I did have three black teammates my senior year in high school when the state of Oklahoma integrated its public schools, so I had some idea of what it was like to compete with and against black athletes. I unfortunately had almost no contact with Gautt at summer camp, but the word among the troops was that he was bright, personable, a nice guy, and a very good soldier. I caught him once or twice in the barracks minus his shirt, and he most certainly possessed the best physique I had ever seen.

It turns out that the culprits who concocted the consummately misguided, malevolent, cockamamie, out-and-out racist ritual were A&M classmates. There may have been others involved, but I remember at least one, whose name will go unmentioned to protect the innocent, had a Lufkin connection. Lufkin, like Cleveland, Vidor, and several other neighboring cities in East Texas, was a hotbed of racial hatred and hostility so commonplace well into the 1950's and 1960's and beyond.

Near midnight that fateful evening, the perpetrators of this incident donned makeshift Ku Klux Klan apparel and paraphernalia and harassed Gautt with their white outfits, pointed hats, and attendant racial taunts and epithets. For their part in the debacle, the guilty parties were dismissed from summer camp and their A&M military contracts terminated, punishments richly deserved and highly justified. I wholeheartedly agreed with the extent of the punishment, and the swiftness by which it was dispensed was most gratifying. The powers-that-be sent a swift, powerful message about how A&M and the military felt about this issue.

As for Gautt, this incident was hardly his first exposure to racism, and he responded throughout with the class and decorum mentioned in the earlier quotes by Jakie Sandefer. Gautt returned to OU for a highly successful senior season, played seven years of professional football, one year with the Cleveland Browns and six with the St. Louis (now Arizona) Cardinals. Gautt eventually earned the PhD degree in Psychology from the University of Missouri, and spent most of his professional life as Special Assistant to Commissioners of both the Big Eight and Big Twelve Conferences. Prentice Gautt died of flu-like symptoms in 2005 at the age of sixty-seven. A year prior to his death, the Big Twelve named a graduate scholarship in his honor. The award is worth $7,500 and goes annually to a male and female athlete from each of the conference schools. The 2011 winner was Ryan Tannehill, the outstanding quarterback on the A&M football team who now plies his considerable skills with the NFL Miami Dolphins. All told, twenty-six Aggie athletes have been recipients of the Prentice Gautt award.

Weekend Leaves with Larry Guseman. The only other thing of consequence I remember about summer camp was being allowed to leave Fort Hood on weekends if we did not have KP or guard duty. I ended up hanging out most of the time with Larry Guseman, a mathematics and computer whiz and later a professor at A&M. Larry was a sociable, extroverted Italiano, nice looking, bow-legged, bright, funny, and we hit it off nicely. Interestingly, and in spite of the great fun and camaraderie we enjoyed in the summer of 1959, Larry and I were never running mates once we returned to campus after summer camp nor as fellow A&M faculty members.

The two of us spent one weekend that summer in the east Texas town of Mineola where he had somehow arranged dates for us with a couple of locals. He was quite taken with his date and she fixed me up with a friend who was the "Watermelon Queen" from Mineola, an honor to be sure. Have you ever wondered how many small towns have their "Watermelon Queen" and are hailed as "The Watermelon Capital of the World?" Recently, curiosity about that issue got the best of me so I Googled "Watermelon Capital" to see what turned up. Not too surprisingly, I found several pretenders to this highly coveted throne. When I was growing up in Oklahoma, I knew Rush Springs made its claim, and I assumed at that time it had to be the only one of its kind. Google burst my bubble when I found out about Mineola, which it turns out has competition within its own state from both Hempstead and Luling. To support its claim to the title, Luling has a watermelon water tower. Incidentally, the city is also home to the Luling City Market which arguably serves absolutely the best barbecue on the planet! If the reader gets a chance to pass by Luling, the brisket and sausage at the City Market are to die for.

Hope, Arkansas, the hometown of President Bill Clinton, has staked its own claim to watermelon supremacy as has Cordele in Georgia, Hermiston in Oregon, Shartlesville in Pennsylvania, Green River in Utah, Hampton County in South Carolina, and Muscatine in Iowa (which, for some reason, has since relinquished its claim). Anyway, I was honored to have a date with Mineola's version of the "Watermelon Queen." I also learned as the evening wore on that I liked watermelon far more than I did the reigning watermelon aristocracy.

On another weekend, Larry and I went to Austin and attended a friend's wedding. At the reception, he and I drank far more champagne than we should have, and I suspect my continuing aversion to that bubbly brew is traceable to the summer of 1959.

Larry went on to Rice University from A&M and put his mathematics background to work familiarizing himself with the new and burgeoning computer technology. His PhD was conferred in 1968 by The University of Texas and his dissertation topic was entitled "Spaces of Affine Continuous Functions." Now I know why Larry and I never continued our friendship after those halcyon summer camp days; we spoke different languages!

I remember a party in College Station thrown in Larry's honor shortly after he had enrolled at Rice (or maybe it was when he joined the Mathematics faculty at A&M). During the evening's festivities, Larry held forth about this new-found technology, the computer, one he said was going to revolutionize the world. None of us at that moment could imagine the profound ramifications of that prophetic pronouncement.

Around ten or eleven that night, I decided to make the 150-mile journey to Texas City, which was still home. Since I had no means of transportation at the time, hitchhiking was my only option. I did not want to reveal my plans to anyone at the party for fear they would make a big brouhaha out of my decision, so I walked from the party site to a vantage point on Texas Avenue in front of the main entrance to the university (i.e., "East Gate"). Once there, I optimistically stuck out my thumb to catch a ride. After an hour or two of little traffic and boatloads of rejection, my optimism waned; it was clear I was not going to make it to Texas City that night. I then formed a makeshift bed in some shrubs where I passed the night in a sound sleep, believe it or not. Around eight the next morning, I was up and about and got a ride almost immediately, arriving in Texas City around noon.

My friend, Larry Guseman, spent twenty-three productive years on the faculty in mathematics but died prematurely in 1991 of what has long been reported as congestive heart failure. In a shocking turn of events, a source I consider reliable told me Larry was actually one of those unwitting victims of AIDS, which was essentially a death sentence in those days. It seems that Larry was undergoing heart surgery and received HIV-contaminated blood. Larry Guseman was in his mid-fifties, a good guy with a fine mind who died far too young.

Commanding Officer
ARNOLD D. LE UNES

CORPS OF CADETS COMPANY COMMANDER, 1959-1960

The Senior Year

School-wise and Corps-wise, the senior year was pretty uneventful. I stayed afloat academically, kept my unit running smoothly (with a lot of help from my friends), and figured out what I was going to do with the rest of my life, knowing all the while that graduation loomed large on the horizon. All things considered, it was a good year.

As mentioned several times in some detail, I was an unsuccessful candidate for the position of Corps Commander which was neither personally coveted nor deserved. However, I did eventually land a position I wanted rather badly. To my utter delight, I was named Commanding Officer (CO) of my home unit, C-1, for the academic year 1959-1960. As CO, it was my duty to corral the minds and occasionally misguided priorities and energies of seventy-five to one hundred rambunctious young men. Thank goodness I was ably assisted in these tasks by my Executive Officer and long-time roommate, Dorsey Blue, who had my back, for sure. Dorsey more than made up for my shortcomings when it came to attention to detail, decorum, drill, and dress. Another key piece of the puzzle was my First Sergeant, Donald Michael (Mike) Ogg. Between Blue and Ogg and their combined leadership skills, it was hard to go wrong. Dorsey Blue has received his due elsewhere but I would like to say a few words at this time about my friend, Mike Ogg.

Mike Ogg, First Sergeant Nonpareil. My First Sergeant, Mike Ogg (1938-2008), was an absolute gem of a human being. He was a kind, considerate soul from the aforementioned city of Lufkin, a Physical Education major, and a leader in the truest meaning of the word. Mike was maybe 5' 9" and weighed around 180 pounds. He had an unusually large head, a pocked, acne-scarred face, and the muscular build one would expect of a good high school football player which Mike had been, according to reports.

Beyond his considerable personal attributes, one of the things I admired most about Mike was his ability of make my job incredibly easy. He was a true leader of men, loved the responsibility associated with being in charge, and enforced the unit and Corps rules and regulations with a judicious blend of toughness and fairness. As testimony to the budding leadership I had the good fortune to witness during my tenure as CO, Mike was named the outstanding Company Commander in the entire Corps of Cadets his senior year. I was not surprised when I heard the news of his selection for I always believed if you were drawing up specifications for how a Corps leader ought to look and act, Mike Ogg would be the gold standard.

Though unintentional on their part, Dorsey Blue and Mike Ogg taught me, through some nebulous, indefinable, osmotic process, that the best way to run an organization is to surround oneself with the most capable people you can find and turn them loose to do their jobs. I have never for the life of me figured out why some leaders surround themselves with boot-licking lackeys, sycophantic martinets, and outright incompetents who only make their jobs more difficult. In my own experience, the latter model is more common than the former which is unfathomable, in my humble view, as a leadership strategy. This discussion is not meant as an indictment of the Corps leadership, and is aimed at a much more general audience that includes the military, our public schools, sports teams, and business corporations.

After graduating in 1961, Mike Ogg spent a little over a year on active duty in the army at good old Fort Hood, my home base for nearly three years. After being released from active duty in 1963, Mike joined the Texas National Guard which became one of the passions of his life for the next forty years. He held many positions of leadership and repeatedly received recognition for his efforts on behalf of the Guard. As a final reward for his exemplary service, Mike was promoted to Brigadier General in 1991. I attended his promotion ceremony, as did Dorsey Blue who himself was a Lieutenant Colonel in the Guard. We basked in Mike's success and I somewhat selfishly like to think I might have contributed to it in some small way. I always felt Mike sought and respected my opinion when we worked together as Company Commander and First Sergeant in the school year of 1959-1960, and hoped some of what I taught or modeled served him well.

After the award ceremony, Blue and I adjourned to the bar in a local hotel and drank a bit, or in Blue's case, more than a bit. I drank my usual quota of beer but I noticed that Dorsey was ordering and essentially chugalugging double drinks of bourbon (or perhaps it was the vilest of alcoholic beverages, scotch). In any case, I have no idea how many of those concoctions he consumed but I eventually had to drag him to his room and put him to bed to keep him from trying to drive back to Dallas. There is a stereotype of the drunk who has to be carried out of a bar with his feet dragging behind him; that was my man Blue that night. I surmised my old roommate had issues with alcohol as a result of that episode. I was told by his son in the previously mentioned visit that such was the case, though it never got in the way of job performance or family life.

In civilian life, Mike became a highly respected educational leader in Texas, serving as principal of junior high or high schools in Gladewater, Lake Highlands, College Station (A&M Consolidated), and Montgomery. Mike also served a stint as superintendent of the Gilmer school district. He was an accomplished leader in many areas with his faculty, but students who knew him always raved about his ability to memorize each and every one of their names, a daunting task considering the size of some of the schools in which he worked.

Mike retired from both the National Guard and Montgomery High School, and died suddenly on March 8, 2008, at the age of sixty-nine from what I assume was cardiac failure. Mike was a devoted family man, an outstanding military leader, and a much-admired icon in the field of public education, and the world is less well off with his passing.

In Memory
Don Michael "Mike" Ogg
September 11, 1938 - March 04, 2008.

MIKE OGG OBITUARY

I have met few people I think more highly of than Mike Ogg. He was a great person and though we went our separate ways and only saw each other on rare occasions over the years, I miss him. He was a genuinely good man and an inspiration to those of us fortunate enough to have crossed his gentle path. He always treated me with friendly respect and I think the admiration I felt for him seemed shared; I choose to think it was, at least.

Uncle Jimmy Serves Up Some Cold One's. My senior year started off with a bang in late August, 1959, thanks to some friends who celebrated its beginning perhaps a bit too enthusiastically. I had returned to campus from my home in Texas City and found a note attached to my door indicating three high-spirited boys from the nearby city of Brenham, Ken Stufflebeme, Ray Murski, and Bill Seeker, were kicking off the new school year at Uncle Jimmy's with more than a couple of beers. Uncle Jimmy's was one of the few places one could buy a beer around the A&M area in 1959; it was a hybrid, sort of a cross between a beer joint, a dive, and a dump. It was situated on Texas Avenue across from the A&M golf course. Aggies of today would recognize the area where Uncle Jimmy's was located in the general vicinity of the popular Mexican cantina, On the Border.

Before that evening was over, the band of beer-guzzling Brenham boys had consumed eighteen beers each, give or take, and I lagged behind by maybe a six-pack. Since my friends had a substantial head start, I was the most sober of the group and inherited the dubious honor of loading my beefy buddies into a car and driving them back to the dorm which fortunately was nearby. The task was not easy; Bill Seeker was of relatively normal size, maybe 180 pounds, but my friends Stufflebeme, of German heritage, and Murski, of Polish ancestry, weighed in collectively at nearly 500 pounds. Gathering the strength to muscle this third of a ton of humanity in and out of the car was a daunting task, but I somehow got us all back to the dorm safe and sound.

Uncle Jimmy's was pretty much our hangout for much of that last year. Dorsey Blue, Joe Watson, Earl Yarbrough, the aforementioned Ken Stufflebeme, Joe Saunders, unnamed others, yours truly, and our Academic Advisor, Dr. H. O. Kunkel from the College of Agriculture, were regulars there several nights a week for most of the school year. Dr. Kunkel, who went on to become Dean of the College of Agriculture, was our academic advisor, and a facilitative one at that. As part of a university initiative to forge good relationships between faculty and students, Corps units were assigned faculty advisors and Dr. Kunkel was our man. He would give wise academic and life counsel to the younger troops for an hour or two on selected evenings, at which time the seniors among us would adjourn to Uncle Jimmy's for a beer or two (or three!). We were, of course, pleased that someone of Dr. Kunkel's considerable stature in the university would take an interest in us as beer-drinking companions. Though I am not sure of my facts here, I think Dr. Kunkel was still single at that time, which would partially account for his availability. In any case, his wise counsel and camaraderie were much appreciated.

Poor Dr. Kunkel was the unwitting recipient of one of my most egregious lapses in judgment, and I still to this day experience guilt over my misstep in etiquette. It seems that the night before graduation, several of us were celebrating the upcoming event by imbibing a bit at a local watering hole. Dr. Kunkel drove up to where we were drinking and sent an emissary, Earl Yarbrough, to coax us away for a goodbye meal. I sandbagged and hem-hawed for a while and after much pleading, Earl and Dr. Kunkel eventually gave up their ill-fated quest and drove off. I owed Dr. Kunkel my attendance at that proposed meal as payback for his kindness, camaraderie, and mentorship. Every time I saw him on campus when I rejoined the faculty, I would feel pangs of guilt for my decade-old faux pas. Unfortunately for my mental well-being about this incident, I never did work up the courage to offer Dr. Kunkel an apology. Perhaps I have overblown the incident, but it remains in my memory bank as a low point in my undergraduate experience. I have the feeling this was not the first or last time over-imbibing led to lapses in judgment.

Final Memories of A&M. Several other significant events stand out from that year, and one was the aforementioned Texas Aggie Bonfire, that symbol of every Aggie's undying love for his (or her) university. A time-honored tradition associated with that event was attaching an outhouse to the top of the stack prior to its immolation. Another Bonfire tradition, though of lesser glitz and glitter, was hoisting a makeshift flag atop the obligatory outhouse shortly before the entire stack was set ablaze. Tradition further dictated that the flag was to be made from a bed sheet belonging to the commander of Company C-1, which was moi! Three-and-a-half years of college life had taken a serious toll on my supply of bedding, and I ended up donating my last sheet to the underclassmen so they could draw up a proper adornment for the 1959 bonfire. This act of tradition-driven largesse forced me to sleep on my mattress sans bed sheets from Thanksgiving when the bonfire was set ablaze until May graduation. On those rare occasions when our unit underwent military inspection during those last six months, I borrowed sheets from friends just long enough to meet the requirements for a neatly made-up bunk. Watching my last sheet going up in flames sort of wiped the slate clean in one area. I could travel light after graduation, comforted by the fact I did not need to fret about taking any bedding home!

Another thing I remember was receiving a nice gift from my troops during Parents' Weekend, a hallowed event even today dedicated to rewarding moms and dads for their sacrifices in the name of their offspring. It was traditional for the underclassmen in each unit to kick in a small contribution to buy their CO a nice wrist or pocket watch (my choice) to be awarded during the mid-April festivities. Little did I know that seventeen months later, the watch would go to a watery grave at the hands of one of the worst weather catastrophes to ever hit the Texas Gulf Coast, little Miss Hurricane Carla.

My dad and stepmother, June, attended the Parents Weekend ceremony, and I know they were proud of my modest accomplishments. It also provided another opportunity for my father to remind me for the umpteenth time about my wanting to quit school four years earlier, thanks to the hazing and the Kyle Field smoke-in-the-face fiasco involving the aforementioned Will Elias. My dad never tired of telling that story, even as he reached his eighties.

What Are Friend's For? Another interesting recollection from that senior year was a short but relatively intense relationship I had with of a more-or-less steady girlfriend by the name of Audrey

Little, aka "Little Audrey." Audrey was attractive and I liked her well enough, but I must confess to seeing, for whatever reason, little long-range potential in our relationship. When Christmas vacation rolled around that year, I spent the holidays in Oklahoma ostensibly visiting my mother though I spent far more time renewing old high school friendships than I did visiting with her. As she so eloquently described it one evening as I was going out the front door: "You have a beautiful back because that is all I ever get to see of you." I had a wonderful time in Oklahoma but upon my return after New Year's Day, I found that Audrey was going steady with my close friend, Joe Saunders. It seems I had asked Joe to keep tabs on Audrey from time to time while I was away for Christmas, and he apparently took my request to heart. But then, what are friends for if they can't steal your girlfriends while you are away? In actuality, I was rather pleased with Joe's intervention as it freed me of having to make a decision about our future status. I think the romance, such as it was, had pretty much run its course, was headed nowhere, and Joe's intervention gave me a comfortable, non-controversial out.

I Graduate!!

Graduation finally rolled around in May, 1960, and the ceremony was about as perfunctory as it gets; all males, mostly military, no bright colors, drab, drab, on top of boring, mind-numbing drab! I was thrilled to finally be there though, and my dad and June enjoyed seeing me walk across the stage and watching me wrap my grubby little paws around the long-awaited diploma. Attendance at graduation was mandatory in those days, but it was something I would not have missed anyway. I felt I owed that brief episode of pomp and circumstance to my dad and June for the sacrifices they made in getting me to that point. It was a nice payback for all their emotional and financial support.

I do lament a bit the loss of decorum and the unrepentant narcissism characterizing graduation ceremonies today, what with the names and slogans all over the hats ("Please look at my hat decorations. Aren't I cute?"), cell phones chirping, mindless texting taking place with its attendant drivel (or is palaver a better term?), people getting up to buy cokes and, even worse, parents permanently departing immediately after their own child receives his or her diploma. It would not take much to go with the flow for two hours at a once-in-a-lifetime event. I am happy to say that the power poobahs at A&M have apparently tired of the disrespect, too, and have put strictures in place to ensure that everyone treats graduation with proper respect. For example, I am told that people who leave early have to hand over their diplomas, only to receive them somewhat later in the mail. Not much of a penalty, really, but it does apparently have some clout with parents and new graduates.

For me, graduation served as a signal that the price of poker was getting ready to escalate. Reality hit home like a shot from an NFL linebacker. The soft life was over. I was done with school. I was done with the Corps. I would never again lay eyes on the vast majority of these people with whom I had lived, labored, languished, lazed, and lamented for so long and so ardently. Also, the safety net of emotional and financial support I had enjoyed for four years was kaput. My father had always told me he would support me financially through the bachelor's degree, but I was on my own from then on. He died in 2006 never having gone back on his word, and I cannot fault him in the slightest. He cut me a hell of deal for an undergraduate education and helped make those some of the greatest years of my life.

I had no idea what was looming ahead other than my military obligation which had been deferred in order for me to attend graduate school. But I knew deep down I had just spent the best four years of my life and it had ended all too quickly and unceremoniously. Welcome, Arnold Dallas LeUnes, to the real world. Or was it to be the cold, cruel world?

Favorite Professors

At this time, I would like to pay tribute to those professors with whom I had the good fortune to learn academic and life lessons from as an undergraduate student at A&M. My personal and professional lives have been greatly influenced by their teachings, philosophies of life, and mostly compassionate responses to young people. I owe these dedicated professionals a huge debt of gratitude for what they taught me about their subject matter and, more importantly, what they imparted about life. Interestingly, I do not think these people are all that different from what students at all universities experience. There are some universal traits that professors share regardless of where they toil, and I suspect the readership will readily identify with my own mentors.

The Motley Crew Earns Their Nicknames

Professors in my undergraduate days were characterized by at least two salient markers. First of all, they were a motley crew, by any measure. Only half of the A&M faculty members had earned the PhD degree; many professors had master's degrees and, more often than not, the highest degree earned was conferred by A&M. To put it kindly, at least in terms of their academic credentials, the faculty in the 1950's was a ragtag group with more than its share of run-of-the-mill "good old boys." Secondly, professors who had any status in the eyes of the students were accorded nicknames borne usually of affection and almost always recognizable by the majority of the student body. For whatever reason, the Department of History had more than its share of these "prestigious" namesakes.

Milton "No Notes" Nance. Prominent among the motley crew was the long-time chair of the Department of History, Dr. Milton "Notes" Nance. Dr. Nance was also sometimes referred to as "No-Notes" Nance for both the alliterative qualities of his nickname, his voluminous class lecture notes, and his affinity for writing 600-page books, two-thirds of which were devoted to footnotes. In defense of Dr. Nance, his colleagues of my acquaintance have assured me his books on Texas History were scholarly, well-researched, and highly-regarded by other scholars in his area of expertise.

Dr. Nance served as Head of the Department of History for several decades, and he was a legend among his peers. Nance stories abound, some of which show him in less than the most positive light. One has to remember that Dr. Nance served at a time in A&M's evolution when racism, ethnocentrism, anti-Semitism, and provincialism were pretty much the order of the day.

One anecdote concerning the man comes from the late 1960's or early 1970's. It seems Dr. Nance decided to clean up his act, language-wise, by ceasing to refer to African-Americans as "niggers", choosing instead to use the term "nigra" which apparently was an attempt on his part to reconcile his history and personal philosophy with changing American folkways and mores and the beginnings of the wave of political correctness so salient today.

Yet another Nance vignette, however apocryphal, has been relayed to me by my friend and History colleague, Dr. Arnold Krammer. It seems that in the early 1970's, Dr. Nance hired two young, neophyte historians who were to later distinguish themselves in their respective sub-fields. One was the aforementioned Arnold Krammer, a Jew of Hungarian descent, who grew up in Chicago. Arnie Krammer authored a dozen books on the Holocaust during his thirty-plus years at A&M and prior to his retirement in 2015. The second astute Nance hire was a promising scholar whose focus was on British history, Dr. Ralph James Quincy Adams, known affectionately to his colleagues as "Quince." To this day, "Quince" Adams is stylishly foppish in a decidedly British way, always exquisitely dressed to the nines. He has a full head of sandy-red hair streaked with the inevitable gray, and sports a prominent reddish-gray handlebar mustache that curls on the ends and protrudes beyond the confines of each side of his face. Quince was widely known to be professionally ambitious, but he also had a reputation among his peers to be highly attuned to social nuances, a bit of a social climber, and always acutely tuned in to powerful others around the university. At the same time, he seemed well-liked and respected by his colleagues despite his sometimes socially manipulative ways. In my own case, I have always liked Quince, greatly appreciate his quirkiness and, to this day, find him to be an interesting guy.

It seems in the 1960's and 1970's, Dr. Nance was known in local social circles for hosting a fancy Yuletide party in his home, with invited guests from the History faculty as well as prominent and influential people from other walks of life. Formal faculty invitations to those events were placed in their mail boxes a few weeks before the big social event, but Dr. J. R. Q. "Quince" Adams found himself on the outside looking in each Christmas when party time rolled around. For several years, he failed to receive an invitation to the soiree! No one I know would have taken such a snub more personally than the social animal, "Quince." At some point a couple of years into the sequence of the Christmas parties, Dr. Nance let it slip to someone that the reason he did not invite Dr. Adams was because he was "that Jew from Chicago." Someone informed Dr. Nance that "Quince" Adams was not from Chicago nor was he a Jew, but instead a Protestant from Indiana. He was further informed that he must have confused Dr. Adams with my Hungarian Jew amigo, Dr. Arnie Krammer. Guess what? When the party invitations were passed out the next December, "Quince" Adams received the long-awaited invitation and Arnie Krammer found his mailbox empty! One can only speculate as to how Dr. Krammer got hired in the first place, given his heritage.

I recently brought this tale to the attention of "Quince" Adams and he adamantly denies the events ever took place. On the other hand, Dr. Krammer is equally vociferous in his defense of the story, which he loves to recite. Where, then, must the truth lie? But even if the words are apocryphal or an elaborate fabrication, they capture well certain aspects of the personality of Dr. Milton "Notes" Nance.

Dr. Nance supervised the master's thesis of my first wife, Barbara, which was a history of the local private and one-time military training school, Allen Academy. As part of her research, it seems that one of the pictures Barbara wanted to include in her thesis was of the Allen Board of Directors in 1905 or some such year early in the twentieth century. All board members were men and listed by initials, and Dr. Nance required Barbara to find out first and middle names of each of those individuals rather than citing them by their initials. Such a quest proved pedantic, problematic and time-consuming for Barbara (half of one summer) and a source of considerable aggravation for Dr. Nance when one inconsiderate soul on the board had the gall to possess only initials. Dr. Nance ranted and raved about the obviously misguided and primitive parents who would assign initials to a child in lieu of a proper first and middle name!

Other History luminaries included Lloyd "Ivy League" Taylor, "Screaming Al" Nelson, and "Red Ass" Bass. I did not get to know Drs. Nelson and Bass other than by reputation but Dr. Lloyd Chamberlain "Ivy League" Taylor, Jr., one of Dr. Nance's hires, was easily my favorite undergraduate professor.

Lloyd "Ivy League" Taylor. Dr. Taylor received all three of his degrees from Lehigh University in Bethlehem, Pennsylvania, including the PhD in History. He was the professor for my very first college course, History 105, which covered the American Colonial Period to the Civil War. The students in that class were all beginning freshmen attending their first college lecture and none of us had the foggiest notion of what to expect. Thus, we awaited Dr. Taylor's arrival with an air of nervous anticipation. Our soon-to-be professor strode quietly but confidently into the classroom, introduced himself, and checked attendance. He concluded his introductory remarks by announcing to the group that athletes were free to attend but should expect nothing higher than an F if they stayed in the class. As I think about Dr. Taylor and the possible origins of this bias, he was slight of build, a bit effeminate in demeanor and, as I was to discern later, gay at a time when such things were hush-hush at best. As a result, I suspect he was never involved in sports, or at least the "manly" ones, and was probably bullied by athletes as a young boy or adolescent. In any case, that first-day pronouncement sent a shock wave through the group, and several athletes immediately bolted for the door. I had no idea professors entertained such biases and was certainly unaware they exerted that level of control over their classes and, by default, the students.

As I said, "Ivy League" was not imposing physically, a tad on the effeminate side, average in height and weight, a nice-looking guy in an eastern, preppy, Ivy League way, hence his nickname. He had a very heavy, dark beard, immaculate and closely trimmed black hair, and showed up for class without exception in a freshly pressed shirt with button-down collar, colorful but tasteful striped tie, and Ivy League pants with the buckle in the back so fashionable among preppy types in the 1950's. Interestingly, when Dr. Taylor finished his classes each day, he would immediately go to his office and change into penny loafers sans socks, Ivy League shorts with the obligatory buckle on the back, and a white dress shirt. The sleeves of his shirt were always rolled up above the elbows and the shirt-tail inevitably remained untucked.

Rumors floated about that Dr. Taylor had attended a fancy exclusive eastern prep school with Jacqueline Bouvier before she became Jackie Kennedy, which added to his mystique. His association with Jackie Kennedy may have been more apocryphal than true but one thing was certain: "Ivy League" Taylor clearly came from a world we small-town Texans knew little about.

I struggled to make a gentleman's C in Ivy League's course but enjoyed his lectures immensely. I also liked him personally and entertained hopes of enrolling later in another course he might be teaching. It was not to be, however, and as we shall see shortly, it was my loss.

"Ivy League" had a reputation as a bit of a drinker and rumor had it that at his peak in the 1960's and 1970's, he typically consumed a six-pack of beer and a fifth of bourbon each and every day. He also spent many a Friday evening at The Texan, an upscale restaurant with easily the most elegant cuisine to ever hit the Bryan-College Station area. Even today, the so-called upscale restaurants in the area, Christopher's and The Republic, cannot hold a candle to The Texan for elegant food. The Texan, long since out of business, was the brainchild of an A&M Physics Instructor by the name of Robert Tapley.

Prior to becoming The Texan, the business was a seedy drive-in with shabby, torn, and patched upholstery in most of the booths and a menu that added new meaning to the term pedestrian. My friends and I often went there as undergraduates to hang out and drink coffee, but seldom to eat for fear of ptomaine poisoning. When Tapley took the place over in the mid-1960's, he spruced it up a bit, though almost all improvements were confined to the interior of the restaurant not the exterior. The building retained its appearance as a real dive, the parking lot remained rough and uneven, potholes and all, but the inside dining environment was beyond elegant.

Though the food was absolutely phenomenal, my wife and I ate there only on special occasions, say birthdays or anniversaries. For two people, the tab ran upwards of one hundred dollars for appetizers, main courses, desserts, and a couple of drinks, a hefty chunk of money by 1970's standards. When we were able to save up enough shekels to dine there, Judy and I ordered without exception and with great glee and anticipation the Caesar salad and a bowl of their signature onion soup. I have dined in a fair number of fine restaurants in many of the big cities in the US, Canada, Australia, New Zealand, and a fair portion of Europe and have found nary an eating establishment that could create Caesar salad or onion soup rivaling what was served in that humble local restaurant. The salad was a major production, literally a work of art, prepared at the table by one of the always well-trained, attentive, almost always officious waiters. The soup was served with a delicious broth, ample amounts of onions, and a crusty layer of cheese baked on top and running down the sides of the serving bowl. Words do not do justice to those two delicacies. Once done with the soup and salad, I chose as my entrée the "Shrimp of Two Kinds", an absolutely delightful mixture of equal amounts of perfectly boiled and exquisitely battered fried shrimp. Judy was partial to the elegant lobster dishes which were wonderful in their own right. I have never been much of a lobster guy myself.

Tapley was truly a culinary genius but when he passed away, his deft touch with the elegant cuisine, along with his finely tuned restaurant management skills, passed along with him. Both the service and the quality of the food began to deteriorate, and the business closed for good not too long after Mr. Tapley died, maybe a year. Some things should never die, and The Texan restaurant is one of them.

It is said that "Ivy League" Taylor often invited a favorite student to dine with him at The Texan on Friday nights, and those evenings out constituted a major part of his social life. A friend, former banker, and local businessman, Bill McGuire, worked at The Texan as an undergraduate student and Dr. Taylor always asked for him as his waiter. The staff eventually hung the nickname "Bud" Taylor on Dr. Taylor because he expected two Budweiser's to be placed on his chosen table immediately upon entering the restaurant. Bill also indicated that the two beers were not the only ones "Bud" Taylor drank during those evenings out.

As was noted earlier, it was widely believed that Dr. Taylor was gay at a time when such intimations were only discussed in hushed terms, and I suspect the assertion was true. I cannot affirm or deny the suspicion nor do I care, but what I do know for certain is that he was a brilliant, private, reclusive man with a touch of mystery and an elegant ability to express himself in the classroom.

"Ivy League" was a long-time jogger and it was not unusual to see him running on campus, sporting his skimpy white shorts and cheap white running shoes. Unfortunately, he died one afternoon in the late 1970's while jogging near the recently-razed local landmark, G. Rollie White Coliseum. Reports were that he had eaten a hefty lunch at the Memorial Student Center (MSC) prior to going on his daily run. While navigating the campus, he apparently got violently sick, began to vomit, and reports indicated he probably choked to death. I prefer to believe that Dr. Taylor was smarter than to go running right after a meal, but who knows? I have also wondered from time to time if the rumored high levels of alcohol consumption might have played a role in his premature demise. Dr. Taylor was his mid-fifties, seemingly in good health, and died far too young. He remains one of the fondest memories of my many days in academia.

In the spring semester of 1960, A&M offered a philosophy course for the first time ever, essentially an introduction to the major schools of philosophical thought. Students of today would probably recognize the course as Philosophy 111, Contemporary Moral Issues. Dr. Taylor was asked to teach one of the two sections, no doubt due to his classical, Ivy League liberal arts education and the fact that there were no faculty members specifically trained in the discipline of Philosophy at that time. I had the option of signing up with him but decided for reasons I could neither explain nor understand then or now to branch out and try the professor who was teaching the other section. At the time I made that decision, I had no idea it would be one of the worst mistakes I ever made in my 297 hours of college coursework. What could I have possibly been thinking? Why would you pass up an opportunity in your final semester to take a course from your favorite, most esteemed professor? Why would you risk taking a course from a person with no track record in the classroom? I honestly cannot tell you what my thought processes were at the time, nor can I tell you today. Temporarily insanity and taking leave of my senses are the best I can come up with to explain my mental lapse.

The other "professor", the one I signed up for, was a retired Protestant minister who announced at the start of the first class period that there was too much material to cover and, for that reason, he would not entertain questions or observations from the floor. We soon learned what he really meant to say was he was going to read the book aloud while the few of us who brought our books to class would read along silently with him. Every once in a while on a completely random basis, he would look up, staring at no one in particular, and ask the class, "You see?" The frequency with which he posed this rhetorical inanity was striking so I devoted one entire "lecture" to counting the "You sees" by marking down four vertical lines and then crossing them with a slanting diagonal line to denote the number five. The count eventually got up to 143 "You see's" with fifteen minutes remaining in the class, and I was struck with an epiphany. It occurred to me that I really did not see, probably was never going to see, and, most importantly, did not want to see.

This triple epiphany led me to walk out of class that brilliant late March day, never to return, thus earning my first and only grade of F in college. I genuinely did not see, did not want to see, would never see and, most importantly, did not need the course to graduate. I thus walked away from the wreckage that was Introductory Philosophy, retired-preacher style. I could only imagine what torture it must have been to be in that man's congregation where the "You see's" must have been staggering in number and frequency.

Anyway, the class was interfering with my golf game! Now I could join up with fellow duffers, Joe Watson, Bob Underwood, Earl Yarbrough, and the rest of the guys playing the A&M course or the Municipal (Muny) course in Bryan! Muny was a favored option because there were times we would play eighteen holes, venture over to nearby Martin's Place for some barbecue and a beer or two, and return for eighteen more. Martin's began as a family-owned business in 1925 and to my knowledge is the only eatery still open in Bryan and College Station that was operating during my days as a student at A&M.

Aside from the most eccentric Milton Nance, Loyd Taylor, and their colorfully nicknamed colleagues in the Department of History, there were other colorful characters in abundance around campus. Among them were D. B. "Dusty Butt" Cofer and Sid "Wolfman" Cox in English, "Daddy-O" Dowell and Emil "Mammy" Mamaliga in Physical Education, Walter "Marvel" Varvel in Psychology, Sidney O. "SOB" Brown in Biology, Eugene "Blue Book" Benton in Political Science, and "Cigar Dan" Davis in Sociology. Just referring to them in conversations with your peers as "Cigar Dan", or "Dusty Butt", or "Screaming Al", or "SOB" was sufficient identification; no further elaboration was necessary!

Jimmy Brautigam. Another "professor" I was fortunate enough to meet that first semester of my freshman year was not a professor at all but rather a young graduate student by the name of Jimmy

Brautigam whose kindness and counsel helped me through Algebra 101. This kind man, not much older than me, literally saved my academic bacon. A mid-semester average of 42 in algebra suggested I was in need of help, so I wisely (for once) sought Mr. Brautigam's guidance. As a result of his patient mentorship, I eventually was able to pass the course by the skin of my teeth; 70 was a D in those days and I squeaked by with a 69.75 average. I am not positive I would have been allowed to return to A&M for the spring semester had I made an F in that course, so as I said, Jimmy Brautigam may have unknowingly altered the course of my life!

Miss Barbara McKinney. My first English professor, Miss Barbara McKinney, was one of only four female faculty members on the campus in the academic year 1956-1957. The others were Mettie Rodgers, also a lecturer in English, who had been at A&M since 1947, Judith Ann Bell in Spanish, and Mrs. K. D. Reel in Electrical Engineering who was the wife of an officer assigned to the Department of Military Science. I struggled mightily with Miss McKinney's course at first, but my grades continued to get better and better as I learned (relearned?) more and more about the proper use of the King's English. At the end of the semester Miss McKinney stopped me in the hall to offer her congratulations for my excellent work on the final exam. Excited by the news, I optimistically blurted out: "I guess that means I might make a C in the course, huh?" She let me know in no uncertain terms, however kindly, that I had made considerable progress during the semester but a C was not in the cards. I made a D and felt pretty good about it as she gave no A's, nary a B, seven C's, seven D's and ten F's. To put it in other terms, right at seventy percent of the class made a D or F. The best thing that came out of the whole experience was I learned so much from her, thus making the rest of my English courses pretty much a breeze. Hopefully, some of what she taught me will be evident in this humble document.

Miss McKinney was either a graduate student or a beginning professor, young, single, pretty much average in size and not especially striking in appearance. However, there were no female students at A&M at that time, the local *femme fatales* shunned us like we had cooties, and we seldom got to go home that fall semester, so female companionship was in short supply. As a result, my plain Jane English professor underwent some sort of convoluted mental transmogrification in my head and became almost a Marilyn Monroe look-alike by Thanksgiving. Maybe all the girls really do get prettier at closing time!

"Cigar Dan" Davis. My first Sociology professor was an intriguing chap by the name of Dan Davis. For most of his adult life, he had been an avid, addicted, hard-core cigar smoker and this life-long affinity for a smoking stogie earned him the nickname, "Cigar Dan" Davis. However, his egregious cigar habit had taken a horrific toll on his teeth and gums, and eventually forced him to abandon his affinity for the nicotine monster. Shortly after kicking the habit, he replaced what was left of his original but embattled teeth with an attractive set of bright new dentures.

"Cigar Dan" was not a particularly engaging teacher, but was famous for one lecture in which he spent the entire fifty-minute class period regaling the troops about the evolution of the wheel as a historical and sociological phenomenon. Listening to him drone on and on for the better part of an hour about the numerous and subtle nuances of the invention and continuing development of the wheel was pretty much edge of the chair stuff, to say the least!

William Merl "Daddy-O" Dowell. Another memorable professor was "Daddy-O" Dowell who may well have saved my life without knowing it. I took a health course with Mr. Dowell as a sophomore and one of his lectures dealt with snakebites. As part of that recitation, "Daddy-O" brought a highly-poisonous coral snake to class after capturing it in his yard the previous evening. The viper was safely contained in a Mason jar with holes punched in the top for aeration, and Mr. Dowell talked at length about the coral snake's brilliant colors. Most importantly, he gave us a mnemonic device guaranteed to provide positive identification if confronted by one of the slippery critters in the wild. He told us if you suddenly come upon a snake of color, you should invoke the following mantra to assess the seriousness of the situation: "Red and black, venom lack. Red and yellow, kill a fellow" (also iterated sometimes as "Red and yellow kills a fellow. Red touches black, friend of Jack").

To my knowledge, I have never seen a coral snake in the wild. However, I recently spotted a gorgeous, brilliantly colored snake slithering across the road near our house, and I instantly thought of the handy little mnemonic "Daddy-O" had given us some fifty-five years earlier. The snake in my path had alternating red and black stripes rather than the to-be-feared red and yellow ones, so I knew immediately my life was not on the line. Kudos go out to "Daddy-O" Dowell for giving me that serendipitous pearl of wisdom six decades ago.

Emil "Mammy" Mamaliga. "Mammy" was one of my favorite professors of all-time, a good, down-to-earth, pragmatic teacher and a real sweetheart of a guy. "Mammy" was an All-American swimmer at The Ohio State University in his undergraduate days, and later received a master's degree at A&M where he stayed on as professor for the rest of his life. I took a couple of courses with "Mammy" as an undergraduate but really got to know him much better when I joined the faculty and became a colleague of sorts.

The name Mamaliga itself has an interesting history. It seems that "Mammy's" father was a Romanian by the name of Teflian and his favorite dish was a cornmeal mush called "mamaliga." At some point and for reasons not clear to anyone, the parents changed the family name from Teflian to Mamaliga.

"Mammy" knew most of what there was to know about one of his specialties, sports injuries, and he supplemented his academic expertise with doses of good old common sense and an abundance of street smarts. Over the course of several years, I was able to witness a couple of examples of his down-to-earth, common sense wisdom. On one occasion, I stopped by his office in the late 1960's to seek his opinion about why my knees were suddenly stiff and sore and giving me minor fits. It was the week after Thanksgiving and "Mammy" surmised that I had probably spent a fair amount of time during the holiday with my legs propped up on a coffee table or a hassock grading term papers. He diagnosed my condition as a mild hyperextension of the knees for which he recommended I quit propping my knees up on assorted objects to grade papers. I did as he recommended and the stiffness and soreness dissipated right away, never to return.

On another occasion, I brought complaints of mild shoulder and elbow pain to his attention. "Mammy" said, "I'll bet you sleep with your right arm curled up under your body with your elbow between your head and the pillow." Sure enough, that was a common sleeping position for me. As best I could I quit positioning myself that way and, as predicted, the shoulder and elbow pain subsided. These examples of the street wisdom from my man "Mammy" are only two of many attributed to him by various people.

"Mammy" died at the age of sixty-three as the result of an inoperable cancer located near the base of his tongue. "Mammy" was widely known for the signature cigar dangling visibly from his lips, day after day, month after month, year after year. I cannot remember ever seeing him without a cigar, though it was seldom lit. Unfortunately, the habit came back to bite him badly, and he died a slow and, from what I have been told, painful death from the cancer.

Sid "Wolfman" Cox. Mr. Cox, an English professor, was another most interesting chap. He had a lupine face and eyes, hence his nickname. He had a personality to match, at least on the surface, though after being in his Logic course for a couple of weeks I figured out his bark was far worse than his bite. Mr. Cox always showed up for class wearing a more or less white dress shirt and slacks, with the shirt sleeves unbuttoned and rolled up near his biceps. Rather than rolling his sleeves up in a systematic fashion with orderly folds, Mr. Cox would push them up above his elbows using his thumb and forefinger, and shortly afterward, they would fall back around his forearms. Again, he would push the sleeves up, repeating the ritual over and over. Apparently, he did not wash his shirts on a regular basis and as the shirt sleeves fell from above his elbows to near the wrists, each wrinkle revealed a tell-tale, multi-hued discoloration, thus giving his shirts a modified rainbow or a ROY G BIV, colors-of-the-spectrum effect. Students in the class joked that you could tell the age of his shirts by the number of multi-colored rings on the sleeves, much as you would by counting rings on an old tree.

Mr. Cox was regaling us with the nuances of logic one day and made a comment that struck one of my classmates, Stan Wied, as wrong. Stan uttered a more or less rhetorical "bullshit" under his breath to no one in particular, assuming the epithet was inaudible. Mr. Cox somehow picked up on Stan's momentary editorializing, and from that day on, every time the class roll was called, he would say "bullshit" when he got to Stan's name…no Stan, no Wied, no Mr. Wied, just "bullshit." Stan Wied went on to a career as a pilot for one of the major airlines and I was fortunate enough many years later to have one of his daughters in class. Fortunately, she was not built like her father who, proportionally, may have had the broadest and most muscular shoulders I have ever seen. Stan was a decent-sized guy, maybe six feet one and two hundred pounds and very athletic-looking but his shoulders belonged on someone a half foot taller and fifty pounds heavier. He was an early and somewhat smaller version of the fictional character Jack Reacher, the famous creation of novelist Lee Child. As a fan of Jack Reacher, I am appalled that the wimpy actor and resident Scientologist, Tom Cruise, was recently cast as Jack Reacher in the movies. If anything, Tom Cruise is the anti-Jack Reacher. Casting Cruise as Lieutenant Colonel Claus von Stauffenberg, the German aristocrat and military leader who attempted to kill Adolf Hitler during World War II, is almost as egregious.

Wimpy Cruise as the fictional Jack Reacher and the larger-than-life Baron von Stauffenberg, both great examples of men's men? You have got to be kidding me!

Despite his idiosyncrasies, I really liked Mr. Cox. I thought he was a good teacher and a good man. I say good man because, among other things, Mr. Cox spent many a noon hour reading aloud to his wife's special education students in the College Station schools. That gesture of kindness suggests there was a good man behind that lupine-like, rough and tumble, almost always unkempt exterior.

Dr. Ewens. One other professor merits some attention, but not for the right reasons. His name was Dr. Ewens (given name not remembered) and I took Educational Psychology (I think) from him. Professor Ewens was lecturing along one morning and made a casual comment that parents should never spank their children. One of my classmates, a Korean War veteran and A&M football player named Merle Locke, took polite exception with that particular professorial pearl of wisdom. He said, "Professor Ewens, I respectfully disagree with what you just said about spanking children. I have a five-year-old at home and I do not spank him very often or very hard, but there are times when I think a mild slap on the rear end teaches him a few things about right and wrong." The reply to this commentary from our professor went roughly as follows: "Please see me after class, Mr. Locke. You have been rude, disrespectful, and out of line and if it is within my power as a Professor, I am going to do my best to have you permanently expelled for insubordination."

Merle Locke, who died a few years back, was not expelled from school but the incident had a major impact on the way I looked at the field of psychology, or at least Texas A&M's brand of it. It seemed to me that freedom of thought and open inquiry did not exist in Dr. Ewens' class, and through guilt by association, I reasoned that such must also be the case with the entire field of Psychology. I thus took my remaining required course in that discipline, Adolescent Psychology, by correspondence from Southern Methodist University (SMU) in Dallas, more or less as an act of defiance against people like Ewens. Since I was not much of a fan of Political Science either, I decided to double my "pleasure" for that summer by taking Texas Government at the same time.

Much to my delight, Dr. Ewens took a job elsewhere the next year, I think Oklahoma A&M. Perhaps Merle Locke's "insubordination" was too much for him. It was pretty raffish stuff, by any standard, and Locke may have well deserved being stoned in the courtyard or impaled on a sarcophagus for having the chutzpah to politely disagree with a professor.

Speaking of correspondence courses, students of today would likely view today's on-line courses as an appropriate analogue. In my day, you completed a lesson, sent it to the professor by what is known currently as "snail mail." Most likely, the professor would then sit on the lesson for a while, returning it at his or her leisure. At the other end, the student (i.e., me) often lacked the discipline to sit down and complete the next lesson. The pairing of lackadaisical students with procrastinating professors was not a good one, and did not bode well for courses taken by correspondence. By late August, it was clear I was not going to complete the either of the two correspondence courses by the start of fall classes at A&M. I figured on completing them as time allowed during September and

October, if needed. However, sometimes the best laid plans of mice and men go awry. Shortly after arriving back on campus, I got a summons from the iron maiden in the Office of the Registrar, a woman named Caroline Mitchell who everyone knew must be obeyed at all costs. Ms. Mitchell was a legend on campus for her unbending, no-nonsense, and often dictatorial approach to dealing with wayward students (and I suspect faculty of the same ilk), and many of us felt her wrath as we crossed her path in the late 1950's.

The aforementioned summons was a request to appear in her office posthaste. Ms. Mitchell greeted me in her most stern, grim-faced, business-like manner, letting me know in no uncertain terms I was in violation of A&M regulations about number of hours one could take in any given semester. According to Ms. Mitchell, I was signed up for eighteen hours at A&M (which was true) and six at SMU (which was also true). The total of hours was thus twenty-four or six too many in light of my overall grade point ratio. She let me know, again with absolute certainty, that I had a week to drop six of the A&M hours or complete the two correspondence courses. I, without hesitation, got on the stick and wrapped up the six hours at SMU, thus allowing me to keep the eighteen for which I was enrolled at A&M. Ms. Mitchell lit a much-needed fire under my happy little procrastinating ass, thank goodness.

Walter Alphonso "Marvel" Varvel and Walter Andrew Varvel. Of all the professors with interesting nicknames, I knew Walter Alphonso "Marvel" Varvel (1908-1990) the best for we were departmental colleagues for fifteen years until his retirement in 1981. Unfortunately, I did not have the good fortune as an undergraduate to take a course with Dr. Varvel. To this day I regard him as a major mentor at A&M, along with Dr. Albert Casey, and I prevailed on him for words of wisdom many times during my first few years as a professor. Walter was a brilliant but unpretentious, down-to-earth man who grew up on a farm in rural Kansas where he acquired one of life's greatest assets in my opinion, a great work ethic. Against considerable financial odds, he was able to work his way through undergraduate school at the University of Kansas where he later earned his master's and doctoral degrees. The Kansas alumni magazine once ran an article featuring Walter as one of six people who had received three degrees from that university without making a grade lower than A. Walter once allowed he had made a B at mid-semester in a graduate course in statistics, by his own admission not one of his strengths. He, of course, eventually turned that B into an A by the end of the semester, thus keeping his perfect record intact.

Walter was the consummate Renaissance man, having taught virtually every course in Psychology at A&M, as well as several in English and Chemistry during World War II due to a shortage of professors in those areas. He knew his own discipline backwards and forwards, could give the genus and species of all flora and fauna during walks across campus, quoted philosophers and poets liberally, sang (badly but enthusiastically) in the choir at his church, and could recite at will the batting averages or pitching statistics of many past and current major league baseball players. He was a daunting intellect and an immensely generous and giving man.

Walter was married to his childhood sweetheart, Nelly, and they had two girls and a boy. His son, Walter Andrew, was a talented, multi-sport high school athlete who later pitched for the A&M baseball team for four years. Young Walter, as we in the department called him, ultimately earned a PhD in Economics and retired a few years ago as Chief Operating Officer for the Federal Reserve Bank in Richmond, Virginia. Young Walter was as good a man as his father, adding support to the old time-worn adage that the apple does not fall very far from the tree.

I was able to partially repay Varvel the Elder for his boundless friendship by doing Walter the Younger a big favor shortly after he was drafted into the army in the late 1960's. Once basic and advanced infantry training were completed, young Walter was assigned to Fort Hood, Texas. He carried an infantry Military Occupational Specialty (MOS) and was ticketed for an infantry unit at the height of the Vietnam War. The 1960's was not a good time to be a "grunt" or "ground pounder", army appellations often used to describe infantrymen. I would suggest there is no good time to be an infantryman!

As will be noted elsewhere later, I left Fort Hood as Special Services Officer for the First Armored Division in 1964, but I still had contacts there throughout the remainder of the 1960's. When Walter Alphonso told me that Walter Andrew was going to be assigned to Fort Hood, I phoned Ed Hickman, the post Athletic Director, and called his attention to young Walter's impending arrival. After hearing my recitation about Walter's intelligence, character, and high school and college sports background, Ed Hickman went to the personnel people and persuaded them to have him assigned to his sports operation. I know Old Walter appreciated my efforts on behalf of Young Walter, and it was a small payback for all his guidance and friendship. Walter Alphonso "Marvel" Varvel retired in 1981 and passed away nine years later. His wife Nelly preceded him in death by several years.

Friends and Classmates Killed in Vietnam: A Belated Tribute

"No one is ever forgotten as long as someone still has memories of them."

Ed Worthington

For several of my classmates, that cold, cruel world we discussed and sometimes joked about came all too soon and with a vengeance, for they were killed in Vietnam between 1963 and 1969. That awful and indefensible war, as are most, was the source of much dissent, rancor, and periodic violence in many segments of American society in the 1960's. Even as late as October, 2008, I received an email over the Internet in which Jane Fonda was being lapidated for her alleged role in assisting the Viet Cong with their anti-US propaganda program forty years earlier. My feeling is: Let it go! Yes, there are people with long memories of the mistreatment of their friends and relatives by the North Vietnamese, but a time comes to let it go. The Prisoner of War (POW) issue became the subject of much talk during the 2008 John McCain presidential campaign in which his heroism under fire was told and retold.

Floyd Kaase and Byron Stone

Captain Floyd Wayne Kaase and Captain Byron Stone were two classmates killed in Vietnam, and I had more than a passing acquaintanceship with both guys. Floyd Kaase was a country boy from the small town of Schulenberg, and I knew him best from his four-year stint as a waiter in the Duncan Mess Hall. Floyd was a helicopter pilot who suffered fatal injuries in a non-hostile crash. He was married at the time of his death on May 28, 1967. He was, sadly, only twenty-eight years old.

Byron Stone, a native of Houston, was in an Infantry unit on campus, and I remember him best as an energetic, vibrant, wiry guy, one of those athletic acrobats who constantly amused his occasional impromptu audiences by performing kips and back flips in the quadrangle in the middle of the Corps dormitories. As such, Byron's athleticism made him seem eternal and indestructible. Byron Clark Stone was killed on August 20, 1964 in a fierce fire fight with the Viet Cong. He was twenty-six at the time of his death and was buried two weeks later in Arlington National Cemetery. For his valor, Byron was awarded the U.S. Army Distinguished Service Cross for "extraordinary heroism in action against an enemy of the US."

Jim Vrba

I knew Jim Vrba better than either Floyd Kaase or Byron Stone for he was a Physical Education major, as was I, and we had quite a few classes together. I remember Jim as a tall, blond, and handsome, happy-go-lucky, loosey-goosey, carefree guy. However, the thing I recall most about Jim is his stealing the affection of the love of my life at the time, a beautiful young woman from Lake Jackson named Patsy (last name remembered but omitted).

Patsy had married shortly after high school and her new husband was a shot putter on the A&M track team. According to Patsy, the husband tried to shot put her across the hotel room in a moment of wrath on their wedding night. Predictably, the marriage went rapidly downhill from there. After the divorce, she stayed on at A&M as secretary to Dr. Carl Tischler, the head of the Department of Physical Education. Since most of my classes were near Dr. Tischler's office on the second floor of G. Rollie White Coliseum, I spent a lot of time kibitzing and flirting with Patsy, as did quite a number of other potential suitors. She was a beauty, a green-eyed brunette with a drop-dead gorgeous figure.

Largely due to my lack of sophistication and *savior faire* in matters where females were concerned, our relationship proved to be brief, mostly consisting of daily chats in her office. However, she decided to visit her parents in Lake Jackson one weekend in late April of 1958, and invited me to come down and spend some time with her. Needless to say, I was flattered and ecstatic at the prospect of getting to know the lovely Miss Patsy on a more intimate basis, with a lot of emphasis on intimate!

I forget what we did on Saturday night, probably the first date obligatory movie, but we agreed to get together early Sunday and make a day of it at the beach. I volunteered to pick her up at her parents' home but she insisted on meeting me at my hotel room before we adjourned to soak up some rays in the sand. Being equal parts gallant and naïve, I held my ground and eventually argued her out of the idea of coming to the hotel. It never dawned on me in my naiveté that she almost certainly had in mind a romantic interlude in my room. She put up a valiant fight about who was picking up who and where, but unfortunately I "prevailed." I picked her up at her home, we went to the beach for a few hours, and I returned to A&M later that day by way of Texas City. On the drive home, I could not shake the feeling that the day had not gone well. Subsequent events supported my assumption as I was to find out the next day.

It was clear on Monday that the relationship had cooled noticeably and within a short time, Patsy started dating handsome, genial Jim Vrba. Though I may have initially harbored some resentment toward Jim for his intervention, I knew deep down the culprit who killed the relationship with Miss Lake Jackson was Arnold Dallas LeUnes, not James Matthew Vrba. Of course, I could never have imagined in my wildest dreams that ten short years later, Jim would be killed in Vietnam.

Major Jim Vrba was thirty-one, married (not to Patsy), a veteran of six years in the Army, and had been deployed for eighteen weeks when he was killed by enemy small arms fire near Vinh Long,

South Vietnam, on January 31, 1968. It was a truly sad day for me when I first heard of Jim's death, and any ill feelings I may have had about events related to our tussle over the affections of Patsy a decade earlier had largely been forgotten and completely forgiven. Things that seemed earth-shattering at one moment can seem awfully trivial in retrospect.

Words cannot capture the psychic pain I feel when reflecting in quiet moments on how guys like Kaase, Stone, Vrba, and countless thousands of other American soldiers were never able to savor the good fortune I have experienced over the past five decades since that ugly, needless war ended….children, grandchildren, family life, great male and female friends, a rewarding career, travel, fine restaurants, beautiful music, and other adventures far too numerous to mention.

Other Classmates

Three other classmates also died in the Vietnam conflict, though I have no recollection of knowing any of them personally. One of these victims was First Lieutenant Billy John Coley from Ennis who was killed in the crash of his 01-E FAC airplane on December 20, 1963, at Soc Trang Airfield in South Vietnam. The FAC designation stood for Forward Air Controller, aka the flying bird dogs, whose task it was to rescue soldiers on the ground at risk for being killed or captured by the enemy. Married at the time of this death, Lieutenant Billy John Coley was buried in his hometown and, like the other fallen comrades mentioned here, his name can be found on the Vietnam Memorial in Washington, D.C. As well, his and the other five names mentioned here are among the many featured on a memorial located adjacent to the Corps of Cadets dormitories on the A&M campus.

The second member of my class from the "unknown group" was Gregg Hartness of Dallas. His plane took a serious hit over a target in Laos on November 26, 1968 and, in an act of heroism, he was able to get his co-pilot Allen Shepherd out of the plane prior to its crashing into the jungle. It is now apparent Major (later Colonel) Hartness never made it out of the plane. After years of speculation as to his fate, a search team located and identified him through the process of dental forensics. Major Hartness was thirty-one at the time of his death and he was accorded a military burial in the Arlington National Cemetery on September 14, 2005, some thirty-six years after his extraordinary act of heroism had saved the life of his co-pilot. His wife and Shepherd were among fifty family members and friends who attended the ceremony in Washington, D.C.

The third of these "unknown" classmates was Lieutenant Colonel Donald Alfred Luna of Houston. On February 1, 1969, the thirty-year-old Captain Luna was flying a mission over Savannakhet Province in Laos when his plane disappeared. A subsequent search revealed no traces of his aircraft and he was immediately declared missing in action. Thirty-one years later, in 2000, his remains were identified though it is not clear if he died in the crash or as a result of imprisonment in a Vietnamese prisoner of war camp.

These six classmates were among many other Aggies who died needlessly in that conflict which took almost 60,000 American lives along with those of three or four million North and South

Vietnamese, and nearly two million Laotians and Cambodians. The carnage was rationalized as essential to halting the Chinese Communist military intrusion throughout Asia. The reasoning, later to be proven flawed, was that if Vietnam fell, all of Southeast Asia would fall like dominos, hence the term "domino theory" invoked so often by the Pentagon to justify a clearly indefensible war.

Perhaps the following words written in 1979 by David Skocik, himself a combatant in Vietnam, would have special meaning for Comrades Hartness and Luna, creating a fitting epitaph for both of them. No doubt, the words would also resonate with Billy Coley, Floyd Kaase, Byron Stone, and Jim Vrba as well. Though many, many years have passed since the death of these valorous classmates, I offer this borrowed poem as my partial apology for ignoring them for so long:

The Last Forgotten Soul

They're coming for me now, I'm going home.
I've waited oh so many years, thank God, I'm going home.
I arrived in '68, a lot of us moved in.
Mostly young and idealistic, unknown to battle's din.
We came here out of high school to do a noble chore.
But there was no glory in combat in an ugly, teen age war.
Our country was behind us then, we had a job to do.
I remember the day I arrived, half boy, half man, still new.
My friends who went to college just could never understand.
We were inspired with a mission, to free a foreign land.
I've heard some were spit on, some upbraided and abused.
I thought we served our nation well, but some held another view.
But I forgave my country, I loved it more than life.
Even though I really felt betrayed by the protest and the strife.
I traveled over Vietnam, from Khe San to Saigon.
I fought in the A-Shaw Valley and partied at Cam Rahn.
I saw action in the Delta and did battle at Phan Rang
Just when I thought I'd seen it all I bought it at DaNang.
From the stilled hope of glory to the darkness of the grave.
I tried to do the best I could, it's a hard thing to be brave.
I expect no rousing welcome, just a single moment's pause.
A minute of reflection upon a long forgotten cause.
My soul is squared away with God, now they've finally found my bones.
Yes, I was killed in '69, Oh thank God, I'm going home.

American Life in the 1960's

Population of United States: 178 Million
The Annual Average Salary: $4,700
Average Annual Teacher's Salary: $5,200
Life Expectancy in US: For Males 66.6 Years, Females 73.1 Years
Minimum Wage: $1 Per Hour
Seventy Million Baby Boomers Become Teenagers and Young Adults
Sylvia Plath Writes *The Bell Jar* and Betty Friedan *The Feminine Mystique*
To Kill A Mockingbird, Catch-22, One Flew Over the Cuckoo's Nest are Best Sellers
Games People Play, Valley of the Dolls, In Cold Blood are Popular Titles
Clear Creek (TX) School District Allows Visibly Pregnant Woman to Teach
Burt Lancaster (Elmer Gantry) and Elizabeth Taylor (Butterfield 8) Win Oscars
It's Now or Never by Elvis Presley is the Song of the Decade
Boris Pasternak, Emily Post, and Albert Camus Die
Skateboards, Barbie Dolls, Bouffant Hairdos, Go-Go Boots, Nehru Jackets Are the Rage
Civil Rights Act of 1964 Major Legislation of the Decade
Martin Luther King and Malcolm X are Leading Civil Rights Activists
John and Robert Kennedy Assassinated
Hippies, Marijuana, LSD, Zen and Transcendental Meditation (TM) are Trendy
Beatles, Jimi Hendrix, Bob Dylan, Bobby Darin, Aretha Franklin Dominate Music Scene
Popular Dances Include The Twist, Watusi, Mashed Potato, Jerk, and Monkey

Summer of 1960

The summer of 1960 was one of if not the most carefree periods of my life. I was totally unshackled from the baggage associated with having a girlfriend (thanks in some measure to the aforementioned Joe Saunders), had minimal financial worries, and held a good-paying summer job which allowed me, among other things, to purchase a new car. Actually, the car was not new but new to me; we called them used cars in 1960 but they are now euphemistically called "pre-owned" vehicles. My "new" set of wheels was a 1954 two-tone, light and dark green Oldsmobile gas guzzler made marginally affordable by the fact that gas sold for twenty to twenty-five cents a gallon at that time. No one thought about such mundane stuff as depletion of the world's natural resources, alternative fuels, global warming, and the myriad environmental issues we face today. Having some money, my own car, and no female attachment allowed me to hang out, drink beer, play poker, stay out late on weekends, and generally party my life away for one final all-too-short, care-free summer.

Falstaff Beer, "The Chief", and Brewmaster Tom Griesedieck

Through his many labor union contacts in the area, my father landed me a summer job as a laborer at the Falstaff Brewery in Galveston. As well, he arranged for me to live in one of the fraternity houses at the University of Texas Medical School. Falstaff paid well but the work was physically demanding, tedious, and largely brain-dead, and beer consumption during working hours was prohibited for those of us with so-called dangerous jobs. On the other hand, it was the custom among the other employees to drink as they pleased during working hours, and some of their personal beer steins were eye-catching and ingenious in design. Even the stein makers in Munich, Germany, would have viewed the collection with some degree of envy, I suspect.

The Falstaff plant brew master was a guy named Tom Griesedieck, a member of the famous Griesedieck beer-brewing family of St. Louis. The family brewed Budweiser, Falstaff, and Griesedieck Beer, though the latter did not stay on the market long. As you might guess, the name Griesedieck was the subject of considerable derision and off-color humor, some of which involved a major brewing competitor, Joseph Schlitz, the maker of the highly popular Schlitz beer. As an example, there was an old and awful joke floating around dives, dumps, and saloons during the 1950's that went something like this:

1960 Music & Movie Favorites

Music

The Twist - by Chubby Checker

Save the Last Dance for Me - by The Drifters

Stay - by Maurice Williams & The Zodiacs

Stuck on You - by Elvis Presley

Teen Angel - by Mark Dinning

Alley-Oop - by The Hollywood Argyles

Are You Lonesome Tonight? - by Elvis Presley

Cathy's Clown - by The Everly Brothers

El Paso - by Marty Robbins

Georgia on My Mind - by Ray Charles

Movies

- **The Apartment**
  Academy Award Winner
- Psycho
- Spartacus
- The Magnificent Seven
- The Time Machine
- The Little Shop of Horrors

SeekPublishing — Remember When — 1960

POPULAR SONGS AND MOVIES, 1960

First drunk: "Did you hear about the couple who got in a horrible fight in a bar the other night?"
Second drunk: "No, what happened"?
First drunk: "This woman slapped her date right in the face. He was trying to put his Griesedieck into her Schlitz."

Yikes and God Save the Queen!

I never got to meet Tom Griesedieck, but my immediate boss was a guy we knew only as "Chief" Taggart. Taggart had an exceptionally curvaceous secretary who was a Jayne Mansfield (Marilyn Monroe?) clone, a real head-turner, to say the least. Our Jayne Mansfield look-alike, Galveston variety, was a diminutive, curvaceous, blue-eyed blond who was built like the proverbial brick outhouse. On occasion, as our sins of commission or omission warranted, "Chief" Taggart would call us peons into his office for an ass-chewing, and the boss always made sure he conducted these sessions in front of Jayne Mansfield, I suppose to impress her with his power. From time to time, she would chime in as he lapidated us with a nicely choreographed, "You're so right, Chief" or "I could not have said it better, Chief" or "Way to go, Chief" or "You are so marvelous, Chief." The more "Chief's" she could invoke, the more Taggart would swell up like a big, fat toad. His ego was dependent on hearing a lot of "Chief's" and Jayne Mansfield knew how to use them to her advantage.

The medical students at the fraternity house were an interesting lot, too. They had their own agendas so we had next-to-nothing to do with each other socially that summer. I did find it interesting that their modus operandi for studying each night was to leave the fraternity house with a medical textbook or two in one hand and a bottle of bourbon or scotch in the other. I once inquired about the significance of the liquor and its relationship to studying, and the students indicated the rule of thumb was that when the bottle was empty, it was time to put the books away for the night. This seemingly cavalier approach to the consumption of alcohol gives one pause, particularly when statistics about physicians with substance abuse problems are so well-documented.

The Terrace Drive-In

Mostly, I spent my time after work with my Texas City friends at a local hangout known as The Terrace Drive-In where we sat in our cars, listened to music, ate hamburgers or corny dogs, and drank root beers or real beers. The standard modus operandi for an evening at The Terrace was to flit from car to car, visiting with friends and acquaintances as they showed up there. If you wanted to see someone who was anyone, all you had to do was hang out for they would almost certainly end up at The Terrace at some point in the evening. A steady stream of vehicles continuously circled the place, with occupants gawking about to see who else was there. It was truly the meeting place for a majority of the early-twenties crowd in Texas City.

On those nights when no one had to work the next day, we would leave The Terrace around midnight and head off to LaMarque, just across the railroad tracks from Texas City, to eat at a popular all-night restaurant. Johnny Garton, Jimmy "Monk" Martin, "Dirty Earl" Yarbrough,

Richard "Crow" Koehler, Johnny DeZengotita, Joe Saunders, who knows who else, would pile in one or two cars, leaving The Terrace behind for another night. Once our midnight snack was dispatched, we would go elsewhere, often to "Crow" Koehler's home, and play poker for the rest of the night. It did not get much more laid back and irresponsible than that. We all knew a day of reckoning was out there somewhere in time and distance but it seemed an eternity away in those wonderful, halcyon, carefree days.

You would think girls would be of paramount importance for a bunch of healthy, normal college guys but few of us really had a "steady" girlfriend at that time. If we did take a girl friend or date out for the evening, it was virtually mandatory if you wanted to retain your membership in the good old boys club that you take your lady friend home before closing time to meet the guys at The Terrace or, if running late, at our all-night gathering place in LaMarque. Some of the best times I had as a young guy involved having a steady girlfriend but those periods where it was just me hanging out with the guys were priceless, too.

During the course of the summer, I decided to attend graduate school at North Texas State College (NTSC) in Denton where I planned to seek a master's degree in Educational Administration. The decision to attend North Texas was based not so much on academics as it was social reasons. To wit, I had a number of friends from Texas City attending school there, most of whom hung out with me at The Terrace every summer. Several had also been Aggies prior to becoming academic or hazing casualties, so North Texas seemed like a socially safe and acceptable academic alternative.

Graduate School, 1960-1961

As the end of that idyllic summer of 1960 loomed ominously on the horizon, my father and I visited one of the banks in Texas City where he co-signed a note for $3,000 which I planned to use (with success, by the way) to finance my master's degree. With money in hand, I loaded my meager belongings into the aforementioned gas-guzzling, two-tone green Oldsmobile and headed off for North Texas State College (NTSC) in Denton, Texas.

The university was originally founded in 1890 as the North Texas Normal School, charged with the mission of producing well-trained public school teachers. At the time of my enrollment, the institution was known as NTSC. When I started my doctoral studies there in 1964, it had become North Texas State University (NTSU), and is now known as the University of North Texas (UNT). I am going to refrain from referencing the sometimes confusing NTSC, NTSU, UNT trichotomy for the remainder of the narrative by using the latter when referring to my cherished alma mater.

As stated above, the institution was originally charged with the responsibility for turning out public school teachers, a mission that is still firmly in place though greatly broadened in scope. For example, the School of Music has achieved national prominence for many years and young musicians from all over Texas flock to UNT to be a part of that scene. Prominent music alumni who have gone on to distinguish themselves include 1950's and 1960's heart throb Pat Boone, Grammy Award-winning singer and musician Don Henley of The Eagles, country and western icon Ray Wylie Hubbard of "Up Against the Wall, Redneck Mother" fame, singer and guitarist Roy Orbison whose credits include "Pretty Woman", "Ooby Dooby", and "Crying", the aforementioned Michael Martin Murphy of "Wildfire" fame, Grammy-Winning vocalist Norah Jones, trombonist Tom "Bones" Malone of *Saturday Night Live* and *Late Show with David Letterman* fame, and the Eli Young Band made up of James Young, Chris Thompson, Mike Eli, and Jon Jones.

A short list of UNT notables in other fields include actor Joe Don Baker, actresses Joan Blondell and Ann Sheridan, *Lonesome Dove, The Last Picture Show*, and *Terms of Endearment* author Larry McMurtry, television journalist Bill Moyers, NFL Hall of Famer "Mean" Joe Greene, prominent professional golfers of the 1960's Don January and Billy Maxwell, the 1971 Miss America and one-time sports announcer Phyllis George, and well-known Texas politician and humorist Jim Hightower.

Culture Shock Redux

I thought I had landed on Uranus when I first set foot on the UNT campus; the culture shock was overwhelming, in some ways surpassing that which I felt upon my arrival at Texas A&M four years earlier. Transitioning from a sterile, stultifying, uninspiring, all-male, military environment to what struck me as a more normal one was a welcome change. Unlike A&M at the time, UNT had professors with doctoral degrees from reputable schools who were wonderful, caring, and inspiring teachers. There were also a fair number of female professors, in stark contrast to Aggieland with its four distaff faculty members! UNT had music, drama, and art majors! UNT had fraternities and sororities! UNT had an abundance of beautiful women! UNT had a wonderful jazz tradition in the One O'clock Lab Band with links to greats of that music genre such as Stan Kenton and, later, the Marsalis brothers! Ah, the wonderment of it all! The opportunity to experience such a new and vibrant academic and social climate was exhilarating after four years in backwater Brazos County and the academically challenged and militarily drab and dreary Texas A&M.

Speaking of music, 1960's vintage UNT students were beyond enamored with blues musician Jimmy Reed and it was often said that he would have been elected president of the university by a landslide had he chosen to run.

The Koehler Boys and the KA's

As noted elsewhere, I had negotiated a deferment with the Army to attend graduate school, and UNT was chosen largely out of convenience because quite a few of my friends were there, all still laboring in search of assorted undergraduate degrees. Chief among these friends were Richard "Crow" Koehler and his little brother, Jimmy. I had known Richard since childhood, but we really became good friends through weekend visits, holidays, and vacations during my undergraduate days. Richard and Jimmy were members of the local Kappa Alpha (KA) chapter and their lives revolved around the fraternity. Though they did not live in the fraternity house, the two of them spent many an hour over there with their KA brothers.

The UNT fraternities and sororities were huge, socially and psychologically if not numerically, and I thought a bit on the snobbish side. Just being around them with their rituals and idiosyncrasies was totally new to this alien Texas Aggie from an all-male, mostly military school. Their snobbish exclusivity struck me as their least redeeming feature. In any case, every Monday was dress-up day for the fraternities, and that occasion necessitated an obligatory, grand appearance in the Student Union Building, each group clad in garb specific to their organization. For example, the Lambda Chi's had a penchant for all black outfits, the Sigma Nu's sported dress suits with ties, and the Sig Eps (Sigma Alpha Epsilon) were known for their red blazers. The Sig Eps were also the only one of the nine fraternities, according to hearsay, possessing an aggregate grade point ratio above a 2.00 or C average. Their combined average was rumored to be around 2.60 so the other fraternity members decided the Sig Eps must be gay, for surely only guys with a swishy persuasion and limp wrists would take their studies seriously. This mentality says something about gay relations in the 1960's, does it not?

The sororities were pretty tame for the most part, at least when compared with their male Greek counterparts. For one thing, being conditioned by family and society to be conscientious, the females actually studied and all of the sororities save one had an aggregate grade point average above 3.00. The Zeta's (Zeta Tau Alpha) were known widely for their abundance of beauty pageant contestants. A fair number had participated in the Miss Texas Pageant, and there was actually a "Miss Texas" or two in the group. The Zetas were a sight to behold for a guy who had spent the previous four years looking at hairy legs and bald heads.

The creators of "Animal House" must have used the UNT fraternity life as a template when they made that outrageously popular movie. The institutional rules and regulations guiding fraternity behavior were flaunted or broken on a regular basis, and several chapters were on local and/or national probation. One or two of the houses burned down that year, and there were strong if unsubstantiated rumors that the PiKA's (i.e., the "Pikes") were operating a combined bootlegging and prostitution operation out of their house. I cannot vouch for the prostitution operation but the bootlegging part was a reality. Denton County was dry and the opportunistic "Pikes" bootlegging operation filled a real void by keeping a good supply of beer on hand for their thirsty patrons.

YOURS TRULY AND RICHARD KOEHLER ON GALVESTION BEACH, SUMMER, 1957

Interestingly, Coors Beer was new on the market in 1960 and had become the rage, largely because of its novelty and scarcity in the Lone Star State. People actually drove from Texas to southern Colorado just to buy a few cases of Coors, which I assume is a manifestation of the forbidden fruit thing. I can remember paying $24 a case at a time when you could get equal amounts of other more pedestrian beers like Budweiser, Miller's, or Schlitz for a fourth or fifth of the asking price for Coors. When the initial burst of enthusiasm wore off and its distribution became common in Texas, the sales of Coors dropped below Budweiser and it became just another beer among many. As well it should have…

I lived with Richard Koehler, little brother Jimmy, and a chap from Wichita Falls I remember only as "Spanky" in a two-story duplex just off campus near the School of Business and a couple of blocks south of the main students hangouts, UNT's answer to A&M's popular North Gate. "Spanky" acquired his nickname from fraternity brothers who thought he was the reincarnation of the lead character in *Spanky and our Gang*, the famous child comedy series first created in the era of silent movies and later transitioned to television in the 1950's. Those original shows were way ahead of their time because women and minorities were accorded key roles at a time when neither group had many rights in American society.

In its heyday, many parents felt they had a child who would be the perfect fit for the original cast of *Spanky and Our Gang*, and superstars Mickey Rooney, Judy Garland, and Shirley Temple all tried out unsuccessfully for parts. One famous actor who was selected was Robert Blake, nee Gubitosi. Blake was also notable for his role in the movie adaptation of Truman Capote's Pulitzer Prize-winning book, *In Cold Blood*, and for his portrayal of the lead character in a popular television series, *Baretta*. In 2005, Blake gained further notoriety when he was tried in criminal court for the murder of his wife. Though acquitted, he was found liable that same year for her wrongful death in a civil court case.

The 1960's UNT version of "Spanky" earned his nickname pretty honestly thanks to *Spanky and our Gang*, but several of his fraternity brothers had acquired theirs based on visible handicaps. One brother was known as "Speedy" because of the pronounced limp he had acquired as a result of the polio epidemic of the 1950's, and another had lost an eye in an accident, leading him to answer to "Cyclops."

I was taken aback at some of the antics of my KA friends. For one thing, their house reeked of racism dating back to the days of slavery. The yard was festooned with mementos glorifying the Confederacy and the Old South, including a Little Black Sambo, Stepin Fetchit-like statue near the steps leading up to the front entry to the house. For those of you not familiar with Stepin Fetchit, his real name was Lincoln Theodore Monroe Andrew Perry (1902-1985) and he made over fifty films spanning fifty-one years. Perry became the first black millionaire actor and was good friends with Will Rogers and, much later with Muhammad Ali, and has a star on the Hollywood Walk of Fame. However, as mores and folkways changed regarding racial issues, his Stepin Fetchit character was lampooned and spoofed and became the symbol of the shuffling, subservient black man who said "Yassuh" and "Nossuh" to the always superior white man.

Niggers and Jews and Sigma Nu's, A Hangin' from a Tree. Another noteworthy KA idiosyncrasy, one no doubt linked to its segregationist roots, was a raunchy, racist melody sung at the fraternity mixers I attended as guest of the Koehler boys. At these less-than-sober socials, the KA brothers would consume copious amounts of keg beer, and upon reaching the feel-good stage, they would gather around arm in arm in the spirit of camaraderie, singing a song that began with the refrain, "Niggers and Jews and Sigma Nu's, a-hangin' from a tree", and so the song went. I do not remember the rest of the lyrics and can find no recapitulation of the song on the Internet or anywhere else. I am assuming the KA's have abandoned that unbelievably politically incorrect and tasteless song.

On occasion, I have inquired of current Aggie KA's about the status of that ditty in their chapter lore, and the general response is one of shock and surprise that something like that could have been promoted by their past brothers. However, I cannot shake the nagging feeling the song is out there somewhere, given the racism that occasionally occurs even today in fraternity skits and programs. For example, the KA chapter at A&M received a lot of bad press nationally for an ugly racial incident a few years ago in which blacks were parodied, a la Stepin Fetchit, in a skit performed at one of their social events. As I read about the episode, I could not shake the lingering suspicion that "Niggers and Jews and Sigma Nu's, a-hanging from a tree" is still alive and "well" somewhere out there in space.

The Boys in the Boarding House

My UNT social life was focused for the most part on the boarding house next door to the duplex where "Spanky", the Koehler boys, and I lived. The house was a large two-story structure with students seemingly tucked away in every nook and cranny. Several small-town Texans became good friends for that memorable year. Chief among them were Clayton Duke from Lampasas and Dean Wallace from Crawford. Clayton was of average height, nice-looking, personable, and aspired to attend law school upon graduation. He was an amiable sort, with a big smile and a folksy, small town demeanor and I enjoyed our brief friendship. I never heard of Clayton after leaving Denton in 1961.

As for Dean Wallace, he was my closest friend and constant companion for the year. Dean was a country boy from Crawford where ex-President George W. "The Shrub" Bush now (but not then) has his ranch. Dean was quite intelligent but hid it behind a Gomer Pyle "Gee Whiz" and "Aw, Shucks" country boy persona. Dean had thick, wavy brown hair, a pleasant face, and a perpetual grin featuring the David Letterman-like gap between his two upper front teeth. We shared a lot of good times together.

Dean and I went to Dallas one fall afternoon to attend a football game between SMU and A&M and we proceeded to drink entirely too much cheap, rot-gut bourbon, vile stuff that sold for $2.50 a fifth. I do not think I have ever been so sick on alcohol in my life. I threw up most of the next day to the point that only green gastric juice remained to be purged. Being a quick learner (sometimes), I have kept my distance from all forms of bourbon, rot-gut or elegant (if there is such a thing), since that memorable occasion.

Dean had aspirations, later realized, of going to Optometry School at the University of Houston. Dean completed his studies at what Aggies love to call "Cougar High" and left Houston to set up shop in Bryan-College Station in the late 1960's. In addition to his general optometry practice, Dean was hired by the A&M athletic department to assist the coaches on matters related to the visual health of their athletes. In this connection, I once visited Dean for an eye checkup, and as we were talking he told me a story about a prominent Aggie basketball star of the period, Jimmy Gilbert. Jimmy was both talented and tall (six feet nine inches) and played center for his high school team in nearby Huntsville. The fact that Jimmy played so close to the basket enabled him for years to hide some fairly severe visual problems which Dean apparently unearthed during a routine eye examination.

The coaching staff, suspecting something was amiss with his vision, referred Jimmy to Dean for assessment and a problem was detected that had been with our erstwhile roundballer for most of his life. As Dean relayed it to me, since Jimmy was tall and dominant near the basket ("in the paint"), almost all of his shots were launched from pointblank range. The fact that all Jimmy could see was a round, circular, orange or black blur passing for a rim was of minor importance. A whole new world opened up for Jimmy once his visual deficiencies were treated, and he went on to star status at A&M

where he eventually also graduated. As a side note, Jimmy's 6' 4" daughter, Carla, graduated from A&M Consolidated High School in College Station in 2010 and played basketball for Coach Gary Blair and the Aggies. Carla was named a McDonald's All-American while in high school, which is quite an honor for any basketball player. She used up her college eligibility and in 2014 joined her father as a graduate of A&M. Mother Nelda had been a star player at UNT, so Carla had plenty of basketball genes.

Dean Wallace and I drifted apart over the years for no particular reason, really, and I had not seen him in more than a decade until recently when I spotted him across the room at a local fundraiser of some kind. It is ironic that two people can be inseparable for a year and have virtually nothing in common after that. Sort of reminds me of the relationship I shared with Larry Guseman in the summer of 1959.

Scrabble. Another guy I remember from the boarding house was Larry Edgerton who was not so much a friend as he was a friendly rival in Scrabble. Larry and I locked horns in some monumental Scrabble matches with each of us winning about half the time. The two of us had pretty much decimated the available competition in my duplex and the adjoining boarding house, so our friendly confrontations were occasions for major fandom from the other guys. We each had our own loyal cheering sections, and they got to witness our last and greatest match of the year in late April as the spring semester wound down. After several hours of matching wits with Larry, I ended up on the short end of a colossal struggle, losing 376 to 375 in our Super Bowl of Scrabble. Because the school year was coming to a close and to accord the 376-375 skirmish its proper place in our own personal posterities, Larry and I agreed to never play each other again.

TV Westerns. Despite its considerable social and intellectual significance, Scrabble came in a distant second to the real action in the boarding house, early evening television. Clayton, Dean, a guy named "Country" from Whitesboro, and yours truly would congregate along with an ever-changing assortment of other guys every evening at 1800 hours, bodies draped at all angles across chairs, sofas, and the carpet to watch the rage of that era in televisions, wall-to-wall westerns. We would spend two or three hours each weekday evening watching *Bronco, Cheyenne, Gunsmoke, Have Gun, Will Travel, Laramie, Lawman, Rawhide*, and *Wagon Train. Bronco* was of some passing personal interest because its star, Ty Hardin (nee Orison Hungerford) attended A&M for a short time where he was also a member of the football team. None of my UNT friends were impressed, but after Ty Hardin/Orison Hungerford left A&M he went on to bigger and better things on television which gave me some minor bragging rights as a fellow Aggie. Ah, what lengths will we go to bask in reflected glory!?

Another impressive star of those halcyon days of the television western was the gargantuan Clint Walker who played Cheyenne Bodie in the *Cheyenne* series. Clint Walker was tall, dark, chiseled, with pitch black hair and a voice so deep it sounded as if he was talking from the bottom of a deep well. In real life, Clint Walker was six feet six inches tall and weighed 240 pounds which made him a giant of a man in that era. Being youthful, hormonal, macho males, we were beyond enamored with his massive size, bulging, sinewy muscles, and deep voice. To a man, we all would have loved to have been Clint Walker.

For sheer impressiveness, it was hard to get past *Gunsmoke*, and its sterling array of stars, James Arness, Milburn Stone, Amanda Blake, Dennis Weaver, and Burt Reynolds. Ditto *Have Gun, Will Travel* in which Richard Boone played a professional gunfighter by the name of Paladin. Two other series, *Rawhide* and *Wagon Train*, had their share of well-known actors including, respectively, a guy who later achieved some degree of stature in the world of film by the name of Clint Eastwood and his side-kick Ward Bond. Our final two shows, *Lawman* and *Laramie*, were not as sensational as the others and the stars of those two shows were not as well-known, including actors such as Peter Brown, John Russell, John Smith, Robert Fuller, and Bobby Crawford. Gee, did we ever love those old westerns! They were a staple in our lives for that year, and the communal gathering in front of the boarding house television set gave us the opportunity to do some serious male bonding.

The westerns ran their course by 2000 or 2100 hours each evening and Dean and I would mosey a couple of hundred yards north of the boarding house to the student hangouts to see if we could drum up some female company or do some additional male bonding over a cup of coffee or a fountain Coke. Coffee and soft drinks where the order of the day in Denton County for, as noted earlier, it was dry, alcohol-wise, much like the rest of north Texas. To slake the beer thirst, students would drop by the aforementioned PiKA house or make the hour run to Dallas to the south or the Oklahoma state line to the north to stock up for the week or month, depending on one's consumption capabilities and cash availability.

When it came to women, my master's degree days at UNT were largely non-descript/boring with a couple of small, fleeting exceptions. Sometime early in the fall semester, I became quite infatuated with a blond, blue-eyed, pixie-ish coed from Pampa, Texas, by the name of Linda Gail Fain. Unfortunately, her fascination with the glamour of fraternity life was greater than her valence for me, and nothing but temporary, fleeting frustration came out of the relationship. In the spring, I had a brief fling with a girl named Patsy from the metropolis of Gorman, west of Fort Worth, but nothing much came of that one either. All in all, the vast majority of the year was spent male bonding, watching TV westerns, playing Scrabble, and just hanging out. Little did I know what fate held in store for me, woman-wise, before I got out of Denton, and that topic will be addressed shortly.

My Introduction to Graduate School

To be brutally honest, I had no idea what I had gotten myself into when I went to UNT for graduate work. I was certain I no longer wanted to be a coach but staying in the broad field of education seemed like a viable option. Thus, I chose to major in Educational Administration which ostensibly would prepare me to be a principal or superintendent in the public schools. In all honesty, I was pretty clueless about my long-range career goals and did not have the foggiest notion of where it all would lead. What I did know was I liked university life, I enjoyed learning, and wanted to get some additional education while I was in the groove.

If my memory serves me right, the Graduate Record Exam (GRE) was not required for admission and the grade requirements must have been minimal or else my undergraduate grade point ratio of 2.83 on a 4.00 scale would not have been sufficient. As near as I can remember, the only prerequisites for graduate school at that time were having an undergraduate degree, enough money in your pocket to pay for tuition, and vital signs.

My first professor in graduate school was a distinguished gentleman by the name of Dr. Robert Toulouse whose primary duty was serving as Dean of the Graduate School when he was not teaching his one class. I felt both lucky and intimidated by being in the presence of such as esteemed scholar and administrator, but I took an immediately liking to Dr. Toulouse. He was middle-aged, not handsome or homely, just a regular-looking guy with the outgoing personality stereotypically associated with someone of French heritage. He took an immediate liking to me that seemed, in retrospect, to be part professorial and part paternal. Academics are often drawn to students who seem to have high potential for achievement, and I guess Dr. Toulouse saw in me latent traces of electrical activity that hinted of excellence. He was to remain throughout both my UNT degrees a seldom seen but eternally supportive figure. The man was always effusive in his response to me when we happened to meet on campus, and I always enjoyed his good-natured banter and quirky sense of humor.

As it turns out, Dr. Toulouse served as Dean of the Graduate School from 1954 through 1982, at which time he became Provost, the second highest ranking administrator at the UNT, and he ultimately retired from that position. Several months ago, I read that my esteemed mentor died on April 11, 2017, at the age of ninety-eight. He was preceded in death by his wife, Virginia, in 2015. Prior to their deaths, they established an undergraduate scholarship program in Religious Studies, the Toulouse Scholars Program Fund to assist faculty with their research, and a charitable trust to support graduate student education. Dr. Toulouse loved his university, served loyally on its behalf for many years, and his support continues in perpetuity. I must confess to choking up a bit when I read in *The North Texan*, the UNT alumni magazine, he had died. He was one of the finest men I have ever met and his influence on me was considerable. Over the years, I made occasional half-hearted attempts to see if he was still alive so I could thank him personally for his kindness, generosity, collegiality, mentorship, and inspiration, but was unfortunately not successful. The loss is mine!

We students took a battery of tests in his course, including one measuring intelligence (California Test of Mental Maturity; CTMM) and the other personality (Minnesota Multiphasic Personality Inventory; MMPI). With regard to the CTMM, I must have been in the zone that day as my IQ came out to be 148 and I think this score, however accurate/inaccurate, may be where Dr. Toulouse first saw the potential alluded to earlier. As for the MMPI, it is an oft-used and highly researched instrument with a long history in the assessment of psychopathology, or abnormal behavior. Given its intent to assess psychopathology, I could never figure out why it was administered to a class of what struck me as relatively normal graduate students. I still have the visual representation of my MMPI responses from that fall day in 1960 in my files. It is reassuring to realize my responses did not suggest I needed emergency institutionalization those many years ago!

I do not think you can go to graduate school without being apprehensive and intimidated, and my first semester professors did absolutely nothing to allay my initial misgivings. After leaving that first class with Dr. Toulouse, I met my other four professors and was left wondering what I had done to myself. The course requirements Dr. Toulouse outlined seemed absurdly ponderous and difficult and I was not sure they were manageable in one semester. I went from his class to the next one and came out wondering how I could possibly complete those requirements, never mind the ones spelled out by Dr. Toulouse. Then I went to class number three and left there even more intimidated than I had been by the first two. I left classes number four and five with much the same feeling and was convinced no human being regardless of intellect and motivation could possibly get through those five courses in a lifetime, let alone a single semester.

I quickly learned to manage my time effectively (other than when watching TV westerns and goofing off with my friends), combining a tad of intellect and a modicum of dedication with a dose or two of hard work. As noted earlier, my undergraduate courses tested me a bit at first but soon became manageable and I experienced the same thing with graduate school. It took a semester to figure out I could do it and from then on it became essentially an endurance contest. I think I made three A's and two B's the first semester, followed by three A's, one B, and one C in the spring, and two A's in the one summer session I needed to complete my 36-hour master's degree. I was a decent student and I loved every moment of graduate school. I could have gone to school forever but the pay seems well below minimum wage.

Another professor I seemed to have impressed and, in turn, was most taken with was Dr. Jack Watson in the Department of Physical Education. He was a graduate of Columbia University, and his academic credentials were most impressive to someone of my limited experience with such matters. I say limited because I am certain there were no Columbia PhD's in Dewey, Oklahoma, where I grew up nor at Texas A&M where such pedigrees were scarce sixty-plus years ago. Even more impressive than Dr. Watson's academic credentials, though, was his affable, low-key, soft-spoken demeanor, and I took an immediate liking to him. I do not remember whether we were required to have a minor area of concentration in my major or if I just chose one, but I took four Physical Education courses as part of my master's degree, and two were with Dr. Watson. He, like Dr. Toulouse, seemed to be in my corner, always going out of his way to be personable and make me feel welcomed whenever we crossed paths. It is professors such as Dr. Toulouse and Dr. Watson who, by their implicit and explicit support, spur students to excel. Both men were truly inspirational and I thank them profusely.

It is with great sadness that I recently learned of the death of Dr. Watson in July of 2017. He lived a long life, made a difference in the lives of young people, and will be greatly missed.

Yet another professor of note is unfortunately nameless due to my ever-increasing memory deficits. This man taught me the virtue of attending class regardless of what the course content was or how well it was presented. He was a reasonably interesting lecturer but the course content was on the dry side, to put it kindly, making it difficult to get excited about being there each class period. During one particular lecture, Professor Anonymous got off on one of his pet topics, what he called the "law of minor concessions." Essentially he was saying there are many issues worthy of concession and damned few really worth fighting about. To put it another way, some battles are worth fighting, most are not. Where the concession is minor, he would say, just concede the point and move on smartly. The famous twentieth-century author and educator, Jonathan Kozol said the same thing in slightly different words: "Pick battles big enough to matter, small enough to win." This admonition from my old professor (and Jonathan Kozol) has served me well throughout my adult life; I spend little time jousting (tilting?) with what I perceive to be immovable windmills.

Another professorial recollection is not a particularly happy one, thanks mostly to me. I had a class in counseling techniques from a nice man, perhaps too much so, who also happened to be our landlord. Somewhere along the line, I had gotten pretty full of myself, perhaps due in part to having been so warmly embraced by Drs. Toulouse and Watson. I had become a bit arrogant, to say the least, and my professor/landlord became the target of my newly-acquired chutzpah. In his class, he required each student to make a presentation on a counseling theory or method. From time to time, the class presentations were weak or, alternately, played loose with the facts. There was little in-class feedback from the professor, and when things were presented poorly or erroneously by my peers, they were pretty much allowed to pass without comment. This lapse in professional judgment bothered me a great deal, so at about the mid-point in the semester, I decided to go to the professor to strike a compromise. I proposed accepting a "C" in the course if the professor would exempt me from some course requirements I did not want to complete. I also agreed to continue attending the class and taking examinations. I cannot imagine allowing a student to treat me so condescendingly, but, for whatever reason, he let me get away with it. He kept his end of the bargain, awarding me one of only two C's I made while pursuing my two final degrees. A more appropriate response might have been to flunk me on the spot and kick my arrogant, perhaps insufferable ass out of the class (and the duplex the Koehler brothers, Spanky, and I inhabited).

The spring semester went by swimmingly and summer school came and went. I was soon to receive a master's degree in a field I had no intention of entering; I was dead certain a career in school administration was not my calling. Fortunately, in the process of completing the degree requirements in Educational Administration, my interest in Psychology was ignited, and I decided to make it my third and, hopefully, final area of academic concentration when I got out of the Army several years hence. That decision pretty much required me to literally start over, but such a course of action seemed to be the only way to go.

Barbara Laverne Blythe (March 11, 1942-May 28, 2017)

Shortly before completing those final two courses that summer of 1961, I was lounging around the Student Union Building with a compadre named Chet Atkins (not the famous guitar player of that era). Chet was short in stature, maybe five feet five or six, but long on athletic and dancing talent. He had been a state-caliber athlete in several sports in high school and was the reigning university champion in table tennis. In his spare time, he doubled as a professional dance instructor. I saw Chet dance a time or two, engaging in his best Fred Astaire imitation, seemingly unfazed by the fact that he was often shorter than his female partners.

Chet and I were sitting around talking, batting the breeze, chewing the fat, or solving the world's problems over coffee one afternoon when two attractive coeds walked into the student union lounge. I nudged Chet in the ribs, urging him to take a peek at the sudden infusion of palpable pulchritude. Though both young ladies were attractive, I was particularly taken by one of the two, a shapely brunette. Chet informed me (1) one of them was his girlfriend and (2) the one I liked best was not only his girlfriend's best friend but was also my blind date the following Monday. Things went well enough that fateful Monday, I suppose, for Barbara Laverne Blythe and I were married less than a year later.

Barbara was known by friends as "Bobbie." When I met her, she was dating a talented young musician by the name of Bob Blanton from her hometown of Sherman, Texas. That relationship soon faded in part due to my intrusion, and Barbara and I became inseparable for the remainder of the summer and beyond. I finished my coursework at UNT, said my goodbyes (for the time being) and returned to Texas City to work at the Monsanto Chemical Company refinery until time came for my January 1962 entry into the Army. I had no clear idea where Barbara and I were headed in our relationship but I knew it was the real deal, so to speak.

Hurricane Carla

I did not have the foggiest notion my life was going to get turned upside down in unimaginable ways and to an unfathomable degree when I left Denton in late August. Texas City had taken a major hit in 1947 with the explosions at the Monsanto Chemical Company plant chronicled elsewhere in which six hundred people were killed. Nearly fifteen years later, the city was to experience yet another catastrophic event, beginning innocently and benignly enough right after I arrived from Denton on September 3, 1961, with the formation of a tropical depression in the western Caribbean Sea. The growing menace moved slowly on a northwesterly course, became a tropical storm on the fifth of September, and evolved into a hurricane the following day. The National Weather Service dubbed her Carla.

Initially, Carla was a relatively weak storm, but after skimming over the Yucatan Peninsula, entered the Gulf of Mexico where she quickly gathered strength. By September 11, Carla possessed sustained winds of 175 miles per hour, making her the eighth strongest storm of its kind to ever strike the United States, a genuine Category Five hurricane. Later that same day, the storm weakened a bit and made landfall at Port O'Connor, Texas, as a Category Four storm. Carla hit the Texas coastline with winds of 173 miles per hour, dumping upwards of twenty inches of torrential rain on Galveston and Texas City over the next four days. Storm surges of over twelve feet were recorded.

Thanks to an efficient early warning system and an orderly evacuation, there were "only" forty-three deaths attributed to the storm, thirty-one in Texas and a dozen from tornados spawned in Kansas and Missouri where the monster eventually petered out. Property damage was estimated at around $325 million. That same dollar figure would translate out to over 2.5 billion dollars by today's standards.

Prior to its arrival in Texas City, it was clear to the locals Carla was going to be an unbelievably bad storm. Most of us had ridden out several lesser storms in other hurricane seasons but there was something very special and eerily ominous about Carla. I was first alerted to the gravity of the situation by the steadily rising water in our front yard. There had never been flooding anywhere near our house with any of the other hurricanes I had experienced but the water was rising visibly throughout the neighborhood. The thing that made this water surge particularly scary was the fact that Carla was still twenty-four hours out in the Gulf of Mexico. You did not need to be a meteorological wunderkind or hurricane expert to figure out Carla was a very serious storm, one sufficiently threatening to warrant mass evacuation.

Because we had always ridden out these storms at home in the past, I wished to do so again. However, my father requested I chauffeur the family out of harm's way, and his wise decision probably saved me from multiple snakebites or possibly even death by drowning or sheer terror. As things turned out, when we returned home after the storm, my room was the least damaged. Water only rose in my closet to the level of the hems of my sport coats and shirts, so I probably would have survived the ordeal had I stayed. However, the storm surge filled the rest of our house with flotsam and jetsam liberally laced with an assortment of snakes, eels, fish, and other forms of aquatic life. Co-existing harmoniously with the numerous snakes could have been a dicey proposition at the peak of the hurricane.

My father had some important labor union business to transact in Galveston before the storm hit land, hence his request to have me drive stepmother June and my two young half-siblings, Nancy June and George Wayne, to a safe haven. However, when the storm surge started splashing over the seawall onto the second floor windows of the Galvez Hotel, he decided he had seen enough of Galveston for a while. He then left the island with hopes of eventually hooking up with the family somewhere along the line.

The media had issued an alert indicating housing might be available at A&M, three hours away, so we headed to College Station where we found the dormitories already full of people fleeing the storm. We then pushed on to Hearne, Marlin, Mart, and Waco in search of motel accommodations, again without any luck. Finally, I placed a phone call to my sister, Jo, in Dallas, asking her to let us ride out the hurricane at her place for a few days. She agreed to provide us safe harbor, our father tracked us down, and the temporarily itinerant family was reunited.

Several days later, the authorities determined it was safe to return to Texas City, so my father and I left Dallas to survey the damage. What we found was a house that looked reasonably intact from the front view but, upon entry, was missing the entire back wall. The storm surge had knocked out the rear portion of the house and swept away most of our belongings, including a washer and dryer purchased just the week before. Flotsam and jetsam reigned throughout, and imbedded in the waist-deep debris were the aforementioned snakes and assorted aquatic life. We hauled out all the effluvia, hosed down the house, got in the car, and drove away for good. The house was within twelve months or so of being paid off, and my dad just walked away and left the remains to the bank. Insurance policies did not cover such a calamity in those days and no federal handouts were available, so any losses incurred pretty much accrued to the individual home owner.

Unfortunately, the bottom inch or two of all my shirts and coats were ruined by the bleaching effects of the rising salt water. Also lost in the debacle were several scrapbooks from my youth baseball and high school football days which were essentially irreplaceable. Another casualty was the treasured pocket watch given to me by my troops during Parents Weekend at Aggieland in April of 1960. The clothing, scrapbooks, and pocket watch were simply no match for the invasive and destructive salt water.

My father also had a vacation house on Jamaica Beach in Galveston. It was constructed on stilts as were many similar area dwellings and thus avoided the water damage. However, the combination of high winds and rising water had turned the house about ninety degrees, causing the front door to face a totally new direction. As was the case with our home in Texas City, the beach house was a total loss.

The hurricane signaled the end of our days in Texas City. Just a few days before Carla exacted her toll, I had gone to work at the Monsanto Chemical Company plant as a laborer, and as laborers go, I was a pretty well-educated one by then, what with the master's degree in hand. I chose to work at Monsanto for the four months prior to reporting for Army active duty because the best paying jobs around were in the highly-unionized Gulf Coast petrochemical industry. I had been promised a nice hourly wage with plenty of opportunity for overtime and even double overtime, and the prospect of being to work long hours pretty much guaranteed me a sizable nest egg by the end of my stint with Monsanto and the start of the tour of duty with the U.S. Army.

Unfortunately, Carla threw a serious kink in my plans. When the hurricane surge hit the refinery, it displaced most if not all of the oil and chemical storage tanks, causing them to release their petroleum-based contents into the rising water. Since oil and many related derivatives float on water, they rose with the storm surge, finally reaching a height throughout the refinery that may have been five or six feet. When the bay water subsided, a thick coat of petroleum-based goo was deposited on virtually every structure in the facility. My job then switched from general laborer to assisting in the removal of those assorted petroleum by-products.

By the end of work each day, my clothes and body were completely saturated with oily residue. I could get the stuff off of me, though not without considerable effort, but there was no way to remove it from my clothes. To complicate matters, since our homes in Texas City and Galveston had been rendered unlivable, I was forced to take up temporary residence in nearby LaMarque with my father's old friend, Frank Simmen. It did not take long to figure out I was trashing out Frank's home, much to the chagrin of his wife, though she never really said anything to me. Also, my meager supply of work clothes was dwindling at the rate of one outfit per day.

These events led me to trade the gritty, grimy, gross high-paying job in Texas City for a clean one with low pay, hawking toys for a J. C. Penney store in the Big Town shopping center in Big D (Dallas). The money I made there, essentially minimum wage, was a mere pittance compared to what I would have earned at Monsanto had it not been for Carla. For all practical purposes, my weekly salary at Penney's was equivalent to what I would have made each day had I been able to hang on in Texas City. Thanks to the kindness of my sister, Jo, and her husband, Andy, I was able to live with them for my three-month tour of duty with Penney's.

Uncle Sam Comes A' Calling

Fort Benjamin Harrison: The Winter of My Discontent

January 2, 1962, signaled the start of another fascinating chapter in my life, active duty with the U.S. Army. Shortly after Christmas, I reported for duty at Fort Sill in Lawton, Oklahoma, only to be informed I had misread not only when I was to report but also where. It turns out I was to make my military debut at Fort Benjamin Harrison in Indianapolis, Indiana, a few days hence. Thus, I got a welcome three-day reprieve which I spent in virtual seclusion with the woman I suspected deep down was my wife-to-be, Barbara.

Finally, the day of reckoning arrived. I had no car and not enough spare cash to take a plane, so I was pretty much forced to travel by Greyhound bus from Dallas to Indianapolis and my new home-away-from-home, Fort Harrison. This decision turned out to be not all that good, for the day I left Dallas was one of the coldest on record, something like two degrees below zero. As luck would have it, the heating system on the Greyhound had gone kaput and the inside temperature rivaled that on the outside which "warmed up" to a balmy zero by the time the Greyhound made it to Indianapolis twenty-four hours later.

To compound the misery, authorities at Fort Harrison were not expecting any new arrivals until the following day so they had not turned on the heat in our accommodations, the Bachelor Officer's Quarters (BOQ). Several other officers arrived at the same time I did, and we all shared a similar fate, temperature-wise. However, we made it through the night by burying ourselves underneath whatever sheets, blankets, and spare clothes we could reconnoiter.

Things quickly settled into a routine at Fort Harrison, with the days full of military training and the nights filled mostly with camaraderie fueled by drinking beer, playing poker, and shooting pool. One of my close compadres was an older officer, a Captain Butters, who was maybe thirty-ish and quite a good pool and table tennis player. Butters had become an officer through the Officer's Candidate School (OCS) option whereas the rest of us were Reserve Officers Training Corps (ROTC) products, wet-behind-the-ear, college-boy trainees. Butters quickly assumed the role of *de facto* father figure, social chairman, and primo beer drinker, so I spent a lot of time in his company for those ten weeks in the frozen tundra.

My closest friend at Fort Harrison, however, was Lieutenant John Poff of Whitesboro, Texas. Johnny Poff was a graduate of Hendrix, a small college in Arkansas, and a decent distance runner.

He and I shared what I now see as a childish Johnny Reb mentality about the Civil War and we loved hazing the Yankees in the Fort Harrison group when we could. John and I were both in excellent shape and could run a six-minute mile in combat boots with relative ease. Each morning when it came time to run, John and I would sprint to the head of the pack with the goal of setting a pace designed to leave our Yankee friends from New York and New Jersey, several of whom were overweight and out of shape, both nauseated and exhausted. We took great pleasure in torturing the out of shape, lard-asses in our midst, particularly those of Yankee persuasion. The weaker among them would often throw up during or after the run, thus affording John and I a rather perverse version of the runner's high.

The military has long been known for its indelicate use of the King's English and the officers in charge of our training were no exception. They were always yelling threats at Poff and me to the effect: "OK, you two. Knock that shit off. You're making these assholes in the back lose their fucking breakfast and it is not a pretty sight. You know who I mean…Poff, you and LeUnes. Slow it down, goddamit!" Johnny Poff and I would flash a sly, perverse grin at each other, reduce our pace for maybe a hundred yards, and then accelerate back to the original killer pace, if a six-minute mile can be called a killer; perhaps one man's leisurely run is indeed another man's killer pace. As close as Lieutenant Poff and I we were for those ten weeks, I never saw or heard of him again (or Captain Butters) after Officer's Basic Training at Fort Harrison.

Then there was the Lieutenant (whose name I am choosing to omit to protect the potentially innocent), a rugged, strapping, muscular, athletic-looking guy with a lot of charisma, bluster, and bravado who was inordinately fascinated with his sister-in-law who lived in Terre Haute, up the road a bit from Indianapolis. Any time there was a break in the training, he would boogie up to Terre Haute to tryst with the wife's apparently willing and able sister. Having a relationship with one's sister-in-law was relatively unheard of in the limited world view of most of my associates, though one of my A&M classmates my freshman year had allegedly maintained an on-going sexual relationship with a young woman while concurrently diddling her mother. In this latter instance, our perp was able to escape a potentially sticky wicket by absconding to the U.S. Military Academy at the end of the spring semester. Sexual shenanigans involving girlfriends and their mothers were novelties for most of us for sure, but the situation was largely seen as a sterling example of extremely good fortune. Sort of like having your cake and eating it, too.

One of my A&M friends, Hazel O'Neal Munn, aka O'Neal Munn, Class of 1961, departed Fort Harrison shortly before my arrival, and tipped me off to a delicacy he urged me to try at the first opportunity. It seems there was an all-night restaurant near the base featuring spaghetti and chili which was about as close to southern or Texas cooking as it got in Indianapolis. I tried O'Neal's recommendation on two occasions, found his assessment to be right on target, and thanked him for the tip when we met up later at Fort Hood. O'Neal also gave me a heads-up about an added extra at that same restaurant, a young and attractive waitress with what he described as a "healthy appetite for sexual activity" and a fascination with men in uniform. For a variety of reasons neither here nor there, and for better or worse, I confined my sampling of the goods in Indianapolis to the spaghetti and chili.

The weather in Indianapolis was positively frigid by the standards by which Texans measure cold. My feelings can be summed up most succinctly as follows: If the sun was out in the morning, the high temperature would be ten or fifteen degrees below zero. If the cloud cover at daybreak was heavy, the temperature would be a tepid ten or fifteen above zero. I know the numbers are exaggerated, but they fairly portray what we experienced, weather-wise. Also, there were far more cloudy days than fair ones and, exaggerating again only slightly, I think I saw more sunlight coming through Missouri in March on my way to my next destination, Fort Hood, than I did the entire stay in Indianapolis. I am playing loose with the facts again, but not by much. Succinctly put, Indianapolis was cold and bleak, end of story!

In all fairness to the great state of Indiana, the city of Indianapolis, and Fort Benjamin Harrison, I was deployed there a second time eighteen months later for the entire month of September, and the weather was absolutely delightful. In stark contrast to Fort Hood, the grass was green, the temperatures moderate, and it actually rained from time to time. I played golf almost every day, a task made even more enjoyable by the lovely fall weather.

But I digress. The biggest thing to occur while I was in the frozen tundra, Indianapolis-style, was the news from Barbara in late February; she was pregnant! This is what my friends in Germany would call a "Heilige Scheisse" or "Holy Shit" moment! This news was overwhelming though not totally unexpected given the frequency and unprotected nature of our sexual relations over the preceding months. The pregnancy soon became the subject of numerous back and forth phone calls. I cannot say that I was thrilled but I was not dismayed either. I loved Barbara and the prospect of getting married sounded reasonable enough. I had never really visualized getting married at anything more than the most superficial level, but that is precisely what we did when I got back to Texas!

Good Old Fort Hood, Texas

I had experienced a healthy dose of Fort Hood in the summer of 1959 at the aforementioned ROTC summer camp, so I knew pretty much what I was getting into with regard to my new assignment. The first item of business upon my return from Fort Harrison, however, was to get married. Of course, we did not want to break the news to the parents, especially hers. As I look back, coming clean and being totally honest probably would not have devastated them as much as we thought. They were good, forgiving people and would have adjusted to the news. I suspect they probably knew something was up, anyway, though it was never mentioned.

When I first got back to Fort Hood, Barbara and I wandered around central Texas off and on for a few days trying to figure out what we should do about getting married. Finally, we bought a marriage license and found a bored, detached Justice of the Peace in Cleburne, of all places, who performed the marriage service in a manner far beyond perfunctory. It was a bland, emotionless ceremony, and the names "Blythe" and "LeUnes" gave the poor man fits. His inability to pronounce our names lent an almost surreal touch to an already strange set of circumstances. Do you Barbara Blythel take this man, Arnold Loons…?

FIRST ARMORED DIVISION ("OLD IRONSIDES") INSIGNIA

Being legally married took a burdensome load off our collective shoulders. Of course, to protect the secret and the unborn child who was due in late September or early October, we trumped up a hokey story indicating we had secretly been married since shortly before I went to Fort Harrison the preceding January. Our carefully selected time frame provided legitimacy to the baby, and got us off the hook as bad people, or so we thought. Looking back, I suspect few if any bought into our far-fetched, feeble fabrication.

Next on the agenda after getting the marriage monkey off our back was finding a place to live, which was a daunting task at that time. The conflict in Vietnam was heating up, Killeen, the city where Fort Hood is located, was swamped with a huge influx of soldiers, and housing was in short supply. We were told during our search that some soldiers and their families were living in railroad boxcars with latrines made from holes cut in the floor. We were a bit luckier, finding a modest, decent two bedroom frame rural home in nearby Copperas Cove. The house was livable enough, but I never quite got accustomed to having my hand covered with cockroaches every time I reached into a cabinet to retrieve something, but again, beggars can't be choosers. We could have ended up living in a box car or a tent!

Copperas Cove was small back then, maybe 5,000 people, and was a fifteen-minute commute through the countryside from the base. My job title at Fort Hood was Special Services Officer and my duties were to provide sports and recreation activities for the men of "Old Ironsides", the First Armored Division. I actually had two offices on the post, one in the Headquarters of the 501st Administration Company to which I had been assigned, and another in the gymnasium where a number of our sports activities were held. I spent a great deal of time going back and forth between the two offices, but I felt most at home when in the gymnasium, such as it was.

As a young second lieutenant, I was taking home the princely sum of $235 per month, a third of which went to pay off the $3,000 bank debt I had encumbered to pay for graduate school. Another third went for rent, leaving us with less than a hundred dollars each month to buy food, gasoline, and necessities for the new arrival. We allocated a fair portion of what money was left over to gasoline for the rusty, trusty Chevrolet Corvair we had purchased from Barbara's dad who owned a used car dealership. It was not a fancy vehicle but the mileage was good, and it provided reasonably reliable transportation from Killeen to Sherman virtually every weekend. I do not know if Barbara's parents knew how destitute we really were, but their generosity was pretty much the only reason we got to eat during that financially strapped first year.

I still owned that same Corvair when I started my professorial career at A&M in 1966. The rusting pile of junk had become old, decrepit, and I think it gave up hope while tenaciously holding on to the belief that it was eventually going to spend eternity in some Chevrolet Corvair Cemetery in a galactic constellation somewhere. The pile of junk posting as a car sat on the street in front of our house for at least a year after its long overdue demise, but one day good fortune struck. It seems that a quartet identifying themselves as garbage collectors knocked on our front door and inquired about the possibility of taking the beloved Corvair off my hands, but only if the price was right. They said they had noticed the car had not moved in a long time and figured maybe I no longer was using it. They were correct; I had no use for it but did not know how to get rid of the old heap.

Though it had some sentimental value, the opportunity to get the Corvair off the street and thus out of our lives was impossible to pass up. Allowing that it was not in good running order and would have to be towed or pushed away, I asked for the princely sum of $25. They thought my offer was more than generous, handed me the money, and went back to the street to further inspect and admire their new purchase. A few minutes later, I heard another knock on the door, and the guys asked if I would be willing, as part of the deal, to throw in the bottle of wine they found in the trunk. The wine was not remotely of the expensive variety, had been there for at least a summer and a winter and surely had turned to vinegar by then, but the guys seemed genuinely ecstatic with my act of largesse. The last time I saw my old beloved Corvair, four guys were pushing it (and the bottle of wine) down Rosemary Lane in College Station to some unknown destination. A big part of my life has just disappeared, and it felt like I had just lost a battered but beloved old comrade.

The summer of 1962 was one of the hottest on record in the history of Texas, and to compound the misery, we had no air conditioning in our home in Copperas Cove. There were countless days in which the temperature was still in the low hundreds at sundown. It is a miracle Barbara and the unborn child, to be known as Leslie Katherine (the middle name given in honor of my mother), survived.

As an index of just how hot it was, the three worst years in recent history for heat-related deaths in Texas were 1955, 1962, and 1980 (I am sure 2011 has since been added to the list!). To compound the heat problem, the dearly beloved Corvair mentioned earlier in such reverential terms was black with a black interior, and getting in it after work (or any other time late in the day) was like sitting in front of a blast furnace in the midst of a tropical rain forest. Some of the exterior paint buckled and much of the interior, particularly along the exposed dash board, split under the blistering heat rays. Surely human beings were not meant to live in Texas! Or North Dakota, but for very different reasons!

On September 28, 1962, Leslie Katherine LeUnes was born. She weighed nearly nine pounds and was almost twenty-three inches long. The day we brought her home from the hospital, Baskerville, our Dachshund, disappeared. We never figured out if he was kidnapped or just took off because he was jealous or felt displaced. The late summer temperatures continued to be outrageous but we did the best we could with lots of heat, a new baby, little food, and swarms of friendly kitchen cupboard cockroaches.

DUTIES OF SPECIAL SERVICES OFFICER

I did not adjust well to the duties of being a new father, and had considerable trouble accepting the new family member. I do not know what one does *a priori* to become a good father; mostly it seems to be on the job training. I was a slow learner but eventually figured out most of what it took to do the job right. Patience is the first requisite trait, I think, and it took some time, maybe eighteen months or so, for me to figure that out. I was not much of a father at first, bordering on the abusive at times due to temper outbursts. However, time and the birth of our second child, Natalie Jean, on Christmas Day of 1963 helped me to further adjust to being a father. I think I became quite good at it, actually, as I went along. I came to be patient and learned to cherish each of the developmental stages the two little girls went through, and to experience those moments with them as much as possible.

Captain William "Bulldog" Turner, Sergeant Dean R. Gardner, the "Unknown Soldier", PFC Larry "I Don't Know if Natalie Would but I Would" Birr, and Specialist Five Art Parrack. In my job as Special Services Officer, I was responsible for was administering the sports and recreation program for the 15,000 troops in the First Armored Division. With help from my mostly capable enlisted men, I operated a gymnasium and conducted league and tournament play in approximately two dozen sports. I also played, coached, and officiated a bit in my spare time, and once finished eighth in the post badminton tournament. I held the title of Special Services Officer for six months or so, at which time a man of higher rank was transferred to the post, and he took the title and I became his assistant.

My new superior officer was Captain William Turner of Virginia. He was known as "Bulldog" Turner by the troops, though he bore absolutely no resemblance to a bulldog or the old professional football legend bearing the same nickname. Actually, in Captain Turner's case, the sobriquet was coined tongue in cheek by specialist Five Art Parrack, for our man was much more wimp than warhorse, the complete antithesis of a bulldog. He was of average size, had an oversized bulbous nose, wore thick glasses, and did not appear to have an athletic bone is his body. I doubt he ever played sports and the overall effect was more geek than gladiator.

I remember an incident that entrenched Captain Turner's nickname in the minds of the troops. In the course of everyday discussion, he had told us of his morbid fear of hypodermic needles. Such a phobia can be a huge problem in the military because you are always lining up for the latest inoculation against the flu, cholera, malaria, tetanus, and only God knows what else. One morning shortly after the workday began, it was announced that the next round of shots was scheduled for late that same afternoon. In a moment of unadulterated perversity with the aim of torturing Captain Turner firmly in mind, the enlisted men in the unit located a huge, formidable fake syringe perhaps a foot long with an intimidating four-inch needle. They then strategically placed the imposing paraphernalia on a table near the area where we were to line up for our shots. When "Bulldog" Turner walked in, PFC Larry Birr pointed to the needle and said: "Jesus, Captain, Sir. Have you ever seen a needle this big? I don't know what disease they are trying to prevent but it must be a real motherfucker! Sir!" Captain Turner, always the bulldog, turned as white as a sheet, his legs wobbled and gave way, and we were barely able to get him to a nearby chair before he temporarily passed out. I do not know if he ever figured out the syringe was a fake, but his status as "bulldog" and "warrior" took a serious hit that day.

"Bulldog" Turner's immediate superior officer was a Major by the name of Marsh who we all called "Swampy." Major Marsh was an amiable, middle-aged career soldier with a substantial beer gut and a red nose, clearly twin by-products of his career-long affinity for happy hour at the Officer's Club. My daily interactions with both Captain Turner and Major Marsh, the latter very much an Elmer Fudd look-alike, were benign for the most part. I liked both of them well enough and they performed their jobs ably and created a reasonably hospitable workplace. "Bulldog" Turner was eventually assigned to another base and I spent my last year at Fort Hood as the major domo, the boss man, the Special Services Officer once again.

Behind every good military officer is a loyal, take-charge non-commissioned officer, or NCO. In my case, the man who assumed the role of shepherding the troops around while making my life easier was a veteran of the Korean conflict named Dean R. Gardner. Master Sergeant Gardner was maybe mid-forties, scrawny as a sick chicken, with a prominent Adam's apple, bloodshot eyes, and the dissipated look of someone who partied way too late and drank far too much. The visage was accentuated by a noticeable limp from combat injuries acquired during the so-called Korean peacekeeping exercise. Isn't it interesting how the government officials have a never-ending supply of euphemisms for what is really war?

Sergeant Gardner had become an expert at getting things done when going through channels was either cumbersome or not an option. One of the most important jobs in the entire army and one for which there is no formal title is that of "scrounger." People who can acquire goods without going through formal channels, i.e., "scroungers", are worth their weight in gold. It is hard to put a price tag on the value of an adept scrounger, but Sergeant Gardner was a master practitioner of the art. When I needed something and could not requisition it through channels, all I had to do was walk up to Sergeant Gardner and say, "Hey, Sarge. I'm having trouble locating X, Y, or Z. Any chance you might know where we could find it?" Shortly afterwards, X, Y, or Z would suddenly show up, no questions asked. Sergeant Gardner would simply grin, and offer up a terse question (to which he already knew the answer) followed by a brief question: "Is that what you were looking for Lieutenant?" He would then limp away, in search of some other mischief with which to occupy his time.

I remember an incident that captures the essence of Sergeant Gardner's more perverse side, and his was ample. He was immensely proud of his late model Cadillac and treated it with kid gloves. It was literally his baby and he talked about it all the time. However, late one night, some inconsiderate asshole leaving the parking lot at a watering hole/tavern/saloon/dive/dump in Waco backed into his prize possession, badly denting a fender. This misfortune rightfully did not set well with Sergeant Gardner, so a day or two later after a night of drinking and reveling, he backed the Cadillac into the barracks building where he and my other troops lived three times from different angles, thus insuring that there would be three newly-dented fenders to match the previously damaged one. Satisfied with his handiwork, Sergeant Gardner took the prized Cadillac into his favorite local body shop for repairs to the four dented fenders. For all his quirky idiosyncrasies, Master Sergeant Dean R. Gardner was immensely loyal and I would not have traded him for any other NCO of my acquaintance. He could be terribly aggravating but his loyalty to me transcended all his sins. "Is this what you were looking for, Lieutenant?"

There was an enlisted man who worked for me for a short time who will remain unnamed to protect his loved ones who might possibly still be alive. The man in question, a Sergeant First Class, had been in the army for nearly twenty years, was rough around the edges and dumb as dirt. I think he was divorced and lived in the barracks with the other much younger enlisted men where he spent many an hour in the barracks grousing about this, that, and the other, but focusing often on the food in the mess hall. One night he asked no one in particular what was in store for the evening meal and was told "Hamburgers, Sarge. How's that sound?" Our Sergeant friend responded, "Sounds horrible to me. Pork! Won't the Army ever run out of fucking pork?" Someone asked him what he meant by that comment, and he said, "You know, Hamburgers! Ham! Ham! You know, ham is pork which comes from fucking pigs." When not waxing eloquent about mess hall menus, I was told by my other enlisted men he would sit on his foot locker at night, pull out his wallet, and stare longingly at a picture of his teen-age daughter. He accompanied the lascivious leering with rhetoric about how much he would like to have sex with her, though the descriptors he used to express his incestuous yearnings were far more explicit and X-rated than the polite language I have chosen to use here to protect those of you with more tender ears and sensibilities.

Another memorable office character was Private First Class Larry Birr from Appleton, Wisconsin. Private Birr was perhaps nineteen, and resembled one of those enlisted men depicted in Ernie Pyle's World War II cartoons. Or maybe even better, Beetle Bailey of comic strip fame. Birr, as everyone called him, was a good-natured sort, with an eternal buck-toothed, goofy grin on his face. He almost always greeted Sergeant Gardner or me, or sometimes both of us, at the start of each day with his favorite salutation: "Good morning, Sarge/Lieutenant. I don't know if Natalie Wood but Larry would." Natalie Wood was the heart throb movie starlet of the day, and obviously the apple of PFC Birr's eye. But, then, Natalie Wood was the apple of a lot of eyes in her heyday.

I had a young lady in class many years ago (Leslie Bruno?) who could have passed for the long-lost, separated-at-birth identical twin sister of Natalie Wood, and I once asked her if that comparison was common. She said, "Yes, I get asked this question all the time." I suspect my coed friend tired of the comparison, but she could have done far worse, for sure. I am positive PFC "I don't know if Natalie would but I would" Birr would agree.

The most talented of the enlisted men who worked for me by a country mile, as they say, was PFC, later Specialist Fourth Class, then Specialist Fifth Class, Arthur "Art" Parrack of Missouri. Art was blond, maybe six feet two inches tall and 180 pounds, with the largest hands and fingers I had ever seen on a man his size. Those remarkable hands and fingers seemed more fitting for a blacksmith than a clerk-typist saddled with typing memos on an old Royal manual typewriter, still state of the art (pardon the pun) in 1962. Art had actually won several state typing championships in high school competitions and, after graduation, wrote sports for the student newspaper at the University of Missouri. Art could flat make a typewriter smoke and almost never made a mistake which was so critical in those days of manual typewriters and carbon paper duplicates.

Art left the university without earning his degree, though I am not sure why, given his considerable intellect which was at least as good as mine. He then served a short tenure as the youngest General Manager in all of professional baseball, administering the front office of the Tampa (Florida) Tarpons, a minor league farm team in the Cincinnati Reds organization. His brief baseball career was interrupted by the military draft, an oft-repeated scenario for many young men during the Vietnam era. Like so many others, Art had dropped out of college which was an ill-advised decision for it immediately earned you the unenviable perch at the top of the draft list. That is how Art Parrack ended up in the Army and at Fort Hood.

A number of the players who passed through Tampa during Art's tenure there became key cogs in the "Big Red Machine" as the Cincinnati Reds were known in the 1970's, the years when they dominated major league baseball. Perhaps the most famous of those players was the controversial Pete Rose who went to be one of the greatest hitters of all time. His status as a potential Hall-of-Famer is cloudy only because of bad judgment involving betting on his own team's games. Minus that baggage, he would have been in the Hall a long time ago. It is my hope that he makes it to Cooperstown while still alive. Other Reds players who spent time in Tampa during Art's tenure included Hall-of-Fame catcher Johnny Bench, heavy-hitting outfielder Ken Griffey, Sr., and slick-fielding shortstop Dave Concepcion.

Art's main cohort in Tampa, and the team field manager from 1960 to 1962, was Johnny "Double No-Hit" Vander Meer, legendary in baseball lore for the back-to-back no-hit games he pitched in June of 1938 while himself a member of the Reds. Apparently, the two of them spent a lot of time together and Art came away from the relationship with many fond memories and some great baseball war stories.

For all practical purposes, Art was my day-to-day *de facto* Deputy Special Services Officer. Having him around was like having another officer in the section, and in this particular case, one at least as talented as the man to whom he had to report, me! It always struck me, somewhat painfully I must admit, that I did not stand out among young officers nearly as much as Art did among enlisted men. Frankly, I met scant few from either group with his intelligence, talent, work ethic, sense of humor, and *savior faire*.

Because of his intellect and personality, Art related well to officers and enlisted men alike. As an indicator of how highly he was regarded by those of us who performed his job evaluations, Art made Specialist Five in less than two years, a most unusual accomplishment. Our division commander, Major General Ralph Haines, remarked on several occasions that he thought Art behaved more like an upwardly mobile young officer than an enlisted man, and he pushed hard to get Art to apply for Officer Candidate School. However, Art was a civilian at heart and a military career held little appeal. On this point, as well as many others, Art Parrack and I were simpatico. We were never shy in voicing our collective desire to rejoin civilian life at the earliest possible juncture!

In addition to our work relationship, Art and I became good friends, sharing many similar interests. Given our sports backgrounds, it is not surprising we found common ground in baseball and football. Being a sports writer for the University of Missouri student newspaper, Art was particularly knowledgeable about the legendary football coach at the University of Oklahoma, Charles "Bud" Wilkinson. Since I had grown up in the heyday of OU's 47-game winning streak in the 1940's that made a coaching icon out of Wilkinson, Art's revelations and insights into his personality resonated with me.

Also, Art had a great sense of humor that jived nicely with my own, and we shared many a laugh in those two years. Art was released from his military obligation a few months before me, and his departure left a big hole in our operation and a sizable gap in my life; I missed the guy terribly. As is too often the case with friendships, ours was transient and short-lived. Art and I met only once after we became civilians, and unfortunately never touched base again. I can only hope he has been successful in life, given his positive intellectual and interpersonal qualities.

The Fort Hood Boxing Team. The Post Athletic Director, Ed Hickman, in conjunction with the Post Commanding General and the Commanding Generals of the two Armored Divisions, decided to start a team to represent Fort Hood in the "gentlemanly" art of boxing. A couple of Sergeants with both civilian and military boxing experience were selected as the trainers/coaches and I was asked to be Officer in Charge (OIC). The latter struck me at the time as both an honor and a novelty since I had no formal boxing experience.

The trainers were a most interesting group, loaded with war stories about the boxing business. As for me, my position was largely titular and certainly not based on any past prowess as a fighter. I was involved in a couple of minor tiffs as a teenager, and my record was an undistinguished zero wins and four losses. One of those fights took place immediately after a heated high school basketball game, and I got an ass-whipping to end all ass-whippings, a trouncing to end all trouncings, a beating to end all beatings…you know, the steak-on-the-black-eye kind of butt-kicking. That incident pretty much put an end to my non-illustrious, pansy-ass, pugilistic career.

Actually the fight (or non-fight) that truly put me into permanent retirement as a "fighter" took place several years later at The Terrace Drive-In in Texas City, our aforementioned summer hangout. On that fateful evening, I was heading to someone's vehicle to visit when I heard a voice behind me say, "Any of you sons-of-bitches think you're tough?" I assumed the voice was that of friend not foe, so I turned and answered with a jovial, "Damned right, pal. Bring it on." The author of that question was a total stranger and seemingly did not have my best interests at heart and, as I turned slightly in the direction of the voice, found myself flat on my back from a right hook to the side of the head. Some stranger had stunned me with one punch. I gave up fighting for good that night.

Ed Hickman put out the call for boxing tryouts throughout the post, and it was interesting to watch our fighters go through the selection process and start their workouts. After a couple of weeks of training, the trainers made their decisions about who they thought were the best fighters, and we scheduled our first fights. In that connection, Mr. Hickman asked me if I would be willing to sit at ringside and serve as the timer for knockdowns. My job was to start counting when a fighter went down, and it was incumbent on the referee to pick up the count from me once the fighter who was left standing retreated to a neutral corner. I enjoyed the job and had it all the way through the all-military championships which, incidentally, were won by our own Fort Hood team. Our guys out-boxed the best fighters from the Army, Navy, Air Force, Marines, and Coast Guard, which we all thought was quite an accomplishment.

Our pool of fighters had an interesting cast of characters, and they were the source of some life-long memories. One of my more positive recollections centers on the most accomplished fighter in our stable. His name unfortunately eludes me now but he was a welterweight, which meant he weighed between 140 and 147 pounds. He had been involved in over 350 amateur fights and his only losses reportedly had occurred at tryouts with national, international, or Olympic implications. However apocryphal his accomplishments, he was a whale of a fighter, a poor man's version of the boxing icon of the era, Sugar Ray Robinson, and he gave me a vivid object lesson about what is popularly known as the "killer instinct." I had always heard the term but did not know its true meaning until I had the good fortune to watch this boxer in action.

During a fight, our Sugar Ray Robinson surrogate would dance around the ring, throwing a few jabs while sizing up his opponent. At a certain juncture in the fight, he would spy an opening, and his opponent would be rendered unconscious within sixty seconds, give or take. Sitting at ringside, I soon learned to anticipate the beginning of the end for these unfortunate adversaries. Our gladiator would dance about, looking for a weakness, and when the opening occurred, his eyes would light up like star sapphires. This signal meant he had sensed the kill and the fight was about to end. From the moment those star sapphires lit up to the time he had rendered his opponents unconscious was almost always measured in seconds, not minutes. I have never seen a better example of the killer instinct. It was truly fascinating to behold, remindful of what it must be like to a lion in the wild finally when he or she locates and subsequently isolates the weakest, most vulnerable eland from the herd.

Two other fighters were almost as good as my welterweight but they left something to be desired in the character department. One of them was an 118-pounder, a black Private First Class from Philadelphia, who fought as a bantamweight. Unfortunately for him, he got caught breaking into the Commanding General's office to make long distance calls to his family and "homies" in Philly. These indiscretions led our commander, General Jablonski, to call me early one morning, angrily informing me he had caught the perp in the act the previous night. His subsequent thoughts on the matter were voiced roughly as follows, "Lieutenant, get that son-of-a-bitch off the post and out of the Army today. If you fail in this assignment, I will see that your ass is sent packing instead." I was not looking to leave the Army under that or any other stipulation, so I called my friends in Personnel and explained the problem. Six or seven hours later, our bantamweight was on his way to hang out with his "homies" in the City of Brotherly Love.

The second boxer of note fought in the 154-160 pound class, a very accomplished middleweight. He was a strikingly handsome black man with a muscular physique and a mustache that framed a mouthful of sparkling gold-capped teeth. It seems that our muscular middleweight was enjoying some time off one afternoon when his wife unexpectedly came home early from her job and found him in the throes of passion and lust with the family canine. She understandably took offense at this lapse in marital manners and reported him in to his commander. Shortly after that, I got the anticipated call: "Lieutenant, this is General Jablonski. Your middleweight has a problem. He has an affinity for dogs and I want the son-of-a-bitch off this post today. If he isn't gone by 1700 hours, you are."

The General said he wanted this latter pugilist off the post but did not ask for his dismissal, so my friends in Personnel transferred him to Fort Chaffee, Arkansas. I suspect the decision to grant reassignment rather than dismissal was based on the fact that he was a Sergeant First Class with career aspirations rather than some expendable, street-tough PFC off the streets of Philadelphia. Our muscular middleweight with a mind for making it with mutts proceeded to come to Fort Hood on several occasions during the next year or two and beat up on our replacements in his weight class. As a postscript, I am told that the Fort Hood team we started in 1963 has consistently been the best in the entire armed services, winning the boxing title year after year.

Badminton: Old Sarge Teaches Me a Lesson in Sport Psychology. Badminton was quite popular at Fort Hood in my day, and the best player on the entire post was a wily old middle-aged sergeant whose name also eludes me after all these years. "Old Sarge" (he was forty-ish) once bet me he could beat any and all challengers among the 40,000 troops on the base without moving his pivot foot from a fixed position on the badminton court. As might be expected, there were times when he could not get to a few well-placed shots because of the stationary pivot foot, but he lived up to his promise by never, in my presence at least, losing a match as a result of his self-imposed immobility. Unfortunately, he shredded an Achilles tendon one day in the middle of a match and pretty much lost his edge over the other troops after that.

However, "Old Sarge" poignantly demonstrated with his pivot foot ploy that the person who wins athletic events is not necessarily the youngest, biggest, fastest, or ablest, but rather the smartest and most experienced. I regard this lesson as formative in my views of how psychology interacts with sport performance. "Old Sarge" reinforced the notion I was beginning to figure out that success in sports is not always a king of the mountain affair. Yes, being big, strong, and fast are important attributes, but intelligence, street smarts, artifice, and guile also play huge roles in athletic success.

Two of the best badminton players on the post other than the NCO mentioned above had been accomplished collegiate athletes at Trinity University in San Antonio. One was a Lieutenant named Francisco Cruz-Aedo who had been one of the top youth tennis players in his home country of Mexico. Trinity was a major power in both men's and women's tennis in the late 1950's and early

1960's, and it was quite an honor to be recruited to play there. Another top competitor from that school was a former collegiate basketball player, a Lieutenant by the name of Jim Potter, who was a starter on the post basketball team. Jim was a genuinely nice guy who, after leaving the Army, went on to a distinguished career in athletic administration at his alma mater in San Antonio before retiring a few years ago.

Though Lieutenant Cruz-Aedo was an accomplished athlete whose racket skills made him one of the best tennis and badminton competitors on the post, his talents did not extend to golf. I took him out to the post golf course one afternoon for his maiden voyage at that most challenging, humbling, and aggravating sport. After sixteen holes, Lieutenant Cruz-Aedo had taken 168 strokes, plus or minus, at which point we agreed to cease counting. Francisco later told me he pretty much felt his first effort at golf was also going to be his last. He probably was not the first person to hang up the clubs so prematurely!

My Two Quasi-Combat Experiences

I was fortunate enough to avoid the gruesome and consummately indefensible Vietnam conflict, but divisions such as the First Armored were required to be combat-ready on a moment's notice if fighting broke out somewhere on the globe. I was thus provided with a couple of interesting "near-war" or mock combat experiences, one near Savannah, Georgia, and the other in the Mojave Desert in California.

Cuban Missile Crisis, 1962. The First Armored Division, "Old Ironsides", was deployed on two occasions for long periods of time during my nearly three years of active duty. One of these events took place in early October of 1962 when it was announced (with virtually no advance warning) that we were deploying from Fort Hood in favor of the friendly confines of Fort Stewart, Georgia, near Savannah. The division was to be a part of the lead invasion force should action against Cuba be deemed necessary by the Pentagon. Prior to my leaving for Georgia, Barbara and I decided it would be best if she and young Leslie moved in with her parents in Sherman for the duration of my stay at Fort Stewart or, heaven forbid, Cuba. We thus gave up our cockroach conservatory in Copperas Cove and bid adieu to our cordial cabinet inhabitants.

The Cuban Crisis that prompted our relocation was brought about because the Russians, under the leadership of Commissar Nikita Khrushchev, had joined with the Cuban Communist leader, Fidel Castro, in arming that country with numerous strategically-placed missiles. This major arms buildup posed an immense threat to the security of the US mainland and forced the Pentagon to consider military intervention to remove the missiles. The First Armored Division was thus designated to be part of the lead invasion force should negotiations deteriorate, hostilities escalate, and World War III break out. One can only speculate after the fact what role ground forces would have had in what almost certainly would have been a nuclear war had hostilities broken out.

Fortunately, Mr. Khrushchev and the U.S. President, John F. Kennedy, resolved the missile crisis without triggering off what many thought would be a nuclear holocaust. In all likelihood, such a war would have produced catastrophic results. This capacity for catastrophe reminds me of the words of Albert Einstein who once said: "I know not with what weapons World War III will be fought, but World War IV will be fought with sticks and stones." Fortunately, World War III, or some ugly variant, was circumvented by diplomacy which is almost always the preferred solution for resolving conflict.

After six weeks of waiting for the proverbial other shoe to drop, we were returned to our home base, Fort Hood, though there was a time when I was not sure we were going to get back at all. The military plane carrying us from Georgia to Robert Gray Army Airfield, a stone's throw outside of Killeen, encountered seemingly unending turbulence like I had never experienced before and only once since. The enormous winds said to be as high as one hundred knots tossed our plane around like a rag doll. I was too young and too dumb to realize what dire straits we were in, but I know I felt great relief when we put down in Killeen after those tumultuous hours on the roller coaster ride posing as an airplane flight.

When I sent Barbara the news that I would be returning from Georgia, she arranged to meet me in Killeen, prevailing on her parents to look after Leslie for an extra day or two. She picked me up at Gray Airfield and we spent the night in a local hotel enjoying a long overdue reunion. While visions of sugar plums danced about in my head, someone broke into the car and stole my M-1 rifle. Do not ask me why I left my weapon in the car, but I did! I again violated one of the cardinal rules of being a soldier just like I had done three years earlier at ROTC summer camp…never let your weapon out of your sight. Of course, I received the requisite major league ass-chewing from my superiors at Fort Hood. Thanks to the soon to be mentioned Colonel Jung's considerable talents for verbal assault, the ass-chewing was minor, but forking over a hard-earned one hundred bucks for the stolen weapon hurt badly when you were making second lieutenant pay.

After the soiree at Fort Stewart and subsequent events surrounding the theft of my rifle, I was tired, burned up, bummed out, and in a blue funk. I could not force myself to get up and go back to work for several days, no doubt due to extreme mental and physical exhaustion. Captain Turner and Specialist Four Parrack reached out to me after several days, suggesting I had better get my ass in gear and report back to the company or I would damn well be declared AWOL (Absent Without Leave) and charges against me would have to be filed, which no one wanted to do except as a last resort. A long conversation with Captain "Bulldog" Turner and Major "Swampy" Marsh ensued, ending with an acknowledgment on their part that I had been an excellent soldier up to that point and thus deserved a second chance sans any disciplinary charges other than those associated with repaying Uncle Sam for the missing M-1 rifle.

Shortly after the Fort Stewart and quasi-AWOL episode, Barbara and I were offered a chance to move into a fairly new house in a nice residential area in Killeen. A sergeant with whom I was acquainted invited us to live in his house while he and his family were away for a tour in Germany, and we lived there for the duration of my Army stay. We were essentially homeless after leaving the cockroach conservatory in Copperas Cove and regarded ourselves as indeed fortunate to have such an opportunity fall into our laps.

Operation Desert Strike, 1964. A second major deployment took place in the spring of 1964 when "Old Ironsides" was sent to the Mojave Desert in California for maneuvers. We were joined there by troops from other posts and divisions as well as those from the U.S. Air Force in an operation that was known as Desert Strike. A 1964 *Time* magazine article reported the exercise cost sixty million dollars, and involved 90,000 army troops, 10,000 air force personnel, 780 aircraft, 1,000 tanks, and 7,000 other wheeled vehicles. In the same article, the scene was described as follows:

> "Hordes of 52-ton tanks churned up choking waves of orange dust over California's Mojave Desert. Oil-drum devices released mushroom clouds to simulate atomic attack. In the 105-degree heat, smoke generators threw up acrid screens. Fighter-bombers singed the sand with the blast of their afterburners. The normally green Colorado River turned brown with machine-swirled mud, black with slicks of oil. Helicopters chattered, machine guns clattered and men swore."

This was not war but it was a damn convincing approximation in my mind. In breaking the news of our deployment to the troops someone high up in the chain of command, most likely our Commanding General, announced that the purpose of Desert Strike was to familiarize us with desert warfare. The rationale for the exercise was put to the troops as follows: "We are going to have to fight the Arabs over their oil one day." That pronouncement has turned out to be eerily prophetic, particularly in light of the repeated assertions from the most recent Bush administration that our incursions into Iraq had nothing to do with oil. The American public was told the goal was to rid Iraq of weapons of mass destruction while simultaneously freeing the Iraqi people from the clutches of an evil dictatorship. I find it both ironic and a touch humorous that our government attempts to liberate people from the clutches of evil dictators only if they are in possession of oil or other precious commodities not found in sufficient quantities in the US.

Our encampment was smack dab in the middle of the desert west of Needles and a bit north of the Marine base at Twenty-Nine Palms near Ludlow on Route 66 (now known as I-10). We arrived there in mid-April, set up our bivouac, and upon waking the first morning found ourselves snowed in for the first few days. The snowfall was totally unanticipated and we had not been instructed to bring any cold weather gear, so it was a bit frosty for a day or two. Fortunately, the snows rapidly disappeared, to be replaced by predictably hot weather and its partner in the desert, low humidity. Those among us from the Gulf Coast in Texas were accustomed to sweltering, almost suffocating humidity so the lack of it in the desert was noteworthy and refreshing. Helicopters were often grounded until mid-morning because it took several hours after sunrise for the humidity to rise to a level sufficient to support an aircraft lift-off, or so I was told.

The wind was brutal, and started up each day around 1000 hours. The gales cause tents to collapse and weapons to be fouled, as were typewriters, jeep windshields, and anything else with moving parts. We heard later that every single one of those wind- and sand-damaged items had to be replaced upon the return to Fort Hood. Thankfully the winds died down in the early evening as if someone had hit a switch, and from 1800 hours each day, peace and tranquility reigned. The evenings were typically gorgeous, with moderate temperatures and stunning sunsets.

My desert duties were two-fold: Perhaps the most important task was to make sure the officers in the Division Headquarters and related administrative units had plenty of beer. As was the case in Texas, Coors was new to California in the early 1960's, and my jeep driver, Private First Class Birr of "I don't know if Natalie Wood but Larry would" fame, Specialist Five Parrack, Master Sergeant Gardner, and I would make periodic runs to the U.S. Marine base at Twenty-Nine Palms for cerveza and other provisions.

I was also assigned a second major task, that of providing recreation for the troops minus any sports activities which were not feasible due to nature of the combat exercises. Thus, my enlisted men showed movies most evenings, but on one occasion I was dispatched to Las Vegas to review some casino acts to be brought out to the desert. The well-known comedian of the day, Jerry Colonna, a popular Vegas musical group known as Freddy Bell and the Bellboys, and the reigning Miss Nevada were three of my selections. The special services officers with other units also made arrangements to bring in acts from Vegas, and one of my peers chose a topless dance troupe as part of the entertainment menu for his troops. Most of us lieutenants were envious of his good fortune and congratulated him on hitting the jackpot, but his unit chaplain was not at all pleased with his choice of amusement for the troops. We later heard through the grapevine that the young lieutenant was severely chastised by his superior officers for his dastardly departure from 1960's decorum.

As a small reward for taking part in the selection process, several of us officers were given a night in Las Vegas. I was stone broke with nary a penny to my name, and Las Vegas is not much fun if you have no money. As a result, I retired to my room at an early hour to take full advantage of a real shower, the porcelain pot, and sleeping for the first time in weeks in a bed complete with mattress and clean sheets. Shortly after retiring, I got a breathless phone call from what I was sure was a lady of the evening telling me she had seen me in the lobby, thought I was dashing way beyond Clark Gable (or was it Cary Grant?), and wanted to know if I would like to get together later on for a meal and some drinks. Any temptations I might have entertained about such an arrangement were rendered moot by two things; first of all, I had a wife at home and secondly, my financial wherewithal was way beyond woeful. My situation brought to mind the plight of the python that got separated from his charmer; like the big snake, I did not have a pit to hiss in.

One of my peers ended up taking one of these young women up on her flattering offer, and came to my room about 0300 hours wanting to know if he could borrow $50 to get out of hock with his pulchritudinous playmate for the evening. I told him I could not help him even if I had wanted to; he was flat out of luck talking to me. I am not sure how he ever resolved that dilemma.

We played soldier in the Mojave for those several weeks and there were thirty-three fatalities associated with the mock exercises. Six soldiers died in aircraft crashes and five others drowned in the Colorado River despite repeated warnings to stay away from that inviting, seductive body of water and its dangerous riptides and undertows. Five others died in truck accidents and two soldiers were run over by tanks after passing out on the desert floor due to extreme fatigue and, I suppose, delirium from induced by lack of sleep. There were also several suicides. Casualties from Desert Strike (100,000 personnel) were proportionally quite close to those associated with Desert Storm in Kuwait in 1991, with its 500,000 real-life combatants. The awareness that mock exercises could produce casualties similar to those associated with actual combat is really quite scary to contemplate.

Though everyone in the Army is first and foremost a combat soldier, my section was pretty much exempt from engaging in the mock war exercises. Thus, our days in the Mojave were pretty humdrum except for those times when our tent would be blown away by the incessant pounding of the daily gale-force winds. But the cessation of the winds in the evenings, as noted earlier, made for some pretty relaxing times. I would begin a typical evening after dinner by hanging out with the Division Chaplain, an affable Irish Catholic named Father Sheehan. The good padre was a native of New York and an avid major league baseball fan who also had a monk's affinity for beer. From time to time, I would grab a six-pack of Coors and head over to his tent to quaff a beer or three and engage in some serious baseball talk with our friendly, outgoing chaplain. On other occasions, I moseyed over to talk to the cooks about food and recipes.

Food was a major obsession, attributable I am sure to our sub-standard rations. Most of what was served to the troops was powdered….powdered eggs, powdered potatoes, powdered milk, powdered everything, or so it seemed. Also, I think the Army must have had a huge stockpile of unused Vienna sausages for we were served those delightful delicacies once a day in sort of a predictable cycle. To start with, they would be served at breakfast, almost always covered in white gravy. The next day, they would show up at lunch, smothered in brown gravy. On the third day, they would be served at the evening meal, disguised in yellow gravy. These Vienna sausages were not those "beauties" packaged and sold by Hormel or some other big company; these were big, ugly, low-bid Army Vienna sausages, rendered no less scary by the presence of an assortment of gravies.

At other times, we ate C-Rations (now known as MRE's, or Meals Ready to Eat) which at that time consisted of things like tuna, beanie-weenies, cheese and crackers, and different desserts. These time-honored concoctions actually tasted pretty good in comparison with their powdered counterparts and those butt-ugly, low-bid, virtually inedible Vienna sausages, a la the US military. Every once in a while, in a fit of ravenous hunger, Specialist Five Art Parrack, Master Sergeant Gardner, and yours truly would grab an entire case of C-Rations, jump in our jeep, and have our driver, PFC Larry "I don't know if Natalie Would but I would" Birr, take us out to Route 66 where we would make trades with farmers passing by for heads of lettuce and some good old ripe tomatoes.

I got so hungry at one point I sat down and wrote a letter home that began; "Dear Barbara. Hamburger, steak, chocolate cake, pizza, French fries, corn, spinach, bananas, peaches, etcetera, ad infinitum, ad nauseum". Three full pages of food items later, I tersely and succinctly signed off, "Love, Arnold."

At the end of Desert Strike, some of the more unlucky troops rode back to Fort Hood in jeeps or trucks, bivouacking as they went, but for some unknown reason I was among the fortunate few who was chosen to make the return trip by train. We ate well, slept like babies, played some cards and dominoes, and reveled in the scenery from California to central Texas. I am sure it was not intended, but the return trip was a nice reward for ten weeks in the desert, literally a leisurely vacation in its own right.

Natalie Jean LeUnes: Little One Born on Christmas

A most exhilarating event took place late in the second year of my active duty tour. Early on Christmas morning in 1963, Natalie Jean LeUnes made her debut into this wild-and-woolly, crazy, unpredictable world. Leslie was by then fifteen months old, so she and I were left to shift for ourselves during the birth of the baby sister. Fortunately, Barbara's mother, an absolutely exquisite cook, came down from Sherman later that day and brought us a wonderful Christmas feast.

1962 and 1963 were the years my first two kiddos were born, and the policy in place at Fort Hood's Darnall General Hospital was to order prospective fathers off the premises once they brought their expectant wives to the facility. The scenario played out roughly as follows: You would be met by a female nurse the size of an NFL nose tackle, with a mustache and deep, gravelly voice to match. Her message would go something like this: "Lieutenant, we will call you when the baby is born. Prior to that, you are expected to leave the hospital. Husbands are a pain in the ass and they just get in the way, sir. Good-bye and good luck, sir!"

The new fathers were later notified by phone after the babies had arrived, at which time they were allowed in the hospital to see the mother and child. After getting my phone call that morning, I entered the hospital, found Barbara's room, and inquired as to whether the child had been a boy or a girl. She replied "It's a beautiful baby girl." Being a young macho male, I must admit I was temporarily depressed by this news because I so badly wanted a son. As time wore on, I got past this childish notion, but it took two or three hours of driving silently through the countryside with Leslie for my disappointment to subside. And the exquisite cuisine Barbara's mother had so generously provided helped me regain my senses. At some point, the realization hit me that a healthy female child was fine. It was okay! I knew we were not through having children and a healthy baby girl surely did not signal the end of the world.

The poor woman in the hospital bed next to Barbara got a real earful from her husband with the birth of their third child. He walked into the room, asked if the baby was a boy or a girl, and his poor wife reluctantly responded, "It's a girl." His reaction to the obviously disappointing news was to utter a terse, "Goddam you", at which point he stormed out of the hospital. The woman later related to Barbara that this new baby was female child number three. I could not help but marvel at both the unwarranted verbal abuse he heaped on his wife as well as his total ignorance of the role the male plays at the moment of conception in determining gender.

In no time, I became very much at peace with my female-dominated home life, and really enjoyed being with the girls. I spent many an hour pushing Natalie in her stroller as she got older and stronger while Leslie practiced her new-found walking skills. Later on, Leslie got a lot of enjoyment out of a small red wagon which Santa had so generously delivered for Christmas of her second year. One day shortly thereafter, she came in the house complaining that her wagon was broken. I inspected it and ascertained that one of the rear wheels had come off, thanks to a missing nut. While trying to figure out what to do next, I happened to look at Leslie and noticed a touch of tell-tale rust residue around her mouth. I surmised (correctly) that she had swallowed the missing nut. My assumption was if the nut had been swallowed, it would probably pass through the digestive system and reappear at some point. Sure enough, when Leslie used the potty the next day, I heard a metallic clang. Sure enough, the missing nut had found its way back to the light of day, so to speak. I retrieved the nut, washed it off, grabbed a crescent wrench, and had the wagon rolling again in short order. I was quite proud of my amateur detective work in solving this knotty case, and justifiably so, don't you think?

One of our favorite activities as the girls got older was to go into downtown Killeen on pay day and watch the merchants, assorted women in revealing skirts far beyond mini, and the members of the world's oldest profession work the GI's for their small but precious paychecks. Things got so bad the post Commanding General was forced to place severe restrictions on enlisted men leaving the post for downtown Killeen on payday, knowing they would be broke for the entire month in less than a day. Watching the women work the GI's was fun and my girls had no idea what was taking place; all they knew was it was a day out on the town with their dear old dad, I guess.

Minor Aggravations Add Up

Overall, I found military life to be okay in some ways but intellectually stifling overall. I soon found I no longer had any interest in reading anything other than *The Army Times* to see who had been assigned where and my world pretty much consisted of the post, the sports program, and my family. From time to time, I would think of staying in the Army because it offered me a career working in sports and lucrative health and retirement benefits. And retirement at age forty-five or so would allow me to start a second career as still a young man, hopefully in collegiate or professional sports administration. Fortunately, I always came to my senses in time to decide otherwise about a military career.

Like most things in life, it was not the big things about the military that did me in, but the small stuff. For example, there were quite a few mornings when we were required to take an early morning wakeup call, ring up a number of people on our phone tree, and then show up for work at some ungodly hour, maybe 0400 or 0500. This exercise was designed to test our readiness to respond as a team in times of potential emergency. Once everyone had reported, we would sit around grousing and drinking coffee until time to go to work at 0730. At the time, it always seemed to me that conducting war should involve less sleep deprivation but, in retrospect, I can see there was a method in their madness. Responding promptly and well in an emergency would seem to be a sensible and defensible way for military units to proceed.

Another aggravation was the requirement that we run a red carpet from our parking lot into the gymnasium so the Commanding General, Ralph Haines, and the wife could make their grand entry at selected sports events. The carpet started at the jeep stand in the parking lot, ran all the way from there into the gym, along the baseline of the basketball court, at which point it would take a left, ending at their mid-court ringside seats. This was the royal path the General and his wife took to witness sports events. There was something ludicrous about running cheap red carpet into a stark old army barracks trying to pass for a gymnasium. The troops and I also shared a good laugh about the General's wife whose old-style nylon hosiery with a thick seam in the back which, along with her stern visage, gave her sort of a battle-axe persona.

Speaking of the gymnasium, it highlighted another problem that bothered me a great deal about military life. I once sent a memo up the chain of command to General Haines I hoped would highlight the shortcomings of our sports facilities, with particular emphasis on the aforementioned primitive barracks building parading as a gymnasium. Once the document was crafted, it went forward to "Bulldog" Turner who read it and bounced it back with an admonition to soften the language so as to not offend "Major Swampy." I did a rewrite and "Bulldog" forwarded it to the Major's desk. The Major, in turn, bounced it back, saying the rhetoric needed to be modified so it would not offend his boss, a Lieutenant Colonel. The Lieutenant Colonel later bounced it back, urging me to be more diplomatic and less candid as it might offend the Chief of Staff, the much-feared Colonel Wing Foo Jung. Certainly, Colonel Jung was not a man you would want to offend, as the reader will soon see. Once rewritten, Colonel Jung would forward the document to the Deputy Division Commander, a Brigadier General. Shortly thereafter, a note appeared on my desk, asking me to revise and soften once again. Finally, my letter was deemed ready for the consumption of the Commanding General. What had started out weeks earlier as a damning commentary on the state of the gymnasium had miraculously transformed our grubby holdings into state of the art athletic facilities, sort of a Central Texas sports Taj Mahal.

Here I was, a dumbass First Lieutenant writing about sports facilities which in the greater scheme of things are of modest importance. However, I could not help thinking about parallels between what I had experienced at little old Fort Hood and high level decision-making on earth-shaking issues in the Pentagon and the White House. Do memos to people who make life and death decisions get the same treatment as mine concerning a dilapidated, two-bit gymnasium? I always think of the mean-spirited, epithet-spewing, profane, pervasively paranoid Richard Nixon when I reflect back on that letter. I strongly suspect the lower echelon advisors surrounding President Nixon were not about to tell him the truth on vital issues if the information was potentially offensive in some way, particularly if one were to possibly incur his considerable wrath. There would thus be a whitewash throughout the entire chain of command. I can visualize a CIA intelligence memo from a field agent who possessed indisputable evidence indicating World War III with Iran or North Korea was imminent, only to have it mutated by the links in the chain of command and reported to the

President as an impending kumbaya love fest between the rulers of those two countries. People who demand distortion of the truth up the chain of command concerning something as trivial as a rickety barracks building posing as a gymnasium gives me pause where vital life and death decisions are being made at the highest levels of our government.

In this regard, a document attributed to an unknown source recently crossed my desk and it captures the essence of what I have just described. It comes from my friends in Business Management or Industrial/Organizational Psychology who specialize in issues of corporate life. They understand the applicability of "The Creation" to decision-making in business, industry, the military, and other organizations.

The Creation

In the beginning was the Plan
And then came the assumptions
And the assumptions were without form
And the plan was completely without substance
And darkness was upon the faces of the workers
And they spake unto their Group Heads, saying:
"It is a crock and it stinketh!"
And the Group Heads went unto their Section Heads, and sayeth:
"It is a pile of dung, and none may abide by the odour thereof."
And the Section Heads went unto their Managers, and sayeth unto them:
"It is a container of excrement, and it is very strong, such that none may abide by it."
And the Managers went to their Director, and sayeth unto him:
"It is a vessel of fertilizer, and none may abide by its strength."
And the Director went to his Vice-President and sayeth:
"It contains what aids plant growth, and it is very strong."
And the Vice-President went unto the President, and sayeth unto him:
"It promoteth growth, and it is very powerful."
And the President went unto the Chairman of the Board and sayeth unto him:
"This powerful new Plan will actively promote growth and the efficiency
of the Company."
And the Chairman looked upon the Plan and saw that it was good.
And the Plan became Policy.

Yet another annoyance associated with my military duties had to do with dignitaries who visited the post from time to time. It was often my responsibility to make sure our guests were presented with a trophy to commemorate their visit. For the life of me, I could never figure out why a 45- or 50-year old Colonel or General would want a shitty little meaningless trophy, but, being the good soldier I was, it was not mine to reason why; mine was to do or die even if the potential death sentence involved a trivial trinket. In this connection, I was once asked to get a trophy prepared for presentation to a visiting General who was scheduled to receive his treasured memento around 0900 hours on a Monday morning. I put in my order at the sporting goods store in downtown Killeen with full intentions of retrieving the trophy on my way home from work on Friday or during the day Saturday. Unfortunately, I flat forgot the trophy! To add misfortune to misfortune, the store did not open until 1000 hours that Monday, so there was no way I could get the trophy on hand for a 0900 presentation. Upon hearing the news that the trophy would not be ready to present as scheduled, Colonel Wing Foo Jung, our Division Chief of Staff, came looking for me with fangs bared and talons sharpened. I got an ass-chewing to end all ass-chewing's from Colonel Jung and, as a result, I no longer fear ass-chewing's. Once you have endured the worst possible ass-chewing and there is nothing left to gnaw on, all other ass-chewing's pale by comparison. I suspect it is a good thing getting the ultimate ass-chewing out of the way early in life so you no longer have to fear getting an ass-chewing for literally the remainder of your life. And thanks to Colonel Jung, subsequent ass-chewing's, though few in number since the day he lit into me, have had the same effect on me as water on the proverbial duck's back. Once you have experienced the ultimate, quintessential ass-chewing, all other ass-chewing's are rendered meaningless. All ass-chewing's are not created equally; there are ass-chewing's and then there are ass-chewing's, and Colonel Jung knew how to deliver an ass-chewing *par excellence.*

Another anecdote serves to highlight how silly military life can sometimes become. The Post Commander at Fort Hood was a Lieutenant General (three stars) by the name of T. H. R. Dunn. One day General Dunn was motoring around the post, chauffeured by his jeep driver, and he decided the junior officers and enlisted men were not showing proper respect as evidenced by their lackadaisical saluting practices. To rectify this dire disciplinary deficiency, the younger officers, lieutenants, captains, majors, and as I remember even lieutenant colonels, were required to attend Saturday morning saluting practice for the next three or four weeks. The ironic thing about this whole brouhaha was General Dunn had the worst salute I had ever seen by any soldier, anytime, anyplace, anywhere. When he saluted, his hand moved from the tip of his cap outward and he would then curl his fingers, creating the image in my mind of an unfolding parachute or a granddaddy longlegs spider slowly wending its way via its web from mid-air to the ground. Rank has its privileges, I guess.

Another silly incident: Major General Harvey J. Jablonski, one of the Commanders of the First Armored Division during my tenure at Fort Hood, was being driven to work and he casually mentioned to his Aide-de-Camp, a Captain, how nice it would be to jog to work early in the morning and end the run with a dip in a swimming pool. In response to what I am sure was meant to be a random commentary requiring no action, every pool on the base was open at 0700 hours the next morning on the outside chance General Jablonski might want to take an early morning dip. Several weeks after the institution of this knee-jerk, cockamamie order, the General had not once stopped for a swim, and the mandate to open the pools early was rescinded and their hours of operation returned to business as usual.

In the greater scheme of things, none of these minor aggravations were earthshaking, but in combination they did little to inspire a long-term interest in committing to military life. Also, I knew that not all of my military assignments would be in sports and recreation, and that was the major deterrent for me. I did not want any other job in the army, and facing a tour or several tours as a combat infantry officer, postal officer, or personnel officer held no attraction for me. Also, being much more dove than hawk, the increasingly volatile Vietnam War did little to ignite my interest in a combat assignment. In retrospect, I would like to be able to say I had served and survived Vietnam but, at the time, having two children, a devoted wife, many friends, and a deeply-rooted instinct for survival pushed me strongly in the direction of civilian life. As I said earlier, Audie Murphy, I ain't!

PIT BULL AND CLOSE FRIEND, 2016

No More Active Duty for Me!

Toward the end of my original two-year obligation, the Pentagon came up with a plan whereby soldiers could extend their active duty time for up to one year from the time they were to be originally released. Since I had been called up in January of 1962, my active duty was to end that same month in 1964, but I decided for two reasons to stay on for eight additional months. The primary reason for my decision was by getting out in late August, I could start my doctoral studies at UNT with the beginning of the academic year which seemed like a sensible way to proceed, A second reason was an eight-month obligation would almost certainly prevent me from serving a tour in Vietnam which was heating up and becoming increasingly perilous. I was released from active duty late in August of 1964 and, with glee for which there are no words, we headed off for more schooling. Barbara had an undergraduate degree to earn and my sights were set on getting the doctoral degree that would be my ticket to the academic world. To make the process of moving and getting set up go a bit smoother, I had saved up all my vacation time for two years so I got a nice $2000 check the day I left the post.

I have few regrets about my time in the military. Looking back, I wish I had gone to jump school at Fort Campbell, Kentucky, after I finished the Officer's Basic Course at Fort Benjamin Harrison in the winter of 1962. I left Indianapolis in excellent physical shape thanks to help from my running mate, the ruthless, unfeeling, uncaring Johnny Poff, and the three weeks of jump school would have gone by in a trice. However, I was in a big hurry to get back to Texas and get my affairs in order there. Also, I knew I was being assigned to an armored division where the highest point of possible departure for a paratrooper to ply his proficiencies would have been the top of a tank. There simply was not much demand for trained paratroopers in an Armored Division! Also, it made little sense to go through the rigors of paratrooper training if I could not be placed on "jump status" which would provide me with an extra one hundred dollars a month Still, I regret not taking advantage of the jump school option.

It is difficult to have served in the army during that period of time without thinking of the tragedy of the Vietnam War. I wish I could say that I had served there for the experience but it was a dreadful place for anyone to be, let alone a married man with two children. As noted elsewhere, a number of my college classmates paid a severe price for their service in Vietnam.

On a more positive note, I am prouder each year of my military service and the experiences I had at Fort Hood, Fort Benjamin Harrison, Fort Stewart, and Fort Mojave Desert. I met some interesting people, the foremost of whom was Specialist Five Art Parrack, along the way and my intolerance for those who talk, giggle, or play grab-ass during the playing of the National Anthem is a source of great pride for me. Such actions are disrespectful of me as a veteran and a colossal disservice to those who paid with their lives, limbs, or mental well-being, trying to protect the freedoms these consummately disrespectful people seem to take for granted. I am not always proud of my biases, but I am exceedingly fond of and greatly cherish greatly my intolerance of those who tarnish the playing of the National Anthem.

The trend of late among professional football players in which they refuse to honor the flag and the anthem is particularly irksome for me. There are all sorts of points of view about San Francisco 49er Colin Kaepernick's refusal to stand for the anthem, but my own view was expressed perfectly by an unnamed NFL executive who said when he first heard of his act of disrespect, "Fuck Kaepernick." Beautifully and succinctly stated and I hope Kaepernick's actions are factored into the equation whereby he never gets another job in professional football anywhere. He is a spoiled brat and a second-rate talent who makes millions of dollars and lives an extravagant lifestyle because of the country in which he lives and symbolically by the flag and anthem he disrespects.

On a related note, I have nothing but the utmost regard for those who serve or have served and nothing but loathing for the misguided and/or malevolent politicians who send young soldiers into harm's way for no real purpose. Do you hear me, 'Dubya', Dick, and Condy? It would give me great peace of mind to know these three "world leaders" have experienced second thoughts and sleepless nights for what they did to our soldiers and innocent Iraqi civilians. Unfortunately, I am convinced beyond even the slightest doubt their misdeeds have caused them nary a moment of doubt or psychic pain. They were wonderful with the platitudes and bromides about their undying love and support of our military, but I never once believed they felt their pain or experienced even the slightest compassion for our troops or the other victims of war.

George W. Bush strikes me as the ultimate mountebank, or unscrupulous pretender. He ignored reports from the Central Intelligence Agency (CIA) and lied repeatedly to Congress and the American people about the weapons of mass destruction in Iraq. He also lied through his pearly whites about the dangers posed for this country by Saddam Hussein and his supposed harboring of al Qaeda terrorists. In reality, Saddam Hussein and the terrorists were the most unlikely of bedfellows because of their intense hatred for each other.

A German proverb sums up the evils of war well: "A great war leaves the country with three armies – an army of cripples, an army of mourners, and an army of thieves." In this instance, George W. Bush and his sycophantic henchpeople were the "thieves" and they bear sole responsibility for the legions of mourners and cripples created by their immoral war. I find myself sympathetic to the call made by Vince Bugliosi in his book and subsequent audiotape, *The Prosecution of George W. Bush for First-Degree Murder*. Bugliosi makes an absolutely compelling legal case for prosecuting George W. Bush for wantonly contributing to the murder of over 4,000 American soldiers and 100,000 Iraqi civilians. In addition to the huge number of fatalities, untold thousands of American and coalition soldiers and Iraqi citizens are presently suffering and will continue to experience lifelong medical and psychological issues. Young people today, upon reaching their fifties and sixties, will see their Veteran's Administration hospitals full of the "cripples." As is almost always the case in these kinds of things, the "mourners" will continue to grieve while the "thieves" will largely go unpunished. They will continue to write their bestsellers (George W. Bush), make their millions from business and the war industry (Dick Cheney), and enjoy their lucrative professorships at prestigious universities such as Stanford (Condoleezza Rice). In this regard, I have a warm spot in my heart for the students and professors at Rutgers University who rose up in opposition to Dr.

Rice's role in the Iraqi War, leading her to cancel a commencement speech there in 2014. It is gratifying to know there are still some long memories out there for the "thieves."

As much as my heart is warmed by these protests, I am convinced the greater good is ultimately best served by allowing people like Dr. Rice to talk because of freedom of speech. Hear her out and make your own decision as to the merit of her ideas. Bad ideas, along with the good, merit a hearing. As a postscript, the Chancellor of Texas Tech University, Kent Hance, subsequently proffered an invitation to Dr. Rice to deliver a graduation speech at his institution any time she pleased. Shame on Texas Tech and Kent Hance!

Doctoral Student Days in Denton

The LeUnes Family Heads to Denton

After cutting the almost three-year umbilical cord with Fort Hood in August of 1964, Barbara and I packed up our two baby girls, ages two and one, and headed to Denton and good old UNT. I planned to work on a doctorate in Psychology, or the UNT approximation. The university offered only a master's degree in Psychology at the time, so Counseling and Personnel Administration was the closest major I could find that might correspond to my wishes. Virtually every course I took for my doctorate had Psychology as its recognized prefix and, as stated elsewhere, I now have just shy of 300 hours of college credit across my three degrees. As for Barbara, she had designs on finishing her undergraduate degree in Education with an emphasis in English.

Sometime after I received my doctorate in 1969, UNT started offering the PhD degree and I was told that it was possible to change my degree designation from EdD to PhD by displaying my academic credentials, jumping through some bureaucratic hoops, and paying a small fee. I never got around to looking into the issue because I never saw the necessity. Some purists have maintained that the EdD degree is an inferior degree, and I was told from time to time I would not be able to compete with PhD's in Psychology. Fifty-two years later, I am still competing and with a modicum of success.

I dearly loved my three years at UNT (across the two graduate degrees), was quite fond of the city of Denton, and greatly enjoyed my professors almost to a man/woman. I particularly enjoyed the sixteen short months I was in residence as a doctoral student prior to accepting the faculty position at A&M in January of 1966. I worked during those sixteen months as a jack-of-all-trades in the Student Union Building (SUB), in great part because I had no teaching experience and thus was ineligible to be considered for a teaching assistant position. My ineligibility was linked historically to the old teacher's college tradition that placed great emphasis on public school teaching as preparation for doing so in college, and I had no such experience. However, someone was in my corner, putting in a kind word or two with Dr. Harold Farmer, the Director of the Student Union Building (SUB). Dr. Farmer hired me and I have always believed the mystery someone in my corner was the aforementioned and much revered Dr. Robert Toulouse, Dean of the Graduate School and my first Professor in graduate school four years earlier.

As far as my duties in the SUB were concerned, I pretty much did anything that needed to be done though my major responsibility was to collect and count the money generated daily by the numerous food and drink vending machines located throughout the center. I also made sure the machines stayed full of coins to provide the necessary change. I typed, ran errands, and cleaned up spills and messes made by the masses who hung out in the SUB. I forget what I was paid, maybe $300 per month, but with that money, my separation pay from the Army ($2,000), and Barbara's wages from working nights at Ling-Temco-Vaught (LTV), an electronics and aerospace conglomerate in Dallas, got us by. All things considered, we lived well and it helped out immensely that we were able to rent a three-bedroom, two-bath brick home fairly close to the campus for $95 a month plus bills which never exceeded $50.

When Barbara and I got married in 1962, she left UNT needing a year of course work to complete her degree. She was able to complete the requisite courses and do her student teaching during that first year back in Denton (1964-65), but decided against seeking a teaching job since we felt we were only going to be in Denton for a short time. This led her to take the night job with LTV. The job required a short commute of maybe forty-five minutes to Dallas, but the only position available at the time she applied was on the evening shift from 1600 until 2300 Monday through Friday. Thus, she was gone every afternoon and evening five days a week during my last semester in Denton.

With Barbara working those rather odd hours, I was forced to pick up the slack around the house, including babysitting Leslie who was three and Natalie who was approaching two. They entertained each other and were generally low maintenance as young children go. It helped that they had regular feeding and sleeping hours, with bedtime taking place around 2000 hours which allowed me to get in some productive study time once they went to sleep. On a typical day, I would get up, go to a couple of classes, put in three or four hours at my job in the SUB, and make it home in the afternoon in time for Barbara to head to LTV in Dallas.

Friends and Colleagues

During my short stay in Denton while pursuing what sometimes seemed like an elusive doctoral degree, I was blessed with good friends and wonderful colleagues who added richness to my life during those sometimes demanding times.

Jonathan and Jerrianne. To break the routine of school and family life, I would occasionally work in a round of golf with my brother-in-law, Jonathan Sewell, who was married to Barbara's occasionally ditzy, sometimes zany, and always interesting sister, Jerrianne. Jonathan was a golf fanatic, worked hard at honing his game, and was quite a good player. Unfortunately, however, he brought none of the industriousness about golf to his school work. He had earlier spent some time at Texas Tech University where he posted some unspectacular grades. Jonathan proceeded to do the same at UNT and left after a year and insofar as I know never completed his college degree. Jonathan's parents were well-to-do and indulgent so he really never had to apply himself to much of anything other than golf, gambling, and having a good time. Speaking of gambling, Jonathan bet on anything and everything. I think he probably bet on solitaire; nothing was fun for him if money was not riding on the outcome.

The two of us played golf at UNT but occasionally would journey over to the far side of town and play a round or two on the Texas Women's University (TWU) course. The TWU course was definitely created with women in mind, and thus shorter in length than its UNT counterpart. Playing there was a nice change of pace from the longer and more demanding UNT course. My scores did not show it, for I shot about the same at UNT as I did at the ostensibly easier TWU course. Perhaps this admission reveals shortcomings in the old short game, a deficiency common to many duffers.

One morning, Jonathan and I played eighteen holes on the UNT course, and I headed home around noon. Jonathan said he wanted to play another round, or at least part of it, so he ended up playing thirty-six more holes and darkness was falling when he finished. Jonathan knew he should have quit much earlier and devoted some time to studying, or being with Jerrianne and their new baby, Shelley, or at least working around the house. Jonathan knew he was going to catch hell when he got home, so he decided that the best defense is a good offense. Thus he decided to confront Jerrianne in an attack mode. He pulled up in the driveway, got out of the car, loudly threw open the front door, stomped in the house, and shouted at Jerrianne, wanting to know why in hell his dinner was not on the table. Not surprisingly, Jerrianne suggested that his supper was indeed ready but was being served at the nearby Dairy Queen!

My only other golfing memory of those days was the time I was three over par through seven holes on the front nine of the UNT course. Unable to handle prosperity, I told myself that this was not the real me and I was playing over my head. Sure enough, I reverted to form and finished the round with a double bogey and a triple bogey. I shot an eight over par forty-three which was more my speed, and not really a bad score at all for me. Most days I would have been pleased with that score but it was the way I made the forty-three that hurt. Those first seven holes were the best I ever played for any length of time, and the forty-three was among the best nine holes scores I was to record in all my golfing days. My lowest eighteen-hole score ever was at the A&M course where I shot an eighty-six one evening. I never did break forty for nine holes at any time prior to my retirement from the game a decade or more ago.

Jonathan's reach into the golf world extended to a relationship his family had forged with a highly successful professional golfer of the era, Miller Barber. Jonathan's well-to-do parents, among others, were financial backers of Barber in the early days of his career. Barber resided in Sherman at the time and was popularly known on the tour as "Mr. X." because of his low-key, taciturn, and at times mysterious demeanor. Over his long career, Barber won eleven PGA (Professional Golfers' Association) tournaments and enjoyed even more success on the senior tour where he captured twenty-four titles before his retirement. Barber was the eighth golfer on the PGA tour to earn one million dollars, a trivial figure by today's standards where golfers are paid nearly double that amount in some cases for winning a tournament. I might add that the million dollar purses are awarded to males on the PGA; half that amount would be an outstanding purse for a woman winning a LPGA tournament. Dozens of men and nearly a dozen women won a million dollars or more in prize money in 2013; eighteen male golfers made more than $3 million that year!

I have two memories in which Jonathan and Miller Barber were involved, one of which was a high stakes poker game thrown together in the late-1960's by some civic and business leaders of Sherman. Shortly after getting word that the action was on, Jonathan came by the Blythe residence where we were visiting the in-laws and inquired about my interest in taking part in a high stakes poker game being held at a local country club. Knowing Jonathan as I did, I was not sure I could afford to play and was content to be a bystander if the stakes were too high. As it turned out, the stakes were more than excessive; you had to put up $2,500 (a lot of money in the 1960's!) to get in on the action, far more money than a poor Assistant Professor could afford. Thus, I asked if it would be okay if I watched rather than played. After a brief and at times intense discussion, the group reluctantly agreed but told me in view of the money involved, I better have my best poker face on at all times to keep from tipping off the contents of different players' hands. I assured them I had invented the poker face, and I acquitted myself nicely as the evening turned to morning!

Though it has been almost fifty years ago now, I remember one of the players being the Mayor of Sherman and another was the former Head Football Coach and Athletic Director at Oklahoma State University, a fellow by the name of Floyd Gass. Jonathan and four or five other guys made up the rest of the table. As for Miller Barber, he proffered that he never gambled so his role that night was to kibitz, serve food and drinks, and generally help out where needed. Consistent with his reputation as the mysterious "Mr. X", Barber said little and left early and quietly without fanfare.

The festivities commenced a couple of hours before midnight and ended around six or seven in the morning. Over the course of the evening/morning, I sat behind each player and was thus able to size up their poker acumen. Jonathan's assessment and mine generally agreed; there were some good players and a couple of pretty bad ones. Jonathan told me on the way back to the Blythe's home that the game was an annual thing and was designed to take advantage of the deep pockets of two bad players at the table. Jonathan won a few hundred bucks and I had my first high stakes poker viewing. Like most of us, I am content to play where the stakes at the highest are nickel, dime, and quarter.

Another interesting Miller Barber/Jonathan Sewell anecdote concerns a trip to New Orleans where, among other things, we dined at a very fancy restaurant, the Commander's Palace. I am not sure of the total makeup of the group that evening, but Barber, Jonathan, and yours truly were there for sure. We were joined by a handful of Barber's peers on the PGA tour, and I am almost certain two of them were Don January (forty-four professional career wins) and Billy Maxwell (ten wins) who had been teammates on the University of North Texas teams that won the NCAA golf championship from 1949 through 1952. The entourage of golfers and pretenders like me was eventually joined by a diminutive, suave, urbane, dressed-to-the-nines, well-spoken gentleman who held forth for most of the meal. At the end of the festivities, he pulled out four or five one hundred dollar bills to pay the tab and left another hundred as a tip for the waiter. We eventually made our way to the street, and after a few hail fellow well met words, our generous benefactor bid us a hearty farewell. The ever-curious Jonathan who, like yours truly, was somewhat in awe and amazement asked "Who was that masked man?" Miller Barber answered that we had just been regaled for two hours by none other than the Mafia chieftain of New Orleans, Carlos "The Little Man" Marcello (1910-1993). Upon hearing the news, Jonathan said, "Gee. He just seemed like a successful businessman to me." To this, someone in the group offered up the following pearl of wisdom, "He is a businessman---a very big businessman!"

My Pals, John Ed and Sharon. In off hours at school, I hung around with my fellow graduate students, two of whom stand the most. Their names were John Ed Wilhite and Sharon Anderson, and I pretty much spent all my spare time with those two, drinking coffee, studying, kibitzing, and just hanging out. John Ed was single, late twenties or early thirties, and hailed from metropolitan Lueders, just north of Abilene in west Texas. The 1965 population of Lueders is unknown to me but probably not too much different from the 264 who lived there fifty years later. John Ed and I talked a lot over coffee, took most if not all of our courses jointly, and studied together for practically every exam. He was maybe six feet tall, slim, pale, and about as vanilla a personality as you would find anywhere. I would attribute all of his pallor and the majority of his "vanilla-ness" to spending almost all of his life indoors. He was an introvert, quiet, low-key, and not very exciting or animated, but a good guy whose kindness and friendship were much appreciated. Unfortunately, I saw John Ed maybe once or twice after we left UNT. I do not believe he ever finished his doctorate, choosing instead to leave ABD (All But Dissertation) to accept a position on the faculty at Nicholls State University in Thibodeaux, Louisiana, less than an hour drive south and west of New Orleans.

As for Sharon, she was in her twenties, married, and lived in nearby Lewisville with her husband. Sharon was deceptively attractive and would have been even more so if she had worn contact lenses instead of her slightly clunky glasses. She reminds me in retrospect of a television commercial I once saw featuring what is obviously a young professional woman working in an upscale office, dressed formally and professionally, wearing the mandatory thick-rimmed eyeglasses, and putting her hair up in a bun. At the end of the day, she jumps into an expensive sports car, rips off the clunky glasses, lets her hair fall free, and drives off as a suddenly attractive and seductive woman out on the town. That is how Sharon always struck me; conventional but with something exciting lurking beneath that reserved, conservative surface.

Two Sharon stories stand out. In one instance, she and I were taking a course from a senior faculty member who had this idiosyncrasy of not awarding many A's, particularly to male students. Historically, selected females were more likely to get the A, and Sharon was no exception to the rule that semester (I got a C as did most other males). As she left the final exam, Sharon handed the professor a self-addressed postcard and requested he mail it to her home when the final averages were tabulated. A few days later, the postcard arrived in Lewisville but fell into her husband's hands before Sharon got home from school. He was holding the postcard in his hand when she arrived, and politely asked what was going on with her professor up there in Denton. Sharon looked at him, puzzled by his query until she picked up the postcard which read, "You made an A. Now what do I get out of this?" Needless to say, she was taken aback by the message though not totally shocked because rumors had circulated for years about the professor's propensities to hit on his female students. A second rumor suggested that because he was the son of a past president of UNT, he was conferred protection by history and the "good old boys" network. Also, women had fewer protections in those days with regard to sexual harassment. Sharon convinced her husband there was no hanky-panky going on, dismissed the episode without protest, and went on about the business of finishing her degree.

Sharon told me she wrote most if not all of her husband's term papers, themes, and other written assignments. Occasionally, the two of them would also take courses together, and typical of many women of that era, Sharon lowered her expectations and performance, always making sure her husband made slightly higher exam grades than she did. She was a far more diligent student than her husband, but it was not acceptable for women to outdo their spouses in competitive situations in the 1960's, and she was typical in that regard. This lowering of expectations and performance in competitive situations was the subject of considerable research during the early 1970's by a psychologist name Matina Horner, and she labeled her construct "fear of success." My suspicion is that women today not only do not fear success, they seek and revel in competitive situations. Some might even cut your throat, so to speak, to get ahead.

My final two encounters with Sharon took place in the late 1960's. After I left UNT, we crossed paths at a Vocational Guidance convention in San Antonio in the late 1960's, spending the better part of an evening together over dinner. The last time we met was in Denton was when I was back there trying to complete my dissertation. Little did I know when I left UNT it would take three-and-a-half years and 10,000 miles of driving between College Station and Denton to complete the much-anticipated doctoral degree. Occasional if brief visits with Sharon helped ease the pain of the long and boring trips.

Memorable Professors

It is impossible to reminisce about those doctoral student days without reflecting back on the tremendous influence several professors exerted on my personal and professional development. They had names like Bonney, Bellamy, and Beamer, to name only a few.

Merl E. Bonney, Professor Without equal. My favorite professor of all time without question was Merle Bonney (1902-2001), Distinguished Professor of Psychology. Dr. Bonney stood out from his peers because of his scholarship, style of delivery in the classroom, academic rigor, and utter and complete disregard for the traits that supposedly make up the "good teacher." Professor Bonney willfully and egregiously violated every principle of the "good teacher" in every class each and every day and in each and every way.

Dr. Bonney spent the majority of his career during an era when procuring research grants, authoring books and articles, and attaining visibility at the national and/or international level (i. e., "scholarship") was not a priority at UNT. Despite the lack of a university-wide mandate for scholarship, Dr. Bonney published regularly in good psychology journals, authored several books, and even wrote some pieces for some of the more prominent popular magazines of the day, such as *Reader's Digest*. He also taught twelve hours each semester, or four courses, though his normal expected course load was only one or two due to his status as a Distinguished Professor. Like Freud many years earlier, Dr. Bonney viewed psychology as his tyrant. At the same time, he also viewed teaching as his calling.

Dr. Bonney told us in class one day he was the first person in his family to graduate from college. He received his undergraduate degree at Willamette University in Washington, a Master of Arts degree from Stanford, and his PhD degree was awarded by Columbia University in New York City. After graduating from Willamette in 1925, Dr. Bonney taught social science for a brief time at a high school in Hillsboro, Oregon. Upon completion of his master's degree in 1927, he spent four years teaching at the Oregon Normal School. After earning the doctoral degree at Columbia in 1935, Dr. Bonney taught at UNT for twelve years, at which time he left Denton for a faculty appointment at the University of Colorado in Boulder. He was in Boulder for three years but returned to Denton and UNT where he would spend the rest of his long and distinguished professional life.

Physically, Dr. Bonney was pretty much unremarkable. He was of average size, bespectacled, and stereotypically professorial in appearance and dress; I never saw him wear anything other than his slightly ill-fitting dark suit augmented by a conservative tie. He was one of those people you could never visualize without his trademark suit, much like my A&M colleagues, John McDermott in Philosophy and the recently deceased Howard Kaplan in Sociology. Prior to his death in 2011, I actually saw Professor Kaplan dining at the now-defunct Tom's Barbecue, a local restaurant of some repute prior to its unfortunate demise, wearing a pair of Levi's and a casual, collared shirt. To this day, my colleagues who knew him are convinced I experienced an unexplained transient hallucinatory episode, steadfastly refusing to believe the distinguished Dr. Kaplan would lower himself to wear blue jeans.

As for my colleague and friend John McDermott, he is one of A&M's small cadre of Distinguished Professors, and truly a brilliant, well-respected philosopher and scholar in the truest sense of the word. I have known McDermott for maybe thirty of his eighty-plus years and have never seen him anywhere, anytime without his trademark dark suit, vest or sweater, tie, and hat. John is always attired in the dark suit with its assorted accoutrements, but there is no way anyone would ever confuse him with a spiffy dresser. His suit is rumpled from both age and benign neglect, and the vests or sweaters are often festooned with a random assortment of stains and burn holes. McDermott is a long-time pipe smoker and small burn marks in his suits, vests, ties, and shirts bear testimony to occasional carelessness (or bad luck perhaps). Another McDermott trademark is the long, thick, wiry, gray hair which protrudes several inches below the rim of his hat (which I have never seen removed from its perch atop his head). His hair length does not seem to vary much, so he must visit a barber once in a great while, though I do not know that to be true. He has an unmistakable presence as he walks the campus, to say the least.

Years ago, A&M hired Robert Gates, the ex-director of the Central Intelligence Agency (CIA) and later Secretary of Defense in the Obama presidency, as Director of the George Herbert Walker Bush School of Public Policy, so named in honor of the forty-first President. After a short time in that position, Gates assumed the Presidency of A&M before departing in 2008 for Washington, DC, to serve in President Obama's Cabinet. When interviewing at A&M for the first time, he flew into Easterwood, the local airport, where he happened to spot Professor McDermott at a distant point in the waiting area. Dr. Gates had no idea McDermott was one of A&M's forty-one Distinguished Professors when he asked a highly-placed A&M official: "Is that one of College Station's homeless people over there?" John is not going to win any sartorial splendor awards, but his idiosyncratic dress and demeanor are part and parcel of the persona by which he is widely known. As with Howard Kaplan and John McDermott, I cannot wrap my mind around an image of Dr. Bonney in loafers, blue jeans, and a Henley.

Dr. Bonney was a self-appointed social isolate, never seeming to need or seek the company of others. According to legend, he had been married, gotten divorced, remarried the same woman, and in one of the marriages fathered a child, Warren, who followed in his father's footsteps and became a psychologist, though of the clinical private practitioner variety. Dr. Bonney admitted that he had no hobbies; he confessed to trying bowling once but couldn't keep the ball out of the gutter, so he quit. His recreational life consisted of attending local church services on a random basis. He would go to a different church in Denton County each Sunday until he had been through them all, and then would repeat the cycle. He told us he did this because he wanted to know what all the local preachers were talking about, what their points of concern were, and how they expressed observations and ideas to their respective congregations.

Dr. Bonney was trained as a social and personality psychologist, and was greatly interested in sociometry, a social-psychological assessment procedure first advanced by Dr. Jacob Moreno, the Romanian-born psychiatrist, psychotherapist, and Professor at the University of Vienna in Austria. One of Moreno's major disciples was Dr. Muzafer Sherif, a faculty member at the University of Oklahoma, and both he and Sheriff exerted a major influence on Dr. Bonney's professional development.

Essentially, sociometry is a method for assessing the degree of relatedness of people in groups. Considerable emphasis in sociometric measurement is placed on finding out through peer nomination who are the leaders, who are the followers, and importantly, who are the isolates or rejects within a group. As part of Dr. Bonney's course in Sociometry, I conducted a study of a gymnastics team at UNT. True to prediction, the technique proved to be successful in delineating leaders, followers, isolates, and rejects within that sport group.

I first met Dr. Bonney in the fall of 1965, and he was sixty-three years of age at the time. I was about two-thirds of the way through my doctoral studies, and had enrolled in two of his courses, Sociometry and Theories of Personality. Though I had heard rumors about Dr. Bonney, I had no idea what I had let myself in for when I signed up for his courses. One of them would have been plenty and two turned out to be excessive.

He started each of the courses with a statement which I will paraphrase as follows: "Good afternoon, ladies and gentleman. I am Dr. Merl Bonney, and I am your professor for this course. While there are many points of view about what constitutes good teaching, I am convinced after many years in the classroom that learning takes place best under conditions of maximum terror. Rest assured, I will inflict maximum terror on you for the next four months!" Dr. Bonney was true to his word, and then some.

The threats of infliction of maximum terror set a somber enough tone, but Dr. Bonney's course requirements were scary enough in their own right. He started by saying we should be prepared for a major examination each class period; there would not always be one but we had better be prepared just in case. As he so clearly and succinctly put it: "Don't you ever walk into my class without being prepared for a major exam. When there are exams, some will last the entire period and others might take half or a fourth of the class. They might occur at the start of class, or in the last thirty minutes, or in the middle of the period. Just make sure you are prepared every time you walk into my class."

In the sociometry course, we also had to annotate three articles each week on five-by-eight cards, conduct and write up an actual sociometric research study of thirty or forty pages, and engage in periodic writing assignments related to particular daily topics. The requirements in the second course, Theories of Personality, were essentially the same, at least in terms of complexity. The sociometry course met early in the afternoon twice a week for seventy-five minutes but the personality course was a three-hour offering on Thursday nights from 1900 hours to 2200 hours. By the nature of the way the courses were organized, several of us got a double whammy on Thursday because we had to attend and be prepared for exams in both courses.

On top of the seemingly outlandish requirements, Dr. Bonney would engage in humiliation tactics if students were not up to speed on their daily reading. And heaven help you if you did not know an answer to one of his impromptu questions! He also specialized in butchering student last names; John Ed Wilhite was Whitehead, the Greenspan kid was Greenhorn, LeUnes was Levine, and so it went for pretty much everyone in the class.

Another Bonney idiosyncrasy was his exams were almost always short- or long-answer essays. On the short essays, he would put three or four on each page to force the students to be frugal with words while framing their answers. In the middle of the sociometry class one day, he handed out a ten-page exam composed of forty short answer questions. I have always been a fast reader and often finished exams earlier than most people (though my grades did not always coincide with my speed). True to form, I knocked out the forty items in a rapid, orderly, and precise fashion by my estimation, at which time I vacated the classroom, leaving my peers to work their way through the exam. My friends later told me that after I closed the door, Dr. Bonney went to the front of the class, dug into his attaché case, and pulled out a second set of forty questions. He muttered something almost inaudibly that went along the lines of, "Did you see that? Did you see what he did? Levine just walked out of my class early. No one leaves my class early. The class is seventy-five minutes long and Levine cheated me out of fifteen. Here, class, let me hand you the second half of the exam." When the exam results were handed out at the start of the next period, Dr. Bonney wrote that I had done extremely well on the half of the exam I answered but failing to respond to any of the items on the second half had reduced my overall grade to fifty percent which was an F!

On another occasion, I went up to Dr. Bonney with a question about an exam grade. As noted earlier, he typically put four short answer questions per page and I noted a minus one scribbled in red ink right down the middle of the page, running from the top margin to the bottom edge. When I asked Dr. Bonney what I had missed, he dismissed me by saying, "I don't know what you missed, dummy, but you missed something or there wouldn't be a minus one on your paper." I said, "I see, Dr. Bonney", though I did not.

Yet another time, I was comparing my test results with those of my friend, John Ed Wilhite (aka Whitehead). I noticed that John Ed had missed eleven points and made an A-. I had only missed eight points and received a B+ for my efforts. I then went up to Dr. Bonney to inquire about what I mistakenly thought was a grading discrepancy. I said, "Dr. Bonney, John Ed had eleven points counted off and made an A- and I missed eight points and made a B+. I don't understand why his letter grade is better than mine if he missed eleven points and I missed only eight." In his inimitable fashion, Dr. Bonney replied, "It's simple, dummy. His letter grade is higher because he wrote a better paper than you did, hence his A and your B." I said, "I see, Dr. Bonney", which again I did not.

In looking back on those exchanges, I think I really just wanted to dish some of Dr. Bonney's wickedness back to him. Grades mattered to me, but I figured the doctoral degree was going to happen despite him (and others) and the individual class grades were not really all that important in the grander scheme of things. I guess it is good that I was philosophical about grades because I made a B in the Personality course and a C in Sociometry, and both grades were similar to those of most of the students in the two classes. Dr. Bonney in no way subscribed to the prevailing grading zeitgeist which held that graduate students with appropriate effort should usually count on making an A, occasionally make a B, and only in the direst of circumstances, expect to make a C.

Yet another memorable idiosyncrasy of Dr. Bonney's was we were never to come by his office. He made it abundantly clear during the initial lecture he did not meet with students in his office, but indicated he would be willing to field questions or requests as he walked from the classroom. Thus, if a student framed questions or requests properly ahead of time, they might get a response from him as he made his way to the safety of this office. Such was his policy about office hours. From time to time, an unwitting victim would knock on his office door, thus incurring his considerable wrath. You could hear Dr. Bonney all over the building, yelling at the poor victim, "I don't see students in my office. Please get away from my door and do not ever come back."

One of my most favored Bonney stories unfolded early on in the Thursday night course. There were maybe twenty-five of us in the class and I sat next to a local Protestant minister of some persuasion, probably a Baptist or Methodist; I confess total ignorance of the difference between the two denominations. After the first exam, my minister friend unashamedly showed me his paper, and it was a mess of red marks. A grade of F was prominently displayed at top of the first page, and Dr. Bonney had written in big letters with his trademark red ink pen, "This is one of the most poorly written and illiterate papers I have ever read in my forty years of teaching. If your sermons are as poorly constructed and incoherent as your answers to my exam questions, it must indeed be a miserable experience to be a member of your congregation." Yikes!! And I cannot believe the minister shared that little episode with me, essentially a total stranger.

My final Merl Bonney (mis)adventure took place during final exams in January, 1966, just a few scant days before I was to report to my new, supposedly temporary job at A&M. My last final examination was in the aforementioned sociometry course. Shortly before the exam was to be administered, I was trudging up the steps to the classroom when I encountered my classmates, all of whom were engaged in animated conversation as they descended the same flight of stairs. I said, "Where are you guys going? We have an exam coming up in a few minutes." Their response was something to the effect, "Why is it that fifteen people are heading down the steps and only one person is heading up. There is something wrong with this picture. The final began two hours ago and is now over and done with, big boy." It was hard to argue with them, given the tide of humanity going in the opposite direction, so I sheepishly headed toward Dr. Bonney's office. I waited for maybe fifteen minutes until he came out, not daring to incur his considerable wrath by knocking on his door. When he saw me, he immediately inquired as to my whereabouts that afternoon. In answer to his query, I said, "Dr. Bonney, you won't believe what happened. I had the exam down in my planner for 1500 hours and it was obviously given two hours earlier. Can I make it up somehow at a later date?" The idea that he might entertain something as frivolous and heretical as a makeup exam gave me considerable pause, but he acquiesced in part, I think, because of the A&M job recommendation he had given me a few weeks earlier. He glanced cursorily, almost absent-mindedly, at his calendar and, in his own inimitable and curmudgeonly fashion, told me he did not have an opening for an appointment earlier than mid-September. And this was January! I protested politely, suggesting September was eight months removed and thus an eternity. He let me know once again that mid-September was his first opening and I could take it or leave it. Eight months later, I drove from College Station to Denton to take the final exam and Dr. Bonney stayed true blue to his idiosyncratic principles by handing me an exam that, instead of the university-allocated two hours, took five hours and forty-five minutes to complete. He was Merl Bonny to the bitter end, and I could not help but love him for it.

Dr. Bonney was a true scholar and an absolutely flawless, funny, and gifted lecturer, all of which represented the flip side of his idiosyncratic irascibility. He had been asked to teach virtually every other course in his department at one time or another during his long career, and taught most if not all better than the various area specialists. His three-hour Personality class on Thursday night passed as if it were thirty minutes. You took pages and pages of notes while laughing your way through the entire evening (except for the seemingly never-ending exams, of course). He was the consummate lecturer, brilliant, incisive, informed, and incredibly humorous to boot.

One thing Dr. Bonney was fond of saying in his classes resonated at the time and has stuck with me and served me well ever since. He made a statement in class one day to the effect, "In this culture, a few of you will come to harm in confrontations with truly bad individuals but most of you will suffer much more at the hands of the good people. The good people in your life will do you more harm than the bad ones." I am positive, though he never said so directly that Dr. Bonney was influenced by Henry David Thoreau who wrote in his famous book *Walden*: "There is no odour so bad as that which arises from goodness tainted. It is human, it is divine, carrion. If I knew for a certainty that a man was coming to my house with the conscious design of doing me good, I should run for my life as from that dry and parching wind of the African deserts called the simoon, which fills the mouth and nose and ears and eyes with dust till you are suffocated, for fear I should get some of this good done to me-some of its virus mingled with my blood. No, -- in this case I would rather suffer evil the natural way." In my own case, I can say without any reservation whatsoever the "good" people have been far more hurtful in my life than the bad ones. Do-gooders, religious zealots, political conservatives, Fox News "analysts", and the terminally smug abound, shamelessly spewing their mean-spirited hate messages, all aimed at my personal betterment, of course.

My teaching position at A&M had its genesis when I received a rare invitation to visit with Dr. Bonney in his office in mid-November, 1965. He indicated that a representative of my old alma mater, Texas A&M University, had asked if he could recommend a young, promising teaching prospect to fill a one semester position on the psychology faculty. Despite our mildly confrontational run-ins, Dr. Bonney had graciously given them my name along with a most enthusiastic endorsement for the position. Of course, I was flattered by his kindness, and I took A&M up on their offer for a four-month appointment that reached the half century mark in December, 2015.

I have loved my stay as a Professor at A&M, and Merl E. Bonney has my eternal gratitude for his kindness on my behalf those many years ago. I had signed up for two more of his courses for the spring of 1966 but never got to take them because of my new job at A&M. My UNT friends thought I was a glutton for punishment, and perhaps that was true, but I could not get enough of his wisdom and humor, and grades be damned! And they might as well be because he was not going to give many good ones to me or anyone else anyway.

Dr. Bonney stayed on at UNT long after I left, and retired completely in his early nineties. I never saw him again, but did try to communicate through painfully inadequate, ineloquent, abortive letters how much I admired him and the debt I owed him for his mentorship. Finally, when he was ninety-eight or so, I knew time was running out so I sent him the best summation of my thoughts I could muster up, however modest. His caretaker in Boulder, Colorado, a Mr. Baynton answered back on his behalf, indicating that Dr. Bonney was not doing well but he did think he remembered me and was appreciative of my kind and well-intentioned words. Dr. Bonney died not too long after that, just short of his ninety-ninth birthday. I always thought he was too mean to die, but I guess the Grim Reaper gets us all eventually. He reaped a good one, however curmudgeonly, with Dr. Merl E. Bonney.

I would like to end this tribute by mentioning others who viewed Dr. Bonney through pretty much the same positive prism. A Merl E. Bonney Lectureship was created in 1986 and upgraded to the Merl E. Bonney Visiting Professorship in 1993. The goal of the lectureship was to bring in nationally recognized professionals in the field of psychology who would stay for several days and share their expertise with faculty and students. Thanks to legions of loyal ex-students who contributed an initial one hundred dollars per person to kick off the campaign, the Professorship eventually reached the pre-determined goal of $350,000. Almost one-third of that total ($100,000) was generously donated by two devoted former students, Dr. Peggy Ladenberger, a 1961 UNT graduate, and her husband, Charles. Peggy Ladenberger was a psychologist in private practice in the Dallas area at the time she and her husband made the generous donation on behalf of their/our much-admired mentor.

In closing, one of my fellow ex-Bonney students, a private practitioner, summed him up in a few words at a psychology convention a few years ago. There were several of us riding an elevator in the convention hotel and I overheard the psychologist say to a friend: "If you haven't had a course in Psychology from Merl Bonney at the University of North Texas, you shouldn't be allowed to call yourself a psychologist in this state." I could not agree more with the general sentiment expressed by Bonney's admirer, and it is hard to imagine how different my life would be had I not been exposed to and influenced by his wisdom and mentorship.

Roy Q. Bellamy, Abnormalist. Dr. Roy Quentin Bellamy (1920-1971) was another professor I remember with considerable fondness, and his case was both intriguing and, ultimately, tragic. I enrolled in his undergraduate course in Abnormal Psychology in 1964, a couple of weeks after my military separation, to make up some work missing from my previous two degrees which were admittedly light on Psychology courses for reasons explained elsewhere. Dr. Bellamy was in his mid-forties with closely cropped salt and pepper gray hair, a big, boyish, toothy smile, and skin coloration that would make the tanning salon ingénues of today turn green (brown?) with envy. Girls lined up in droves to take his courses; as one of my female friends put it, "I am taking Abnormal Psychology just to stare at him. He is so dreamy!" Seeing men as "dreamy" has never been one of my own quirks, but I had to admit Dr. Bellamy was movie-star handsome. Pictures from his youth, snapshots taken during his military service in World War II, and photos taken while at UNT serve to document my humble assessment and that of his legions of female admirers.

Dr. Bellamy was an engaging lecturer who was fond of frequent exams covering small amounts of material. His exams were usually confined to no more than a chapter and a half, or maybe two at most, and we had eleven of them by the end of the semester. The exams were just that, exams, but my most vivid recollection of Dr. Bellamy's course was the required term paper. He asked for seventy-five typed pages but gave us a three-pronged option to meet the requirement: (1) write 25-page papers on three topics of our choice; (2) write a 50- and a 25-page paper on two topics, or (3) write a 75-page paper on a single topic. I chose option three since it seemed easier to select a broad topic and organize only once as opposed to doing so two or three times. I eventually cranked out a document on juvenile delinquency that ended up being one paragraph short of seventy-five full pages. I typed the paper myself on a manual typewriter, an agonizing task given the fact that I am saddled with five thumbs on my left hand and perhaps one or two functional fingers on the right, at least when it comes to typing. That paper is still in my office file cabinet and celebrated its 50th anniversary in December of 2014. I made an A- on the paper and it remains to this day largely if not entirely unread by anyone other than me.

The reason I say unread is that Dr. Bellamy had several sections of Abnormal Psychology with numerous students. I figured out that to thoroughly read and mark all the papers prior to the due date for final course grades, he would have had to peruse (not scan!) ten of them a day for about two weeks, or roughly 750 pages every twenty-four hours. It did not take a rocket scientist to figure out the likelihood mine would be read thoroughly, with red ink pen poised, was at best remote.

Just before the final exam, Dr. Bellamy disappeared and rumors made the rounds that he had become terribly depressed and had been committed to a private psychiatric clinic in Dallas. There were recurring rumors intimating the exact same thing happened the following year. I suppose it is instructive for the students in a course in abnormal psychology to watch their professor sink into a depressive abyss right in front of their eyes, but I have always told my students that they will not have that luxury. Tragically, Dr. Bellamy died in Denton of a heart attack several years after that second commitment. Roy Quentin Bellamy was a good professor whose life was almost certainly shortened by the psychological baggage and/or detritus of the soul he bore for part or most of his life.

Dr. George Beamer Saves The Day (Or the Dissertation). Professor George Beamer was my committee chairperson and dissertation director. He was a specialist in vocational guidance and personnel selection, but relatively long in the tooth and nearing retirement in 1969. I think it is fair to say he did not take matters as seriously as some of his younger, more eager colleagues who were dead set on solving all the world's problems and changing the course of world events.

I do not have the slightest idea how such a thing could have possibly happened as I look back on my life, but somehow George Beamer ended up being my committee chair and dissertation director, most definitely a double-edged sword situation. On the negative side, I made many trips from College Station to Denton while trying to complete the dissertation, only to find his office dark and locked up tight as a tick. He was variously on the golf course, in an impromptu meeting, consulting in private industry, or otherwise MIA (missing in action). As a result, I made the 450-mile round trip to Denton for no reason on more occasions than I can recount. All in all, I figure I drove around 10,000 total miles in three-plus years trying to wrap up the loose ends of my doctoral degree.

On the other hand, when push came to shove and I needed him most, Dr. Beamer turned out to be my greatest advocate. Let me elaborate. One of the steps in earning a doctorate is to make an oral presentation of a proposed dissertation research topic to a panel made up of one's own doctoral committee. In addition to the regular committee, it was the custom at UNT for randomly-appointed faculty members to serve as devil's advocates during the proposal defense. One such outside antagonist was Dr. Ray Johnson who, among other things, taught the courses in human sexuality.

As part of protocol in these proposal defenses, once the formal presentation ends, it is customary to ask the candidate to leave the room while the committee deliberates his or her fate. I left as requested and it was not long before I could hear loud voices and animated yelling emanating from the meeting room. Being ever astute and blessed with incredible insights, I did not take this not-so-muffled hubbub as a positive sign. It was clear there was not a consensus concerning the viability of my proposal. I learned later Ray Johnson was the most vociferous of the nay-sayers which, of course, came as no surprise based on what I had observed while presenting my proposal. He wanted to scuttle the whole project because of what he perceived to be a weakness in one of the instruments I was using in my study. His misgivings were not without some validity but completely deep-sixing the dissertation might have been excessive. You can bet I thought so!

Finally, a half hour or so into the melee, Dr. Beamer put his ample and authoritative foot down and said in so many words, "We are going ahead with the dissertation idea as is. End of discussion." Sometime later, I finished the project and received the coveted doctoral degree, thanks in no small part to the assertiveness under fire on the part of Professor Beamer. He was in my corner when I needed him most. His other transgressions were wiped clean in one fell swoop!

I should add a note indicating I was struggling with the dissertation data analysis at one point and had sought assistance from a number of resources on the A&M campus who were in the business of helping people analyze and interpret data. I finally tired of spinning my wheels with these well-meaning people and decided to see what a friend in Austin had to say about the matter. To wit, my good friend Norvell Northcutt had been released from the army after a tour in Vietnam and relocated to the University of Texas in Austin. Norvell was among the first people to make use of the new technology known as the computer, and knowing this, I dialed him up on the phone, asking for his assistance in analyzing my data. He said pack up your data cards and bring them on over to Austin and let me take a shot. Three days later, I received word that my analyses were ready to be picked up. Not too many weeks later, the dissertation was ready to submit to Dr. Beamer and the committee for their approval. I literally wrote the entire dissertation in ten days with no feedback from any source other than the data analyses provided by Norvell Northcutt. Thanks, old friend, for bailing me out!

Other Wonderful Professors. In addition to the irrepressible Merl Bonney, the tragic Roy Bellamy, and the assertive-when-it-counted George Beamer, I had the good fortune to be exposed to an array of other truly outstanding teachers who were extremely competent in the classroom and friendly and facilitative when away from their chalk and blackboard. Chief among them were:

> Dr. Earl Kooker who terrorized graduate students with his statistics courses;
>
> Dr. Jack Haynes, a most affable professor whose course in Theories of Learning was a toughie for me;
>
> Dr. Harold Holloway who taught a couple of doctoral courses and was open, friendly, and outspoken about his belief in my potential;

Dr. Sidney Hamilton, the departmental testing specialist who had received his training from one of the most influential figures ever in the assessment of human intelligence, Dr. David Wechsler of New York University;

Dr. Jack Watson, the aforementioned soft-spoken, warm, exceedingly kind individual who taught courses in my secondary field of Kinesiology and from whom I received considerable professional and personal support.

I liked, admired, and respected these men and I owe each a great debt for their excellence as teachers, their patience as mentors, and for generally being good, caring people. Why I am just now giving the roses, I will never know…most or all are deceased and I never told any of them of my fondness and admiration. I think they knew at some level, but it would have taken little effort to put some words behind the emotion. I am blessed that legions of my current and past students are more generous and forthcoming in expressing their feelings about me than I was about my mentors.

As one example, I happened to throw in a comment during a lecture in my abnormal psychology class in the fall of 2016 that I had lost my Aggie Ring some thirty years earlier, most likely in a fire that destroyed our home. Without any awareness on my part, a junior Psychology major named Sophie Roberts created a GoFundMe account and within a day or so raised well over a thousand dollars to replace my long-missing ring. There are few kudos a teacher could receive that would parallel the act of generosity and affection headed up by Sophie and supported by classmates, friends, and others. Tim Gronberg, Head of the Department of Economics, and a friend from the old softball days, emailed me that he thought this was the greatest accolade for a professor he had witnessed in his forty years at A&M. I agree with Tim!

All things considered, my family, my friends, and my wonderful professors made my stay in Denton a memorable one, and words fail me when I try to recapture my feelings. Those were some of the best days of my life, and I am eternally grateful to all who played a part in making so many good things happen.